Engine and Tractor Power

ASAE Textbook Number 3
Published by the
American Society of Agricultural Engineers

Pamela DeVore-Hansen, Technical Editor
Books & Journals

# Engine and Tractor Power

3rd Edition

Carroll E. Goering
University of Illinois

Copyright © 1992 by the American Society of Agricultural Engineers
All Rights Reserved
Manufactured in the United States of America

The American Society of Agricultural Engineers is not responsible for
statements and opinions advanced in its meetings or printed in its
publications. They represent the views of the individual to whom
they are credited and are not binding on the Society as a whole.

This book may not be reproduced in whole or in part by any means
(with the exception of short quotes for the purpose of review)
without the permission of the publisher.
For information, contact:

ASAE
2950 Niles Road
St. Joseph, Michigan 49085-9659 USA
Phone: 616.429.0300  Fax: 616.429.3852  E-mail: hq@asae.org

ASAE Textbook Number 3
THIRD EDITION
LCCN 92-61515  ISBN 0-929355-30-X

Pamela DeVore-Hansen, Editor
Information Publishing Group

This book is dedicated to my sister,
Wellma Hamilton,
a beacon of love, generosity, and courage.

# Contents

Foreword .................................................................. ix

## Chapter

1. Introduction .................................................. 1
2. Basic Thermodynamics of Engines .......... 21
3. Engine Components .................................. 39
4. Practical Engine Cycles and Timing ........ 69
5. Power Efficiencies and Measurement ...... 89
6. Fuels and Combustion ............................. 127
7. Electrical Systems .................................... 161
8. Ignition Circuits ...................................... 207
9. Fuel Systems and Carburetion ................ 229
10. Diesel Engines ......................................... 255
11. Intake and Exhaust Systems ................... 293
12. Cooling Systems ...................................... 315
13. Lubricants and Lubricating Systems ....... 333
14. Hydraulic Systems and Hitches .............. 365
15. Power Trains ............................................ 419
16. Weight Transfer, Traction, and Safety .... 473

Appendix A - Bibliography ................................... 507
Appendix B - Symbols .......................................... 511
Appendix C - ASAE Standard ............................... 515
Subject Index ....................................................... 519

# Foreword

Students in colleges of agriculture and other students with an interest in engines and motor vehicles are the primary audience for whom this textbook was written. Although the primary focus is on engines and farm tractors, many of the concepts also apply to automobiles, trucks, self-propelled farm machinery, lawn and garden tractors, and other vehicles.

Engines and vehicles merit study because they have transformed society. In early American society, it was necessary for nearly everyone to live on farms to produce food and fiber. The mechanization provided by farm tractors gives modern U.S. farmers the ability to grow food and fiber for many people, so that less than 5% of the current population are farmers. The remainder are free to enter industry or become doctors, lawyers, astronauts, and so forth. At the same time, the automobile has given people freedom to travel the length and breadth of the country. In contrast, most of the population in less developed countries must live on the land to produce food, and transportation usually is primitive.

The purpose of the book is to illuminate the principles of construction, operation, and maintenance of engines and tractors. Mathematical equations and problems often provide the best means to illuminate such principles, but the mathematics here is at a level that is accessible to the nonengineer. A prerequisite course in algebra is assumed. A course in physics would also be helpful, but is not essential.

The textbook undoubtedly includes more material than can be covered in a one semester course. Instructors may choose chapters to meet the needs of their own curricula. For example, Chapters 6 through 9 might be omitted if the focus was on diesel farm tractors. Other combinations of coverage are also possible.

The author gratefully acknowledges the contributions of many individuals in the preparation of this third edition of the textbook. One of these is undergraduate student Brett Aukamp, whose expert use of computer graphics produced many of the new illustrations in the third edition. Professors Crowell Bowers of North Carolina State University, Kevin Shinners of the University of Wisconsin, and Elton Solseng of North Dakota State University performed a great service by doing in-depth reviews of the second edition. Their reviews provided the basis for a survey form which was sent to individuals at more than 60 educational institutions in the U.S. and abroad which were current or potential users of the book. The author is grateful to the more than 40% of these individuals who took the time to complete and return the survey form. Collectively, it was the survey responses that guided the preparation of this third edition of the textbook. Further thanks are due to Professors Bowers and Solseng, and to Professor Ralph Alcock of South Dakota State University, for reviewing the first draft of the third edition. Last but not least, the author is grateful to his wife, Carol Ann Goering, for her patience and support during the many hours that were devoted to revising the textbook.

Readers familiar with the first and second edition will notice quite a few changes in this third edition. SI units were the sole units in the first two editions, but the respondents strongly recommended that dual units be used in the third edition. They also recommended that certain chapters should be rearranged in their order of appearance. Coverage was expanded on carburetion and ignition systems for small engines and on electronic fuel injection into multicylinder engines. Additional material was added on power transmission systems. Other chapters were also updated as needed.

All of the known errors in the second edition were corrected. Despite the intensive efforts of the author, the publisher and the reviewers, it is possible and even likely that some errors remain in this edition. Readers who find such errors or who have suggestions for further improving the textbook are encouraged to write to the author so that further improvements may be made in future editions of the book.

Carroll E. Goering<br>
Urbana, Illinois

# 1
# Introduction

## 1.1  OBJECTIVES OF MECHANIZATION

Farm tractors are a key element in the mechanization of farm work. Tractors provide the power for machines that till the soil, plant the crops, control the weeds, and harvest the crops. The mechanization of farm work has three primary objectives:

To reduce the drudgery of farm work.
To increase the productivity of farm workers.
To increase the timeliness and quality of farm work.

The first objective has already been accomplished. A century ago, farm work was so hard and low-paying that many considered farm life something to escape. Human beings cannot live well using only their muscle power. An adult human can produce approximately 150 W (0.2 hp) of power, or 0.15 kW-h (0.2 hp-h) of energy/h while working continuously. A good diesel tractor can produce 3.0 kW-h of energy/L (15.2 hp-h/gal) of fuel. Thus, a human being working as a power unit is equivalent to only 0.05 L/h (0.013 gal/h) of diesel fuel. If fuel costs were $1.00/L ($3.79/gal), a human being would be worth only $0.05/h as a power unit. Fortunately, mechanization allows farm workers to escape a life of drudgery and low pay by multiplying their efforts far beyond what their own muscles could accomplish.

Productivity is increased when farm workers use mechanization. As Figure 1.1 shows, the increasing use of farm mechanization since 1915 has been accompanied by increased productivity per hectare (ac) and per hour of labor. Although improved seeds, fertilizers, herbicides, and other farm supplies have played a role in these

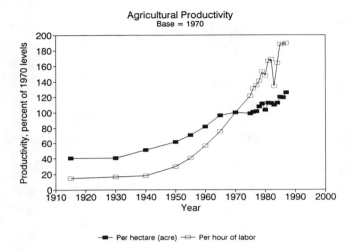

*Figure 1.1–Trends in agricultural productivity. (Data from U.S. Department of Agriculture, Fact Book of Agriculture, Publication No. 1063, 1989.)*

productivity gains, mechanization also has been a contributing factor. Mechanization has been a major contributor to the gains in productivity per hour of labor.

There is an optimum time for performing critical farming operations such as planting and harvesting. Crop yields tend to be highest when these critical operations are done closest to the optimum time. Farmers with high-capacity machines can perform the critical operations quickly and thus accomplish them close to the optimum time. Mechanization can also improve the quality of farm operations. For example, plows pulled by modern farm tractors can till the soil deeper and more thoroughly than the wooden plows that were once pulled by draft animals.

## 1.2 DEVELOPMENT OF THE TRACTOR

Modern farm tractors are a marvel of engineering, and users expect them to be efficient, reliable, comfortable, and safe. How did such tractors come into being? Although the roots of the farm tractor can be traced far back into history, the major developments in tractor design have occurred within the last hundred years. Experiments with engines prior to 1700 were impractical or unsuccessful. Perhaps the first successful development occurred in 1769, when James Watt patented a practical steam engine. A hundred years later, following the U.S. Civil War, the homesteading of the Western prairie lands

*Figure 1.2–Horse-drawn steam engine. (Courtesy of the American Society of Agricultural Engineers.)*

increased the need for mechanization of farming, and steam engines were put to work supplying belt power for threshing machines. Since those early steam engines were not self-propelled, horses or mules were used to transport the threshers and steam engines from place to place (Figure 1.2). In the 1870s, inventors devised clutches, gears, and chains to drive the rear wheels of steam engines, and steering devices were invented to steer the front wheels. By 1880, farmers were buying these steam traction engines in considerable numbers for pulling threshers and for plowing (Figure 1.3).

An important step in the development of internal combustion engines occurred in 1862 when Beau de Rochas, a French engineer, set forth four principles that were essential for efficient operation. These principles were as follows:

1. The combustion chamber should have the smallest possible surface to volume ratio.
2. The expansion process should be as rapid as possible.
3. The compression at the start of expansion should be as high as possible.
4. The expansion stroke should be as long as possible.

The first two principles were intended to minimize heat transfer from the combustion chamber, while the latter two were intended to produce the greatest possible amount of work from each expansion stroke.

Many inventors attempted to embody the Beau de Rochas

*Figure 1.3–Steam-powered plowing. (Courtesy of the American Society of Agricultural Engineers.)*

principles in engines. In 1861 German inventor Dr. Nikolaus Otto conceived the first engine to use ignition of a gaseous fuel after compression. By 1878 he and Eugen Langen had built an engine which used the same four-stroke cycle – that is, intake, compression, power, and exhaust – that is used in most engines today.

Otto's contemporaries thought that having only one power stroke in two revolutions was a serious disadvantage, and experimenters turned their attention to the two-stroke-cycle engine of the explosive type – that is, without compression. Three years after Otto patented his four-stroke-cycle engine, Sir Dugald Clerk built a two-stroke-cycle engine with compression, but he abandoned it due to mechanical difficulties. Joseph Day simplified the two-stroke-cycle engine design in 1891 by using a gas-tight crankcase as the pumping cylinder. Day's engine used the intake and exhaust ports in the cylinder wall that are still used in modern two-stroke-cycle engines. By 1906 the Cushman Company was producing successful two-stroke-cycle two-cylinder spark-ignition engines for use in farm tractors.

In 1892 Dr. Rudolph Diesel, a German engineer, patented an engine designed to ignite the fuel by means of the heat produced by high compression. Diesel originally designed his engine to run on powdered coal, but he quickly switched to liquid fuels. Although Adolph Busch built the first U.S. diesel engine in St. Louis, Missouri, in 1896, it was not until many years later that the diesel engine was adopted for farm tractors.

Around 1890 companies began to manufacture tractors[1] with internal combustion engines (Figure 1.4). Bitter competition began

*Figure 1.4–An early tractor with an internal combustion engine. (Courtesy of the American Society of Agricultural Engineers.)*

to develop between the makers of these gas tractors and the makers of steam tractors. The Winnipeg Tractor Trials, held annually from 1908 to 1912, gave the public its first opportunity to compare steam and gas tractors in the field. The gas tractors could be operated by one person, whereas the steam tractors required an extra person to tend the firebox and boiler. The popularity of steam tractors faded following the Winnipeg Trials. International Harvester Company developed a closed-cycle steam tractor as late as 1924 but chose not to market it.

The period 1910 to 1920 saw most manufacturers beginning to produce tractors much smaller and lighter than the earlier giants. This was also the time when reliable transmissions, ignition systems, lubrication systems, governors, carburetors, and air cleaners were developed. A great variety of chassis arrangements appeared during this period. Some manufacturers sold tractors with steered wheels in the rear and drive wheels in the front (Figure 1.5). Other tractors had only two wheels. There were even rear axle kits sold for converting automobiles to tractors. Many of the freak tractors

---

[1] The word *tractor* has been attributed to several sources. The sales manager of the Hart-Parr Tractor Company used it in an advertisement in 1906 to replace the cumbersome phrase "gasoline traction engine". However, the word *tractor* had appeared earlier in a patent issued in 1890. According to the *Oxford English Dictionary*, the word was first used in England in 1856 to mean one who or that which draws something.

*Figure 1.5–An early row-crop tractor with rear-wheel steering. (Courtesy of the American Society of Agricultural Engineers.)*

disappeared by 1920, as designers began to concentrate on tractors with drive wheels at the rear and steered wheels at the front.

Many of the tractors sold prior to 1920 were so unreliable that pressures began to mount for a federal tractor-testing program. Congress failed to appropriate funds for the program, however, and the need remained unaddressed at the national level. Fortunately, Nebraska farmer E. F. Crozier was among those who had bad experiences with unreliable tractors. Crozier was a member of the Nebraska legislature, and he introduced a bill to provide a remedy. The Nebraska legislature passed the Nebraska Tractor Test Law in 1919, requiring manufacturers to submit their tractors for testing by the University of Nebraska before the tractors could be sold in the state. The Nebraska tests became accepted nationwide as a reliable standard for comparing tractors. Until they were supplanted by OECD (Organization of Economic and Community Development, a European organization) tests in the late 1980s, the Nebraska tests were responsible for many improvements in tractor design and eliminated many tractors of inferior design.

Although the basic form of the tractor had emerged by 1920, many improvements have been made since that time. An important improvement, made in the early 1920s, was the development of the general-purpose tractor, which could be used for cultivating and other row-crop work. Earlier tractors were used primarily for heavy tillage and for belt work. The power take-off (pto) was also developed in the 1920s, and the American Society of Agricultural Engineers (ASAE) published the first pto standard in 1925. Power take-off drives are discussed in Chapter 15.

Pneumatic tires began to replace steel wheels on tractors in the 1930s, increasing the operating speed of tractors in the field and on highways. The first successful three-point hitch was introduced in the 1930s. Hitches are discussed in Chapter 14.

The decades of the 1940s and 1950s brought hydraulic systems, self-starters, improved seating, and other features that made tractors more comfortable and more convenient to operate. Improvements first introduced in the 1950s included power steering, independent pto, and power-shift transmissions.

A strong trend toward the use of diesel engines started in the 1960s, and today, most farm tractors have diesel engines. Also introduced in the 1960s were alternators, turbochargers, hydrostatic transmissions, and roll over protective structures (ROPS).

The 1970s brought a substantial increase in the number of tractors with four-wheel drive on the market and also smaller specialty tractors. Intercoolers were introduced for large, turbocharged diesel engines.

As the size of two-wheel drive tractors increased in the 1980s, mechanically driven front-wheel assists (FWA) came into widespread use. Advances in electronics lead to the introduction of sensors, monitors and electronic controls to improve fuel efficiency and performance of tractors.

## 1.3 TYPES OF TRACTORS

The first tractors were used for few jobs other than plowing and threshing. The development of tractors that could cultivate row crops was a major advance. Other uses for tractors have developed over time, and today there are many types of tractors available for specialized jobs.

The history of the development of *crawler* tractors parallels that of wheel tractors. Crawler tractors with steel tracks are still used on some large farms (Figure 1.6), but they are less popular in agriculture now than they once were. Although large-wheel tractors have largely displaced crawler tractors in agriculture, the latter are widely used in the construction industry. The *belted agricultural tractor* (Figure 1.7) has been introduced to combine the benefits of low ground pressures of crawler tractors with the mobility of wheel tractors.

The *row-crop* tractor can be used for traction work and is also adaptable to many machines used for growing row crops. The *tricycle* design of early row-crop tractors (Figure 1.8) has given way to the use of *wide-front axles*, which are pivoted in the center (Figure 1.9). The *standard* tractor is similar to the row-crop tractor, but is used primarily for traction work and does not have a three point hitch.

Figure 1.6–A crawler tractor being used in agriculture. (Courtesy of Allis Chalmers Corporation.)

*High-clearance* tractors are row crop tractors that have been modified to give extra clearance for working in tall crops.

*Orchard* tractors have a low profile and are sometimes equipped with special, streamlined fenders for working under trees. *Utility* tractors are usually smaller and have less clearance than row-crop tractors. Utility tractors are often used for jobs around the farmstead (Figure 1.10). Garden tractors (Figure 1.11) may be equipped with a mower for mowing lawns, or with a variety of gardening tools.

An implement carrier (Figure 1.12) is a *universal* tractor that is specially designed to carry combines, field choppers, and other implements. Use of a universal tractor avoids the duplication of a separate propulsion unit for each of several self-propelled implements.

Figure 1.7–A belted agricultural tractor (Courtesy of Caterpillar, Inc.)

Introduction

*Figure 1.8–A tricycle-type, row-crop tractor.*

*Industrial* tractors are similar to farm tractors, but they are more rugged in order to withstand the continuous duty encountered in road or building construction or similar jobs. Industrial tractors are often equipped with front-end loaders and back hoes (Figure 1.13). Skid-steer loaders (Figure 1.14) are compact tractors built for the special purpose of moving earth and other materials. They have four-wheel drive and are steered by operating the wheels on one side

*Figure 1.9–A row-crop tractor with a wide front axle. (Courtesy of Case-IH.)*

*Figure 1.10–A utility tractor. (Courtesy of Case-IH.)*

faster than the other. The wheels must skid sideways during turns, which explains the name of this tractor.

Some row-crop tractors are equipped with optional *front-wheel drives* (Figure 1.15). The front wheels are driven hydraulically on some early models and mechanically driven front wheel assists (FWA) are now more popular. The front wheels are usually smaller than the rear wheels.

The *four-wheel-drive* (4WD) tractor is the largest tractor used in agriculture. It usually has equal-size wheels at the front and rear. Some 4WD tractors have four steerable wheels (Figure 1.16), while

*Figure 1.11–A garden tractor. (Courtesy of Deere & Company.)*

Introduction

*Figure 1.12–An implement-carrier tractor. (Courtesy of New Idea Farm Equipment Corp.)*

others pivot the frame in the center to accomplish steering (Figure 1.17). The latter arrangement is called *articulated steering*. Many 4WD tractors are suitable only for heavy traction work, but some manufacturers have produced 4WD row-crop tractors with articulated steering (Figure 1.18).

*Figure 1.13–An industrial tractor. (Courtesy of Case-IH.)*

*Figure 1.14–A skid-steer loader. (Courtesy of Ford-New Holland.)*

## 1.4 FUELS FOR TRACTORS

Tractors must burn fuel to produce power. Steam engines could use a variety of fuels, but wood and coal were the most commonly used.

*Figure 1.15–A two-wheel-drive tractor with optional front-wheel drive. (Courtesy of Deere & Company.)*

Introduction

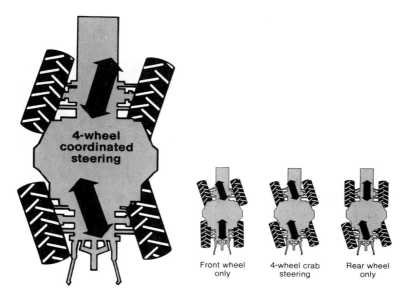

*Figure 1.16–A four-wheel-drive tractor with steerable wheels. (Courtesy of Case-IH.)*

Solid fuels are not practical for use in internal combustion engines. Some of the early engine inventors used turpentine for fuel. In 1792, William Murdock, an engineer for James Watt, succeeded in lighting his house by distilling gas from coal. Such fuel sources would not

*Figure 1.17–A four-wheel-drive tractor with articulated steering. (Courtesy of Deere & Company.)*

*Figure 1.18–A combination row-crop and four-wheel-drive tractor. (Courtesy of Case-IH.)*

have been sufficient to supply the industrial revolution and the mechanization of agriculture; however, in 1859, a new source of energy was found. It was in August of that year that Edwin Drake drilled the world's first oil well in Titusville, Pennsylvania.

Petroleum became the accepted source of engine fuel. Early spark-ignited engines used kerosene and a low-volatility, low-octane,

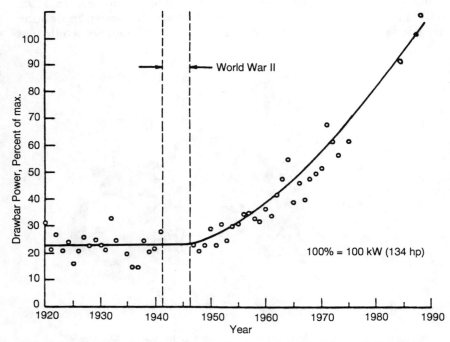

*Figure 1.19–Trends in draw-bar power of new tractors tested at the Nebraska Testing Station.*

Introduction

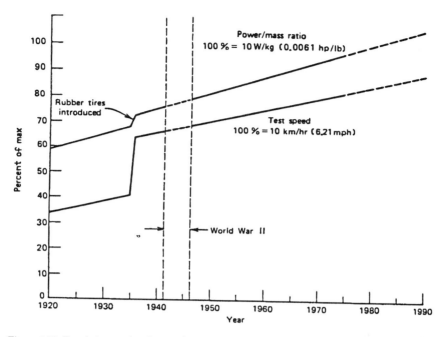

*Figure 1.20–Trends in speed and power/mass ratio of new tractors tested at the Nebraska Testing Station.*

petroleum distillate fuel called tractor fuel. Tractors could not be operated on these low-grade fuels until the engine had been started and warmed on gasoline. The low-grade fuels gave way to gasoline, and, for a time, liquid petroleum gas (LPG) also was a popular fuel for tractors. In recent years, the use of diesel engines has displaced all of these fuels for farm tractors.

All of the petroleum-based fuels are fossil fuels that have been stored in the earth for many centuries. They are nonrenewable and will be depleted at some future date. Production of crude oil in the United States is already declining, and it is expected that world petroleum reserves will be depleted in the twenty-first century. Other sources of fuel energy for engines are being sought.

Solar energy is the most inexhaustible energy source, and it may be used directly or may be stored for later use. Petroleum is an extreme example of stored solar energy. The energy was trapped by plants growing thousands of years ago, and, as will be discussed in Chapter 6, these plants were eventually transformed into petroleum. In direct use, solar energy is used as soon as it is collected. Direct use of solar energy to supply power to a farm tractor is impractical for two reasons. The energy is not concentrated enough to supply a tractor with a reasonably sized collector, and it is unavailable at night or on cloudy days.

Coal, oil shale, and tar sands are fossil fuels that are available in much larger reserves than is petroleum. If these fossil fuels could be extracted from the earth and converted to petroleum-like liquids, the duration of the fossil-fuel era could be greatly extended. The extraction and conversion processes have been demonstrated on a pilot scale. The enormous capital costs of full-scale plants have delayed their construction in the United States, but South Africa produces large quantities of liquid fuel from coal.

Engines can be operated on liquid fuels produced from biomass. Ethanol fermented from farm crops is widely used as a fuel for spark-ignition engines and has been used experimentally in compression-ignition engines. Soybean, sunflower and other vegetable oils have been converted into fuel for diesel engines. Such fuels might become available in sufficient quantities to supply the fuel needs of farm tractors, but not enough would be available to fulfill the needs of transportation, manufacturing, and other industries.

## 1.5 TRACTORS OF THE FUTURE

How will tractors of the future differ from those of the past? One way to make predictions about future tractors is to extrapolate from past trends. Figure 1.19 shows trends in the drawbar power of tractors tested at the Nebraska Testing Station. Continuation of the upward trend in drawbar power would require increased pulling capability and/or increased operating speeds from future tractors. Pulling capability can be increased through the use of more massive tractors or, if tractive devices can be improved, through higher pull/mass ratios. The implication of Figure 1.20 is that tractor power/mass ratios have been increasing primarily due to increased speeds and that tractive improvements have not yielded appreciable gains in pull/mass ratios. Unless breakthroughs in traction research can produce increased pull/mass ratios, reasonable limits on tractor size and speed will cause a leveling off of the upward trend in the drawbar power at some point in the future.

The small, inexpensive digital computers called microprocessors are likely to further increase the use of monitors and automatic controls on farm tractors. If an engine-efficiency monitor was included on a tractor with a hydrostatic transmission, for example, the operator could adjust the transmission speed ratio to maintain peak efficiency from the engine. The next step would be to control the transmission automatically. Use of automatic controls on farm tractors is not a new idea. Engine governors automatically control engine speed, and three-point hitches include automatic control of hitch height. Microprocessors have already been introduced as a component of farm tractors. Will microprocessors eventually permit the automation of tractor steering?

The increasing cost and scarcity of petroleum fuels are likely to lead to changes in engine design. Will engine efficiency be increased through the use of the higher operating temperatures permitted by ceramics and other new engine materials? Will engines become more efficient through the use of slower speeds? Will spark-ignition and diesel engines be supplanted by multifuel engines that can run on whatever fuel is most readily available and least expensive?

Some trends in tractor design may end. For example, as was discussed earlier, the upward trend in drawbar power may level off. Innovations have led to improvements in design throughout history, however, and such improvements are likely to continue.

## 1.6 SUMMARY

Farm tractors reduce the drudgery of farm work, increase the productivity of farm workers, and increase the quality and timeliness of farm work. Although the roots of the development of the farm tractor can be traced far back into history, the major developments have occurred in the last hundred years. Tractor development was aided by the Nebraska Tractor Test Law, which was passed in 1919 and subsequently helped to eliminate tractors of inferior design.

The first farm tractors were designed to power threshing machines and pull heavy tillage implements. In the 1920s, general-purpose tractors, which could also accomplish cultivation of row crops, were designed. Now, many specialized tractors are available for doing a wide variety of jobs in agriculture and construction.

The steam engines in the first tractors burned wood or coal. The first oil well was drilled in 1859, and petroleum became the fuel for internal combustion engines, which succeeded steam engines in the early 1990s. Diesel fuel has become the dominant fuel for farm tractors in recent years. New sources of fuel are being sought already in anticipation of the depletion of worldwide petroleum reserves.

Reasonable limits on tractor size and speed will cause a leveling of the upward trend in drawbar power of tractors unless breakthroughs in traction research can produce increased pull/mass ratios. However, future tractors will have many improvements. Microprocessors will provide better monitoring and control of tractor operation. Engines will become more efficient to conserve scarce fuel. Multifuel engines may be introduced to allow farmers to use whatever fuel is least expensive and most readily available.

## QUESTIONS

Q1.1 (a) Certain groups in society benefit when the primary objectives of mechanization are realized. Consider the first primary objective of mechanization as given in Chapter 1, and state whether the primary beneficiaries are farm workers or consumers of farm products or whether both groups benefit about equally. Briefly explain your answer.

(b) Reconsider part a and state who would benefit the most from the second primary objective of mechanization.

(c) Reconsider part a and state who would benefit the most from the third primary objective of mechanization.

Q1.2 The earliest tractors had steam engines, but modern tractors have internal combustion engines. Briefly explain why steam engines lost the competition, and identify the time period when their disadvantages became apparent.

Q1.3 Who was the inventor of the four-stroke cycle for engines? Name the four strokes and the year by which the inventor had perfected a working model of the engine.

Q1.4 A standard tractor has an appearance similar to a row-crop tractor with a wide front axle. What is the primary difference between the standard and row-crop tractors?

Q1.5 Briefly describe the differences between an articulated four-wheel-drive (4WD) tractor and a tractor with front-wheel assist (FWA).

Q1.6 Could James Watt's engine have been as successful if he had patented an internal combustion engine instead of a steam engine? Briefly explain your answer.

Q1.7 Pneumatic tires were first introduced on farm tractors in the 1930s and have now replaced the steel, lugged wheels that were used earlier. What are the primary advantages of pneumatic tires that caused them to displace the steel wheels? (*Hint:* See Figure 1.18.)

## PROBLEMS

P1.1 In 1970, a farmer using a two-row combine with a corn head could easily harvest 0.75 ha (1.85 ac)/h and a typical corn yield was 5000 kg/ha (80 bu/ac). Before 1940, most corn was harvested by hand and a skilled person could harvest 250 kg (10 bu)/h. Calculate the productivity ratio. That is, the hand harvesting rate is what percentage of the rate of harvest in 1970? Compare your answer to the appropriate curve in Figure 1.1.

P1.2  At noon on a cloud-free summer day, sunlight intensities at the earth's surface are nearly always less than 940 W/m$^2$ (0.12 ht$^2$).

(a) At this intensity, if the solar collector and electric motor could convert 10% of the collected solar energy to mechanical power, how large a collector would be required on a tractor to supply 100 kW (134 hp) of mechanical power?

(b) If the length of the collector was twice its width, what would be the dimensions of the collector?

# 2
# Basic Thermodynamics of Engines

## 2.1 INTRODUCTION

You will not need to learn an excessive amount about thermodynamics to understand engines. There are, however, a few basic thermodynamic equations that can provide you with good insights into the operation of engines. One such equation, for example, shows that the efficiency of gasoline engines is unlikely to ever reach 50%. Another equation can be used to reveal the conditions under which a diesel engine will start or fail to start. Thus, your study of the material in this chapter will be rewarded by better insights into engine performance.

Calculation of engine performance requires the use of certain basic and derived quantities and units of measurement. The tractor industry is well along in the conversion to the metric system, and so SI units will be the primary units used in this book. SI is an abbreviation for "Le Systeme International d'Unites", the official name in French for the modern metric system. Customary units will be shown in parentheses for those who have not yet converted to the SI system of units.

## 2.2 BASIC QUANTITIES AND UNITS OF THERMODYNAMICS

The SI system includes four basic quantities that are needed in the study of tractors, and other quantities will be derived from these four. The four basic SI quantities are length, time, mass, and temperature. The four basic customary quantities are length, time, force and temperature.

Length and time are familiar quantities that need no elaboration. Although the meter (m) is the basic SI unit of length and tractor part dimensions are usually given in millimeters (mm), the centimeter (cm) and the kilometer (km) are also used. In customary units, the primary unit of length is the foot (ft) but inches (in.) and miles are also used. In either system of units, the second (s) is the basic unit of time, but minutes (min) and hours (h) are used as well.

Mass refers to the quantity of matter that is in a body or substance and, in SI units, it is measured in kilograms (kg). Description of the customary mass unit will be deferred until after the introduction of force. Mass should not be confused with weight. The weight of a body is the force exerted on it by gravity. Thus, when a given body is taken to outer space it becomes weightless, but its mass remains unchanged.

The degree Celsius (°C) is the most familiar unit of temperature in the SI system, but it cannot be used in thermodynamic calculations. Instead, the absolute temperature in degrees Kelvin (°K) is used. Zero absolute is the temperature at which all molecules cease to move. In customary units, the degree Fahrenheit (°F) is familiar, but the absolute temperature is given in degrees Rankine (°R). The following equations can be used for converting between temperature scales:

$$°K = °C + 273 \qquad (2.1A)$$

$$°R = °F + 460 \qquad (2.1B)$$

Linear *speed* and *acceleration* are derived quantities. Speed is distance traveled per unit of time. Typical SI units of speed are meters per second (m/s) or kilometers per hour (km/h). Customary units of speed are feet per second (ft/s) or miles per hour (mph). Linear acceleration is the change in speed per unit of time. Linear acceleration is given in meters per second per second (m/s$^2$) in SI units, or feet per second per second (ft/s$^2$) in customary units. The acceleration of gravity is 9.80 m/s$^2$ (32.2 ft/s$^2$).

*Area* and *volume* are familiar derived quantities. The typical unit of area is the meter squared (m$^2$) in SI units or feet squared (ft$^2$) in customary units. The typical unit of volume is the meter cubed (m$^3$) in SI units or cubic feet (ft$^3$) in customary units. However, engine displacement volumes are typically given in liters (L) in SI units, or cubic inches (in.$^3$) in customary units. The following are some useful volume conversion equations:

Basic Thermodynamics of Engines

$$1 \text{ m}^3 = 1000 \text{ L} \qquad (2.2\text{A})$$

$$1 \text{ ft}^3 = 1728 \text{ in.}^3 \qquad (2.2\text{B})$$

*Force* is a derived quantity in the SI system of units. The derivation makes use of Newton's Second Law and states that one unit of force is required to accelerate a mass of one kilogram at one meter per second per second. The derived unit of force is thus kg·m/s$^2$, and this combination of units has been given the name of newton (N). The newton is such a small unit that forces are frequently measured in kilonewtons (kN).

In the customary system of units, force is a basic quantity and mass is a derived quantity. The basic unit of force is the pound (lb$_f$). Mass is derived by means of Newton's second law, which states that the mass that is accelerated at 1 ft/s$^2$ by 1 lb$_f$ is 1 lb$_f$·s$^2$/ft or a mass of one slug. In actual practice, the slug is seldom used to indicate quantity of matter. Instead, the weight of the quantity of matter is used and customary scales are calibrated in pounds (lb$_f$). Thus, for example, the flow rate of fuel would be given in pounds per hour (lb$_f$/h) in customary units. For convenience, the subscript f will be implied throughout the remainder of this book, i.e., the notation lb will always indicate pounds of force. A fuel flow rate of 70 lb/h from a fuel tank, for example, would mean that the quantity of fuel flowing in 1 h, if put on a scale at the earth's surface, would weigh 70 lb.

*Work* is accomplished when a force acts through a distance. Thus, the derived unit for work is the newton meter (N·m), and this combination has been given the name joule (J). *Energy* is a capacity for doing work and has the same units as work. Since one joule of work or energy is rather small, the kilojoule (kJ) or megajoule (MJ) are often used as measures of work or energy. When using customary units, work and energy are given in foot pounds (ft-lb).

*Power* is the rate of doing work. That is, it is the amount of work accomplished per unit of time. The SI unit for power is the watt (W), but a watt is so small that tractor is usually given in kilowatts (kW). Power is typically stated in foot-pounds per second (ft-lb/s) or horsepower (hp) in customary units. To rate his steam engine in familiar terms, James Watt established the relationship that 1 hp = 550 ft-lb/s. Much more will be said about power in Chapter 5.

*Pressure* refers to the amount of force exerted on a unit area by a gas or other fluid. Thus, the derived unit for pressure is the newton per meter squared (N/m$^2$), and this combination of units has been given the name pascal (Pa). One pascal of pressure is so small that pressures are more frequently given in kilopascals (kPa) or megapascals (MPa). In customary units, the basic unit of pressure is pounds per square inch (psi).

The earth is at the bottom of a deep pile of air called the atmosphere, and *barometric pressure* is the pressure that air exerts on any body in the atmosphere. A tire or other vessel may contain air trapped at a pressure greater than that of the atmosphere. Typical gages used to measure the trapped pressure will indicate only the excess of the trapped pressure over the barometric pressure, and the pressure so measured is called *gage pressure*. However, the total pressure or *absolute pressure*, in the tire is the sum of the gage pressure plus the barometric pressure:

$$\text{absolute pressure} = \text{barometric pressure} + \text{gage pressure} \tag{2.3}$$

In reporting pressures, it is necessary to specify whether the pressure is gage or absolute, because the units are the same for both kinds of pressure.

Other derived units are used in calculating the performance of engines and tractors. These units will be discussed in Chapter 5.

## 2.3 IDEAL GAS LAW

The gases trapped in a combustion chamber undergo great changes in volume, pressure, and temperature. Many experiments have shown that these changes are interrelated. According to the kinetic theory of gases, pressure results from the frequent collisions of gas molecules with each other and with the walls of the container. At a given temperature, pressure increases as the volume of the chamber is reduced because collisions are more frequent in a smaller chamber. Increasing the temperature gives the molecules more energy, and they move faster. The number and violence of collisions therefore increases with temperature and causes an increase in pressure. The molecules have no energy at zero absolute temperature, and thus the pressure is also zero.

All of the interrelationships of pressure, volume, and temperature of a gas can be expressed by the *ideal gas law*:

$$pV = MRT \tag{2.4}$$

where
$p$ = absolute pressure of the gas in kPa (psi)
$V$ = volume of the gas in m$^3$ (ft$^3$)

# Basic Thermodynamics of Engines

M = quantity of the gas in kg (lb)
R = specific gas constant
T = absolute temperature of the gas in °K (°R)

The specific gas constant varies depending upon the molecular weight of the gas. However, the product of the R times molecular weight is a universal gas constant with the value 8.314 (10.72). Thus, R for any specific gas is a 8.314 (10.72) divided by the molecular weight of the gas.

One application of the ideal gas law is in finding the density of air at a given temperature and barometric pressure. *Density* is defined as mass per unit volume, and the gas constant for air is 8.314/29 (10.72/29). Therefore, the air density is:

$$\rho_a = \frac{M}{V} = \frac{p}{RT} = \frac{K_p \, p}{T} \tag{2.5}$$

where
$\rho_a$ = air density in kg/m³ (lb/ft³)
$K_p$ = units constant = 3.488 (2.705)

**Example Problem 2.1**
Given that the barometric pressure is 100 kPa (14.5 psi) and the air temperature is 20° C (68° F), find the density of the air in the atmosphere.

**Solution:** The absolute temperature is 20° C + 273 = 293° K (68 + 460 = 528° R). The absolute pressure of the air is 100 kPa (14.5 psi). Thus, the air density is:

$\rho_a = 3.488*100/293 = 1.190$ kg/m³

or

$\rho_a = 2.705*14.5/528 = 0.0743$ lb/ft³

## 2.4 PRESSURE CHANGES IN A POLYTROPIC PROCESS

The mass of gas trapped in a combustion chamber during the compression or expansion strokes is essentially constant. If the temperature were to remain constant, Equation 2.4 shows that the product of pressure times volume also would be constant. The term *isothermal* has been given to a constant-temperature compression or expansion process. The temperature actually changes, however, and the polytropic rule is used. It is:

$$pV^n = \text{constant} \quad (2.6)$$

Many experiments have shown that, if the combustion chamber was insulated to prevent any heat transfer, the value of exponent n would be 1.4. The term *adiabatic* has been given to processes in which no heat is transferred. The true value for n in a running engine must always be between 1.0 and 1.4 and, for the compression stroke, is close to 1.3.

It is not necessary to have a value for the constant in Equation 2.6 because the equation is generally used to compute changes in gas pressure during a compression or expansion, and the product $pV^n$ is the same at both ends of the change. Therefore, for a polytropic compression:

$$p_2 = p_1 \left[\frac{V_1}{V_2}\right]^n \quad (2.7)$$

where
- $p_1$ = pressure at the beginning of the compression
- $p_2$ = pressure after the gas is compressed from volume $V_1$ to volume $V_2$

Equation 2.7 could also be used for polytropic expansions of a gas.

## 2.5 TEMPERATURE CHANGES IN A POLYTROPIC PROCESS

Combining the polytropic rule (Equation 2.6) with the ideal gas law (Equation 2.4) gives a rule for temperature changes in a polytropic process:

$$T_2 = T_1 \left[\frac{V_1}{V_2}\right]^{n-1} \quad (2.8)$$

One of the applications of Equation 2.8 is to calculate whether a diesel engine has sufficient compression to ignite the fuel.

# Basic Thermodynamics of Engines

## Example Problem 2.2

The self-ignition temperature (SIT) of a fuel is, as discussed in Chapter 6, the temperature at which the fuel will self-ignite. A diesel engine will not start unless the temperature at the end of the compression stroke is greater than the SIT of the fuel. Given that the SIT of diesel fuel is 387° C (729° F) and that the air temperature in the combustion chamber is 20° C (68° F) at the beginning of the compression stroke, will the air be hot enough to ignite the fuel if it is compressed to one-sixteenth of its initial volume? (Assume n = 1.3)

**Solution:** The absolute temperature $T_1 = 20°$ C + 273 = 293° K ($T_1 = 68°$ F + 460 = 528° R). The temperature $T_2$ at the end of the compression stroke (Figure 2.1) is:

$$T_2 = 293[16/1]^{1.3-1} = 673° \text{ K} \quad (T_2 = 528[16/1]^{1.3-1} = 1213° \text{ R})$$

or

$$T_2 = 673° \text{ K} - 273 = 400° \text{ C} \quad (T_2 = 1213° \text{ R} - 460 = 753° \text{ F})$$

The temperature $T_2$ is above the SIT of the fuel, and therefore the fuel will self-ignite from the compression.

## 2.6 COMPRESSION RATIOS AND DISPLACEMENT VOLUME

Engines are most efficient when the pressure is maximized at the beginning of the expansion stroke (see the Beau de Rochas principles in Chapter 1). Maximum pressures produce the greatest amount of work from a given amount of air-fuel mixture. Pressures are maximized by releasing the fuel energy into a small, highly pressurized volume at the end of the compression stroke. The volume of gas in the cylinder when the piston is at *head dead center* (HDC) is called the *clearance volume* (Figure 2.1). Likewise, the volume of gas in the cylinder when the piston is at *crank dead center* (CDC) is called the *maximum volume*. Based on the pressure-volume diagrams introduced later in this chapter, the symbol $V_1$ is used to indicate the maximum volume and $V_2$ indicates clearance volume. The ratio of maximum volume to clearance volume is called the *compression ratio* (r):

$$\text{compression ratio} = r = \frac{V_1}{V_2} \tag{2.9}$$

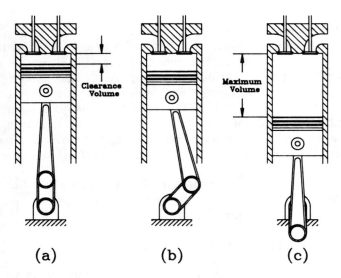

*Figure 2.1–Illustration of clearance and maximum volumes in a combustion cylinder.*

As Equation 2.7 and the preceding discussion indicate, compression pressure and engine efficiency can be increased by increasing the compression ratio.

The volume swept out by the piston as it moves from CDC to HDC is called the *displacement* of the cylinder. The displacement can be calculated from the bore (diameter) of the cylinder and the stroke length:

$$\text{displacement/cylinder} = D_c = \frac{\pi}{4} * \text{bore}^2 * \text{stroke length} \quad (2.10)$$

For a multicylinder engine, the total engine displacement (D) is:

$$D = \frac{\pi}{4}(\text{bore})^2(\text{stroke length})(\text{no. of cylinders}) \quad (2.11)$$

The difference ($V_1 - V_2$) in Figure 2.2 is equal to the displacement of a single cylinder.

## 2.7 THE THEORETICAL OTTO CYCLE

The *Otto cycle* is the theoretical cycle for spark-ignition engines. Figure 2.2 is a pressure/volume diagram of the cycle. At point 0, the

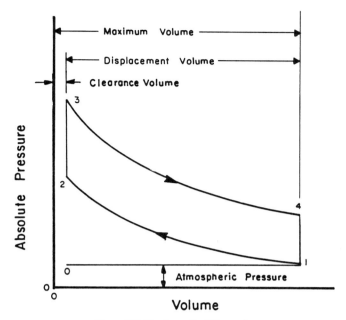

*Figure 2.2–The theoretical Otto cycle.*

intake valve is open and the piston is at HDC. From point 0 to point 1, the piston moves to CDC and draws a charge of air and fuel vapor into the cylinder. The intake valve closes at point 1. The process that occurs between point 1 and point 2 is a polytropic compression stroke. The piston compresses the trapped mixture while moving toward HDC. The spark plug ignites the fuel-air mixture at point 2 and the pressure rises rapidly. Although it is not shown on the diagram, the temperature rises proportionally with the pressure. The process that occurs between point 3 and point 4 is a polytropic expansion stroke. The hot, pressurized gases do mechanical work by forcing the piston toward CDC. At point 4, the exhaust valve opens and the pressure drops to atmospheric as the exhaust gases rush out. The process that occurs between point 1 and point 0 is the exhaust stroke. The piston forces out the remaining exhaust gases while moving toward HDC. The cycle starts over at point 0 as the exhaust valve closes and the intake valve opens.

The *theoretical engine efficiency* – that is, the fraction of the fuel energy that is theoretically converted to mechanical work in the Otto cycle – is given by the following equation:

$$\text{Otto cycle efficiency} = 1 - \frac{1}{r^{n-1}} \tag{2.12}$$

We have now covered enough thermodynamics to calculate the theoretical efficiency of the Otto cycle engine.

**Example Problem 2.3**

Given a four-cylinder Otto cycle engine with a 90 mm (3.54 in.) bore, 100 mm (3.94 in.) stroke, and a clearance volume of 0.106 L (6.47 in.$^3$), calculate the total engine displacement, the compression ratio, and the theoretical cycle efficiency. (Assume n = 1.4)

**Solution:** The displacement of each cylinder is:

$$D_c = \pi/4*[90/10]^2*[100/10] = 636 \text{ cm}^3$$

or

$$D_c = \pi/4*3.54^2*3.94 = 38.8 \text{ in.}^3$$

The total engine displacement is:

$$D = [636 \text{ cm}^3]*[L/1000 \text{ cm}^3]*[4 \text{ cylinders}] = 2.54 \text{ L}$$

or

$$D = [38.3 \text{ in.}^3]*[4 \text{ cylinders}] = 155 \text{ in.}^3$$

The maximum volume per cylinder is:

$$V_1 = D_c + V_2 = 636/1000 + 0.106 = 0.742 \text{ L}$$

or

$$V_1 = D_c + V_2 = 38.8 + 6.47 = 45.3 \text{ in.}^3$$

The compression ratio is:

$$r = V_1/V_2 = 0.742/0.106 = 7.0$$

or

$$r = V_1/V_2 = 45.3/6.47 = 7.0$$

The theoretical cycle efficiency is:

$$\text{efficiency} = 1 - 1/r^{\,n-1} = 1 - 1/7^{1.4-1} = 0.541$$

Thus the cycle efficiency is 54.1%.

Notice that increasing either n or r would raise the theoretical efficiency. However, n cannot be greater than 1.4, the value used in Example Problem 2.3. The compression ratio could be increased by reducing the clearance volume, but then, as will be explained in Chapter 6, the engine could begin knocking. Thus, the theoretical efficiency cannot be much above 50%. Actual efficiency would be considerably less because of energy losses in engine friction and in

# Basic Thermodynamics of Engines

pumping air into and exhaust gases out of the engine. The result is that gasoline engines convert less that half of the energy in the fuel into useful work. Typical overall efficiencies of gasoline engines have ranged from 15 to 30% at full load; efficiencies have been increasing but are limited by the thermodynamic considerations described in Example Problem 2.3.

## 2.8 THE THEORETICAL DIESEL CYCLE

The cycle shown in Figure 2.3 is Dr. Rudolph Diesel's original theoretical cycle for the diesel engine. The cycle is identical to the Otto cycle, except for the processes between points 2 and 4. Also, the pressure at point 2 is much higher in the diesel cycle than in the Otto cycle because of a higher compression ratio. Injecting and burning the fuel at constant volume in the diesel cycle would have caused very high engine pressures and stresses at point 3 because of the high compression pressure at point 2. The excessively high pressures were avoided in the theoretical diesel cycle by injecting and burning the fuel during the expansion stroke. Gas pressures tend to fall during an expansion stroke, but, by injecting the fuel energy at the right rate, pressures were kept constant between points 2 and 3 of the theoretical diesel cycle. Fuel input is stopped at point 3, and

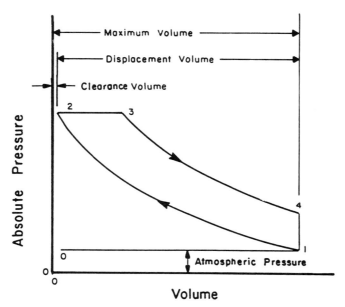

*Figure 2.3–The theoretical diesel cycle.*

the pressures begin to fall, as in a normal expansion stroke. Point 3 is called the *fuel cutoff point*, and the ratio $V_3/V_2$ is called the *fuel cutoff ratio*.

Equation 2.9 can be used to calculate the compression ratio of a diesel engine, and Equations 2.10 and 2.11 can be used to calculate cylinder and engine displacements of the diesel. The theoretical efficiency of the diesel cycle can be calculated from Equation 2.13. Notice that it is identical to Otto cycle efficiency, except for the quantity in brackets:

$$\text{diesel cycle efficiency} = 1 - \frac{1}{r^{n-1}} \left[ \frac{\left(\frac{V_3}{V_2}\right)^n - 1}{n\left(\frac{V_3}{V_2}\right) - 1} \right] \qquad (2.13)$$

## 2.9 COMPARISON OF OTTO AND DIESEL CYCLE

Figure 2.4 is a plot of the theoretical efficiencies of the Otto and diesel cycles. At the same compression ratio, the Otto cycle is more efficient than the diesel cycle. It is more efficient to release the chemical energy of the fuel into a small, constant clearance volume than to release it into an expanding volume while the piston descends toward CDC. The diesel efficiency becomes poorer as the fuel cutoff ratio is increased.

In actual practice, Otto and diesel cycles are not used at the same compression ratio. Compression ratios are typically in the range 6 to 8 for gasoline engines, because higher ratios could cause engine knocking. Ratios of 15 or higher must be used in diesel engines to self-ignite the fuel. Thus, diesel engines overcome their poorer cycle efficiency by operating at a much higher compression ratio than do spark-ignition engines.

## 2.10 THE DUAL CYCLE

The strength of modern diesel engines is sufficient to permit the start of fuel injection and burning before the piston reaches HDC on the compression stroke. At full load, fuel injection and burning continue

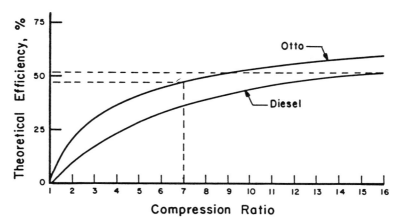

*Figure 2.4–Theoretical efficiencies of Otto and diesel cycles.*

into the expansion stroke. Thus, the dual cycle of Figure 2.5 is more descriptive of the modern diesel engine than of either the Otto or the diesel cycle. The theoretical efficiency of the dual cycle can be calculated from Equation 2.14:

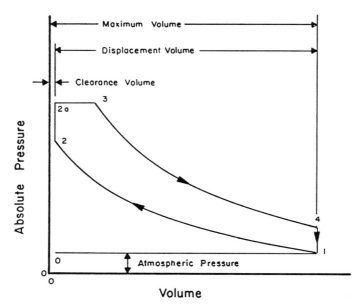

*Figure 2.5–The theoretical dual cycle.*

$$\text{dual-cycle efficiency} = 1 - \frac{1}{r^{n-1}} \left[ \frac{\beta(r_{co}^n - 1) + n(r_{co} - 1)(1-\beta)}{n(r_{co} - 1)} \right] \quad (2.14)$$

where
- $\beta$ = fraction of fuel energy released at constant pressure
- $1-\beta$ = fraction of fuel energy released at constant volume
- $r_{co}$ = $V_3/V_2$ = fuel cut-off ratio

Equation 2.14 is seldom used in calculations because of its complexity, but it has been plotted in Figure 2.6. As shown in Figure 2.6, the efficiency of the dual cycle increases from that of the diesel cycle at $\beta = 1.0$ to that of the Otto cycle at $\beta = 0$. The cycle efficiency of a diesel engine varies with the load on the engine. As the load increases, fuel injection extends further into the expansion stroke, the fuel cutoff ratio increases, and the cycle efficiency declines. The converse statement has interesting practical implications. That is, diesel engines can increase their cycle efficiency at part load. Otto cycle engines do not have that ability. The cycle efficiencies in Figure 2.6 are theoretical and, because of friction and pumping losses, are not attainable by practical diesel engines. Typical overall efficiencies of diesel engines range from 30 to 40% at full load.

## 2.11 SUMMARY

SI units are the primary units used in this book because they are the units used predominantly in the tractor industry. Customary units are also given for those who have not yet converted to the SI system. SI is an abbreviation for "Le Systeme International d'Unites", or the modern metric system. Length, time, mass, and temperature are basic SI quantities. Other quantities derived from the basic ones include speed, acceleration, area, volume, force, work, energy, power, and pressure. Customary quantities are similar, except that force is a basic unit and mass is derived. Absolute pressures and absolute temperatures must be used in thermodynamic calculations.

Interrelationships between absolute pressure, absolute temperature, and the volume of a trapped gas can be studied by means of the ideal gas law and the polytropic rule, which were introduced in this chapter. For example, the equations were used to calculate the density of atmospheric air and to predict whether a diesel engine would start under specific conditions.

The Otto cycle was introduced as the theoretical cycle for spark-ignition engines. The concept of compression ratio was introduced

# Basic Thermodynamics of Engines

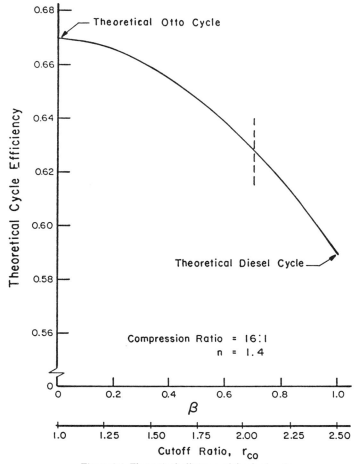

*Figure 2.6–Theoretical efficiency of the dual cycle.*

and used in calculating the efficiency of the Otto cycle. The concepts of displacement volume and clearance volume also were introduced.

The theoretical diesel cycle was shown to be less efficient than the Otto cycle when both are at the same compression ratio. In practice, however, diesel engines run at much higher compression ratios than do Otto cycle engines and thus can be more efficient. The dual cycle was introduced as being more descriptive of modern diesel engines than the theoretical cycle. Unlike the Otto cycle, the dual cycle increases in efficiency at part load.

Because of practical limits on compression ratios, theoretical efficiencies of gasoline engines cannot be raised much above 50%. Actual efficiencies are considerably lower because of inherent energy losses within the engine.

# QUESTIONS

Q2.1    What are the four basic quantities that are used in analyzing engines and tractors? Give the basic SI (customary) unit used with each quantity.

Q2.2    What would the freezing point of water be on the Kelvin (Rankine) scale?

Q2.3    Suppose a sealed container full of air was heated. Would the pressure in the container increase? Would the air density increase? Briefly explain your answers.

Q2.4    If the compression stroke in an engine was carried out so slowly that the temperature of the air remained constant, what value would n have in Equation 2.6?

Q2.5    If the walls of a combustion chamber were insulated and the compression stroke was carried out so rapidly that no heat could be transferred out of the trapped air, what value would n have in Equation 2.6?

Q2.6    Between which two points in the Otto cycle is the chemical energy in the fuel converted into heat?

Q2.7    Between which two points in the diesel cycle is the chemical energy in the fuel converted into heat?

Q2.8    In Example Problem 2.3, what percent of the energy in the fuel was lost as wasted heat?

Q2.9    Why did Diesel design his cycle with constant pressure between points 2 and 3 instead of using constant volume, as in the Otto cycle?

Q2.10   Does the cycle efficiency of a diesel engine increase, decrease, or remain constant as more load is put on the engine? Briefly explain your answer.

# PROBLEMS

P2.1    The barometric pressure at the earth's surface is approximately 100 kPa (14.5 psi). If a gage was used to measure the pressure in a tire and the gage read 200 kPa (29 psi), what would be the absolute pressure in the tire?

P2.2  The volume inside a certain tractor tire is 0.5 m$^3$ (17.7 ft$^3$).
(a) If the air temperature in the tire is 20° C (68° F) and the gage pressure is 200 kPa (29 psi), what is the density of the air in the tire?
(b) How many kilograms (lb) of air are in the tire?

P2.3  If the absolute pressure of the air in the cylinder is 100 kPa (14.5 psi) at the beginning of the compression stroke, what is the air pressure at the end of the stroke if the air is compressed to one-sixteenth of its original volume? Assume the compression is polytropic with n = 1.3.

P2.4  In example Problem 2.2, calculate the minimum temperature T1 at the beginning of the compression stroke that would allow the fuel to self-ignite at the end of the stroke. (Hint: Solve Equation 2.8 for $T_1$ when $T_2$ = SIT of fuel.)

P2.5  A V8 engine in a tractor has a bore of 140 mm (5.51 in.) and a stroke of 127 mm (5.00 in.). Calculate the engine displacement in liters (in.$^3$).

P2.6  A certain six-cylinder engine has a 130.2 mm (5.13 in.) bore, a 127.0 mm (5 in.) stroke, and a clearance volume of 0.119 L (7.26 in.$^3$) in each cylinder.
(a) Calculate the displacement of each cylinder.
(b) Calculate the compression ratio of the engine.
(c) Is the engine a diesel or an Otto cycle engine?

P2.7  If a six-cylinder engine has a total displacement of 4.933 L (301 in.$^3$) and the compression ratio is 15.5:1, calculate the clearance volume. (*Hint*: Note that Equation 2.9 and the equation Dc = $V_1$ - $V_2$ can be solved simultaneously for $V_2$.)

P2.8  Otto cycle engines have compression ratios ranging from 6:1 to 12:1, depending on the design of the engine and the fuel used.
(a) Calculate the theoretical cycle efficiencies over this range of compression ratios, assuming n = 1.3.
(b) Plot cycle efficiencies on the y-axis versus compression ratio on the x-axis.

P2.9 Diesel engines have compression ratios ranging from 14:1 to 22:1, depending upon the size and design of the engine.

(a) Assuming a fuel cutoff ratio of 2.5 and n = 1.3, calculate the theoretical diesel cycle efficiencies over this range of compression ratios.

(b) Plot cycle efficiencies on the y-axis versus compression ratio on the x-axis.

# 3
# Engine Components

## 3.1 INTRODUCTION

Many types and sizes of internal combustion engines have been used since N. A. Otto patented his engine in 1876. The most common type of tractor engine, however, has vertical cylinders arranged side by side, as shown in Figure 3.1. This chapter covers the basic engine parts that are included in such engines. You will learn the functions of basic engine parts, reasons for selecting one type of part over another, how to install and adjust certain parts, and how to decide when the repair or replacement of certain parts is needed.

## 3.2 THE CYLINDER BLOCK

The *cylinder block* is the backbone of the engine. It supports most of the other engine parts and holds them in proper relationship to each other. The block also may act as part of the framework of some tractors and support the front wheels (Figure 3.2). Cylinder blocks for farm tractors usually are one-piece castings made from gray cast iron. Hollow passages may be cast into the block for circulation of cooling water, and enlargements are cast into the walls of the block so that oil galleries may be drilled.

Any one of the following arrangements may be used for the cylinders in which the pistons move:

Cast-in-block (enbloc)
Dry liner
Wet liner

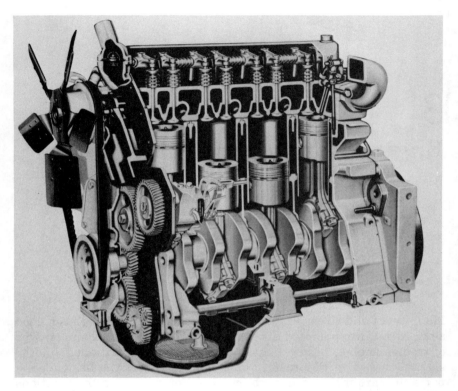

*Figure 3.1–A cutaway view of an internal combustion engine. (Courtesy of Deere & Company.)*

These arrangements are shown in Figure 3.3.

Most automotive engines use the *enbloc arrangement*, in which the cylinders are cast directly into the block. The cast-iron walls of the cylinders must be polished to provide a smooth surface for piston travel. A *dry liner* may be pressed into each cast cylinder, as shown in part b of Figure 3.3. This liner, or sleeve, is dry because it does not come into contact with the engine coolant. In contrast, a *wet sleeve* serves as the only wall between the piston and coolant. Seals must be provided to keep the coolant from leaking past the ends of a wet sleeve. The enbloc arrangement is less expensive to construct than are the liner arrangements, but the liners have the advantage of being replaceable (Figure 3.4).

Liners should be replaced (or enbloc engines should be rebored) when excessive wear has occurred or when the liner walls have been deeply scratched or scored. The two most common symptoms of wear are cylinder taper and out-of-roundness. Taper occurs when wear creates a larger diameter at the top of the ring travel zone than at the bottom. Out-of-roundness occurs when wear creates a larger

# Engine Components

*Figure 3.2–A frameless tractor.*

diameter perpendicular to the crankshaft than the cylinder diameter parallel to the crankshaft. Diameters can be measured as shown in Figure 3.5. The manufacturer's specifications should be used as a guideline when you are deciding whether taper or out-of-roundness is excessive. As a general guideline, however, sleeve replacement or reboring is needed when either cylinder taper or out-of-roundness exceeds 0.13 mm (0.005 in.).

New cylinders or liners will have a surface finish similar to that shown in Figure 3.6. The cross-hatched pattern is made by moving a rotating deglazer up and down in the cylinder during the finishing operation. The cross-hatched pattern prevents rings from catching and also provides a surface that retains lubricating oil. Although some vertical polishing normally occurs during engine operation, the liners should not have deep scuff or scratch marks on the surface.

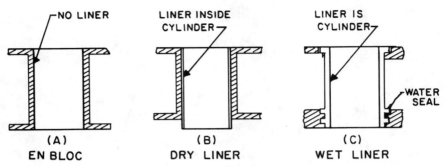

Figure 3.3–Types of cylinder liners.

## 3.3 THE CYLINDER HEAD

The removal of pistons and other parts is simplified by designing cylinders with open ends at the top. The open ends are sealed by means of a *cylinder head* (Figure 3.7). In addition to sealing the combustion chambers, the head contains the valves and passages, or ports, to the intake and exhaust manifolds, which will be discussed in

Figure 3.4–Removal of a cylinder liner. (Photo by Laurie Goering.)

Engine Components 43

*Figure 3.5–Measurement of cylinder liner diameter. (Photo by Laurie Goering.)*

Chapter 11. The head also contains oil passages for conveying lubricating oil to moving parts and water passages for the channeling of cooling water.

Cylinder heads are one-piece castings and are typically made of an alloy of iron and copper or aluminum. The head must be completely sealed to the block to prevent leakage of combustion gases. Excessive warpage of either the top of the block or the mating surface on the head can prevent complete sealing. Therefore, both surfaces must be within the flatness specifications recommended by the manufacturer. Minor warpage can be corrected by planing the head and/or the block to achieve more nearly flat surfaces.

A special *cylinder head gasket* is used between the head and block, as shown in Figure 3.7. Typically, such gaskets are made of asbestos and include metallic rings around each cylinder to aid in sealing in combustion gases. The head is fastened to the block with high-strength head bolts, which must be tightened down gradually and uniformly to ensure good sealing. Generally, manufacturers' manuals number each head bolt location and specify the order in which the head bolts are to be tightened. The normal procedure, as shown in Figure 3.8, is to follow a spiral pattern in tightening the head bolts. This tightening sequence aids in keeping the head flat for a better seal. Manufacturers' manuals will also specify the amount of torque to be applied in tightening each head bolt.

*Figure 3.6–Surface finish of a new cylinder liner. (Photo by Laurie Goering.)*

## 3.4 THE VALVE TRAIN

Valves must seal tightly during the compression and power strokes, but they also must provide minimum flow restriction during the intake and exhaust strokes. Valve timing also is important, as discussed in Section 4.2.1. Operation of the valves is controlled by the valve train, as is illustrated in Figure 3.9.

### 3.4.1 Valve Actuation

The valve train begins at the camshaft. A typical cam profile is shown in Figure 3.10. A valve should be closed when its cam follower (or tappet, as it is also called) rests on the base circle of the cam. The

*Figure 3.7–Cylinder head removed from an engine. (Photo by Laurie Goering.)*

# Engine Components

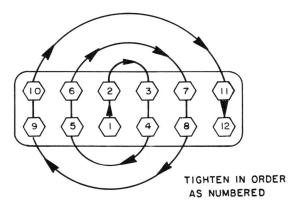

*Figure 3.8–Spiral pattern for tightening head bolts.*

valve opens the maximum amount when the tappet rests on the nose of the cam, as Figure 3.9 shows. The tappet rides in a cylindrical, lubricated guide. Push rods convey the motion of the tappet to the rocker arms, which rock to open and close the valves.

Although they have not been used in tractor engines, overhead camshafts are used in modern automotive engines. Overhead

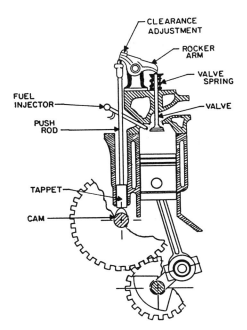

*Figure 3.9–A valve train for an engine with overhead valves.*

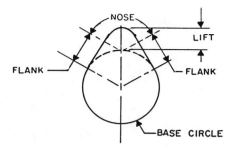

*Figure 3.10–A profile of a cam on a camshaft.*

camshafts simplify the valve train by eliminating the push rods. However, the overhead camshaft is too far above the crankshaft to be driven by a timing gear. Instead, a cogged belt is typically used to drive the camshaft from a pulley on the crankshaft.

### 3.4.2 Valve Seating

Valve terminology is given in Figure 3.11. Sealing occurs when the valve spring presses the *valve face* tightly against the *valve seat*. The seat may be machined directly into the head, or it may be machined into a valve seat insert made of high-grade alloy steel. The inserts reduce wear and are replaceable. The contact area between the valve face and valve seat must be wide enough to provide heat transfer to the guide, but narrow enough to aid in crushing valve deposits. Both valve seats and valve faces can be reconditioned by grinding.

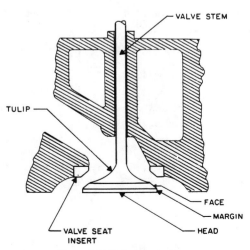

*Figure 3.11–Valve terminology.*

*Figure 3.12–Use of a valve-spring compressor to remove a valve. (Photo by Laurie Goering.)*

Manufacturers' recommendations as to the proper geometry of the reground valve faces and seats should be followed.

### 3.4.3 Valve Stem Clearance

Proper clearance must be maintained between the valve stems and the *valve guides*. Excessive clearance allows lubricating oil to move down the valve stem into the intake or exhaust ports, making oil consumption excessive. However, some oil must move into the valve guide to provide lubrication. Manufacturers' manuals will specify allowable tolerances on valve stem diameters and on the inside diameters of valve guides. A *valve-spring compressor* (Figure 3.12) is used to remove valves for inspection or repair.

### 3.4.4 Valve Cooling

Valves can be damaged by overheating. Each valve must be able to reject the heat that is transferred to it by the hot combustion gases. The shortest and most effective heat rejection path is through the

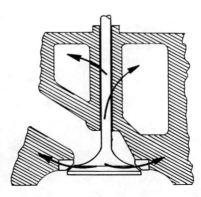

*Figure 3.13–Heat transfer from a valve.*

valve seat to the water jacket (Figure 3.13). Heat can also travel up the valve stem and be transferred through the valve guide to the water jacket. Exhaust valves are especially vulnerable to heat damage because, when they are open while hot exhaust gases are being expelled, no heat can be rejected through the valve seats.

Intake and exhaust valves usually differ in head diameter and in the materials of which they are constructed. Exhaust valves are made smaller to reduce heat transfer from hot combustion gases to the valve. Also, the increased valve opening area of the larger intake valves is needed because, in naturally aspirated engines, less than one atmosphere of pressure is available to push air through the intake valves and into the combustion chamber. Materials for valves include carbon steel, nickel steel or chrome-molybdenum alloys which may be hardened to withstand the high stresses associated with rapid opening and closing of valves. Protective coatings are used on exhaust valves to allow them to resist etching and maintain hardness at elevated temperatures. The valve face and head may be aluminized, that is, a thin layer of aluminum may be applied to resist corrosion. Nickel-chromium alloys may also be coated on the valve head to inhibit corrosion. Iron-, nickel-, or cobalt-based alloys may be applied to the valve seating faces to provide improved corrosion and wear resistance. Since the stem of the exhaust valve is the only heat transfer path when the valve is open, the exhaust valve stem is sometimes made hollow and filled with metallic sodium or sodium-potassium mixtures to improve heat transfer rates.

### 3.4.5 Valve Rotators

*Valve rotators* are used on some engines to cause the valves to rotate when the engine runs. Release-type rotators (Figure 3.14) hold the retainer lock away from the valve stem when the valve is open. Engine vibrations and moving gases then cause the valve to rotate.

Engine Components

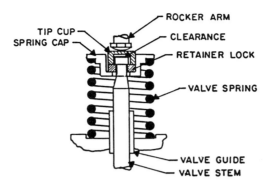

*Figure 3.14—A release-type valve rotator.*

Positive rotators (Figure 3.15) use spring-loaded balls in inclined races to force the valve to rotate slightly each time the valve opens. Rotation of the valves provides a wiping action to keep the valve seat clean and provide better sealing. Because some portions of the valve face are closer to the water jacket than others, valve rotators also help to maintain all parts of the valve head at a more uniform temperature. Some engines only have rotators on the exhaust valves, because intake valves are inherently cooler and cleaner than exhaust valves.

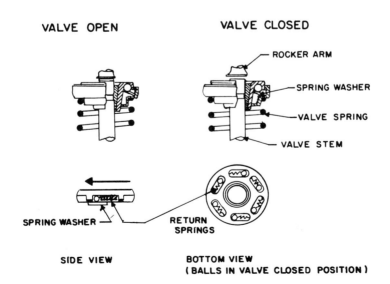

*Figure 3.15—A positive-type valve rotator.*

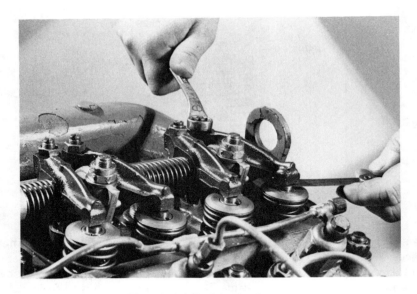

*Figure 3.16–Adjusting valve clearance.*

### 3.4.6  Valve Clearance Adjustment

Heating of the valves during engine warm-up causes the valve stems to extend in length. Clearance must be provided or the increase in stem length would cause the valves to be held open when the engine was warm. Too much clearance would cause noisy operation and would also affect valve timing. Valve clearance can be adjusted and measured, as Figure 3.16 shows. Generally, exhaust valves require more clearance than do intake valves. Necessary clearance also varies with engine temperature. Therefore, manufacturers will specify whether the engine should be cold or hot (warmed up) when valve clearance is set. Typical valve clearances for tractor engines range from 0.25 to 0.50 mm (0.010 to 0.020 in.) for intake valves and from 0.30 to 0.75 mm (0.012 to 0.030 in.) for exhaust valves. Manufacturers' specifications should always be followed for specific engines. Valve clearance cannot be set properly unless the valve tappet is resting on the base circle of the cam. Most manufacturers' shop manuals will describe how to rotate the crankshaft of multicylinder engines so that several tappets will be on their base circles at the same time.

Some automotive engines use *hydraulic lifters* as cam followers (Figure 3.17). A hydraulic lifter receives oil through a passage in the lifter guide and through the use of internal valving, automatically adjusts its length to maintain zero valve clearance. Hydraulic lifters provide quieter valve operation and eliminate the need for valve clearance adjustment. Tractor engines generally avoid the added

# Engine Components

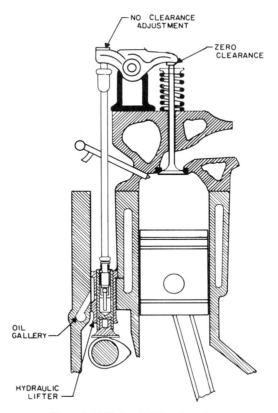

*Figure 3.17–Hydraulic lifters for valves.*

expense of hydraulic lifters by using solid lifters – that is, ordinary cam followers.

## 3.4.7 Timing Gears

Timing gears are used in most tractor engines to time the camshaft to the crankshaft. Typically, alignment marks are stamped on the timing gears to aid mechanics in correctly timing the camshaft. Figure 3.9 shows timing gears, but the timing marks are on the parts of the gears that have been cut away. Typically, when the timing mark on the camshaft gear is aligned with the timing mark on the crankshaft gear with the No. 1 cylinder at HDC between the compression and power strokes, the camshaft will be timed properly. Manufacturers' shop manuals usually describe the correct alignment of the timing marks to ensure correct valve timing.

*Figure 3.18–Piston and connecting rod assembly. (Courtesy of Deere & Company.)*

## 3.5 PISTON AND CONNECTING ROD ASSEMBLIES

A *piston* and *connecting rod* assembly is shown in Figure 3.18. A forged-steel connecting rod converts the reciprocating motion of the piston into the rotating motion of the crankshaft. Connecting rod terminology is given in Figure 3.19. The head has a removable cap for disconnecting the rod from the crankshaft. The cap is held in place by two high-strength bolts that must be tightened to a specified torque during assembly. The connecting rod must not be twisted or bent, the two bores must be parallel within close limits to assure the correct alignment of the piston in the cylinder.

### 3.5.1 Piston Pin Retaining Systems

A *piston pin* joins the connecting rod to the piston. Most tractor engines use a full-floating pin, a pin that is free to rotate relative to both the piston and the connecting rod. Snap rings are used to prevent the pin from sliding endwise in the bore. If the pin is clamped tightly into the connecting rod, it is called a semi-floating pin. A fixed pin is prevented from rotating relative to the piston. When either a fixed pin or a full-floating pin is used, a bushing is usually pressed into the eye of the connecting rod to provide a replaceable wear surface.

Engine Components

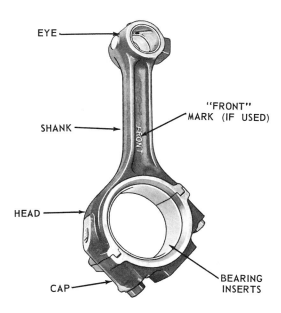

*Figure 3.19–Connecting rod terminology. (Courtesy of Deere & Company.)*

## 3.5.2 Pistons

The piston provides a top area on which the combustion gases can exert pressure, and it also carries piston rings for sealing and wiping the cylinder. Correct piston terminology is given in Figure 3.20. The pistons are made of cast iron or cast aluminum alloys. The angularity of the connecting rod during the power stroke produces a force on the left side of the piston (as viewed from the front if the crankshaft has standard clockwise rotation). Thus, as shown in Figure 3.20, the left side of the piston is called the *major thrust face*, and the opposite side is called the *minor thrust face*. Cylinder liner wear is more rapid on the side rubbed by the major thrust face because the piston exerts greater pressure on that side. The terms thrust and antithrust are sometimes used instead of major thrust and minor thrust, respectively. Typically, the piston pin is not on the centerline of the piston; rather, the pin is offset slightly toward the major thrust face against the liner wall.

The piston should be as nearly cylindrical as possible when it is operating at normal temperature in the engine. The cold piston must be noncylindrical because the piston does not expand uniformly while heating. The top of the piston heats much more than does the lower skirt. Thus, cold pistons are smaller at the top and are said to have skirt taper. Similarly, the minor diameter (see Figure 3.20) expands

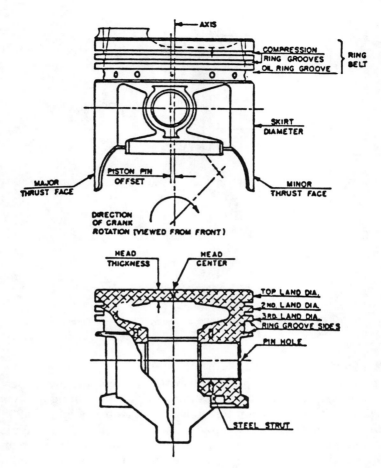
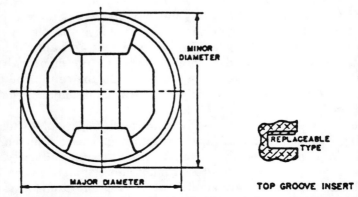

*Figure 3.20–Piston terminology. (Reprinted with permission. © 1984 Handbook, Society of Automotive Engineers, Inc.)*

Engine Components

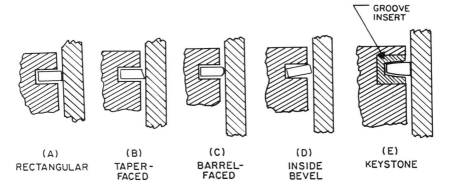

(A) RECTANGULAR  (B) TAPER-FACED  (C) BARREL-FACED  (D) INSIDE BEVEL  (E) KEYSTONE

*Figure 3.21–Types of piston rings.*

more than the major diameter during heating due to the extra material found in the piston pin bosses. Thus, cold pistons have smaller minor diameters than major diameters and are said to be cam ground. The pistons must be slightly smaller than the bore to provide running clearance. The clearance should be at least 0.05 mm (0.002 in.) and typically is about 0.15 mm (0.006 in.).

### 3.5.3  Piston Rings

Typical pistons will include a ring belt containing an *oil control ring* and one or more *compression rings* riding in grooves in the piston. The purpose of the oil control ring is to wipe most of the oil from the cylinder walls during downstrokes and to convey this oil through small holes to the inside of the piston. The function of the compression rings is to provide a seal to reduce blowby (movement of hot combustion gases into the crankcase of the engine). Ring grooves are machined directly into the walls of cast-iron pistons. Some aluminum pistons include a groove insert. The groove insert provides greater wear resistance than does the aluminum piston.

Five major types of compression rings have been used on farm tractor engines, and these are illustrated in Figure 3.21. The rings are made of hardened cast iron and may be plated with chrome to reduce wear. The rectangular ring is the simplest and least expensive ring. The lower edge of the taper-faced ring has positive contact with the liner to provide good wiping of oil on the down-stroke. The taper-faced ring seats quickly, but it has only fair control of blowby. The barrel-faced ring has reduced contact area with the cylinder, which results in greater contact pressures, thereby providing better control of blowby than the rectangular ring provides. The cutout on the inside edge of the inside bevel ring allows this ring to twist in its groove and provide tight sealing during combustion. The inside bevel

*Figure 3.22–Measurement of ring side clearance. (Photo by Laurie Goering.)*

ring is often used as an intermediate ring. The keystone ring is normally used with a groove insert and resists sticking in the carbon that often appears in ring grooves.

Properly functioning rings must be free to move in their grooves. The rings use their own tension and combustion pressure behind the ring to expand outward and press against the liner wall. Rings must have both side clearance and end clearance. Figure 3.22 shows measurement of side clearance, and Figure 3.23 shows end clearance measurement. Manufacturers' shop manuals provide specifications on allowable ring clearances. Typical end gap clearances range from 0.1 mm (0.004 in.) for small pistons to 1.0 mm (0.040 in.) for pistons of large diameters. Excessive side clearance (greater than 0.2 mm or 0.008 in.) leads to excessive oil consumption, because some of the oil in the clearance space is able to move past the ring during the power stroke and be burned.

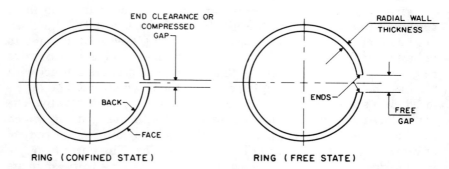

*Figure 3.23–Ring end clearance. (Reprinted with permission. © 1984 Handbook, Society of Automotive Engineers, Inc.)*

# Engine Components

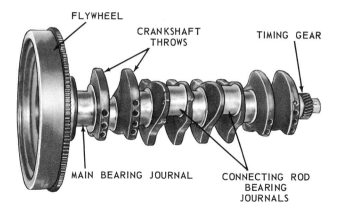

*Figure 3.24–A crankshaft and flywheel. (Courtesy of Deere & Company.)*

### 3.5.4 Piston Cooling

It is necessary to dissipate the heat that is transferred to the pistons by the hot combustion gases. No practical way has been found to provide direct water cooling of the pistons. Some heat travels down to the rings and is transferred through the rings to the cylinder liners and then to the water jacket. Oil dripping off the inside of the piston can also transfer heat from the piston. Some connecting rods include a spray jet to spray oil on the underside of the piston head for cooling. Despite these cooling measures, the piston crown operates at appreciably higher temperatures than do the cylinder liners.

## 3.6 CRANKSHAFTS, FLYWHEELS, AND BALANCERS

The *crankshaft* works in conjunction with the connecting rods to convert the reciprocating motion of the pistons into rotary motion. Typically, crankshafts are forged or cast in one piece from heat-treated steel alloy. As Figure 3.24 shows, a *flywheel* is attached to one end of the crankshaft to smooth out the power impulses from the pistons. The flywheel gains speed and stores energy when cyclic power from the pistons is high. The flywheel loses speed and releases energy when cyclic power is low.

### 3.6.1 Crankshaft Balancing

The crankshaft throws are arranged on the crankshaft to provide the smoothest possible power flows and to match the engine firing order, as will be discussed in Chapter 4. The crankshaft must be properly balanced. Counterweights are located opposite each crank throw to balance the weight of the crank throw and part of the connecting rod. Holes may be drilled into the counterweights to remove metal for more precise balancing.

### 3.6.2 Engine Balance

Counterweights cannot completely balance the inertia forces generated by the acceleration and deceleration of the pistons. The geometry of the piston, connecting rod, and crankshaft system generates both primary and secondary inertia forces, which tend to vibrate the engine vertically. Inertia couples, which tend to rock the engine about a transverse axis, are also generated. In some engines, inertia forces and couples are inherently self-canceling, as shown in

TABLE 3.1. Inherent imbalance of piston engines with vertical cylinders

| Number of Cylinders | Crank End View | Max. Inertia Forces (N) | | Max. Couples (N·m) | |
|---|---|---|---|---|---|
| | | Primary | Secondary | Primary | Secondary |
| One | (1) | k* | $\dfrac{kR}{L}$ | None | None |
| Two | (1, 2) | Balanced | $\left(\dfrac{2R}{L}\right)k$ | ka | Balanced |
| Three | (1, 2, 3) | Balanced | Balanced | 3ka | $\sqrt{3}\,\dfrac{R}{L}\,ka$ |
| Four | (1, 4 / 2, 3) | Balanced | $\left(\dfrac{4R}{L}\right)k$ | Balanced | Balanced |
| Six | (1, 6 / 2, 5 / 3, 4) | Balanced | Balanced | Balanced | Balanced |

m = reciprocating mass (piston plus part of rod) in kg
R/L = ratio of crank radius over connecting rod length
a = distance between cylinders in m
N = engine speed in rev/min
$k = mR\left(\dfrac{\pi N}{30}\right)^2$

* Half of this force can be eliminated by counterbalancing.

Table 3.1. For example, all inertia forces and couples are completely self-canceling in six-cylinder engines. F. W. Lanchester invented a balancer to cancel the secondary forces in four-cylinder engines. The *Lanchester balancer* is used on some larger four-cylinder engines to provide smoother operation. The balancer (Figure 3.25) consists of a pair of counter-rotating eccentric weights that rotate at twice crankshaft speed. The balancer is properly timed to the crankshaft when the eccentric weights are at bottom dead center and any pair of pistons is at head dead center.

### 3.6.3 Torsional Vibration Dampeners

Power impulses from the pistons produce cyclic twisting of the crankshaft. These torsional oscillations are sustained at some natural frequency in the crankshaft. In long crankshafts, the natural frequency may be close to the frequency of power impulses, and then the torsional oscillations may become large enough to cause failure of the crankshaft. Thus, a *torsional vibration dampener* is used on some engines to protect against crankshaft failure. The dampener (Figure 3.26) consists of a small flywheel connected to the front pulley by a rubber ring. Torsional oscillation of the crankshaft is transmitted to the small flywheel through the rubber ring. The rubber dissipates the vibrational energy and reduces the oscillations.

*Figure 3.25–The Lanchester balancer. (Photo by Laurie Goering.)*

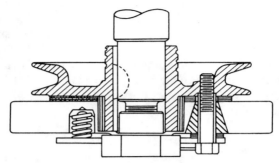

*Figure 3.26–A vibration dampener. (Courtesy of Deere & Company.)*

## 3.7   BEARINGS

Bearings are used in several places in an engine to reduce friction and wear. *Main bearings* hold the crankshaft in proper alignment in the block. *Rod bearings* join the connecting rods to the crankshaft. A bushing may be used to eliminate wear between the eye of the connecting rod and the piston pin. *Cam bearings* are used to hold the camshaft in proper alignment in the block.

Main bearings must be made in two halves to permit installation on and removal from the crankshaft. A bearing cap (Figure 3.27) is bolted to the block to lock the two bearing halves together and hold the crankshaft in place. A locking tang on the bearing ensures that the bearing does not rotate within the cap. The two high-strength bolts on each cap must be tightened to the torque specified by the manufacturer. The portion of the crankshaft that rotates in the bearing is called the journal. The bearing is made softer than the journal so that most of the wear will be confined to the bearing. Most main bearings have a steel backing to which bearing liner material is applied. Typical liners include tin- or lead-based babbit and copper or aluminum alloys. Some bearings have multiple layers of copper or aluminum alloys and silver combinations. Aluminum-lead alloy is a popular new combination. It contains 6% lead, 4% silicon, small amounts of tin, manganese, copper, and magnesium and the balance is aluminum. Some aluminum alloy bearings are one-piece and have no steel backing. Bearing liners should be able to creep to conform to the crankshaft journal and be soft enough to embed small dirt particles without scratching the journal.

Only one of the main bearings in each engine includes thrust resistance to prevent endwise movement of the crankshaft. This

# Engine Components

*Figure 3.27–A main bearing cap. (Photo by Laurie Goering.)*

main bearing may have thrust flanges, or separate thrust washers may be used, as shown in Figure 3.28. There is no standardization as to the location of thrust bearings. Manufacturers may place the thrust resistance at the front main, the rear main, or any of the main bearings between them.

Connecting rod bearings are similar to main bearings. A rod cap is bolted to the head of the connecting rod to lock the two bearing halves together around the crank throw journal. These high-strength bolts must be tightened to the torque specified by the manufacturer.

Main and rod bearings in tractor engines are pressure-lubricated. Oil is pumped through drilled passages in the block to supply the main bearings. Then, the oil moves to the rod bearings through drilled passages in the crankshaft, as shown in Figure 3.29. Grooves in the main bearings (Figure 3.30) allow continued contact of each drilled passage with the oil supply as the crankshaft rotates.

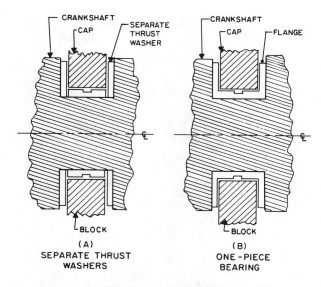

Figure 3.28–Methods for resisting crankshaft end thrust.

## 3.8 SUMMARY

The block is the backbone of an engine. It holds other engine parts in proper relationship to each other, and it also may be part of the tractor framework. The pistons may reciprocate in cylinders machined directly in the cast-iron block, but, more often, tractor

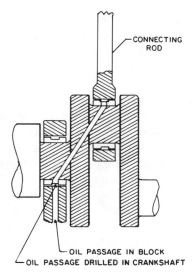

Figure 3.29–Lubrication of connecting rod bearings through main bearings.

*Figure 3.30–Oil groove in a main bearing. (Photo by Laurie Goering.)*

engines have a replaceable wet or dry liner in each cylinder. The ends of the cylinders are sealed by a cylinder head, which contains the valve ports and valves. A cylinder head gasket helps to seal in the combustion gases. The bolts joining the head to the block must be tightened in a specified order and to a specified torque to provide a good seal. Both block and head contain internal oil passages for lubrication and water passages for cooling.

The valve train includes a camshaft, tappets, push rods, rocker arms, valve springs, and intake and exhaust valves. Timing gears on the camshaft and crankshaft provide for the opening and closing of the valves at the proper times. Sealing occurs when the valve springs press the valve faces against the valve seats. The contact area must be small enough to crush deposits, but wide enough to provide heat transfer. Exhaust valves are vulnerable to overheating because, while they are open to release exhaust gases, they cannot reject heat through the valve seat. Valve rotators are often used to keep exhaust valve faces clean and at a more uniform temperature. Sufficient clearance between valve stems and guides is provided to permit entry of lubricating oil, but excessive clearance causes excessive oil consumption. Clearance between each rocker arm and valve stem must be adjusted to allow for the heat expansion of valve stems.

Due to the angularity of the connecting rod, the left side of the piston (as viewed from the front) is the major thrust face and the right side is the minor thrust face. Cylinder wear is more rapid on the side rubbed by the major thrust face of the piston. Usually, the piston pin is offset slightly toward the major thrust face to reduce piston slap against the cylinder wall. Piston shape changes with temperature, and a cylindrical shape is desired when the piston is warm. Therefore, cold pistons are skirt tapered and cam ground to achieve the desired shape when warm. Pistons are cooled by heat transfer through the rings and through the lubricating oil.

Several types of piston rings are available for controlling oil thickness on the cylinder walls and for providing a seal to reduce blowby. Rings must have both side clearance and end clearance to function effectively, but excessive side clearance leads to excessive oil consumption.

The crankshaft has an attached flywheel to smooth power impulses and counterweights to balance the weights of crank throws. Reciprocating forces due to piston acceleration are inherently balanced in some engines, but some four-cylinder engines have Lanchester balances to balance inherent reciprocating forces. Engines with long crankshafts have torsional vibration dampeners to protect against crankshaft failure.

Replaceable split bearings support the crankshaft and join connecting rods to the crankshaft. One main bearing includes flanges to absorb crankshaft end thrust. Oil is pumped through each main bearing and then to rod bearings to provide lubrication. Replaceable one-piece bearings support the camshaft and the piston pins. All of the bearings serve to reduce friction and wear in the engine.

Shop manuals that provide detailed specifications on allowable wear of engine parts are available for each engine. These specifications should be consulted when decisions are being made to recondition or replace worn parts.

## QUESTIONS

Q3.1    What are the primary differences between wet and dry liners?

Q3.2    When should cylinder liners be replaced?

Q3.3    When a cylinder head is installed, what type of pattern should be followed in tightening the head bolts? Why?

Q3.4    Why are exhaust valves more susceptible to heat damage than intake valves?

Q3.5    Do intake and exhaust valves usually have equal or unequal diameters? Briefly explain your answer.

Q3.6    What are the two types of valve rotators? How do they differ in operation?

Q3.7        (a) Why is valve clearance necessary?

# Engine Components

|  | (b) What do the letters H and C mean when used with valve clearances? |
|---|---|
| Q3.8 | Can all valves in a multicylinder engine be set without rotating the camshaft? Briefly explain your answer. |
| Q3.9 | What provisions are usually included on tractor engines to aid in the correct timing of the camshaft? |
| Q3.10 | When is a replaceable bushing used in the eye of a connecting rod? |
| Q3.11 | Often, the piston pin is slightly off-center in a piston. That is, it is closer to the major thrust of the piston.<br>(a) Which is the major thrust face of a piston?<br>(b) Why is the piston pin offset? |
| Q3.12 | (a) What is the meaning of the terms *skirt taper* and *cam ground*?<br>(b) Why do pistons have these features? |
| Q3.13 | (a) What is a groove insert?<br>(b) In what type of piston is the groove insert used?<br>(c) How is the groove insert attached to the piston? |
| Q3.14 | Does the rectangular or barrel-faced ring provide better control of blowby? Why? |
| Q3.15 | What causes piston rings to press against the liner wall? |
| Q3.16 | Figure 5.22 illustrates the measurement of ring side clearance. What is an undesirable result of excessive side clearance? |
| Q3.17 | What is the purpose of the counterweights on the crankshafts of multicylinder engines? |
| Q3.18 | (a) What is a Lanchester balancer?<br>(b) On what type of engine is the balancer used?<br>(c) When the balancer is being installed, how is it properly timed to the engine? |
| Q3.19 | (a) What is a vibration dampener? That is, of what does it consist?<br>(b) On what type of engine is the dampener used?<br>(c) Where is the dampener located on the engine? |

(d) What is its purpose?

Q3.20 (a) Why are main and rod bearings made with two halves?

(b) How are the two halves of each bearing held together?

(c) Why is the bearing made of softer material than the journal?

(d) Why are there grooves in the main bearings (as shown in Figure 3.30)?

Q3.21 What prevents the crankshaft from moving endwise in an engine?

# PROBLEMS

P3.1 Measurements during an engine overhaul show the cylinder bore at the top of ring travel is 120.72 mm (4.7528 in.) parallel to the crankshaft and 120.87 mm (4.7587 in.) perpendicular to the crankshaft. The cylinder bore at the bottom of ring travel is 120.80 mm (4.7559 in.) perpendicular to the crankshaft.
(a) Calculate the cylinder taper.
(b) Calculate the out-of-roundness.
(c) According to the general guidelines, should the cylinder liner be replaced? Why?

P3.2 A six-cylinder engine has a 127.0 mm (5.00 in.) stroke and a 107.9 mm (4.25 in.) bore. According to engine specifications, the compression ratio should be 15.5:1. While overhauling the engine, the mechanic inadvertently installs a head gasket that is 1 mm (0.039 in.) too thick.
(a) Calculate the displacement of each cylinder, the clearance volume ($V_2$), and the maximum volume ($V_1$) of each cylinder.
(b) Calculate the compression ratio of the engine with the thicker head gasket installed. (*Hint*: Calculate the extra volume ($\Delta V$) in each cylinder by multiplying the area of the cylinder bore by the extra thickness of the gasket. In calculating the new compression ratio with Equation 2.9, the $\Delta V$ must be added to both $V_1$ and $V_2$.)

P3.3 Rework P3.2, but assume that the mechanic installs a gasket that is 1 mm (0.039 in.) too thin. (*Hint*: Calculate

ΔV as in the hint in P5.2, but this time, subtract ΔV from both V1 and V2 before using Equation 2.9 to calculate the compression ratio.)

P3.4  Rework P3.2, but assume that the specifications for the new engine give the compression ratio as 7:1.

P3.5  Rework P3.3, but assume that the specifications for the new engine give the compression ratio as 7:1.

P3.6  The force in a spring can be calculated by multiplying the spring rate times the spring deflection. The valve springs on a certain engine have a spring rate of 160 N/cm (90 lb/in.). The free length of the springs, before installation, is 3.88 cm (1.53 in.). The spring lengths are 3.25 cm (1.28 in.) when the valves are closed and 2.36 cm (0.93 in.) when the valves are open.

(a) Calculate the force supplied by the spring in holding the valve closed against the valve seat.

(b) Calculate the force the rocker arm must supply to fully open the valve.

# 4
# Practical Engine Cycles and Timing

## 4.1 INTRODUCTION

Several types of engines could be devised to carry out the theoretical cycles described in Chapter 2. The most common arrangement includes one or more cylindrical combustion chambers in which pistons move with reciprocating motion. The cycles can be carried out in either two or four strokes of a piston. Thus, both two-stroke-cycle and four-stroke-cycle engines have been developed.

In either type of engine, it is essential that certain events are timed correctly with the movement of the piston, or the engine will not run. The valves must open and close at appropriate times to ensure intake and compression of air and ejection of exhaust gases. Fuel must be ignited at the appropriate time to ensure release of chemical energy as the piston is ready to descend. The crankshaft controls the movement of the piston and also drives all other engine components that must be timed to the movement of the piston.

## 4.2 FOUR-STROKE-CYCLE ENGINES

Engines that carry out the cycle in four strokes of the piston are technically described as *four-stroke-cycle* engines, but they are more commonly known as *four-cycle* engines. The operation of four-cycle spark-ignition engines was described in Section 2.6, and four-cycle diesel operation was described in Section 2.8. A four-cycle engine is shown in Figure 4.1. The first successful internal combustion engine was the four-cycle engine developed by N. A. Otto in 1878. Four-cycle engines have continued to dominate the field and are by far the most

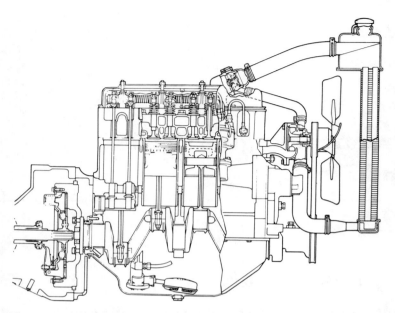

*Figure 4.1–A four-cycle, multicylinder engine. (Courtesy of Allis Chalmers Corporation.)*

common engines found in tractors, trucks, and automobiles today. Four-cycle operation will be assumed for all engines discussed in the remainder of this book, unless two-cycle operation is specifically mentioned.

### 4.2.1 Valve Timing

A commonly used *valve train* is shown in Figure 4.2. Cam lobes on the *camshaft* lift the tappets. Each *rocker arm* translates upward movement of a *tappet* and *push rod* into downward movement of a valve, thereby compressing the *valve spring* and opening the valve. The camshaft must be driven at half the speed of the crankshaft, because there is only one intake stroke and one exhaust stroke for every two revolutions of the crankshaft.

The L-head design used in small engines obviates the need for push rods. The valve stems point downward in such engines and are actuated directly by the camshaft. In recent automotive engines, the use of push rods is avoided by positioning the camshaft in the head above the valves. However, the design shown in Figure 4.2 is common to virtually all tractor engines.

Valves are timed to open and close to achieve the greatest possible airflow into the engine. At extremely low engine speeds, the greatest airflow would be achieved if the intake valve opened exactly at HDC and closed exactly at CDC of the intake stroke and if the

Practical Engine Cycles and Timing

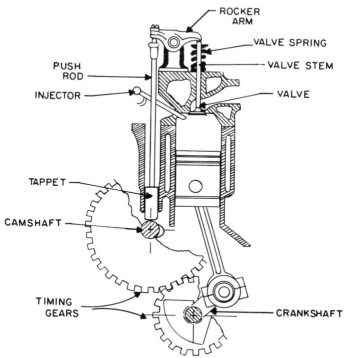

*Figure 4.2–Valve train and camshaft timing in a four-cycle engine.*

exhaust valve opened exactly at CDC and closed at HDC of the exhaust stroke. The ideal valve timing changes with engine speed. Because it is impractical to change valve timing while an engine is running, the valves are usually timed to maximize airflow into the engine at the most frequently used speed.

Typical intake valve timing is shown in the *valve timing spiral* of Figure 4.3, which displays valve timing in relation to crankshaft angle. The intake valve begins opening before HDC so that it can be fully open before the piston begins its high-speed descent. Abrupt opening and closing of valves would cause excessive wear and noise, and so the valve opening and closing periods are spread over a considerable number of degrees of crankshaft rotation. Momentum will keep the air moving into the combustion chamber during the early part of the compression stroke if the intake valve remains open. Thus, complete closing of the intake valve occurs well after CDC.

The typical timing of exhaust valves is also shown in Figure 4.3. The exhaust valve begins opening well before CDC on the power stroke. At high speeds, the loss of power in the hot gases is more than compensated for by allowing early blow down to achieve more

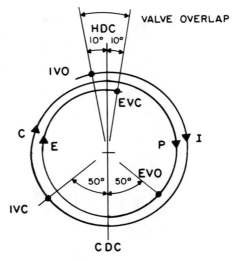

Figure 4.3–Valve timing spiral showing typical valve timing.

complete elimination of the exhaust gases. If the exhaust valve opening is to be kept as large as possible through most of the exhaust stroke, complete closing cannot occur until after HDC.

Notice in Figure 4.3 that there is *valve overlap*. That is, the intake and exhaust valves are open simultaneously for a small part of the cycle. Valve overlap permits some of the exhaust gas to pass through the intake valve and into the intake manifold during the exhaust stroke. This residual exhaust gas reenters the combustion chamber during the intake stroke and dilutes the incoming air. Airflow into the engine is normally so large that the effects of *exhaust gas dilution* are insignificant. When a carbureted engine is idling, however, the amount of incoming air-fuel mixture is so small that dilution by exhaust gases becomes a serious problem. Remedies to this problem are discussed in Chapter 9.

The valve timing in Figure 4.3 is for one model of engine. Manufacturers use calculations and experiments to select the optimum valve timing for each new model of engines. Once selected, the valve timing will produce maximum airflow into the engine at

Practical Engine Cycles and Timing

only one engine speed but will permit adequate airflow over a range of speeds.

## 4.2.2 Ignition Timing

Ideally, nearly all of the fuel energy would be released when the piston was at HDC and ready to begin the power stroke. In the spark-ignition engine, the fuel is premixed with air before entering the combustion chamber and energy release begins when the spark plug is fired. Significant time is required for the flame front to progress from the spark plug to the far side of the combustion chamber, and so the spark plug must be fired before HDC. *Spark advance* refers to the number of crankshaft degrees before HDC at which the spark plug fires. Because initial flame speed is nearly constant, greater spark advance is required at higher engine speeds to allow sufficient time for the flame front to cross the combustion chamber. Greater spark advance is also required for leaner mixtures, because they burn more slowly than chemically correct mixtures. A lean mixture is one in which the fuel to air ratio is less than the chemically correct ratio. The various means for timing the spark are discussed in Chapter 8. Example Problem 4.1 illustrates the need for spark advance.

## Example Problem 4.1

A spark ignition engine is idling at 500 revolutions per minute (rev/min). If the average flame speed is 10 m/s (32.8 ft/s) and the flame front must travel 55 mm (2.2 in.) from the spark plug to consume 85% of the fuel-air mixture, how much spark advance is needed if 85% of the fuel is to be consumed before the crankshaft reaches 10° after HDC? What must the spark advance be if the high idle speed is increased to 2000 rev/min?

**Solution:** The time required for the flame front to advance 55 mm (2.2 in.) is:

t = 55 mm /[1000 mm/m]*[10 m/s] = 0.0055 s

or

t = 2.2 in./[12 in./ft]*[32.8 ft/s] = 0.0055 s

The crankshaft speed at low idle is:

speed = [500 rev/min]*[360°/rev]/[60 s/min] = 3000° /s

The crankshaft rotation in 0.0055 s is:

rotation = [3000°/s]*[0.0055 s] = 16.5°

The required spark advance at 500 rev/min is:

16.5° - 10° = 6.5°

If the flame speed did not change when the engine speed increased to 2000 rev/min, similar calculations show that the required spark advance would be:

66° - 10° = 56°

The flame speed does increase substantially at higher engine speeds due to greater turbulence in the combustion chamber. Therefore, the required spark advance at 2000 rev/min high idle speed would be much less than 56°. With heavy torque load on an engine, spark advance typically ranges from 10 to 20° depending upon speed and design of the engine. When all conditions are considered, including idling and part-throttle operation, spark advance can range from 0 to 35°.

### 4.2.3 Injection Timing

Injector nozzles are used to inject fuel into diesel engines. The fuel does not ignite instantaneously when it is injected into the hot combustion chamber. A delay occurs, during which time the fuel begins to evaporate and mix with the air. Certain pre-flame reactions must also occur to prepare the fuel-air mixture for self-ignition. Because of the *ignition delay*, injection must start before HDC if a high percentage of the fuel is to be consumed before the piston is well past HDC. Timing of the start of injection is selected to optimize performance of each model of engine, but is typically in the range from 15 to 30° before HDC. Proper timing of diesel injections is accomplished by means that will be discussed in Chapter 10.

### 4.2.4 Firing Intervals

Single-cylinder four-cycle engines have only one power stroke in every two revolutions of the crankshaft. A large flywheel must be used to store kinetic energy during the power stroke, and that energy is subsequently released to keep the engine running through the exhaust, intake, and compression strokes. Engines with more than one cylinder can have smaller flywheels, because such engines have smaller firing intervals. The *firing intervals* refers to the number of degrees of crankshaft rotation between successive power strokes. The average firing interval of an engine can be calculated by using the following equation:

Practical Engine Cycles and Timing

| Crankshaft angle, deg | Cylinder No. | |
|---|---|---|
| | 1 | 2 |
| 0 | Power | Compression |
| 180 | Exhaust | Power |
| 360 | Intake | Exhaust |
| 540 | Compression | Intake |
| 720 | | |

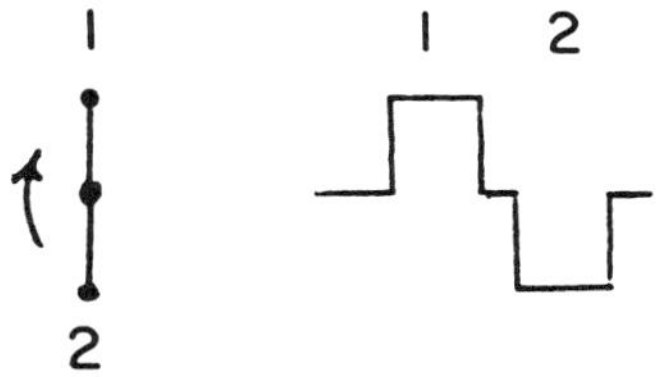

*Figure 4.4–Crankshaft arrangement and sequence of events in a two-cylinder engine.*

$$\text{average firing interval} = \frac{b * 180°}{\text{no. of cylinders}} \qquad (4.1)$$

where
  b = 4 for four-cycle engine, or b = 2 for two-cycle engine

Cylinders must be numbered in a multicylinder engine for purposes of identification. Numbering begins at the front of the engine. Some vehicles have engines mounted perpendicular to the direction of travel. Confusion is avoided if the front of the engine is always taken to be the end opposite the flywheel. On the two-cylinder crankshaft shown in Figure 4.4, for example, crank throw 1 would be near the front of the engine and crank throw 2 would be near the flywheel. The standard direction of rotation of the crankshaft is clockwise, as viewed from the front. Engines can be designed for counterclockwise rotation of the crankshaft, but such designs are exceptions to the general rule.

The average firing interval for the two-cylinder four-cycle engine is 360°, as indicated by Equation 4.1. The actual firing intervals are not evenly spaced, however, as can be seen in Figure 4.4. While piston 1 is producing power, piston 2 is moving to HDC. Thus, cylinder 2 must begin a power stroke or an intake stroke exactly 180° after cylinder 1 fires. In either case, there are two power strokes in

| Crankshaft angle, deg | Cylinder No. | | | |
|---|---|---|---|---|
| | 1 | 3 | 4 | 2 |
| 0 | Power | Compression | Intake | Exhaust |
| 180 | Exhaust | Power | Compression | Intake |
| 360 | Intake | Exhaust | Power | Compression |
| 540 | Compression | Intake | Exhaust | Power |
| 720 | | | | |

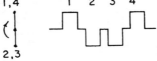

Figure 4.5–*Crankshaft arrangement and sequence of events in a four-cylinder engine with 1-3-4-2 firing order.*

one revolution of the crankshaft and no power strokes in the next revolution. The actual firing intervals are 180° and 540° for an average of 360°. The nonuniform firing can be heard distinctively in slow-running engines. The firing intervals could be equalized by designing a crankshaft with both crank pins in line so that both pistons reached HDC simultaneously. However, such crankshafts are rarely used because of the strong vibration they produce.

The crankshaft arrangement for a typical four-cylinder engine is illustrated in Figure 4.5. The average firing interval for this four-cycle engine is:

average firing interval = 4*180/4 = 180°

The actual firing intervals are uniform. That is, another power stroke begins every 180° of crankshaft rotation.

Six-cylinder, four-cycle engines have an average firing interval of:

average firing interval = 4*180/6 = 120°

The crank throws for the six-cylinder crankshaft are spaced at 120° to match the firing interval. The actual firing intervals are uniform and are less than the 180° needed to complete a power stroke. Thus, the six-cylinder engine has power overlap, as shown in Figure 4.6.

A three-cylinder engine is similar to the six-cylinder engine in that the crank throws are spaced at 120°. The average firing interval for a three-cylinder, four-cycle engine is:

average firing interval = 4*180/3 = 240°

The uniformity of the firing intervals will be discussed in Section 4.2.5.

| Crankshaft angle, deg | Cylinder No. | | | | | |
|---|---|---|---|---|---|---|
| | 1 | 5 | 3 | 6 | 2 | 4 |
| 0 | power | comp | | intake | exhaust | |
| 60 | | | | | | |
| 120 | | | comp | | | exhaust |
| 180 | | | | | intake | |
| 240 | exhaust | power | | | | |
| 300 | | | | comp | | |
| 360 | | | power | | | intake |
| 420 | | exhaust | | | comp | |
| 480 | intake | | | power | | |
| 540 | | | exhaust | | | comp |
| 600 | | | | | power | |
| 660 | comp | intake | intake | exhaust | | |
| 720 | | | | | | power |

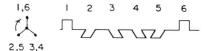

*Figure 4.6–Crankshaft arrangement and sequence of events in a six-cylinder engine with 1-5-3-6-2-4 firing order.*

## 4.2.5 Firing Orders

The mixture in a combustion chamber must be ignited at the proper time, that is, when the piston is near HDC at the end of compression. In a multicylinder engine, the firings must occur in a particular order, called the *firing order*. The arrangement of the crankshaft permits only a limited number of possible firing orders. Other factors, such as balancing airflows to the cylinders, determines which of the possible firing orders is actually used in an engine.

There are two possible *firing orders* for the engine in Figure 4.5. The firing order given in the figure is as follows:

1 - 3 - 4 - 2

Notice, however, that either cylinder 2 or 3 could fire 180° after cylinder 1 fires. Therefore, another possible firing order for the same crankshaft would be:

1 - 2 - 4 - 3

The firing order of an engine cannot be changed without changing the camshaft to ensure that all valves open and close at the appropriate times. The spark plug wires on a spark-ignition engine or the injector lines on a diesel engine would also have to be rerouted when changing firing orders.

A firing order tree provides a convenient way of finding all possible firing orders for a given crankshaft. The firing order tree for the four-cylinder crankshaft of Figure 4.5 would be:

$$1 \begin{cases} 2\text{-}4\text{-}3 \\ 3\text{-}4\text{-}2 \end{cases}$$

Notice that the tree always begins with cylinder 1. Either cylinder 2 or 3 could fire next; so two branches are shown. The next cylinder to fire must be number 4, and then the remaining cylinder in either branch must fire.

The most common firing order for in-line, six-cylinder engines (Figure 4.6) is as follows:

1 - 5 - 3 - 6 - 2 - 4

Development of the firing order tree for the six-cylinder engine is left as a homework exercise. Of the four possible firing orders, those that begin with 1 - 2 would cause uneven airflows to the cylinders and thus are not used.

In Figure 4.6, notice that, if crank throws and columns for cylinders 5, 6, and 4 were discarded, a three-cylinder engine would remain. It would have uniform firing intervals of 240° and a firing order of 1 - 3 - 2. In actual practice, the three-cylinder crankshaft would have crank throws 2 and 3 reversed from those shown in Figure 4.6. Thus, actual three-cylinder engines have uniform firing intervals of 240° and a firing order of:

1 - 2 - 3

## 4.2.6  V-Engines

The length of a multicylinder engine can be reduced substantially by arranging the cylinders into two banks. The two banks form a V, as shown in Figure 4.7. The angle between the banks is typically 60, 90, or 120°, with 90° being the most popular choice. The positioning of the lobes on the camshaft must be appropriate for the angle of the V to ensure that the valves open at the proper crankshaft angles. The distributor or injection pump must also conform to the angle of the V so that the spark or the fuel injections occur at the correct crank angles. The crankshaft has two connecting rods, one from each bank, connected to each crank throw. The crank throws may be spaced at

Practical Engine Cycles and Timing

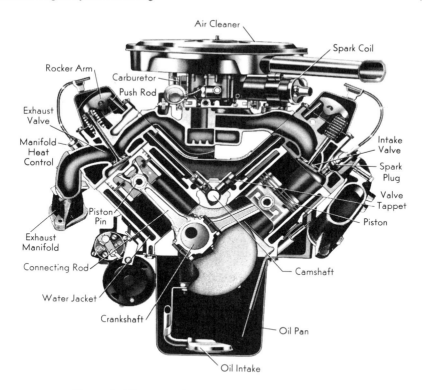

*Figure 4.7–A V8 engine. (Courtesy of General Motors Corporation.)*

90°, as illustrated in Figure 4.8, or at 180°, as in the four-cylinder engine of Figure 4.5. There are also two common schemes for numbering the cylinders. In the scheme shown in Figure 4.8, the cylinders are numbered in the order in which their connecting rods are joined to the crankshaft. Thus, the numbering alternates between the left and right banks of cylinders. Other manufacturers number all cylinders in one bank (for example, 1 through 4) and then number all the cylinders in the other bank (for example, 5 through 8).

The average firing interval is the same for V8 engines as for engines with the same number of cylinders arranged in line. The average firing interval for an eight-cylinder engine is:

average firing interval = 4∗180/8 = 90°

The power impulses for the eight cylinder engine in Figure 4.8 are evenly spaced; so the actual firing intervals are all 90°. The small firing interval produces considerable power overlap, as illustrated in Figure 4.8. It should be apparent that smaller firing intervals provide smoother power flow. Thus, engines with small firing

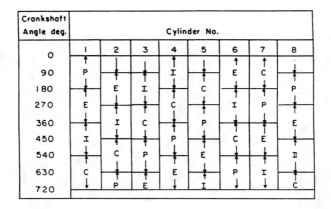

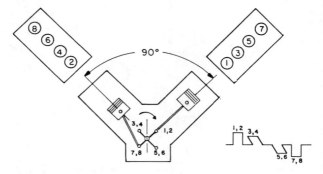

*Figure 4.8–Crankshaft arrangement and sequence of events in a V8 engine with 1-8-7-5-4-3-6-2 firing order.*

intervals can operate with smaller flywheels than can engines with large firing intervals. It is also apparent that uniform firing intervals provide smoother power flow than do unequal firing intervals.

## 4.3  TWO-STROKE-CYCLE ENGINES

Engines that carry out the cycle in two strokes of the piston are technically described as *two-stroke-cycle* engines, but they are more commonly known as *two-cycle* engines. Such engines do not have distinct intake and exhaust strokes. Instead, special means are used for drawing in fresh air and expelling exhaust gases. These special means differ between spark-ignition and diesel engines.

Practical Engine Cycles and Timing 81

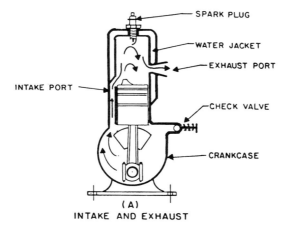

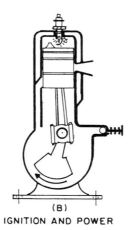

*Figure 4.9–A two-cycle spark-ignition engine.*

## 4.3.1 Two-Cycle Spark-Ignition Engines

The two-cycle spark-ignition engine shown in Figure 4.9 uses the crankcase as an air pump. While the piston is moving upward on a compression stroke, a vacuum is being created in the crankcase, and the check valve opens to admit the air fuel mixture. The check valve closes, and the mixture in the crankcase is compressed as the piston moves downward on the power stroke. The piston uncovers intake and exhaust ports during its descent. When the ports are uncovered, the compressed mixture in the crankcase rushes into the combustion chamber and sweeps the exhaust gases toward the exhaust port. As the piston again rises and covers the ports, the mixture in the combustion chamber is compressed by continued upward movement of the piston. The spark plug fires as the piston approaches HDC, and then the burning mixture forces the piston down to provide power. The use of the crankcase as an air pump interferes with its use as a sump for lubricating oil. The lubrication of moving parts is accomplished by mixing oil with the gasoline.

Two-cycle engines have the advantage of a high power to size ratio. By producing a power stroke during every revolution of the crankshaft, a two-cycle engine can produce much more power than can a four-stroke-cycle engine of the same size. The spark-ignition two-cycle engines idle more erratically, have poorer fuel economy and can be more difficult to start than their four-cycle counterparts. Their use has been restricted to applications where their small size and weight is an advantage, such as in chain saws, string trimmers, some lawn mowers, and outboard engines for boats.

### 4.3.2  Two-Cycle Diesel Engines

A two-cycle diesel engine is shown in Figure 4.10. Instead of the crankcase, a mechanically driven blower is used to pressurize the air. A cam-operated valve in the head is used to expel exhaust gases. When the piston is approximately halfway through the downstroke, the exhaust valve opens to release the exhaust gases and then the intake port is uncovered. Compressed air from the blower rushes into the combustion chamber and sweeps residual exhaust gases through the exhaust valve. The exhaust valve begins closing after CDC, and, while it is closing, the rising piston covers the intake port. Continued upward movement of the piston compresses the trapped air. Fuel is injected as the piston nears HDC and the trapped air has reached the self-ignition temperature of the fuel. The injected fuel ignites, and the released energy forces the piston downward to produce work. Unlike the spark-ignition version, the two-cycle diesel engine uses the crankcase as a sump for lubricating oil. Thus, the two-cycle diesel engine may have a conventional lubricating system.

Two-cycle diesel engines also have a high power to size ratio. Their reduced weight is less of an advantage in the heavy duty vehicles in which diesel engines are normally used. They require the added cost of a blower, but they run as smoothly and efficiently as four-cycle diesels. Two-cycle diesel engines have been a popular engine for busses, where their small size allows them to fit in a compact space at the rear of the bus. They have also been used in some farm tractors and heavy-duty trucks.

### 4.3.3  Timing in the Two-Cycle Engine

There is no valve train in two-cycle spark-ignition engines because the moving piston covers and uncovers the intake and exhaust ports

Practical Engine Cycles and Timing

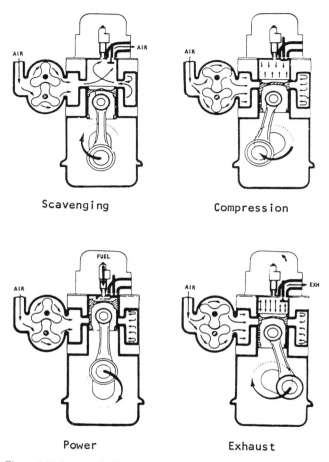

Figure 4.10–A two-cycle diesel engine. (Courtesy of Detroit Diesel Allison, Division of General Motors Corporation.)

in the cylinder wall and thus the timing is set when the engine is built.

Valve timing for a typical two-cycle diesel engine is illustrated in Figure 4.11. These engines have a cam-operated exhaust valve that must be timed. The camshaft rotates at the same speed as the crankshaft. The exhaust valve begins to open at 97.5° before CDC, begins closing at 43° after CDC, and is fully closed at 63° after CDC. The intake port is uncovered after the exhaust valve is closing on the downstroke and before the exhaust valve closes on the upstroke. Thus, approximately 55% of the cycle is used for compression and power; the remaining 45% is used for scavenging exhaust gases and intake of fresh air.

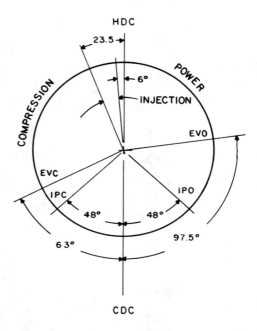

EVO = EXHAUST VALVE OPENS
EVC = EXHAUST VALVE CLOSES
IPO = INTAKE PORT OPENS
IPC = INTAKE PORT CLOSES

*Figure 4.11–Typical timing of a two-cycle diesel engine.*

The spark plug is timed to fire approximately 6° to 8° before HDC in two-cycle spark-ignition engines. Typically, these engines run at full speed when doing work, and no ignition advance system is needed.

Diesel injection begins at 23.5° before HDC in a typical two-cycle diesel engine and ends at 6° before HDC when the engine is running at full load. Thus, injection ends much earlier than in four-cycle diesels, where injection can continue well past HDC at full load. Extending fuel injection into the power stroke of two-cycle diesel engines would not be satisfactory because, as shown in Figure 4.11, the exhaust valve begins opening before the piston is at mid-stroke.

### 4.3.4 Firing Intervals and Orders

The firing interval of a two-cycle engine is half that of a comparable four-cycle engine as indicated by Equation 4.1. Thus, power flow is more uniform in the two-cycle engine. For example, the two-cycle two cylinder engine avoids the nonuniform firing intervals of its four cycle counterpart. Instead, it has the same uniform firing interval of the four-cycle four-cylinder engine.

The firing order of an engine must be compatible with the arrangement of the crank throws on the crankshaft. Thus, the discussion of firing orders for four-cycle engines in Section 4.2.5 also applies to two-cycle engines.

### 4.3.5  Automotive Two-Cycle Engines

The high power to size ratio of two-cycle engines could be advantageous to automobile manufacturers. The reduced weight of the two-cycle engine could improve fuel economy in city driving because automobiles with reduced mass require less energy to accelerate following a stop. Some automobile manufacturers have developed prototype cars which include a two-cycle spark-ignition engine. The engine is similar to the diesel version in that a mechanically-driven blower is used to supply air and fuel is injected directly into the combustion chambers. Four conventional poppet valves are used per cylinder, two for intake and two for exhaust, to improve air handling capacity. An electronic ignition system fires the spark plug in each cylinder once per engine revolution. In addition to the advantage of its high power to size ratio, the new engine has shown reduced levels of $NO_x$ in the exhaust. The engine also has some disadvantages, including higher concentrations of unburned hydrocarbons in the exhaust, and the need to operate the camshaft at twice the speed of a camshaft in a four-cycle engine.

## 4.4  SUMMARY

The theoretical cycles discussed in Chapter 2 can be carried out in either two or four strokes of a piston, and thus there are two-stroke-cycle and four-stroke-cycle engines. Certain events must be timed correctly before either type of engine will run.

Valve timing in the four-cycle engine is accomplished by timing camshaft rotation to crankshaft rotation, with the camshaft rotating at one-half of crankshaft speed. Intake and exhaust valves are each kept open for more than a full piston stroke to maximize airflow into the engine. Valve overlap occurs near HDC, when the intake valve opens before the exhaust valve closes. Valve overlap causes exhaust gases to dilute the incoming mixture in the spark-ignition engine, and thus a richer mixture is required when the engine idles.

Use of the moving piston to cover and uncover ports in the cylinder wall simplifies the timing of intake and exhaust in the two-cycle engine. The spark-ignition engine has no valve train, while the diesel engine has only exhaust valves. Exhaust valves are timed by timing the camshaft to the crankshaft. Both shafts rotate at the same speed in the two-cycle engine. A new automotive two-cycle engine which is being developed combines some of the advantages of the spark-ignition and diesel two-cycle engines.

Ignition must occur before HDC to allow time for burning of fuel before the piston descends on the power stroke. In four-cycle spark-ignition engines, spark advance must be increased at higher engine speeds and for leaner mixtures. Spark timing in two-cycle engines typically is fixed at 6° to 8° before HDC.

Because of ignition delay in the diesel engine, fuel injection must start before HDC to allow time for ignition and burning before the piston descends on the power stroke of four-cycle engines but ends before HDC in two-cycle engines.

Firing interval is the number of degrees of crankshaft rotation between successive power strokes; so increasing the number of cylinders reduces the average firing interval. Four-cycle engines with two cylinders have nonuniform firing intervals. Two-cycle engines have more uniform power flow, because their firing interval is only half that of four-cycle engines.

The firing order of either a two-cycle or four-cycle engine must be compatible with the arrangement of the crank throws on the crankshaft. Construction of a firing order tree exhibits all of the possible firing orders for a given crankshaft.

## QUESTIONS

Q4.1   What is valve overlap, and why do four-cycle engines usually have it?

Q4.2   Why is the intake valve on a four-cycle engine kept open until the piston has moved well into the compression stroke?

Q4.3   Why is the exhaust valve on a four-cycle engine opened well before the power stroke is completed?

Q4.4   Why does spark timing need to be advanced more for lean mixtures?

Q4.5   Why does spark timing need to be advanced more at higher engine speeds?

Practical Engine Cycles and Timing

Q4.6    Consider two-, three-, four-, six-, and eight-cylinder engines. Which of these engines have uniform firing intervals?

Q4.7    Consider two-, three-, four-, six-, and eight-cylinder engines. Which of these engines have power overlap?

Q4.8    What is the standard direction of rotation of a crankshaft as viewed from the front of the engine?

Q4.9    The two-cycle spark-ignition engine has no distinct intake stroke or exhaust stroke. Briefly explain how this engine can receive an air supply and expel exhaust gases.

Q4.10   How is lubrication provided for a two-cycle spark-ignition engine?

Q4.11   In the absence of distinct intake and exhaust strokes, how does a two-cycle diesel engine receive an air supply and expel exhaust gases?

## PROBLEMS

P4.1    A certain engine has the following specifications for valve events: IVO at 12° before HDC, IVC at 40° after CDC, EVO at 45° before CDC, EVC at 10° after HDC.
(a) Calculate the valve overlap.
(b) Draw a complete valve timing spiral. Label all strokes, label all valve events, and indicate overlap.

P4.2    Rework parts a and b of P4.1 using valve timing events as specified by your instructor.

P4.3    For the engine specified in P4.1, calculate the number of crankshaft degrees during which (a) each intake valve and (b) each exhaust valve is open in a cycle.

P4.4    For the engine specified in P4.2, calculate the number of crankshaft degrees during which (a) each intake valve and (b) each exhaust valve is open in a cycle.

P4.5    Make a firing order tree showing all possible firing orders for the six-cylinder engine illustrated in Figure 4.6.

P4.6  Make a firing order tree showing all possible firing orders for the V8 engine illustrated in Figure 4.8.

# 5
# Power Efficiencies and Measurement

## 5.1 INTRODUCTION

Engines are designed to convert fuel energy into useful mechanical power, but typical engines convert less than half of the fuel energy. The remainder is lost in the conversion processes. Various efficiency terms have developed as aids for comparing energy-converting abilities of different engines. Learning these terms will help you to compare and discuss engines intelligently. To give an intelligent discussion of the performance of a tractor engine, you must also know and understand the terms high idle, governor's maximum, governor control, load control, governor regulation, and torque reserve. These terms will be explained in Section 5.8 of this chapter. The measurement of power efficiencies can be accomplished through the use of a number of devices and techniques, as described in Section 5.9 of this chapter. You will learn to interpret and use a tractor test report in Section 5.10.

## 5.2 TORQUE AND POWER

Torque can be described as a turning effort. Torque is exerted, for example when a wrench is used to tighten a nut on a bolt. In Figure 5.1, the torque exerted on the nut is defined by the following equation.

$$T = F * L \qquad (5.1)$$

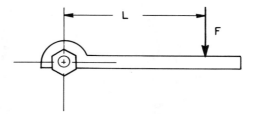

*Figure 5.1–Torque being exerted by a wrench.*

where
    T = torque in N·m (lb-ft)
    F = force in N (lb)
    L = length in m (ft)

Notice that torque could be increased by exerting a larger force on the wrench or by exerting it further from the center of the bolt. Engines must produce torque in order to rotate the drive wheels when a tractor is pulling a load.

In Chapter 2, work was defined as a force acting through a distance. In contrast, torque is a force acting perpendicular to a distance, the distance being measured from a center of turning to the point of application of the force. In customary units, torque is given in lb-ft to avoid confusion with work or energy, whose units are ft-lb. A torque does not necessarily do work. If the nut in Figure 5.1 resisted all movement, for example, a large torque could be exerted without accomplishing any work. Conversely, work would be done if the wrench moved. Suppose that a constant torque was exerted while the wrench traveled one revolution, as shown in Figure 5.2. Then, the force would have traveled a distance equal to the circumference of a circle of radius L. Thus, the work done per revolution (work/rev) would be:

$$\text{work/rev} = [2\pi L] * [F] = [2\pi] * [LF] = 2\pi * T \tag{5.2}$$

That is, the work in joules (ft-lb) per revolution is $2\pi$ times the torque in N·m (lb-ft).

*Power* is defined as the rate of doing work. That is, it is the amount of work accomplished per unit of time. In equation form, power (P) is defined as follows:

$$P = \frac{F * x}{t} = F * \left[\frac{x}{t}\right] \tag{5.3}$$

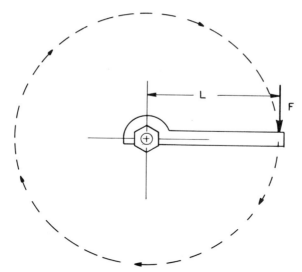

*Figure 5.2–Work being done by a wrench.*

where x = distance traveled by the force (F) in time (t)

A force of 1 newton (lb) moving a distance of 1 m (ft) in 1 s would expend an amount of power equal to 1 N·m/s (ft-lb/s). This combination of SI units has been given the name watt (W) in honor of James Watt. A watt is such a small unit that tractor power is more frequently measured in kilowatts (kW). In customary units, as was mentioned in Chapter 2, it was James Watt who defined 1 horsepower (hp) as being equal to 550 ft-lb/s.

In Chapter 2, linear speed was defined as distance traveled per unit of time. Therefore, Equation 5.3 can be interpreted as showing that linear power is the product of force times the speed with which the force is moving. Equation 5.4 computes linear power in typical units:

$$P = \frac{F * S}{K_{LP}} \qquad (5.4)$$

where
- $P$ = linear power in kW (hp)
- $F$ = force in kN (lb)
- $S$ = speed in km/h (mph)
- $K_{LP}$ = units constant = 3.6 (375)

Just as linear speed is defined as linear distance traveled per unit of time, *rotary speed* is defined as the amount of angular rotation per unit of time. The most common units for rotary speed are revolutions per minute (rev/min).

Rotary power is the product of work/rev (from Equation 5.2) and rotary speed. Equation 5.5 is used to compute rotary power in typical units:

$$P_b = \frac{2\pi * T * N}{K_{RP}} \quad (5.5)$$

where
- $P_b$ = brake power in kW (hp)
- $T$ = engine torque in N·m (lb-ft)
- $N$ = engine rotational speed in rev/min
- $K_{RP}$ = units constant = 60,000 (33,000)

The term *brake power* is used because the first devices for measuring engine power were called prony brakes. The term *flywheel power* is used interchangeably with brake power. Equation 5.5 can also be used to calculate power at the pto if pto torque and speed are used instead of engine torque and speed.

## 5.3 POWER ADJECTIVES

Power can be measured at various places on or in an engine or tractor. The amount of power varies greatly depending on where it is measured. Thus, various adjectives have been coined to describe measured power. The fuel is the source of all engine power (Figure 5.3). *Fuel equivalent power* can be computed from the product of fuel consumption rate and the heating value of the fuel:

$$P_{fe} = \frac{HV * \dot{M}_f}{K_{fe}} \quad (5.6)$$

where
- $P_{fe}$ = fuel equivalent power in kW (hp)
- $HV$ = heating value of fuel in kJ/kg (BTU/lb)
- $\dot{M}_f$ = fuel consumption rate in kg/h (lb/h)
- $K_{fe}$ = units constant = 3600 (2545)

*Figure 5.3–Fuel as the source of engine power. (Photo by Rodney Goering.)*

In customary units, heat energy is measured in BTU (British Thermal Units). The heating value of fuel is the amount of energy that would be released in burning a kilogram (lb) of fuel. Fuel heating values are listed in Table 6.5 and will be discussed in Chapter 6. The fuel consumption rate can be measured on a mass basis, as in Equation 5.6, or on a volume basis. In the latter case, the fuel consumption rate can be converted to a mass basis as follows:

$$\dot{M}_f = Q_f * \rho_f \tag{5.7}$$

where
$\dot{M}_f$ = fuel consumption rate in kg/h (lb/h)
$Q_f$ = fuel consumption rate in L/h (gal/h)
$\rho_f$ = fuel density in kg/L (lb/gal)

Example Problem 5.1 illustrates a typical calculation of fuel equivalent power. The results will be used later in calculations of engine efficiencies.

## Example Problem 5.1

An engine consumes diesel fuel at the rate of 73.1 L/h (19.3 gal/h). The density of the fuel is 0.835 kg/L (6.96 lb/gal), and its heating value is 45 434 kJ/kg (19,533 BTU/lb). Calculate the fuel equivalent power.

**Solution:** On a mass basis, the fuel consumption rate is:

$$\dot{M}_f = [73.1 \text{ L/h}] * [0.835 \text{ kg/L}] = 61.0 \text{ kg/h}$$

or

$$\dot{M}_f = [19.3 \text{ lb/h}] * [6.96 \text{ lb/gal}] = 134 \text{ lb/h}$$

Then, from Equation 5.6:

$$P_{fe} = [45\,434 \text{ kJ/kg}] * [61.0 \text{ kg/h}]/3600 = 770 \text{ kW}$$

or

$$P_{fe} = [19{,}533 \text{ BTU/lb}] * [134 \text{ lb/h}]/2545 = 1028 \text{ hp}$$

The fuel equivalent power is very large. Unfortunately, much of the fuel equivalent power cannot be converted into useful work. Later in this chapter, you will learn where the power is lost. First, however, it is necessary to understand the concept of indicated mean effective pressure and indicated power.

The burning fuel releases energy that is partially manifested as pressure on the top of each piston. Although the pressure varies throughout the power stroke, it is possible to determine an equivalent constant pressure. For reasons to be explained later, this equivalent constant pressure is called the *indicated mean effective pressure* (imep). The mechanical work produced by the burning fuel is:

$$\text{work/cycle} = \text{imep} * A_p * L \tag{5.8}$$

where
  imep = indicated mean effective pressure in kPa (psi)
  $A_p$ = area of the top of each piston in $cm^2$ ($in.^2$)
  L = stroke length in cm (in.)

By multiplying the work produced by the number of cycles per unit of time, the indicated power can be calculated. Therefore, one form of the indicated power equation is:

$$P_i = \frac{\text{imep} * A_p * L \text{ no. of cylinders} * N}{rc * K_{Pi}} \quad (5.9)$$

where
- $P_i$ = indicated power in kW (hp)
- imep = indicated mean effective pressure in kPa (psi)
- $A_p$ = area of the top of each piston in cm² (in.²)
- L = stroke length in cm (in.)
- N = engine speed in rev/min
- rc = crankshaft revolutions/cycle
  - 2 for four-cycle engines, or
  - 1 for two-cycle engines
- $K_{Pi}$ = units constant = $60 \times 10^6$ (396,000)

The product of piston area, stroke length, and number of cylinders is the engine displacement. Therefore, the equation for indicated power can be simplified:

$$P_i = \frac{(\text{imep})(D)(N)}{(rc)(K_{pi})} \quad (5.10)$$

where
- D = engine displacement in L (in.³)
- $K_{pi}$ = units constant = 60,000 (396,000)

It is apparent from Equation 5.10 that designers have only three possible approaches for making more powerful engines. That is, they can design larger or faster running engines or design for higher pressures (imep). The imep can be raised by increasing the compression ratio, increasing the fuel delivery rate, or by other techniques.

Some of the indicated power is absorbed within the engine to overcome friction and to run such accessories as the oil pump, fan, alternator, and so on. All such power is lumped together into a category called *friction power* ($P_f$). By definition:

$$P_f = P_i - P_b \quad (5.11)$$

where $P_b$ is the *brake power* as calculated in Equation 5.5. That is, brake power is the power that is available at the engine flywheel for doing useful work. Thus, by definition, friction power includes that part of the indicated power that is absorbed in the engine and is not available for other useful work. Example Problem 5.2 illustrates the friction power loss in an example engine.

## Example Problem 5.2

The engine of Example Problem 5.1 is a four-cycle engine with a displacement of 15.649 L (955 in.$^3$). While running at 2100 rev/min, it produces 1341 N·m (989 lb-ft) of torque. The imep is 1267 kPa (183 psi). Calculate the indicated, brake, and friction power.

**Solution:** From Equation 5.10, the indicated power is:

$P_i$ = [1267 kPa]*[15.649 L]*[2100 rev/min]/{2*60,000]
= 347 kW

or

$P_i$ = [183 psi]*[955 in.$^3$]*[2100 rev/min]/{2*396,000] = 463 hp

From Equation 5.5, the brake power is:

$P_b$ = 2π*[1341 N·m]*[2100 rev/min]/60,000 = 295 kW

or

$P_b$ = 2π*[989 lb-ft]*[2100 rev/min]/33,000 = 395 hp

Therefore, from Equation 5.11, the friction power is:

$P_f$ = 347 − 295 = 52 kW

or

$P_f$ = 463 − 395 = 68 hp

It may seem improper to include in friction power that part of the 52 kW (68 hp) that is used to run the fan, oil pump, and other accessories. However, the purpose of the engine is to do work and any power used by accessories to keep the engine running properly is not available for doing work. Thus, all such power is included in friction power.

Several other power adjectives have been coined to describe where power is measured on a tractor. Thus, power measured at the drawbar would be *drawbar power* ($P_{db}$) and could be calculated from Equation 5.4. Power measured at the pto shaft would be *pto power* ($P_{pto}$), and power taken out through the hydraulic system would be *hydraulic power* ($P_h$).

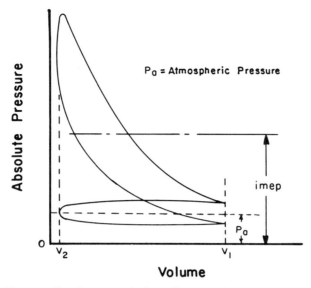

*Figure 5.4–Use of a pressure / volume diagram to determine indicated mean effective pressure.*

## 5.4 MEAN EFFECTIVE PRESSURES

Using Equation 5.9 to calculate indicated power requires that the imep be known. One of the first successful methods to measure imep involved the use of a cylindrical drum driven by the crankshaft. A special instrument measured instantaneous pressures in the combustion chamber and recorded them on a card wrapped around the rotating drum. The resulting diagrams were called indicator diagrams, and, if the ratio of the connecting rod length to the crank throw radius was known, an experimenter could convert such indicator diagrams into a pressure-volume diagram similar to the one shown in Figure 5.4. Note the similarities between Figure 5.4, which was obtained from an actual gasoline engine, and the theoretical Otto cycle of Figure 2.1. A p-v diagram similar to Figure 5.4 could be obtained from a diesel engine. The imep is merely the average height of the p-v diagram. That is, it is the area within the p-v diagram divided by the displacement volume of one cylinder. The indicator diagrams have been replaced by more modern methods, but the mean pressures are still called indicated mean effective pressures.

Other mean effective pressures can be calculated for an engine. *Brake mean effective pressure* (bmep) can be calculated from another form of Equation 5.10:

$$\text{bmep} = \frac{rc * K_{pi} * P_b}{D * N} \qquad (5.12)$$

As in Equation 5.10, $K_{pi}$ = units constant = 60,000 (396,000). Also, *friction mean effective pressure* (fmep) is:

$$\text{fmep} = \text{imep} - \text{bmep} \qquad (5.13)$$

The bmep or fmep cannot be measured directly in an engine; they can only be calculated. They are still useful, however, for describing engine performance. By referring to Equations 5.5 and 5.12, it is easy to show that engine torque varies directly with bmep:

$$T = \frac{D(\text{bmep})}{K_T(rc)} \qquad (5.14)$$

where $K_T$ = units constant = $2\pi$ ($24\pi$)

Thus, for a given size of engine, torque can be increased only by increasing the bmep. A rearranged Equation 5.13 shows that the bmep can be increased by increasing the imep and/or by reducing the fmep. The imep can be increased by raising the compression ratio or the fuel delivery rate by turbocharging or by other means. The fmep is a loss caused by the oil pump, fan, alternator, and so on, and increases with engine speed as shown in Figure 5.5. Thus, both fmep and friction power can be reduced by reducing engine speed. The calculation of mean effective pressures for an example engine is illustrated in Example Problem 5.3.

## Example Problem 5.3

Calculate the bmep and fmep for the engine of Example Problems 5.1 and 5.2.

**Solution:** The bmep can be calculated in either of two ways. It can be calculated from the brake power by using Equation 5.12:

bmep = 2*60,000*295 kW/[15.649 L*2100 rev/min]
     = 1077 kPa

or

bmep = 2*396,000*395 kW/[955 in.³*2100 rev/min]
     = 156 lb-ft

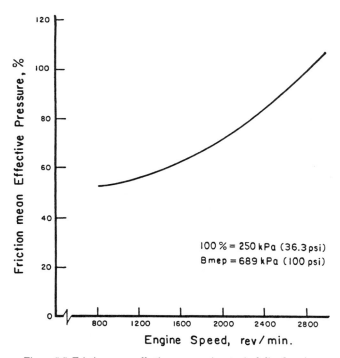

*Figure 5.5–Friction mean effective pressure in a typical diesel engine.*

The bmep also can be calculated from the torque by using Equation 5.14:

$$\text{bmep} = 2\pi * rc * T/D = 2\pi * 2 * [1341 \text{ N·m}]/\{15.649 \text{ L}\} = 1077 \text{ kPa}$$

or

$$\text{bmep} = 24\pi * rc * T/D = 24\pi * 2 * [989 \text{ lb-ft}]/955 \text{ in.}^3 = 156 \text{ lb-ft}$$

Because the imep was previously calculated at 1267 kPa (183 psi), the fmep is as follows:

$$\text{fmep} = 1267 \text{ kPa} - 1077 \text{ kPa} = 190 \text{ kPa}$$

or

$$\text{fmep} = 183 \text{ psi} - 156 \text{ psi} = 27 \text{ psi}$$

## 5.5  POWER EFFICIENCIES

Several efficiency terms have been coined for describing how well engines convert fuel energy into useful power. *Indicated thermal efficiency* ($e_{it}$) is the fraction of fuel equivalent power that is converted to indicated power:

$$e_{it} = \frac{P_i}{P_{fe}} \qquad (5.15)$$

Thus, indicated thermal efficiency is a measure of the combustion efficiency of the engine. For example, the indicated thermal efficiency of an engine could be increased by raising the compression ratio, but not by reducing the friction losses. The latter change would increase the mechanical efficiency.

*Mechanical efficiency* ($e_{bt}$) is the fraction of the newly created indicated power that is delivered as useful power from the engine:

$$e_m = \frac{P_b}{P_i} \qquad (5.16)$$

*Brake thermal efficiency* ($e_{bt}$) is the overall efficiency of the engine in converting fuel power into useful power:

$$e_{bt} = \frac{P_b}{P_{fe}} \qquad (5.17)$$

The brake thermal efficiency, $e_{bt}$, is an indication of the fraction of the energy in the fuel that is converted to power at the flywheel. If the power was measured at the pto instead, Equation 5.17 would give the pto thermal efficiency, $e_{pto}$. Similarly, if the power was measured at the drawbar, the efficiency would be designated the drawbar thermal efficiency, $e_{db}$. The brake thermal efficiency can also be calculated using the following equation:

$$e_{bt} = e_{it} * e_m \qquad (5.18)$$

Thus, for good overall efficiency, an engine must be mechanically efficient and have an efficient combustion process. Figure 5.6 summarizes the relationship of the various efficiencies to the power flow through an engine. Example Problem 5.4 illustrates the calculation of an example engine's efficiencies.

## Example Problem 5.4
Calculate the indicated thermal, brake thermal, and mechanical efficiencies for the engine described in Example Problems 5.1, 5.2, and 5.3.

# Power Efficiencies and Measurement

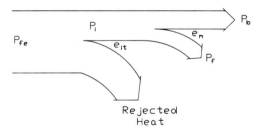

*Figure 5.6–Energy flows through an engine.*

**Solution:** The indicated thermal efficiency is:

$$e_{it} = P_i/P_{fe} = 347 \text{ kW}/770 \text{ kW} = 0.45$$

or

$$e_{it} = P_i/P_{fe} = 463 \text{ hp}/1028 \text{ hp} = 0.45$$

That is, the combustion process converts 45% of the fuel energy into mechanical energy. The remaining 55% of the fuel energy is rejected as heat by the engine. Much of the rejected heat goes out with the exhaust gases, and some heat is rejected through the cooling system.

The mechanical efficiency is:

$$e_m = P_b/P_i = 295 \text{ kW}/347 \text{ kW} = 0.85$$

or

$$e_m = P_b/P_i = 395 \text{ hp}/463 \text{ hp} = 0.85$$

That is, the useful power from the engine is 85% of the mechanical power created by combustion. The remaining 15% is friction power used to overcome friction and to run the oil pump, alternator, and other accessories.

The overall efficiency is called the brake thermal efficiency and is equal to:

$$e_{bt} = e_{it} * e_m = 0.451 * 0.850 = 0.38$$

That is, only 38% of the 770 kW (1028 hp) in the fuel is converted to useful power from the engine.

The mechanical and overall efficiencies of an engine vary with load. The reason becomes clear when we combine Equations 5.11 and 5.16 into the following equation for mechanical efficiency:

$$e_m = \frac{P_b}{P_b + P_f} \tag{5.19}$$

We cannot eliminate friction power from the engine, but it becomes a smaller percentage of total power as the load increases. Conversely, when there is no load, brake power and mechanical efficiency must both be zero. Then, Equation 5.19 shows that the overall efficiency would also be zero! Clearly, engines are most efficient when operated at full load, and they become progressively less efficient as the load declines. In Example Problem 5.4, for example, the fuel equivalent power at zero load would be much less than 770 kW (1028 hp), but all of if would be used as friction power. A practical application of Equation 5.19 is the "shift up and throttle back" technique. When a tractor is operating at less than full load, the operator is advised to shift up and throttle back, that is, to shift to a higher gear and reduce the engine speed to retain the original ground speed. The friction power, $P_f$, then declines (see Figure 5.5), resulting in higher mechanical efficiency and improved fuel economy.

## 5.6 SPECIFIC FUEL CONSUMPTION

The rate at which an engine consumes fuel (in kg/h or lb/h) varies with its efficiency but also with its size and load, that is, a large, heavily loaded engine will always consume more fuel than a small, lightly loaded one. Thus, although engine efficiency affects fuel consumption, fuel consumption alone is not a good indicator of engine efficiency. The term *specific fuel consumption* (SFC) has been developed to indicate fuel consumption in relation to the amount of work that is being done by the engine. SFC is defined as follows:

$$\text{SFC} = \frac{\dot{M}_f}{P} \qquad (5.20)$$

where
 SFC = specific fuel consumption in kg/kW·h (lb/hp-h)
 $\dot{M}_f$ = fuel consumption rate in kg/h (lb/h)
 P = power in kW (hp)

A power adjective must be used with SFC data because, as we discussed in Section 5.3, the amount of power depends upon where on the tractor it is measured. When brake power is measured in engine tests, the SFC is reported as *brake specific fuel consumption* (BSFC). *Indicated specific fuel consumption* (ISFC) would be reported if the indicated power (Equation 5.10) was measured. There are no widely accepted terms for SFC to be reported relative to pto power or drawbar power. For brevity, we will use PSFC for pto specific fuel consumption and DSFC for drawbar specific fuel consumption.

The SFC is related to efficiency, that is, low SFC corresponds to high efficiency. The relationship is clarified by thinking of SFC as the amount of fuel needed to do 3.6 MJ (2.655 × 10⁶ ft-lb) of work. The following equation relates BSFC to brake thermal efficiency:

$$e_{bt} = \frac{K_s}{HV * BSFC} \quad (5.21)$$

where
- $e_{bt}$ = brake thermal efficiency, as defined in Section 5.5
- HV = heating value of fuel in kJ/kg (BTU/lb)
- BSFC = brake specific fuel consumption in kg/kW·h (lb/hp-h)
- $K_s$ = units constant = 3600 (2545)

## 5.7 VOLUMETRIC EFFICIENCY

The power efficiencies discussed in Section 5.5 give an indication of how well an engine converts fuel power into useful power. Volumetric efficiency is a measure of the air-pumping efficiency of an engine. The theoretical air-pumping capacity of an engine is expressed as follows:

$$\dot{M}_{at} = \frac{60 * D * N * \rho_a}{rc * K_{at}} \quad (5.22)$$

where
- $\dot{M}_{at}$ = theoretical air consumption of engine in kg/h (lb/h)
- D = engine displacement in L (in.³)
- N = engine speed in rev/min
- $\rho_a$ = air density in kg/m³ (lb/ft³) (see Equation 2.5)
- rc = crankshaft revolutions/cycle
- $K_{at}$ = units constant = 1000 (1728)

Thus, the theoretical air consumption rate is the amount of air the engine would consume if each combustion chamber were completely filled with atmospheric air during each intake stroke. In a *naturally aspirated engine* – that is, an engine without a turbocharger or supercharger – the pistons create a partial vacuum during each intake stroke, and the combustion chambers do not completely fill with atmospheric air. Therefore, the volumetric efficiency is defined as follows:

$$e_v = \frac{\dot{M}_a}{\dot{M}_{at}} \tag{5.23}$$

where
- $e_v$ = volumetric efficiency (a decimal)
- $\dot{M}_a$ = actual air consumption rate in kg/h (lb/h)
- $\dot{M}_{at}$ = theoretical air consumption rate in kg/h (lb/h)

Calculation of the volumetric efficiency of an example engine is illustrated in Example Problem 5.5.

## Example Problem 5.5
The engine of Example Problems 5.1-5.4 consumes 953 kg/h (2100 lb/h) of air. The air temperature is 25° C (77° F) and the barometric pressure is 97.0 kPa (14.1 psi). Calculate the air density, the theoretical air consumption rate, and the volumetric efficiency.

**Solution:** From Equation 2.5, the air density is calculated as follows:

$$\rho_a = 3.488 * p/T = 3.488 * [97.0 \text{ kPa}]/[25 + 273° \text{ K}]$$
$$= 1.138 \text{ kg/m}^3$$

or

$$\rho_a = 2.705 * p/T = 2.705 * [14.1 \text{ psi}]/[77 + 460° \text{ F}]$$
$$= 0.0710 \text{ lb/ft}^3$$

From Equation 5.22, the theoretical air consumption rate of the engine is calculated as follows:

$$\dot{M}_{at} = 60 * [15.649 \text{ L}] * [2100 \text{ rev/min}] * [1.138 \text{ kg/m}^3]/[2*1000]$$
$$= 1122 \text{ kg/h}$$

or

$$\dot{M}_{at} = 60 * [955 \text{ in.}^3] * [2100 \text{ rev/min}] * [0.0710 \text{ lb/ft}^3]/[2*1728]$$
$$= 2472 \text{ lb/h}$$

Thus, the volumetric efficiency is:

$$e_v = \dot{M}_a/\dot{M}_{at} = 954/1122 = 0.85$$

or

$$e_v = \dot{M}_a/\dot{M}_{at} = 2100/2472 = 0.85$$

That is, the volumetric efficiency is 85% which is typical of a naturally aspirated (not turbocharged) diesel engine. The volumetric efficiency of a naturally aspirated gasoline engine could be as high as 85% at wide-open throttle but would decline as the throttle closed due to the restrictive effect of the throttle. Turbocharging (to be discussed in Chapter 11) can provide large increases in volumetric efficiency. For example, the volumetric efficiency of a turbocharged diesel tractor engine is typically in the range from 150 to 200%. Optimum valve timing, as discussed in Sections 4.2.1 and 4.3.3, is a method used to provide the highest possible volumetric efficiency for a naturally aspirated engine.

High volumetric efficiency is needed to obtain high power output from an engine. The air to fuel ratio required by an engine (to be discussed in Chapter 6) is large and, thus, it is easy to pump enough fuel into the engine to use the available air. It is the quantity of air that can be pumped into the combustion chambers that limits the power output of the engine.

## 5.8 ENGINE GOVERNORS AND GOVERNED ENGINE PERFORMANCE

*Governors* are used on farm tractors to automatically regulate the speed of the engine. Thus, governors have a function similar to the cruise control found on some automobiles. The driver can set the cruise control for any desired speed, and the control will attempt to maintain that speed whether the automobile is going uphill, downhill, or on the level. Similarly, a governor attempts to maintain the engine speed set by the operator regardless of the torque load on the engine. The presence of a governor affects the torque, speed, and power output of an engine as will be explained in Section 5.8.2. The speed governor was invented by James Watt and has been used on farm tractors for many years.

### 5.8.1 Governor Operation

Governors control speed by reducing fuel delivery to the engine when speed is too high and increasing fuel delivery when speed is too low. Most tractor governors use the flyweight principle (illustrated in Figure 5.7a) to control fuel delivery to the engine. Flyweights are hinge connected to the governor shaft which usually rotates at one-half the engine speed. Centrifugal force from the increasing speed causes the flyweights to swing outward and the flyweight arms force the thrust bearing downward. As a result, the governor linkage rotates counterclockwise stretching the governor spring and reducing fuel delivery to the engine. Conversely, reduction in engine speed

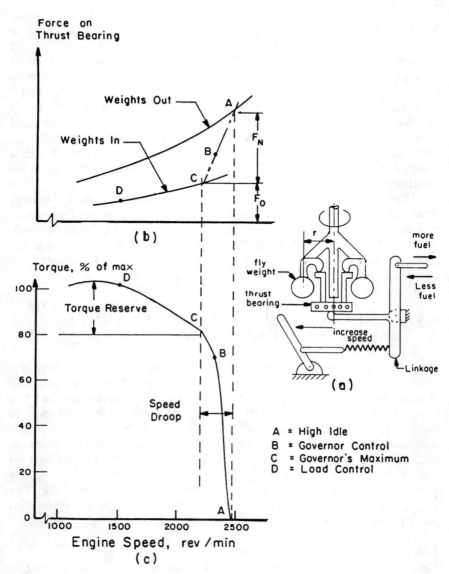

*Figure 5.7–Action of an engine governor.*

allows the spring to contract forcing the flyweights inward and increasing fuel delivery to the engine. The fuel control rod shown in Figure 5.7a could control the carburetor in a gasoline engine or the injector pump in a diesel engine.

The force exerted on the thrust bearing by the flyweights can be calculated by using the following equation:

$$F_{tb} = K * r * N^2 \qquad (5.24)$$

where
- $F_{tb}$ = force exerted on thrust bearing
- $K$ = a constant
- $r$ = radius from center of governor shaft to center of gravity of flyweights
- $N$ = engine speed in rev/min

The thrust bearing force is shown plotted against engine speed in Figure 5.7b. The radius changes, but two limiting cases are shown. The top curve is maximum radius – that is, with the weight swung all the way out – and the bottom curve is for the weights swung all the way in. The actual force must be between these two curves.

### 5.8.2 Performance of Governed Engines

Imagine a tractor connected to a dynamometer and operating with zero torque load but with substantial fuel delivery. Engine speed would be high enough to destroy the engine under such conditions, except that the governor flyweights swing all the way out to limit the fuel delivery. The engine would therefore operate at point A on Figures 5.7b and 5.7c. Point A is called the *high idle point* because the engine speed is high and the engine is idle, that is, not doing any work. Now, suppose that the dynamometer was used to gradually increase the torque load on the engine. The engine would begin to lose speed as the torque increased, but the governor flyweights would begin moving inward and fuel delivery would begin increasing to try to maintain engine speed. Eventually, the flyweights would reach their innermost position, and the governor would not be able to call for any more fuel. With further increases in torque, the engine speed would begin falling rapidly, as shown in Figure 5.7c, and the governor would operate along the weights-in curve in Figure 5.7b. Point C is called the *governor's maximum point*, because the governor is calling for maximum fuel at that point. At all points between A and C (for example, at point B), the speed is controlled by the governor. At all points to the left of C (for example, at point D), the speed is controlled entirely by the load on the engine. Thus, governed engines can operate either in *governor control* or *load control* depending on the torque load on the engine.

No governor can maintain perfectly uniform speed as the load on the engine changes. Figure 5.7c shows the speed variation, or speed droop, allowed by the governor in the governor-controlled range. The *governor regulation*, calculated in Equation 5.25, is a measure of how closely the governor controls the speed:

$$R = 200 * \frac{N_{HI} - N_{GM}}{N_{HI} + N_{GM}} \qquad (5.25)$$

where
- $R$ = regulation in %
- $N_{HI}$ = engine speed at high idle in rev/min
- $N_{GM}$ = engine speed at governor's maximum in rev/min

The calculation of governor regulation is illustrated in Example Problem 5.6.

## Example Problem 5.6

Calculate the governor speed regulation for the torque to speed curve shown in Figure 5.7c.

**Solution:** The high idle speed in Figure 5.7c is 2468 rev/min, and the governor's maximum speed is 2200 rev/min. Therefore, the regulation is:

$$R = 200*[2468 - 2200]/[2468 + 2200] = 11.5\%$$

*Torque reserve* in Figure 5.7c is shown as the difference between peak torque and torque at governor's maximum. Typically, tractor engines are designed to run at governor's maximum. A large torque reserve is desirable so that the tractor can continue to run without stalling if a torque overload is suddenly placed on the engine. Usually, torque reserve is stated as a percentage. A torque reserve of 25%, for example, indicates that the peak torque is 25% greater than the torque at governor's maximum. Typically, torque reserve ranges from 5% on some engines to 30% on others.

The curves in Figure 5.7 show the governor controlling at one speed setting. The operator can select a different speed setting by using the hand lever in Figure 5.7a to change the initial force in the governor spring. Suppose the operator moved the lever to the right to reduce the initial spring force. Then, point C in Figure 5.7b would move to the left along the weights in curve and the entire A to C line would shift to the left. As shown in Figure 5.7a, high idle would shift from point A to point A', and governor's maximum would shift from point C to point C'. The governor would try to control the engine at a lower speed.

Figure 5.8b shows power versus speed curves plotted for the torque versus speed curves of Figure 5.8a. According to Equation 5.5, power is highest when the product of torque and speed is at a maximum. Maximum power generally is achieved near governor's maximum, that is, at point C in Figure 5.8b. At point B, speed is high, but power is declining due to the low torque. At point D, torque is high, but power is declining due to the low speed. Some manufacturers design for nearly constant power by providing enough torque rise in the load-controlled range to offset the decline in speed. The curve of Figure 5.8b has nearly constant power between 2000 and 2200 rev/min.

## 5.9 DYNAMOMETERS FOR MEASURING ENGINE POWER

A *dynamometer* is an instrument for measuring engine power, and it must include at least four essential elements:

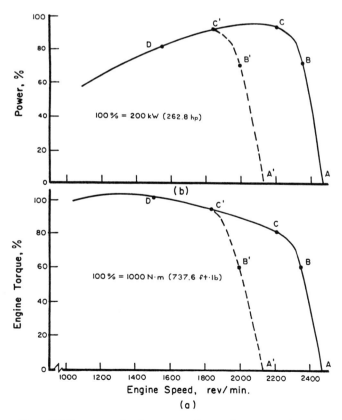

Figure 5.8–Torque-speed and power-speed curves for a governed engine.

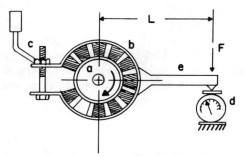

*Figure 5.9–A prony brake dynamometer.*

A means for controlling torque.
A means for measuring torque.
A means for measuring speed.
A means for dissipating the power.

A *prony brake* (Figure 5.9) is the simplest type of dynamometer. The drum (a) is connected to the crankshaft of the engine and rotates at engine speed. Surrounding the drum are brake shoes (b) that create a torque drag on the drum. The torque is controlled by tightening or loosening hand knob (c). The torque is measured by a scale (d) located at the end of a lever arm (e). A tachometer (not shown in Figure 5.9) also must be provided for measuring the engine speed. After the torque and speed are measured, the power can be calculated using Equation 5.5. The prony brake converts all of the power to heat. The brake shoes would soon burn up unless a means was provided for circulating water or some other coolant to carry off the heat.

Prony brakes have been replaced by more modern dynamometers. Figure 5.10 shows an electric generator being used as a dynamometer. The generator has the normal pair of bearings which permit the rotor to turn within the housing. The generator is cradled. That is, the housing is mounted in a second set of bearings. When an electrical load is applied to the generator – for example, by connection to a bank of resistors – the housing attempts to rotate, but it is restrained by a load arm. A scale on the end of the load arm measures the torque. The power is absorbed by the resistors or, in some modern electric dynamometers, the power is fed into the electric power grid. The torque is controlled by regulating the electromagnetic coupling that exists between the rotor and the housing.

An *eddy-current dynamometer* is shown in Figure 5.11. It is similar to the electric dynamometer, except that the electric current

Power Efficiencies and Measurement                                                111

*Figure 5.10–An electric dynamometer.*

is not delivered to an external load. Instead, eddy currents circulate in the rotor and, thus, the spinning rotor absorbs the power. Cooling water must be circulated through the eddy current dynamometer to prevent overheating.

A *portable shop-type dynamometer* is shown in Figure 5.12. This dynamometer uses a water brake principle, that is, the pto shaft drives a pump which pumps water against a controlled restriction. In another type of portable dynamometer, the tractor pto drives a rotating drum. Hydraulically actuated brake shoes are applied inside the drum to produce torque. The brake assembly is connected to a load arm at the back end of the dynamometer. A small hydraulic cylinder at the end of the arm transmits pressure to a large pressure gage which is used to indicate the torque. Many farm equipment dealers have shop-type dynamometers for testing tractors before and after engine overhauls.

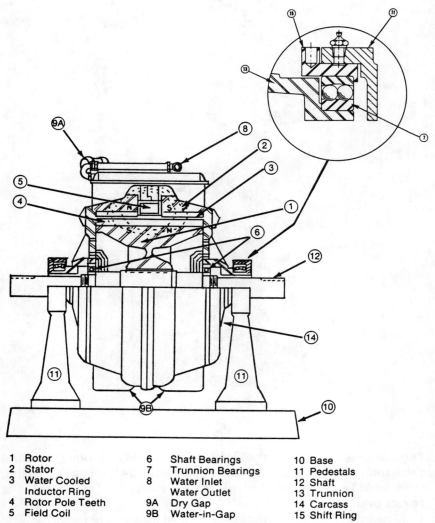

| | | | | | |
|---|---|---|---|---|---|
| 1 | Rotor | 6 | Shaft Bearings | 10 | Base |
| 2 | Stator | 7 | Trunnion Bearings | 11 | Pedestals |
| 3 | Water Cooled Inductor Ring | 8 | Water Inlet | 12 | Shaft |
| | | | Water Outlet | 13 | Trunnion |
| 4 | Rotor Pole Teeth | 9A | Dry Gap | 14 | Carcass |
| 5 | Field Coil | 9B | Water-in-Gap | 15 | Shift Ring |

Figure 5.11–An eddy-current dynamometer. (Courtesy of Eaton Corporation, Electric Drives Division.)

## 5.10 STANDARDIZED TRACTOR TESTS

The 1919 session of the Nebraska legislature passed a bill that required the testing of tractors to be sold within the state and also required the maintenance of service stations for such tractors. As was noted in Chapter 1, the law was prompted by the presence of inferior tractors on the market at that time. The provisions of the law

Power Efficiencies and Measurement 113

*Figure 5.12–A portable shop-type dynamometer. (Courtesy of M&W Gear Company.)*

do not apply to any tractor whose engines develop less than 14.9 kW (20 hp). Tractors manufactured, sold, or used for heavy construction are also exempt unless identical units are sold and used for agricultural purposes.

Concurrent with the development of the Common Market in Europe, the OECD (Organization for Economic Cooperation and Development) in Europe developed a tractor testing procedure that bore many similarities to the one used at the Nebraska Tractor Testing Station. European countries began requiring the OECD test for new tractor models to be sold within their borders. As tractor manufacturing and marketing became global in the 1980s, the OECD test became the most commonly accepted test procedure for worldwide marketing. In 1986 the Nebraska legislature changed their tractor test law to accept either the OECD test or the Nebraska test as a prerequisite to selling tractors in the state. By 1988 the Nebraska testing station became authorized as an official OECD testing station in the United States.

There are a total of five OECD test codes, of which the first two relate to testing of tractor performance. Two others relate to testing of ROPS (roll over protective structures) and another relates to noise measurement. The OECD Test Code II, Restricted Standard Code for the Official Testing of Agricultural Tractor Performance, is the most similar to the Nebraska test procedure. The Nebraska test required a 10-h drawbar test at 75% load while the OECD test requires only a 5-h test. Except for a lugging test on the drawbar, all Nebraska tests were done at governor's maximum. When the engine has more than enough torque rise in load control to offset the falling speed, peak power may occur at a speed in the load-control range and then some OECD tests will be conducted at peak power. The OECD tests also include more detailed tractor specifications, including design data on the engine, power train, brakes, and so forth.

Official OECD tests are too lengthy for distribution to the public. For every tractor which is sold in the state of Nebraska and has an OECD test, however, the Nebraska testing station publishes a summary of the test in a format similar to that of the earlier Nebraska test reports.

Because of manufacturing tolerances in the mass production of tractors, there is variation among tractors produced on the same assembly line. Because of such variation, some procedure must be used to select the specific tractor to be subjected to an official test. With both the Nebraska test and the OECD tests, the manufacturer is permitted to select the specific tractor and to pretest it before it is subjected to an official test. The selection procedure reduces the random variation that could otherwise occur; that is, it is unlikely that a manufacturer would select a tractor with below average performance for official testing. Data in the OECD tests can be used to compare tractors and to decide how to operate a given tractor most efficiently.

Table 5.1 shows an OECD test that was reformatted to be similar in appearance to the familiar Nebraska test reports. If the tractor has a pto shaft, a 2-h test is run at the speed which produces maximum power. Shorter pto tests are also run at rated engine (governor's maximum) speed and at standard pto speed if these differ from the speed at which maximum power occurs. A series of short, part-load pto tests are also run in the governor-controlled range. The engine is also loaded to the torque peak in the load-controlled range so that torque reserve can be reported. For the tractor test reported in Table 5.1, the torque reserve was 31.4% and peak torque occurred at an engine speed of 1700 rev/min. Speed, power, and fuel consumption are recorded during each pto test. By neglecting power losses in the pto drive, the approximate engine torque can be calculated for each test by using Equation 5.5. Since the barometric pressure and ambient temperature affect the air consumption (see Section 5.7) and, thus, the performance of the engine, the average ambient temperature and barometric pressure during the pto tests are recorded. Notice that column four of the pto test results is a listing of the PSFC in each test. Why did the PSFC increase each time the load on the engine was reduced? Because, as Equation 5.19 indicates, the engine mechanical efficiency declines as the torque load declines and becomes zero at zero load. SFC varies inversely

# Power Efficiencies and Measurement

## TABLE 5.1. Nebraska OECD Tractor Test 1619

### POWER TAKE-OFF PERFORMANCE

| Power HP (kW) | Crank shaft speed rpm | Gal/hr (l/h) | lb/hp.hr (kg/kW.h) | Hp.hr/gal (kW.h/l) | Mean Atmospheric Conditions |
|---|---|---|---|---|---|

#### MAXIMUM POWER AND FUEL CONSUMPTION

**Rated Engine Speed—(PTO speed—1002 rpm)**

| | | | | | |
|---|---|---|---|---|---|
| 141.60 (105.59) | 2200 | 8.38 (31.74) | 0.409 (0.249) | 16.89 (3.33) | |

**Maximum Power (2 Hours)**

| | | | | | |
|---|---|---|---|---|---|
| 146.86 (109.51) | 1850 | 8.05 (30.48) | 0.379 (0.231) | 18.24 (3.59) | Air temperature |

#### VARYING POWER AND FUEL CONSUMPTION

| Power HP (kW) | Crank shaft speed rpm | Gal/hr (l/h) | lb/hp.hr (kg/kW.h) | Hp.hr/gal (kW.h/l) | |
|---|---|---|---|---|---|
| 141.60 (105.59) | 2200 | 8.38 (31.74) | 0.409 (0.249) | 16.89 (3.33) | 77°F (25°C) |
| 122.85 (91.61) | 2243 | 7.55 (28.59) | 0.425 (0.258) | 16.27 (3.20) | Relative humidity |
| 93.33 (69.59) | 2276 | 6.29 (23.82) | 0.466 (0.284) | 14.83 (2.92) | 28% |
| 63.12 (47.07) | 2310 | 5.03 (19.06) | 0.551 (0.335) | 12.54 (2.47) | Barometer |
| 31.94 (23.82) | 2338 | 3.78 (14.29) | 0.817 (0.497) | 8.46 (1.67) | 29.12" Hg (98.61 kPa) |
| 0.51 (0.38) | 2363 | 2.56 (21.002) | 34.526 | 0.20 (0.04) | |

Maximum Torque 444 lb.-ft (602 Nm) at 1700 rpm
Maximum Torque Rise 31.4%
Torque Rise at 1000 engine rpm 23%

### DRAWBAR PERFORMANCE
### FUEL CONSUMPTION CHARACTERISTICS

| Power Hp (kW) | Drawbar pull lbs (kN) | Speed mph (km/h) | Crank-shaft speed rpm | Slip % | Fuel Consumption lb/hp.hr (kg/kW.h) | Hp.hr/gal (kW.h/l) | Temp.°F (°C) cool-ing med | Air dry bulb | Barom. inch Hg (kPa) |
|---|---|---|---|---|---|---|---|---|---|

**Maximum Power—12th Gear**

| 122.53 (91.37) | 5126 (22.80) | 8.96 (14.43) | 2199 | 2.41 | 0.473 (0.288) | 14.62 (2.88) | 188 (87) | 74 (23) | 28.84 (97.66) |

**75% of Pull at Maximum Power—12th Gear**

| 94.70 (70.62) | 3843 (17.09) | 9.24 (14.87) | 2254 | 1.80 | 0.518 (0.315) | 13.33 (2.63) | 186 (85) | 76 (24) | 28.84 (97.66) |

**50% of Pull at Maximum Power—12th Gear**

| 64.58 (48.16) | 2562 (11.40) | 9.45 (15.21) | 2291 | 1.17 | 0.611 (0.371) | 11.32 (2.23) | 184 (84) | 77 (25) | 28.84 (97.66) |

**75% of Pull at Reduced Engine Speed—13th Gear**

| 94.72 (70.64) | 3845 (17.10) | 9.24 (14.87) | 1821 | 1.71 | 0.476 (0.290) | 14.51 (2.86) | 186 (86) | 76 (24) | 28.84 (97.66) |

**50% of Pull at Reduced Engine Speed—13th Gear**

| 64.53 (48.12) | 2563 (11.40) | 9.44 (15.20) | 1850 | 1.17 | 0.542 (0.330) | 12.75 (2.51) | 182 (83) | 80 (27) | 28.84 (97.66) |

**Location of Test:** Center for Agricultural Equipment, Lincoln Nebraska 68583-0832, U.S.A.

**Dates of Test:** April-May, 1989

**Manufacturer:** John Deere Waterloo Works, P.O. Box 3500, Waterloo, Iowa 50704

**FUEL OIL and TIME: Fuel** No. 2 Diesel **Cetane No.** 51.1 **Specific gravity converted to** 60°/60°F (15°/15°C) 0.8301 **Fuel weight** 6.912 lbs/gal (0.828 kg/l) **Oil SAE** 15W40 **API service classification** CD/SD **To motor** 4.166 gal (15.768 l) **Drained from motor** 4.122 gal (15.605 l) **Transmission and hydraulic lubricant** John Deere HyGard fluid **Front axle lubricant** John Deere GL-5 Gear Lubricant 85W-140 **Total time engine was operated** 30.0 hours.

**ENGINE: Make** John Deere Diesel **Type** six cylinder vertical with turbocharger **Serial No.** *RG6076T102604* **Crankshaft** lengthwise **Rated engine speed** 2200 **Bore and stroke** (as specified) 4.56" × 4.75" (115.8 mm × 120.7 mm) **Compression ratio** 16.0 to 1 **Displacement** 466 cu in (7634 ml) **Starting system** 12 volt **Lubrication** pressure **Air cleaner** two paper elements **Oil filter** one full flow cartridge **Oil cooler** engine coolant heat exchanger for crankcase oil, radiator for hydraulic and transmission oil **Fuel filter** one paper cartridge and prefilter **Muffler** vertical **Cooling medium temperature control** 2 thermostats and variable speed fan.

**ENGINE OPERATING PARAMETERS: Fuel rate** 56.3-61.5 lb/hr (25.6-27.9 kg/hr) **High idle** 2350-2400 rpm **Turbo boost** nominal 14-17 psi (97-117 kPa) as measured 14.5 psi (100 kPa).

**CHASSIS: Type** front wheel assist **Serial No.** *RW4455P001020* **Tread width** rear 62.0" (1574 mm) to 116.0" (2950 mm) front 60.6" (1538 mm) to 88.0" (2235 mm) **Wheel base** 105.3" (2675 mm) **Hydraulic control system** direct engine drive **Transmission** selective gear fixed ratio with full range operator controlled powershift **Nominal travel speeds mph (km/h)** first 1.45 (2.34) second 2.08 (3.35) third 2.51 (4.05) fourth 3.16 (5.08) fifth 3.64 (5.86) sixth 4.13 (6.65) seventh 4.76 (7.66) eighth 5.47 (8.80) ninth 6.30 (10.13) tenth 7.15 (11.50) eleventh 8.23 (13.25) twelfth 9.21 (14.82) thirteenth 11.40 (18.35) fourteenth 15.94 (25.66) fifteenth 19.73 (31.75) reverse 2.01 (3.24), 2.88 (4.64), 4.37 (7.04), 6.59 (10.60) **Clutch** multiple wet disc hydraulically power actuated by foot pedal **Brakes** multiple wet disc hydraulically power actuated by two foot pedals which can be locked together **Steering** hydrostatic **Power take-off** 540 rpm at 2201 engine rpm and 1002 rpm at 2200 engine rpm **Unladen tractor mass** 15275 lb (6928 kg).

with efficiency and, thus, the PSFC increased as the torque load on the pto shaft declined.

In the OECD drawbar tests (Figure 5.13), the tractor is tested in each gear. The first test reported in the summary (Table 5.1) is for the best pulling gear, that is, the gear which produces the most drawbar power. In Table 5.1, twelfth gear was the best pulling gear and the test was run at governor's maximum (rated engine) speed. The next two drawbar tests reported are also in the best pulling gear,

TABLE 5.1. Nebraska OECD Tractor Test 1619 (con't)

**DRAWBAR PERFORMANCE AT 1850 RPM**
**MAXIMUM POWER IN SELECTED GEARS**

| Power Hp (kW) | Drawbar pull lbs (kN) | Speed mph (km/h) | Crank-shaft speed rpm | Slip % | Fuel Consumption lb/hp.hr (kg/kW.h) | Fuel Consumption Hp.hr/gal (kW.h/l) | Temp.°F (°C) cooling med | Temp.°F (°C) Air dry bulb | Barom. inch Hg (kPa) |
|---|---|---|---|---|---|---|---|---|---|
| | | | | 5th Gear | | | | | |
| 113.25 (84.45) | 14200 (63.16) | 2.99 (4.81) | 2126 | 14.74 | 0.506 (0.308) | 13.66 (2.69) | 185 (85) | 48 (9) | 29.12 (98.61) |
| | | | | 6th Gear | | | | | |
| 121.57 (90.66) | 12794 (56.91) | 3.56 (5.73) | 2083 | 8.53 | 0.467 (0.284) | 14.79 (2.91) | 185 (85) | 48 (9) | 29.12 (98.61) |
| | | | | 7th Gear | | | | | |
| 125.11 (93.29) | 11864 (52.77) | 3.95 (6.36) | 1975 | 7.14 | 0.449 (0.273) | 15.40 (3.03) | 185 (85) | 48 (9) | 29.12 (98.61) |
| | | | | 8th Gear | | | | | |
| 121.45 (90.56) | 10553 (46.94) | 4.32 (6.95) | 1848 | 5.69 | 0.458 (0.278) | 15.10 (2.97) | 185 (85) | 48 (9) | 29.12 (98.61) |
| | | | | 9th Gear | | | | | |
| 122.81 (91.58) | 9134 (40.63) | 5.04 (8.11) | 1852 | 4.62 | 0.451 (0.274) | 15.33 (3.02) | 185 (85) | 48 (9) | 29.12 (98.61) |
| | | | | 10th Gear | | | | | |
| 123.62 (92.19) | 8037 (35.75) | 5.77 (9.28) | 1852 | 3.87 | 0.446 (0.271) | 15.50 (3.05) | 184 (84) | 48 (9) | 29.12 (98.61) |
| | | | | 11th Gear | | | | | |
| 122.93 (91.67) | 6897 (30.68) | 6.68 (10.76) | 1852 | 3.27 | 0.451 (0.274) | 15.34 (3.02) | 184 (84) | 48 (9) | 29.12 (98.61) |
| | | | | 12th Gear | | | | | |
| 126.69 (94.47) | 6338 (28.19) | 7.50 (12.06) | 1851 | 2.93 | 0.437 (0.266) | 15.80 (3.11) | 184 (84) | 48 (9) | 29.12 (98.61) |
| | | | | 13th Gear | | | | | |
| 124.35 (92.73) | 4998 (22.23) | 9.33 (15.02) | 1849 | 2.32 | 0.448 (0.272) | 15.44 (3.04) | 184 (84) | 48 (9) | 29.12 (98.61) |

**DRAWBAR PERFORMANCE AT 1850 RPM**
**MAXIMUM POWER IN SELECTED GEARS—BALLASTED TRACTOR**

| Power Hp (kW) | Drawbar pull lbs (kN) | Speed mph (km/h) | Crank-shaft speed rpm | Slip % | Fuel Consumption lb/hp.hr (kg/kW.h) | Fuel Consumption Hp.hr/gal (kW.h/l) | Temp.°F (°C) cooling med | Temp.°F (°C) Air dry bulb | Barom. inch Hg (kPa) |
|---|---|---|---|---|---|---|---|---|---|
| | | | | 3rd Gear | | | | | |
| 100.17 (74.69) | 17366 (77.25) | 2.16 (3.48) | 2233 | 14.73 | 0.548 (0.334) | 12.60 (2.48) | 186 (86) | 72 (22) | 28.57 (96.75) |
| | | | | 4th Gear | | | | | |
| 118.19 (88.14) | 15455 (68.75) | 2.87 (4.62) | 2176 | 7.70 | 0.488 (0.297) | 14.16 (2.79) | 186 (85) | 71 (22) | 28.57 (96.75) |
| | | | | 5th Gear | | | | | |
| 122.40 (91.28) | 15064 (67.01) | 3.05 (4.90) | 2001 | 7.15 | 0.464 (0.282) | 14.90 (2.93) | 189 (87) | 72 (22) | 28.72 (97.26) |
| | | | | 6th Gear | | | | | |
| 123.94 (92.42) | 14374 (63.94) | 3.23 (5.20) | 1851 | 6.28 | 0.453 (0.276) | 15.25 (3.00) | 187 (86) | 68 (20) | 28.72 (97.26) |
| | | | | 7th Gear | | | | | |
| 126.10 (94.03) | 12474 (55.49) | 3.79 (6.10) | 1854 | 4.90 | 0.443 (0.269) | 15.61 (3.07) | 187 (86) | 65 (18) | 28.72 (97.26) |
| | | | | 8th Gear | | | | | |
| 121.04 (90.26) | 10335 (45.97) | 4.39 (7.07) | 1851 | 3.98 | 0.462 (0.281) | 14.97 (2.95) | 190 (88) | 74 (23) | 28.72 (97.26) |
| | | | | 9th Gear | | | | | |
| 121.52 (90.62) | 8959 (39.85) | 5.09 (8.19) | 1851 | 3.30 | 0.462 (0.281) | 14.96 (2.95) | 190 (88) | 76 (24) | 28.72 (97.26) |
| | | | | 10th Gear | | | | | |
| 122.44 (91.31) | 7918 (35.22) | 5.80 (9.33) | 1852 | 2.96 | 0.455 (0.277) | 15.19 (3.00) | 190 (88) | 76 (24) | 28.72 (97.26) |
| | | | | 11th Gear | | | | | |
| 120.82 (90.10) | 6753 (30.04) | 6.71 (10.80) | 1851 | 2.62 | 0.460 (0.280) | 15.02 (2.96) | 190 (88) | 79 (26) | 28.73 (97.29) |
| | | | | 12th Gear | | | | | |
| 124.94 (93.17) | 6219 (27.66) | 7.53 (12.13) | 1854 | 2.36 | 0.449 (0.273) | 15.40 (3.03) | 189 (87) | 80 (27) | 28.73 (97.29) |
| | | | | 13th Gear | | | | | |
| 120.97 (90.21) | 4846 (21.55) | 9.36 (15.07) | 1852 | 1.83 | 0.458 (0.278) | 15.10 (2.98) | 189 (87) | 85 (29) | 28.73 (97.29) |

**REPAIRS AND ADJUSTMENTS:** No repairs or adjustments.

**REMARKS:** All test results were determined from observed data obtained in accordance with official OECD, SAE and Nebraska test procedures. For the maximum power tests, the fuel temperature at the injection pump return was maintained at 129° F (54° C). This tractor is equipped with a variable speed cooling fan. Since engine power is influenced by fan speed, all power tests were conducted at approximately the same ambient air temperatures. This tractor did not meet manufacturers 3 point lift capacity claim of 6550 lb (2971 kg) or 8470 lb (3842 kg) with lift assist cylinder. The performance figures on this summary were taken from a test conducted under the OECD restricted standard test code procedure.

We, the undersigned, certify that this is a true and correct report of official Tractor Test No. **1619**, Summary 057, December 22, 1989.

LOUIS I. LEVITICUS
Engineer-in-Charge

K. VON BARGEN
R. D. GRISSO
G. J. HOFFMAN
Board of Tractor Test Engineers

but with the pull reduced to 75% and then to 50% of the pull at maximum power. Notice that, as the load was reduced, the governor allowed the engine speed to increase somewhat. For the next two tests, the tractor was shifted to a higher gear (13th gear) and the engine speed was reduced to maintain the same travel speeds as in

TABLE 5.1. Nebraska OECD Tractor Test 1619 (con't)

### DRAWBAR PERFORMANCE AT 2200 RPM
### MAXIMUM POWER IN SELECTED GEARS—BALLASTED TRACTOR

| Power Hp (kW) | Drawbar pull lbs (kN) | Speed mph (km/h) | Crank-shaft speed rpm | Slip % | Fuel Consumption lb/hp.hr (kg/kW.h) | Fuel Consumption Hp.hr/gal (kW.h/l) | Temp.°F (°C) cooling med | Temp.°F (°C) Air dry bulb | Barom. inch Hg (kPa) |
|---|---|---|---|---|---|---|---|---|---|
| | | | | 3rd Gear | | | | | |
| 100.83 (75.19) | 17446 (77.60) | 2.17 (3.49) | 2233 | 14.53 | 0.548 (0.333) | 12.61 (2.48) | 186 (86) | 71 (22) | 28.57 (96.75) |
| | | | | 4th Gear | | | | | |
| 118.09 (88.06) | 15218 (67.69) | 2.91 (4.68) | 2198 | 7.31 | 0.488 (0.297) | 14.17 (2.79) | 186 (85) | 71 (22) | 28.57 (96.75) |
| | | | | 5th Gear | | | | | |
| 121.02 (90.24) | 13287 (59.10) | 3.42 (5.50) | 2200 | 5.47 | 0.478 (0.291) | 14.45 (2.85) | 187 (86) | 70 (21) | 28.72 (97.26) |
| | | | | 6th Gear | | | | | |
| 122.79 (91.56) | 11759 (52.31) | 3.92 (6.30) | 2200 | 4.56 | 0.471 (0.287) | 14.66 (2.89) | 187 (86) | 66 (19) | 28.72 (97.26) |
| | | | | 7th Gear | | | | | |
| 123.72 (92.26) | 10198 (45.36) | 4.55 (7.32) | 2200 | 3.81 | 0.468 (0.285) | 14.77 (2.91) | 186 (85) | 65 (18) | 28.72 (97.26) |
| | | | | 8th Gear | | | | | |
| 118.59 (88.43) | 8454 (37.60) | 5.26 (8.47) | 2200 | 3.13 | 0.490 (0.298) | 14.12 (2.78) | 189 (87) | 76 (24) | 28.72 (97.26) |
| | | | | 9th Gear | | | | | |
| 118.44 (88.32) | 7299 (32.47) | 6.09 (9.79) | 2200 | 2.70 | 0.488 (0.297) | 14.15 (2.79) | 190 (88) | 76 (24) | 28.72 (97.26) |
| | | | | 10th Gear | | | | | |
| 118.12 (88.09) | 6394 (28.44) | 6.93 (11.15) | 2200 | 2.44 | 0.486 (0.296) | 14.22 (2.80) | 189 (87) | 76 (24) | 28.72 (97.26) |
| | | | | 11th Gear | | | | | |
| 116.75 (87.06) | 5466 (24.31) | 8.01 (12.89) | 2198 | 2.09 | 0.489 (0.297) | 14.13 (2.78) | 190 (88) | 79 (26) | 28.73 (97.29) |
| | | | | 12th Gear | | | | | |
| 119.65 (89.23) | 5005 (22.26) | 8.97 (14.43) | 2196 | 1.83 | 0.479 (0.291) | 14.44 (2.84) | 190 (88) | 82 (28) | 28.73 (97.29) |

### TRACTOR SOUND LEVEL WITH CAB

| | dB(A) |
|---|---|
| Gear closest to 4.7 mph (7.5 km/h)—7th Gear | 74.5 |
| Maximum sound level | 76.5 |
| Transport speed—no load—15th Gear | 77.0 |
| Bystander in 15th Gear | 87.0 |

### LUGGING ABILITY IN 10th GEAR

| Crankshaft Speed rpm | 2200 | 1978 | 1755 | 1542 | 1321 | 1101 |
|---|---|---|---|---|---|---|
| Pull—lbs (kN) | 6394 (28.44) | 7221 (32.12) | 8302 (36.93) | 8501 (37.81) | 8502 (37.82) | 8180 (36.39) |
| Increase in Pull % | 0 | 13 | 30 | 33 | 33 | 28 |
| Power—Hp (kW) | 118.12 (88.09) | 119.60 (89.19) | 121.54 (90.63) | 109.25 (81.47) | 93.60 (69.80) | 75.07 (55.98) |
| Speed—Mph (km/h) | 6.93 (11.15) | 6.21 (10.00) | 5.49 (8.84) | 4.82 (7.76) | 4.13 (6.64) | 3.44 (5.54) |
| Slip % | 2.44 | 2.62 | 3.13 | 3.13 | 3.13 | 3.13 |

### THREE POINT HITCH PERFORMANCE (SAE Static Test)

| | | | | | |
|---|---|---|---|---|---|
| Observed Maximum Pressure psi. (bar) | | | 2530 (174) | | |
| Location | | | remote outlet | | |
| Hydraulic oil temperature °F(°C) | | | 144 (62) | | |
| Location | | | transmission sump | | |
| Category | | | II | | |
| Quick attach | | | No | | |
| Hitch point distance to ground level in. (mm) | 8.7 (221) | 15.7 (399) | 22.4 (569) | 30.4 (772) | 37.4 (950) |
| Lift force on frame lb.  "    "    "    "    " (kN) | 7550 (33.6) | 7482 (33.3) | 7199 (32.0) | 6526 (29.0) | 6175 (27.5) |
| | | with lift assist cylinder | | | |
| Hitch point distance to ground level in. (mm) | 9.0 (229) | 16.0 (406) | 22.3 (566) | 30.4 (772) | 37.4 (950) |
| Lift force on frame lb.  "    "    "    "    " (kN) | 9833 (43.7) | 9872 (43.9) | 9540 (42.4) | 8633 (38.4) | 8077 (35.9) |

the corresponding part-load tests in the best pulling gear. What was accomplished by shifting to a higher gear? The answer can be found by comparing the DSFCs. At 75% load in 12th gear, for example, the tractor was traveling at 14.87 km/h (9.24 mph) while producing 70.62 kW (94.70 hp) of power with a DSFC of 0.315 kg/kW·h

TABLE 5.1. Nebraska OECD Tractor Test 1619 (con't)

| TIRES AND WEIGHT | With Ballast | Without Ballast |
|---|---|---|
| Rear Tires—No., size, ply & psi (kPa) | Four 18.4R42; **; 12 (85) | Two 18.4R42; **; 16 (110) |
| Ballast—Duals (total) | 1710 lb (776 kg) | None |
| —Cast Iron (total) | 1000 lb (454 kg) | None |
| Front Tires—No., size, ply & psi (kPa) | Two 14.9R30; ***; 30 (205) | Two 14.9R30; ***; 30 (205) |
| Ballast—Test Equip (total) | 115 lb (52 kg) | None |
| —Cast Iron (total) | 100 lb (45 kg) | None |
| Height of Drawbar | 18.5 in (470 mm) | 18.5 in (470 mm) |
| Static Weight—Rear | 12630 lb (5729 kg) | 9825 lb (4456 kg) |
| —Front | 5570 lb (2526 kg) | 5450 lb (2472 kg) |
| —Total | 18200 lb (8255 kg) | 15275 lb (6928 kg) |

### THREE POINT HITCH PERFORMANCE
### (OECD Static Test)

CATEGORY: II
Quick Attach: None

| | | |
|---|---|---|
| Maximum Force Exerted Through Whole Range: | 5504 lbs | (24.5 kN) |
| | *7281 lbs | (32.4 kN) |
| i) Opening pressure of relief valve: | NA | |
| Sustained pressure with pump stalled: | 2530 psi | (174 Bar) |
| ii) Pump delivery rate at minimum pressure: | 27.0 GPM | (102.2 l/min) |
| iii) Pump delivery rate at maximum hydraulic power: | 25.7 GPM | (97.3 l/min) |
| Delivery pressure: | 2100 psi | (145 Bar) |
| Power: | 31.5 Hp | (23.5 kW) |

*with lift assist cylinder                    *with lift assist cylinder

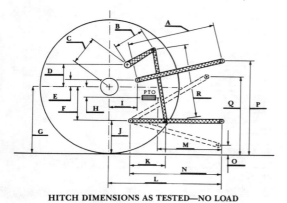

| | inch | mm |
|---|---|---|
| A | 26.6 | 676 |
| B | 11.5 | 292 |
| C | 11.3 | 287 |
| D | 10.9 | 278 |
| E | 5.6 | 143 |
| F | 10.2 | 259 |
| G | 35.1 | 892 |
| H | 6.5 | 165 |
| I | 14.3 | 362 |
| J | 24.9 | 633 |
| K | 23.1 | 587 |
| L | 41.6 | 1056 |
| M | 22.0 | 558 |
| N | 37.1 | 942 |
| O | 10.3 | 262 |
| P | 45.0 | 1143 |
| Q | 37.5 | 953 |
| R | 32.8 | 833 |

**HITCH DIMENSIONS AS TESTED—NO LOAD**

John Deere 4455 Powershift Diesel

Agricultural Research Division
Institute of Agriculture and Natural Resources
University of Nebraska–Lincoln
Darrell Nelson, Dean and Director

(0.518 lb/hp-h). The tractor traveled at the same speed and produced the same drawbar power during the test at 75% load in 13th gear, but the DSFC dropped to 0.290 kg/kW·h (0.476 lb/hp-h) for a 7.9% savings in fuel. The results of the two tests at 75% load illustrate the

*Figure 5.13–The drawbar test of a tractor at the Nebraska Tractor-Testing Station. (Courtesy of University of Nebraska Tractor Test Laboratory.)*

usefulness of the old adage, "shift up and throttle back", for saving fuel while a tractor is doing light drawbar work. The reader can calculate that even larger savings were achieved by the "shift up and throttle back" technique at 50% load.

The next series of drawbar tests reported in Table 5.1 is for maximum power in selected gears. For the tractor of Table 5.1, maximum power occurred when the engine was lugged down to 1850 rev/min. The initial series of tests in selected gears was run when the tractor was not weighted with ballast. Results were not reported for gears in which the wheel slip was more than 15%. The test in 5th gear was not quite a maximum power test, that is, the load was reduced (allowing the engine speed to increase to 2126 rev/min) until the slip fell below 15%. Results of the two highest gears, 14th and 15th, were not reported because the speed would have been more than 24 km/h (15 mph).

The fully ballasted tractor was also tested for maximum power in selected gears. Static weights on the front and rear axles of the unballasted and ballasted tractors are reported on the second page of the test report. Adding ballast reduced the wheel slip. The added ballast allowed the tractor to be operated in 3rd and 4th gears without exceeding 15% wheel slip.

The fully ballasted tractor was again tested for maximum power in selected gears when the engine was operating at governor's maximum, that is, at 2200 rev/min. The governor was able to hold the engine speed very close to 2200 rev/min in all but 3rd gear (when the engine was deliberately unloaded to keep the slip below 15%). You will note that, in the previous two series, the engine was operating in load control and the speed varied somewhat from the desired 1850 rev/min.

The final series of drawbar tests in Table 5.1 is a test of lugging ability on the drawbar. Beginning at governor's maximum, the engine was gradually lugged down into the load-controlled range until the torque rose to a peak and then fell. The torque increased 33% at the peak, which compares closely with the 31.4% torque reserve reported in the pto tests.

Some information can be gained by comparing the results of drawbar tests and pto tests. For example, why did the tractor produce 141.60 kW (105.59 hp) when running at 2200 rev/min in the pto tests but only 118.12 kW (88.09 hp) when running at 2200 rev/min in the drawbar lugging ability tests? The engine was running at governor's maximum in both cases and, thus, was producing the same amount of power. The drawbar power was less because the total of power losses in traction, in the transmission, differential, and final drive was greater than power loss through the pto drive.

Some useful supplementary information is shown in Table 5.1. Reports of sound level measurements are reported under a variety of standard conditions. The lifting capacity of the three-point hitch is reported. Certain specifications are reported on the first page of the report. Information is given concerning the tractor manufacturer. Data are given on the tractor fuel and oil, including the specific gravity of the fuel; in Chapter 6, you will learn to calculate the heating value of the fuel from its specific gravity. A description of the engine is given, including its bore, stroke, displacement and compression ratio. If the engine is turbocharged, the measured boost is reported. In Chapter 11, you will learn to use the boost to estimate the air consumption of the engine. Finally, information is given concerning the chassis tread width, wheel base, nominal travel speeds in the available gears, and information on the clutch, brakes, steering, and pto drive.

## 5.11 SUMMARY

Torque is a turning effort that, when accompanied by rotary speed, produces power. Power adjectives must be used because the amount of power varies depending on where it is measured. Engines typically convert less than half of the fuel equivalent power (power in the fuel) into indicated (mechanical) power and the remainder is lost as rejected heat. Part of the indicated power is lost as friction power due to parasitic losses within the engine and only the remaining brake power is available for useful work. Indicated thermal efficiency, mechanical efficiency, and brake thermal efficiency are measures of the efficiency of energy conversion and transmission in the engine. Mechanical efficiency is zero at zero load, but it increases to a maximum at maximum power. Thus, engines become more efficient with increasing load. Specific fuel consumption (SFC) indicates the amount of fuel needed by the engine to do a certain amount of work. SFC varies inversely with efficiency, that is, SFC is lowest when efficiency is highest.

Volumetric efficiency is the air-pumping efficiency of an engine. High volumetric efficiency is desirable to achieve the highest possible power from an engine. Turbocharging and optimum valve timing are two means of providing high volumetric efficiency.

Gas pressures on a piston vary greatly through a combustion cycle but, for purposes of calculation, can be replaced with an equivalent constant pressure called the indicated mean effective pressure (imep). The imep is merely the average height of the p-v diagram for a combustion cycle. Designers have only three avenues for increasing engine power: They can design larger engines, faster engines, or engines with higher imep. Other mean effective pressures can be calculated and are useful for describing engine performance. Brake mean effective pressure (bmep) varies proportionally with engine torque. Friction mean effective pressure (fmep) increases with engine speed. Thus, friction power can be reduced and mechanical efficiency can be increased by reducing engine speed.

Engines in farm tractors have a governor that attempts to maintain the speed set by the operator, regardless of engine load. Typical governors include flyweights that swing outward against spring tension and reduce fuel delivery when the engine speed is too high. Conversely, the spring pulls the flyweights in and increases fuel delivery when the engine speed is too low. Governor regulation is the percentage change in speed between high idle, when there is no load on the engine, and governor's maximum, when the flyweights have reached the limit of their inward travel. When torque exceeds that at governor's maximum, the governor can have no effect and the speed is controlled only by the load. Thus, tractor engines have two speed ranges: the governor-controlled range and the load-controlled range. When operators set the speed control lever, they are actually setting the high idle speed. The governor controls the actual speed until torque exceeds governor's maximum.

A dynamometer is an instrument for measuring engine power and includes four essential elements: means for controlling torque, means for measuring torque, means for measuring speed, and means for dissipating power. Prony brakes, eddy-current dynamometers, electric dynamometers, and shop-type dynamometers are available for measuring engine power.

The Nebraska Tractor Test was developed to provide a uniquely independent source of data for studying tractor performance. With the globalization of tractor manufacturing and marketing, the Nebraska Test has been supplanted by OECD tests. Data from the Nebraska test or OECD tests can be used to compare tractors or to choose how to operate a given tractor most efficiently. Test data show that SFC falls as either pto load or drawbar load is increased. When a tractor is pulling a light drawbar load, the test data show that fuel can be saved by shifting up and throttling back.

# QUESTIONS

Q5.1   Torque and work are both the product of a force times a distance. How does torque differ from work? Explain briefly.

Q5.2   What two quantities must be multiplied together to obtain the fuel equivalent power?

Q5.3   According to Equation 5.10, there are only three possible methods for increasing the power of an engine. What are these three methods?

Q5.4   The indicated thermal efficiency is the fraction of the fuel equivalent power that is converted into indicated power. What is the fate of the remainder of the fuel equivalent power?

Q5.5   (a) How is mechanical efficiency calculated?
(b) What does mechanical efficiency indicate?

Q5.6   What is the fate of that part of the indicated power that is not converted into brake power?

Q5.7   (a) What is bmep?
(b) Can it be measured directly in an engine?
(c) Briefly explain how bmep can be determined.

Q5.8   (a) What is fmep?
(b) Can it be measured directly in an engine?
(c) Briefly explain how fmep can be determined.

Q5.9   (a) If the torque output of an engine was doubled by applying a heavier load, would the bmep change?

(b) If so, how much would it change?

Q5.10 (a) What is volumetric efficiency?
(b) Why is high volumetric efficiency desirable?

Q5.11 (a) What is the purpose of a governor on a farm tractor engine?
(b) What is the meaning of the term *governor's maximum*?
(c) What controls the speed when the torque is greater than that at governor's maximum?

Q5.12 What are the four essential elements of a dynamometer for measuring engine power?

Q5.13 Eddy-current dynamometers and most portable shop-type dynamometers use the same method for dissipating the power that is absorbed from an engine. How is the power dissipated in these dynamometers?

Q5.14 Do provisions of the Nebraska Tractor Test Law apply to small garden tractors? If so, how? Briefly explain your answer.

Q5.15 (a) When a new model of tractor is to be subjected to an OECD test, how is the specific tractor selected?
(b) Would the specific tractor be likely to have less than, the same, or more power than the average of all similar models produced by the manufacturer? Briefly explain your answer.

Q5.16 The tractor manufacturer's representative generally chooses to shut off the air conditioner when the tractor is being subjected to an official test. Briefly describe the effect, if any, on the indicated thermal efficiency, the mechanical efficiency, the brake thermal efficiency the BSFC when the air conditioner is turned off.

# PROBLEMS

P5.1 Suppose you are using a wrench to tighten a nut on a bolt, as in Figure 5.1.

(a) If you apply 40 N (9 lb) of force at a distance 0.2 m (7.9 in.) from the center, how much torque are you applying?

(b) If the nut is rusted to the bolt and will not turn, how much work is being done with the wrench?

(c) If the nut breaks free and the same torque as in part a is exerted through one complete revolution, how much work has been done?

P5.2  A tractor is traveling 8 km/h (5 mph) while pulling a plow that exerts 20 kN (4500 lb) of pull on the drawbar. Calculate the linear (drawbar) power.

P5.3  An engine is being tested on a dynamometer. The engine is running at 2400 rev/min and the torque load is 450 N·m (332 lb-ft). Calculate the brake power.

P5.4  During a test, an engine consumes 23 L/h (5.9 gph) of fuel whose density is 0.836 kg/L (7.1 lb/gal). The heating value of the fuel is 45 410 kJ/kg (19,523 BTU/lb). Calculate the fuel equivalent power in the engine.

P5.5  A four-cycle 10.455 L (638 cubic in.) engine is producing 670 N·m (494 lb-ft) of torque while running at 2100 rev/min. Through use of special instruments, the imep is measured, and it is 1000 kPa (145 psi). Calculate (a) the indicated power, (b) the brake power, and (c) the friction power.

P5.6  For the engine in P5.5, calculate (a) the bmep, (b) the fmep, and (c) the mechanical efficiency.

P5.7  During a test, the four-cycle, 15.649 L (955 cubic in.) engine in a large tractor consumes 73 L/h (19.3 gal/h) of diesel fuel while running at 2100 rev/min and producing 1160 N·m (856 lb-ft) of torque. The imep during the test is 1110 kPa (161 psi). The fuel density is 0.835 kg/L (7.0 lb/gal), and its heating value is 45 434 kJ/kg (19,533 BTU/lb). Calculate (a) the fuel equivalent power, (b) the indicated power, (c) the brake power, (d) the friction power, (e) the indicated thermal efficiency, (f) the mechanical efficiency, and (g) the brake thermal efficiency.

P5.8  A four-cycle, 5.866 L (358 cubic in.) engine consumes 19 kg/h (42 lb/h) of fuel and 413 kg/h (910 lb/h) of air while running under full load at 2400 rev/min. The air temperature is 24.2° C (75.6° F), and the barometric pressure is 98.13 kPa (14.2 psi). Calculate (a) the air density, (b) the theoretical air consumption, and (c) the volumetric efficiency.

P5.9   The engine in P5.7 is a turbocharged and intercooled engine. It consumes air at the rate of 1650 kg/h (3634 lb/h). The air temperature is 24.4° C (75.9° F) and the barometric pressure is 97.02 kPa (14.1 psi). Calculate (a) the air density, (b) the theoretical air consumption, and (c) the volumetric efficiency. (*Note*: The volumetric efficiency of turbocharged engines is greater than 1.0 — that is, greater than 100% at full load.)

P5.10   Assume the test in P5.7 was carried out by connecting the tractor pto to an eddy-current dynamometer. Further assume that 88% of the brake power is delivered to the pto shaft.
   (a) How much power does the dynamometer absorb?
   (b) What happens to the power that is absorbed by the dynamometer?

P5.11   The high idle speed of an engine is 2862 rev/min, the rated (governor's maximum) speed is 2600 rev/min, and the peak torque occurs at 1550 rev/min. The rated torque is 720 N·m (530 lb-ft) and the peak torque is 910 N·m (670 lb-ft). Calculate (a) the governor regulation, (b) the percent torque reserve, and (c) the percent of rated speed at which peak torque occurs.

P5.12   Rework P5.11, but assume that the high idle speed is 2240 rev/min, the rated (governor's maximum) speed is 2100 rev/min, and the peak torque occurs at 1466 rev/min. Also, assume that the rated torque is 1165 N·m (859 lb-ft) and the peak torque is 1515 N·m (1117 lb-ft).

# 6
# Fuels and Combustion

## 6.1 INTRODUCTION

Fuels for mobile vehicles must have certain characteristics if the vehicles are to operate successfully. The fuels must have a high energy value so that a sufficient supply of energy can be stored in a reasonably small source on the vehicle. The fuels must vaporize and ignite easily in the engine, yet they must be reasonably safe to handle. Nearly all engine fuels today are derived from petroleum. World petroleum reserves are diminishing, but larger quantities of tar sands, shale oil, and coal remain in the earth. After suitable processing and refining, these latter fuels will have properties similar to petroleum. Eventually, however, all fossil fuels will be depleted, and alcohol and other renewable fuels may come into widespread use.

Fuels may be in gaseous, liquid, or solid form. All three types have been used in vehicles in the past. At present, and for the foreseeable future, however, liquid fuels will be dominant. Some gaseous fuels will also be used, but there will be little use for solid fuels in internal combustion engines.

You will not need to memorize the chemical structures of hydrocarbons presented in this chapter. The structures are presented principally for the insights they provide into the differences between diesel fuel and gasoline and the reasons for engine knock. You will learn to balance combustion equations, but the balancing is not difficult. It is simply a matter of counting atoms to ensure, for example, that the same number of carbon atoms are in the exhaust products as were in the fuel. Finding the results of combustion chemistry calculations will provide you with valuable insights that you will need in order to understand carburetor adjustments, fuel economy, exhaust emissions, and other practical aspects of engine operation.

## 6.2 CRUDE OIL AND REFINING

Crude oil is found in rock formations that were floors of oceans thousands of years ago. Organic matter from the sea was trapped by the rocks and subjected to high pressure. Through progressive cracking of the molecules and elimination of oxygen, the organic matter eventually became petroleum. All petroleum is made up of approximately 86% carbon and 14% hydrogen. The *hydrocarbon molecules* in crude oil are found in a wide variety of sizes and are accompanied by dirt, water, sulphur, and other impurities. Thus, it is necessary to refine crude oil to produce fuels suitable for use in engines.

The molecular structures illustrated in Figure 6.1 include most of the molecular families found in refined fuels. Chemical formulas for these families are as follows:

Paraffin: $C_nH_{2n+2}$
Olefin: $C_nH_{2n}$
Diolefin: $C_nH_{2n-2}$
Naphthalene: $C_nH_{2n}$
Aromatic: $C_nH_{2n-6}$

When n is 4 or less, the molecules are small enough to form gases at normal temperatures and pressures. The boiling point of hydrocarbons increases with n – that is, with molecular weight – and this is the principle on which refineries work.

A flowchart for a typical refinery is shown in Figure 6.2. The crude oil is heated beyond the boiling point of the heaviest hydrocarbon and fed into a fractioning tower. The hydrocarbons repeatedly recondense and revaporize as they pass upward through the plates in the tower. In moving up through the tower, the hydrocarbons encounter progressively cooler temperatures which permit only the progressively smaller molecules to revaporize and continue rising. Thus, heavier hydrocarbons can be withdrawn near the bottom of the tower, and lighter hydrocarbons can be withdrawn near the top.

A *distillation curve* shows the percentage of hydrocarbons that boil and distill at various temperatures. A distillation curve for one sample of crude oil is shown in Figure 6.3. For proper engine performance, fuels must have boiling points within the approximate ranges shown in Figure 6.3, that is, from 30° C (86° F) to 230° C

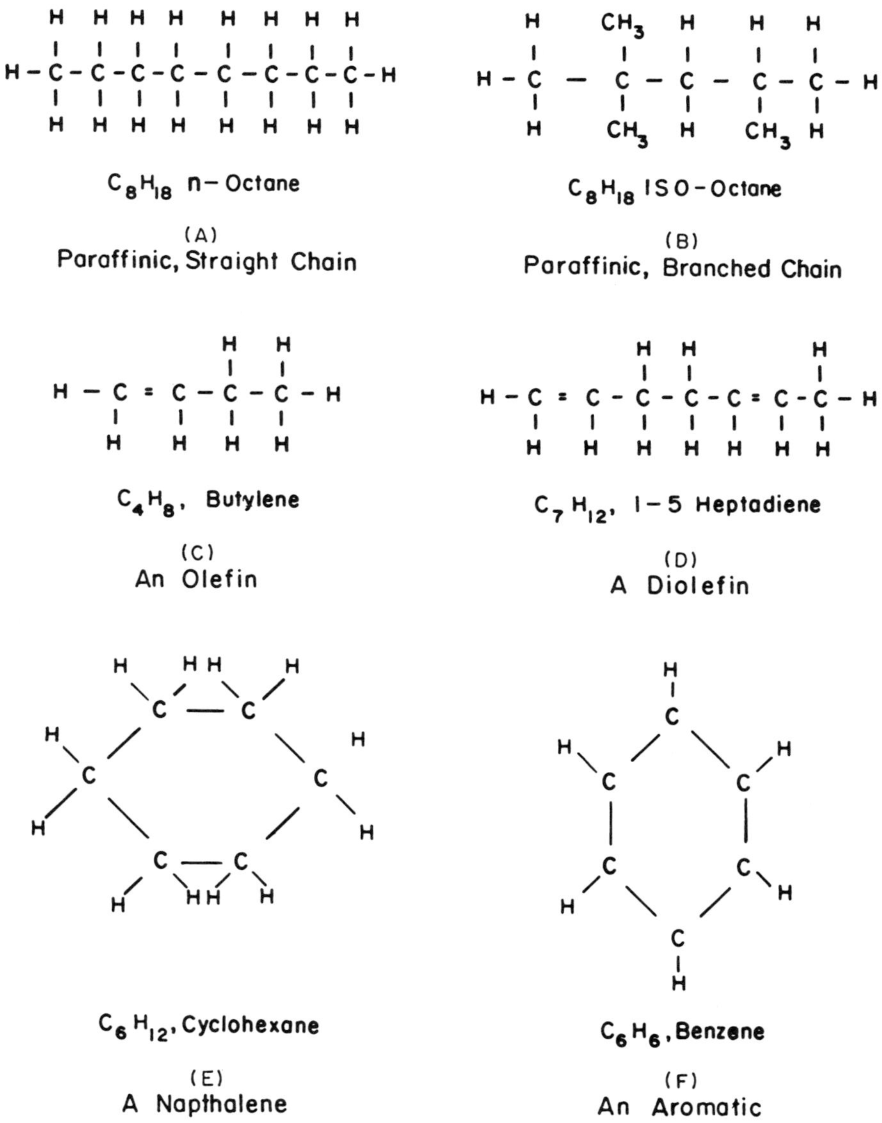

## Fuels and Combustion

**(A) $C_8H_{18}$ n-Octane** — Paraffinic, Straight Chain

**(B) $C_8H_{18}$ ISO-Octane** — Paraffinic, Branched Chain

**(C) $C_4H_8$, Butylene** — An Olefin

**(D) $C_7H_{12}$, 1-5 Heptadiene** — A Diolefin

**(E) $C_6H_{12}$, Cyclohexane** — A Napthalene

**(F) $C_6H_6$, Benzene** — An Aromatic

Figure 6.1–The molecular structure of some hydrocarbon families.

(446° F) for gasoline and from 230° C (446° F) to 370° C (700° F) for diesel fuel. Typical crude oil yields about equal volumes of gasoline and diesel fuel as Figure 6.3 shows. But, historically, the United States has needed much more gasoline than diesel fuel to provide fuel for automobiles. The *cracking unit* in Figure 6.2 uses catalysts with elevated temperatures and pressures to crack larger

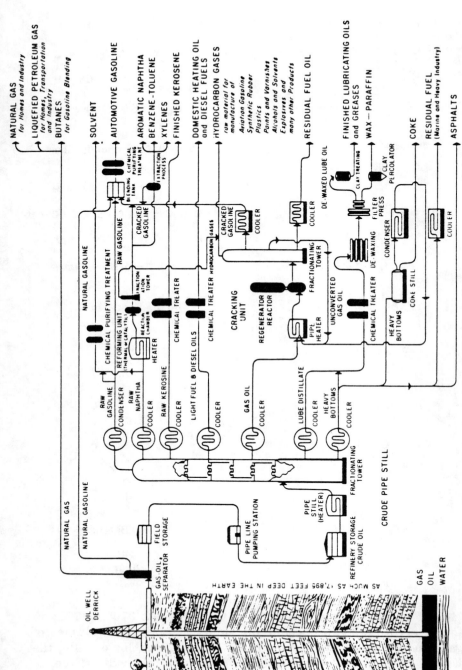

Figure 6.2–A flow diagram of a typical petroleum refinery.

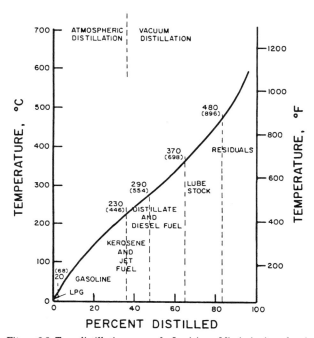

Figure 6.3–True distillation curve of a Louisiana-Mississippi crude mix.

hydrocarbon molecules into smaller ones and, thus, shifts more of the refinery yield into the gasoline range.

## 6.3   COMBUSTION AND EXHAUST EMISSIONS

Combustion is the chemical reaction of carbon and hydrogen in the fuel with oxygen in the air to form water and other exhaust products. The process liberates heat, which raises the cylinder pressure and drives the piston downward during the power stroke. The actual combustion process is a complex one in which many intermediate species form and then disappear in subsequent reactions. However, insight can be gained by considering *ideal combustion*, in which all of the hydrogen in the fuel is converted into water and all of the carbon is converted into carbon dioxide. As a further simplification, air is assumed to be 21.3% oxygen and 76.9% nitrogen by weight, and all other trace elements are ignored. Air contains 21% oxygen and 79% nitrogen on a volume basis. Thus, in air, there are 3.76 molecules of nitrogen for every molecule of oxygen.

Atomic and molecular weights of certain elements are needed in combustion chemistry, and acceptable values are given in Table 6.1.

TABLE 6.1. Atomic and molecular weights of some elements

| Element | Atomic | Weight | Molecular | Weight |
|---|---|---|---|---|
| Carbon | C | 12 | C | 12 |
| Hydrogen | H | 1 | $H_2$ | 2 |
| Oxygen | O | 16 | $O_2$ | 32 |
| Nitrogen | N | 14 | $N_2$ | 28 |
| Air (apparent) | | | | 29 |

Actual petroleum fuels are mixtures of many hydrocarbons. However, the hydrocarbon molecules listed in Table 6.2 are commonly used to represent petroleum fuels when combustion processes are being illustrated. The alcohols listed in Table 6.2 are pure substances. Methyl soyate is an alternative fuel for compression-ignition engines. More specifically, it is the methyl ester of soybean oil and is formed by a chemical reaction involving soybean oil, methyl alcohol, and a suitable catalyst.

The combustion of gasoline is illustrated as follows:

$$C_8H_{18} + 12.5O_2 + 47N_2 \Rightarrow 47N_2 + 8CO_2 + 9H_2O$$

```
1(114)   12.5(32)  47(28)     47(28)   8(44)   9(18)
1        3.51      11.54      11.54    3.05    1.42
```

For simplicity, one fuel molecule is used. Eight molecules of $CO_2$ must be created to use the carbon in the fuel, and nine molecules of water must be created to use the hydrogen. Then, 12.5 molecules of oxygen must be supplied to provide the oxygen in the $H_2O$ and $CO_2$. Finally, each of the 12.5 molecules of oxygen is accompanied in the air by 3.76 molecules of nitrogen for a total of 47 molecules of $N_2$. The first row of numbers below the chemical equation shows the total mass of each reactant and product to be its molecular weight times the number of molecules present. The second row of numbers is the mass relative to the mass of fuel. For example, the mass of oxygen used is 3.51 (12.5*32/114) times the mass of fuel used in the reaction. Notice that although the dominant exhaust product is

TABLE 6.2. Representative molecules for combustion calculations

| Fuel | Molecule | Formula | Molecular Weight |
|---|---|---|---|
| Natural gas | Methane | $CH_4$ | 16 |
| LPG | Propane | $C_3H_8$ | 44 |
| Gasoline | Octane | $C_8H_{18}$ | 114 |
| Kerosene | Dodecane | $C_{12}H_{26}$ | 170 |
| Diesel fuel | Cetane | $C_{16}H_{34}$ | 226 |
| Methanol | Methyl alcohol | $CH_4O$ | 32 |
| Ethanol | Ethyl alcohol | $C_2H_6O$ | 46 |
| Butanol | Butyl alcohol | $C_4H_{10}O$ | 74 |
| Methyl soyate | | $C_{19}H_{36}O_2$ | 296 |

nitrogen, for each kilogram (lb) of fuel, 1.42 kg (lb) of water are produced. In a suitably warmed-up engine, the water would exit through the exhaust system as water vapor. Also, notice that the *stoichiometric* (chemically correct) air to fuel ratio is:

$$A/F = (3.51 + 11.54)/1 = 15.05$$

The air-fuel mixture in an engine is seldom perfectly uniform. That is, there may be leaner areas where the air to fuel ratio is lower. Gasoline engines are sometimes operated on a ratio richer than 15.05:1 to obtain more power. In other words, extra fuel is supplied to ensure the consumption of all of the oxygen in the combustion chamber. With *rich combustion*, there is not enough oxygen to convert all of the carbon to $CO_2$. Therefore, CO (carbon monoxide) appears in the exhaust. Even *lean combustion* is not uniform or complete enough to eliminate all CO from the exhaust. Thus, engines must operate in a properly ventilated area to avoid carbon monoxide poisoning.

Calculations similar to those for gasoline show the *stoichiometric air to fuel ratio* for diesel to be 14.88:1. However, diesels are operated on a much leaner than stoichiometric ratio to achieve more complete combustion of the fuel. Thus, some *free oxygen* will be found in the exhaust from diesel engines.

The *exhaust emissions* from engines will contain products in addition to those just described. Small quantities of fuel will escape combustion and will appear in the exhaust as gaseous, unburned hydrocarbons. At high temperatures, some of the nitrogen will react with oxygen to form nitrous oxide (NO) and nitrous dioxide ($NO_2$). The combination of NO and $NO_2$ is indicated as $NO_x$ by emissions analysts. Also, some of the carbon in the fuel may appear as soot (free carbon) in the exhaust. The federal government has established limits as to the amount of CO, $NO_x$, and unburned hydrocarbons that may appear in the exhaust of automobile and truck engines. Since there are far fewer tractor engines in the country to produce exhaust emissions, the federal government has not regulated emissions from tractor engines. The state of California has begun to regulate emissions from all types of engines. The federal government has begun to regulate exhaust emissions from large trucks and it is probable that exhaust emissions from farm tractor engines may also be regulated in the future.

Calculation of the stoichiometric air to fuel ratio and the theoretical exhaust emissions for ethyl alcohol are illustrated in Example Problem 6.1.

## Example Problem 6.1
Calculate the stoichiometric air to fuel ratio and the exhaust products when ethyl alcohol is used as an engine fuel. Show the balanced combustion equation.

**Solution:** The formula and molecular weight for ethyl alcohol are given in Table 6.2. The exhaust products will include $N_2$, $CO_2$, and $H_2O$.

$$C_2H_6O + 3O_2 + 11.28N_2 \Rightarrow 11.28N_2 + 2CO_2 + 3H_2O$$

| | | | | | |
|---|---|---|---|---|---|
| 1(46) | 3(32) | 11.28(28) | 11.28(28) | 2(44) | 3(18) |
| 1 | 2.087 | 6.866 | 6.866 | 1.913 | 1.174 |

$$A/F = (2.087 + 6.866)/1 = 8.95$$

Three water molecules are created to use the hydrogen in the fuel, and two $CO_2$ molecules are created to use the carbon. The $H_2O$ and $CO_2$ require seven oxygen atoms; one of these is supplied by the fuel, and six atoms must be supplied from the air. Each oxygen molecule in the air is accomplished by 3.76 molecules of $N_2$. The stoichiometric air to fuel ratio is only 8.95:1. Ethyl alcohol thus burns so much richer than gasoline that a gasoline engine would have to be modified to run correctly on ethyl alcohol.

Electronic instruments used for analyzing exhaust gases typically work on a dry volume basis. The theoretical exhaust gases can be analyzed on a similar basis by counting exhaust molecules, because each molecule occupies a definite volume. In the theoretical combustion of ethyl alcohol, for example, 11.28 molecules of $N_2$ and two molecules of $CO_2$ are produced. Thus, there are a total of 13.28 molecules, not counting those in the water. The theoretical composition of the dry exhaust gases is therefore:

$$11.28/13.28 * 100 = 84.9\% \text{ nitrogen}$$
$$2/13.28 * 100 = 15.1\% \text{ carbon dioxide}$$

The exhaust from most engines is primarily nitrogen.

## 6.4 FUEL PROPERTY MEASUREMENTS

The internal combustion engine was invented more than one hundred years ago, and numerous improvements have been made since its invention. The development of fuels paralleled the development of the engine. Many standards concerning the required properties of engine fuels and tests for measuring those properties have been set. Most of the standards were developed through the cooperative efforts of the *American Society for Testing Materials* (ASTM), the *Society of Automotive Engineers* (SAE), and the *American Petroleum Institute* (API). Only the most important of the many standards will be discussed here. Some standards apply to only one type of fuel. For instance, fuel viscosity is relevant only to diesel fuel. Other standards, such as heating value, apply to all types of fuels.

## 6.5 SPECIFIC GRAVITY OF FUELS

*Specific gravity* is a measure of the density of liquid fuels. It is the ratio of the density of the fuel at 15.6° C (60° F) to the density of water at the same temperature. The density of water is 1 kg/L (8.34 lb/gal) and thus, in SI units, the specific gravity of a fuel is equal to its density in kg/L. Density of liquids decreases slightly with increasing temperatures. Therefore, densities must be measured at the standard temperature of 15.6° C (60° F) or must be corrected to that temperature.

The API has devised a special scale for gravities. It is expressed in API degrees and is calculated as follows:

$$\text{API}° = \frac{141.5}{\text{SG}} - 131.5 \tag{6.1}$$

where SG = specific gravity of fuel at 15.6° C (60° F)

The *gravity* of a fuel is measured with a *hydrometer*. The hydrometer in Figure 6.4 is calibrated in API degrees and is read at the liquid level. Some hydrometers include a thermometer and correction scale, which permit the measurement of gravity at any temperature and correction to 15.6° C (60° F).

## 6.6 HEATING VALUE OF FUELS

The purpose of fuels is to release energy for doing work. Thus, the heating value of fuels is an important measure of their worth. Heating values can be measured by burning the fuel in a bomb calorimeter similar to the one shown in Figure 6.5. The combustion creates water, as discussed in Section 6.3, and energy from the fuel is used to convert that water to vapor in the bomb. The heating value measured by the bomb is therefore called the *lower*, or *net*, *heating*

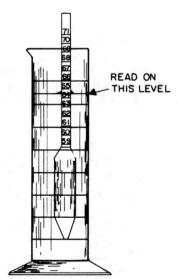

*Figure 6.4–A hydrometer for measuring specific gravity of a fuel. (Data from E. L. Barger, Kansas Engineering Experiment Station Bulletin 37.)*

*value* of the fuel. The *gross*, or higher, heating value is found by adding to the net heating value the latent heat of vaporization of the water created in combustion. When engine efficiencies are calculated, as was done in Chapter 5, it is important to state whether the higher or lower heating value of the fuel is used in the calculation. Published *heats of combustion* are usually higher heating values and, therefore, are often used to calculate engine efficiencies.

Equations have been developed for estimating the heating value of petroleum fuels from their API gravity. The equations are:

$$HHV = K_{F1} + K_{F2} * [API - 10] \qquad (6.2)$$

$$LHV = 0.7190 * HHV + K_{F3} \qquad (6.3)$$

where
- HHV = higher heating value in kJ/kg (BTU/lb)
- LHV = lower heating value in kJ/kg (BTU/lb)
- API = API gravity in degrees
- $K_{F1}$ = constant = 42 860 (18,440)
- $K_{F2}$ = constant = 93 (40)
- $K_{F3}$ = constant = 10 000 (4,310)

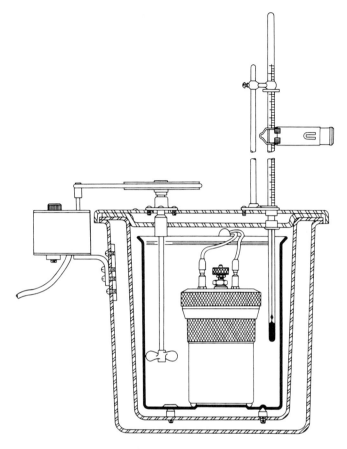

*Figure 6.5–A bomb calorimeter for measuring the heating value of a fuel. (Courtesy of Parr Instrument Company.)*

The calculation of typical heats of combustion is illustrated in Example Problem 6.2.

## Example Problem 6.2
Estimate the higher and lower heating values for the diesel fuel used in OECD Nebraska Test No. 1619 (Table 5.1).

**Solution:** The specific gravity of the fuel is given in the OECD Nebraska Test Report under the heading, "Fuel, Oil and Time". Number 2 diesel fuel was used in the test, and its specific gravity at 15.6° C (60° F) is 0.8301. By using Equation 6.1, the API gravity can be calculated:

API = [141.5/0.8301] - 131.5 = 39.0°

By using Equation 6.2, the estimated HHV can be calculated:

HHV = 42 860 + 93*[39.0 - 10] = 45 557 kJ/kg

or

HHV = 18,440 + 40*[39.0 - 10] = 19,600 BTU/lb

By using Equation 6.3, the estimated LHV can be calculated:

LHV = 0.7190*45 557 + 10 000 = 42 755 kJ/kg

or

LHV = 0.7190*19,600 + 4,310 = 18,402 BTU/lb

The HHV could be used in computing the thermal efficiency of the tractor used in OECD Nebraska Test No. 1619. The procedure was given in Section 5.5.

## 6.7 FUEL VOLATILITY AND FLASH POINT

Fuels must vaporize before they can burn. *Volatility* refers to the ability of fuels to vaporize: Fuels that vaporize easily at lower temperatures are more volatile than are fuels that require higher temperatures to vaporize. Reid vapor pressure and distillation curves are both indicators of fuel volatility.

### 6.7.1 Vapor Pressure of Fuels

*Reid vapor pressure* is measured with the vapor pressure bomb shown in Figure 6.6. Fuel is placed in the bomb, and the bomb is immersed in a water bath at 37.7 ± 0.1° C (100 ± 0.2° F). With proper technique, the pressure gage indicates the vapor pressure of the fuel. The Reid vapor pressure test is used on gasoline. Winter gasolines typically have vapor pressures in the range of 60 to 80 kPa (9 to 12 psi). Vapor pressures of summer gasolines are typically 15 to 20 kPa (2 to 3 psi) lower to reduce the tendency for gasoline to vaporize in fuel lines and cause vapor lock of the fuel pump. Vapor lock is discussed in Section 6.7.2.

Reid vapor pressure expresses volatility with a single number, but a *distillation curve* gives a more complete picture of fuel volatility. The apparatus shown in Figure 6.7 is used for distillation tests. A 100 mL sample of fuel is placed in the distilling flask and heated. A thermometer is inserted through the stopper to measure the temperature of vapors rising from the fuel. Vapors pass through a side tube in the neck of the flask and are condensed by passing

Fuels and Combustion 139

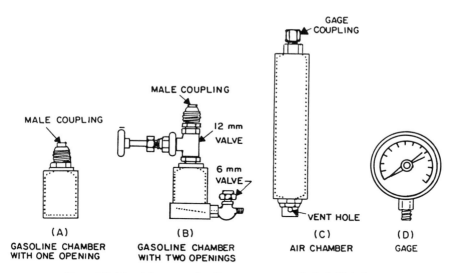

Figure 6.6–A bomb for measuring the vapor pressure of a fuel. (Data from ASTM Standard D323.)

through a metal tube immersed in an ice bath. Then, the condensed fuel is caught in a graduated cylinder. The thermometer is read when the first drop falls into the graduated cylinder, and this temperature is called the initial boiling point. Sample heating continues, and the thermometer is read as each one-tenth of the sample is distilled. The end point is the highest temperature read and is reached just as the last volatile portion of the fuel boils away. Nonvolatile residues may remain in the bottom of the flask; the recovery in the graduated cylinder is then less than 100%.

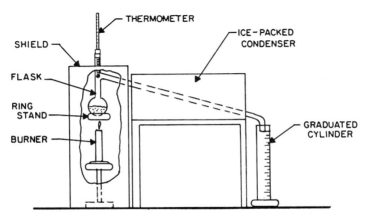

Figure 6.7–Apparatus for conducting distillation tests of fuels.

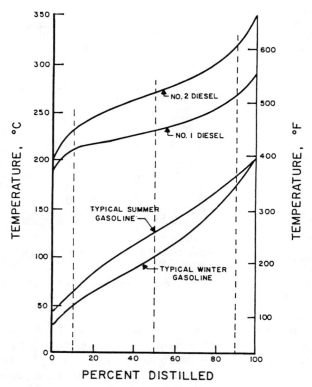

*Figure 6.8–Distillation curves for several fuels.*

### 6.7.2 Interpretation of Distillation Curves

Results of distillation tests are plotted as shown in Figure 6.8. The curves are especially important for gasoline, and three points on the distillation curve are of special interest. The points $T_{10}$, $T_{50}$, and $T_{90}$, respectively, refer to the temperatures on the curve at which 10, 50, and 90% of the fuel has been distilled. For the easy starting of a gasoline engine in winter conditions, the $T_{10}$ *temperature* must be sufficiently low to allow enough fuel to evaporate to form a combustible mixture. The T50 point is associated with engine warmup: a low $T_{50}$ *temperature* will allow the engine to warm up and gain power quickly without stalling. The $T_{90}$ *temperature* is associated with the crankcase dilution and fuel economy: if the $T_{90}$ *temperature* is too high, the larger fuel molecules will condense on the cylinder liners and pass down into the lubricating oil in the crankcase instead of burning. Gasoline volatility is adjusted by petroleum refiners to suit the season and location. Gasoline sold for use in summer or at high elevations is made less volatile because evaporation is easier under such conditions and vapor lock must be avoided. *Vapor lock* is the formation of fuel vapor bubbles in the fuel line, which prevents the fuel pump from working. Conversely, gasoline must be made more volatile for use in winter conditions and/or at lower elevations when vaporization is more difficult. Refiners adjust volatility through blending techniques, for example, more butane and lighter hydrocarbons are blended into gasoline to reduce the $T_{10}$ temperature.

The volatility of diesel fuel is important, although it is not as critical as the volatility of gasoline. Diesel fuel must be volatile enough to ensure vaporization in the combustion chamber. But, if the fuel is too volatile, fuel droplets will evaporate too quickly to permit adequate spray penetration in the chamber. A low $T_{10}$ temperature will permit easier starting of a diesel engine. A low $T_{50}$ temperature helps to minimize diesel smoke and odor. A low $T_{90}$ temperature helps to minimize crankcase dilution and improve fuel economy.

### 6.7.3  Flash Point of Fuels

The *flash point* varies with fuel volatility but is not related to engine performance. Rather, the flash point relates to safety precautions that must be taken when handling a fuel. The flash point is the lowest temperature to which a fuel must be heated to produce an ignitable vapor-air mixture above the liquid fuel when exposed to an open flame. At temperatures below the flash point, not enough fuel evaporates to form a combustible mixture. Insurance companies and governmental agencies classify fuels according to their flash points and use flash points in setting minimum standards for the handling and storage of fuels. Gasolines have flash points well below the freezing point of water and can readily ignite in the presence of a spark or flame. Diesel fuels must have flash points exceeding the minimums listed in Table 6.3, unless governmental agencies specify higher minimums for the region in which the fuel is used.

## 6.8  FUEL VISCOSITY

*Viscosity* is a measure of the flow resistance of a liquid. For example, water has low viscosity, but honey or syrup has very high viscosity. Techniques for measuring viscosity will be discussed in Chapter 13. Fuel viscosity is an important consideration when fuels are injected into combustion chambers by means of high-pressure injection systems as in diesel engines. The viscosity must be high enough to ensure the proper lubrication of the injector pump. If viscosity is too low, the fuel will flow too easily and will not maintain a lubricating film between moving and stationary parts in the pump. If viscosity is

TABLE 6.3. Limiting requirements for diesel fuels[A]

| Property | ASTM Test Method[B] | Grade[C] 1-D | Grade[C] 2-D |
|---|---|---|---|
| Flash point, °C (°F), Min. | D 93 | 38 (100) | 52 (125) |
| Water & Sediment, %$_v$, Max. | D 1796 | 0.05 | 0.05 |
| Distillation Temp.  Min.<br>at 90% point, °C (°F) Max. | D 86 | —<br>288 (550) | 282 (540)[D]<br>338 (640) |
| Kinematic viscosity[D], Min.<br>@ 40° C (104° F), mm2/s [E] Max. | D 445 | 1.3<br>2.4 | 1.9<br>4.1 |
| Ash, %$_m$, Max. | D 482 | 0.01 | 0.01 |
| Sulphur, %$_M$, Max. | D 2622 | 0.50[F] | 0.50[F] |
| Copper Strip Corrosion | D 130 | No. 3 | No. 3 |
| Cetane Number, Min[G]. | D 613 | 40[H] | 40[H] |

[A] To meet special operating conditions, modifications may be agreed upon between purchaser, seller and manufacturer.
[B] The test methods indicated are standard. Other methods may be acceptable. Values in SI units are to be regarded as standard and values in parenthesis are for information only.
[C] Grades 1-D and 2-D (but not the low-sulphur 1-D and 2-D grades) are required to contain a sufficient amount of 1, 4-dialkyl amino anthraquinone (blue dye) so its presence is visually apparent.
[D] When a cloud point less than $-12°$ C (10° F) is specified, the minimum viscosity shall be 1.7 mm$^2$/s and the minimum 90% recovered temperature shall be waived.
[E] 1 mm$^2$/s = 1 cSt (centistoke)
[F] Grades Low-Sulphur 1-D and 2-D shall contain a maximum of 0.05% sulphur by mass. On all grades, other sulphur limits may apply in selected areas in the United States and in other countries.
[G] Where cetane number by Test Method D 613 is not available, Method D 4737 may be used as an approximation.
[H] Low ambient temperatures as well as engine operation at high altitudes may require use of fuels with higher cetane ratings.
[I] Grades 1-D and 2-D must have cloud point 6° C (°F) above tenth percentile minimum ambient temperature for region of use. Grades Low-sulphur 1-D and 2-D must meet cloud point requirement or have minimum cetane index of 40 or maximum aromatic content of 35%.

too high, the injectors may not be able to atomize the fuel into small enough droplets to achieve good vaporization and combustion. Injection line pressure and fuel delivery rates also are affected by fuel viscosity. Viscosity limits for diesel fuel have been established by the SAE; they are listed in Table 6.3.

## 6.9  CLOUD AND POUR POINTS

As a liquid is cooled, a temperature at which the larger fuel molecules begin to form crystals is reached. With continued cooling, more crystals form and agglomerate until the entire fuel mass begins to solidify. The temperature at which crystals began to appear is called the *cloud point*, and the *pour point* is the highest temperature at which the fuel ceases to flow. The cloud point typically occurs between 5 and 8° C (10 and 15° F) above the pour point. Cloud and pour points become important for heavier fuels in the higher boiling ranges (Figure 6.3). Thus, although the pourability of gasoline is not a problem, the SAE gives guidelines for specifying pour points of diesel fuel (Table 6.3).

## 6.10 FUEL IMPURITIES

Crude oil contains many impurities that could be harmful in the storage and use of petroleum fuels. Refining removes most but not all of the impurities. Therefore, fuel specifications must include the permissible concentration of each impurity.

### 6.10.1 Sulphur

Sulphur compounds are present in crude oil, but most of the sulphur is removed during refining. Sulphur is undesirable in fuels. *Sulphur oxides* formed during combustion can convert to acids and cause corrosion of engine parts and accelerated wear of rings and cylinder liners. Typically, sulphur concentrations in gasoline are much smaller than in diesel fuel. In the United States, the sulphur content of gasoline averages less than 0.03% by weight and nearly always is less than 0.15%. The SAE maximum for sulphur content of No. 1 or No. 2 diesel fuel is 0.5% by weight, as listed in Table 6.3. Recently, low-sulphur grades of No. 1 and No. 2 diesel fuel have been developed to meet more stringent emissions requirements. Specifications of the new grades are similar to those of No. 1 and No. 2 diesel fuel listed in Table 6.3, except that the maximum allowable sulphur is 0.05%. Potential corrosivity of sulphur is measured by immersing a copper strip in the fuel for 3 h at 50° C (122° F) and then comparing the resulting corrosion with that on standard corroded strips. Standard strips are numbered, with higher numbers indicating more corrosion. As Table 6.3 shows, the SAE requirement for diesel fuel is that corrosion shall not be worse than that on the No. 3 standard strip.

### 6.10.2 Ash

*Ash* consists of small solid particles and oil or water-soluble metallic compounds found in fuel. Ash is measured by burning a small quantity of the fuel until all the combustible material has been consumed. The unburnable residue is designated as ash and is reported as a percentage of the weight of the fuel sample burned. Ash is particularly harmful in diesel fuel. The abrasiveness of ash can contribute to wear of the close-fitting parts in the injection system and can contribute to plugging of the fuel filter and injection nozzles. The SAE limits for ash in diesel fuel are 0.01% by weight, as indicated in Table 6.3.

### 6.10.3 Water and Sediment

Water and sediment can enter fuel during handling and storage. Water vapor can move into storage tanks through vented openings and condense into liquid when air temperatures drop. Rain may also leak into some tanks, and ground water may seep into leaky underground storage tanks. Sediment can consist of rust from metal tanks and/or small dirt particles that enter tanks with air or through careless handling. The presence of water in petroleum promotes the formation of slime and other organic sediment. Gasoline should be visually free of undissolved water and sediment; it should be clear and bright when observed at 21° C (70° F). The SAE limits for water and sediment in diesel fuel are 0.05% by volume as listed in Table 6.3.

### 6.10.4 Gum

*Gum* is a viscous liquid or semisolid that forms in petroleum fuels containing unsaturated hydrocarbons. Thus, gum is more likely to form in gasoline that is made by cracking. Usually, the gum is soluble in gasoline, but leaves a sticky residue in carburetors and on intake valves when gasoline evaporates. Gasoline usually has a negligible gum content after refining, but gum may form during storage. High temperatures, the presence of oxygen, and passing time are all conducive to gum formation. The ASTM has developed a standard test for identifying existent gum in gasoline and an oxidation stability as an indicator of the gum-forming tendency of gasoline. Most commercial gasoline contains antioxidant additives to retard gum formation, but extended storage of gasoline is not recommended. In the past, diesel fuel was more chemically stable and can be stored for much longer periods than gasoline. Increasing demand for distillate products has led to the use of cracked compounds in diesel fuel and, consequently, antioxidants are also beginning to be used in diesel fuels.

## 6.11 OCTANE RATING AND ENGINE KNOCK

*Octane rating* is a measure of the knock resistance of gasoline. Knock is avoided in a spark-ignition engine when burning starts at the

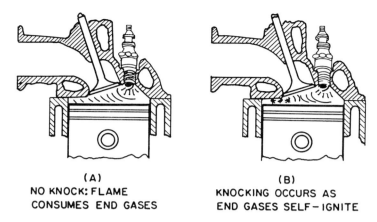

Figure 6.9–Smooth combustion and knocking combustion in a spark-ignition engine.

spark plug and a flame front sweeps smoothly across the combustion chamber to consume the fuel (Figure 6.9a). *Knock* occurs when the end gases – that is, the gases ahead of the flame front – ignite spontaneously and generate a rapid, uncontrolled release of energy. The quick release causes a sharp rise in pressure and pressure oscillations, which may lead to an audible ping or knock. Under what conditions does knock occur or not occur? That question is answered next.

### 6.11.1 Cause of Engine Knock

Burning behind the flame front typically releases enough energy to raise the temperature of the end gases above their *self-ignition temperature* (SIT). Fortunately, end gases do not immediately ignite upon reaching their SIT. Rather, there is an ignition delay, during which certain pre-flame reactions must occur. If the end gases are sufficiently patient – that is, if their ignition delay is long enough – the flame front will sweep through to consume the end gases before they can self-ignite, and knocking will not occur. Knocking is most likely to occur during acceleration from slow speeds. Slow engine speeds reduce turbulence in the combustion chamber and reduce the speed of the flame front. Thus, more time is available for the ignition delay to be completed. Also, the pressure and temperature increase in the combustion chamber during acceleration, and these increases tend to reduce the length of the ignition delay. A variety of other conditions can promote knocking. Knocking is more likely to occur with the higher cylinder pressures and temperatures associated with high compression ratios. Lean mixtures also promote knocking, because the relative scarcity of fuel molecules retards the speed of the flame front. Sustained knock in an engine is audibly annoying and can cause burning of piston crowns and other engine damage.

### 6.11.2 Knock Reduction Techniques

Several techniques are available for reducing the likelihood of engine knock. For example, the wedge-shaped combustion chamber (the design shown in Figure 6.9) provides more surface area for cooling the end gases and lengthening the ignition delay. Gasolines with higher octane ratings also reduce the likelihood of knock. Hydrocarbons with branched-chain molecules (Figure 6.1b) or ring-structured molecules (Figures 6.1e and 6.1f) have considerably longer ignition delays than do straight-chain hydrocarbons (Figure 6.1a). Thus, gasolines with reduced percentages of straight-chain hydrocarbons are more knock-resistant and are assigned higher octane numbers.

### 6.11.3 Measurement of Octane Rating

Octane ratings are measured using a special single-cylinder engine, similar to the one shown in Figure 6.10 (except the engine is a spark-ignition engine), that runs at a fixed speed and has an adjustable compression ratio. The octane rating of a sample of gasoline is determined by comparing its performance to that obtained with blends of iso-octane and normal heptane. Iso-octane is extremely knock-resistant and has been assigned an octane rating of 100, while normal heptane is very knock-prone and has been assigned an octane rating of 0. To measure the octane rating of a sample of gasoline, the sample is burned in the special engine and the compression ratio is increased until the knockmeter indicates that a standard level of knocking has been attained. Then, blends of the reference fuels are burned until a blend of iso-octane and normal heptane that gives the same knock as the gasoline sample is found. The octane rating of the sample is equal to the percentage of iso-octane in the blend of reference fuels.

### 6.11.4 Octane Rating Scales

Two different methods have been developed by the ASTM for measuring octane ratings of gasoline. Both methods use the same engine, but different operating conditions. The motor method is more severe and results in a lower octane rating than does the research method. The *Research Octane Number* (RON) is typically about eight numbers higher than the *Motor Octane Number* (MON) for a given gasoline sample. Many service stations now post an antiknock index on their pumps. The *antiknock* index is simply the numerical average of the RON and MON.

*Figure 6.10–CFR engine for measuring cetane ratings of fuels. (Courtesy of Waukesha Engine Division of Dressler Industries.)*

### 6.11.5 Octane Requirements

Octane requirements of an engine vary with altitude. The reduced air pressure at higher elevations reduces cylinder pressures and makes knocking less likely. The API has divided the country into a number of regions based on altitude. Gasolines sold in regions with higher altitudes typically have RONs that are several numbers lower than those sold for use in regions with lower altitudes.

## 6.12 CETANE RATING

Octane number is not a good measure of the knock resistance of diesel fuel, because diesel combustion differs from spark-ignited combustion. There is no spark plug in a diesel chamber. Rather, the fuel is injected and its temperature must be raised above the autoignition point by use of high compression ratios. Self-ignition temperatures and critical compression ratios for several fuels are shown in Figure 6.11. Typically, fuel injection does not begin until the chamber temperature exceeds the SIT of the fuel, but the fuel

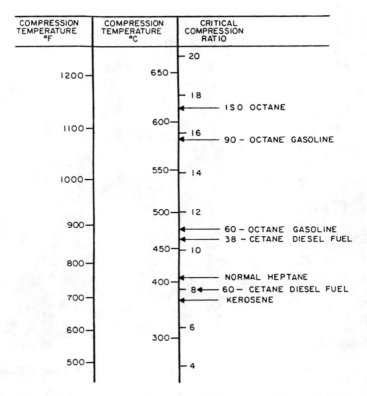

*Figure 6.11–Critical compression ratios and temperatures for several fuels. (Data from Pope, A. W. and J. A. Murdock, Compression-ignition characteristics of ignition-engine fuels, SAE Transactions 27:136. 1932.)*

does not ignite immediately upon injection. A two-part ignition delay, a physical and a chemical delay, must be completed before the fuel will self-ignite. During the physical delay, the fuel is atomized into droplets and begins to vaporize and mix with air in the chamber. Then, the chemical delay begins; this is a pre-flame reaction similar to the total ignition delay in a spark-ignition engine. For fuels of normal viscosity, the physical delay is much shorter than the chemical delay.

### 6.12.1 Combustion and Knock in Diesel Engines

In contrast to spark-ignition engines, knocking in a diesel becomes worse as the ignition delay is increased. The reason can be deduced from Figure 6.12, which is a plot of the rate of energy release from the fuel in a running diesel engine. Typically, injection might begin at 20° before HDC. During the delay, fuel evaporates and mixes with air, and preflame reactions occur to prepare a quantity of

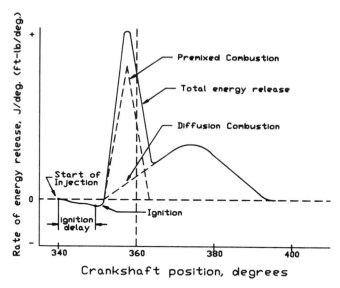

*Figure 6.12–Rate of energy release from fuels in a compression-ignition engine.*

combustible air-fuel mixture. When compression ignition occurs, all of the prepared mixture burns quite suddenly to produce the triangular-shaped peak identified in Figure 6.12 as *premixed combustion*. For combustion to continue, fuel vapor must diffuse into the burned-out zones from one side and air must diffuse in from the other. The diffusion process slows the continuing combustion, which is identified in Figure 6.12 as *diffusion combustion*. Thus, diffusion combustion is smoother and quieter than premixed combustion. As shown in Figure 6.12, the combination of premixed combustion and diffusion combustion give the total energy release. The ignition delay controls the proportioning between premixed and diffusion combustion; the longer the ignition delay, the higher the percentage of the fuel that burns in premixed combustion and the lower the percentage that burns in diffusion combustion. Since diesel knock comes from the rapid, premixed combustion, it follows that a longer ignition delay gives more knocking and a shorter delay gives less knocking.

### 6.12.2 Cetane Number of Fuels

The *cetane number* is an indicator of the antiknock qualities of diesel fuels. High cetane ratings are achieved by blending fuels with higher percentages of straight-chain hydrocarbons (Figure 6.1a), because these have shorter delays. It should be apparent that fuels with high cetane numbers will have low octane numbers, and the reverse is also true.

### 6.12.3 Measurement of Cetane Number
Cetane number is measured in a special engine (shown in Figure 6.10). Originally, the cetane number of a sample of diesel fuel was determined by comparing its performance to a blend of cetane and alphamethylnapthalene. The latter fuel consists of ring-structured molecules and has been assigned a cetane rating of 0. Cetane consists of straight-chain molecules and has been assigned a cetane rating of 100. To measure the cetane rating of a sample of diesel fuel, the fuel is burned in the special engine and the compression ratio is adjusted until ignition occurs at HDC. Injection is always set to begin 13° before HDC. After the compression ratio is set, blends of the reference fuels are tried until a blend that has the same ignition delay as the test is found. The cetane rating of the test fuel is equal to the percentage of cetane in the blend of reference fuels. The procedure was modified in 1962 by replacing alphamethylnapthalene with heptamethylnonane. The latter fuel has a cetane rating of 15. Thus, the following equation is used to calculate the cetane numbers from the reference blend:

$$\text{cetane no.} = [\% \text{ n-cetane}] + 0.15 * [\% \text{ heptamethynonane}] \qquad (6.4)$$

### 6.12.4 Effect of Cetane Rating
The cetane rating of a diesel fuel affects more than diesel knock. If the cetane rating is too low, the ignition delay may be so long that the piston is moving downward on the expansion stroke before the delay is completed and starting of the engine may be difficult or impossible. The appearance of white smoke, consisting of unburned fuel droplets, in the exhaust during starting is an indication of low cetane fuel. Use of excessively high cetane fuel also can cause difficulty. Then, the ignition delay may be too short to allow the adequate mixing of fuel with air, and incomplete combustion may result. Also, a short ignition delay shifts more burning into the diffusion mode and diffusion burning is less efficient than premixed burning. The black smoke in the exhaust of a heavily loaded diesel engine comes from diffusion burning. The SAE minimum for cetane rating of diesel fuels is 40 as given in Table 6.3. The cetane number of commercial diesel fuels seldom exceeds 50 and should not exceed 60.

## 6.13 FUEL ADDITIVES

Many additives have been developed to improve the performance of petroleum fuels. Until 1970, nearly all automotive gasoline sold in the United States contained TEL (tetraethyl lead) to increase knock resistance and raise the octane number. Fuel refiners were able to use a wide variety of lower octane hydrocarbons in gasoline and then use lead additives to boost octane ratings to acceptable levels. However, lead poisons the catalysts in catalytic emission control systems, and, in 1970, petroleum suppliers began to market unleaded gasoline. Various lead substitutes have been investigated, and MTBE (methyl tertiary butyl ether) has come into commercial use as an octane booster. The use of tetraethyl lead in gasoline has been discontinued. Other commonly used gasoline additives are listed in Table 6.4.

Some gasoline additives (for example, antioxidants, metal deactivators, and rust inhibitors) are also used in diesel fuel. Ignition accelerators are used to raise the cetane rating of diesel fuel. Several nitrates are available to reduce the SIT of the fuel by serving as local ignition points. Reducing the SIT boosts the cetane rating of the fuel. Additives are available to reduce the pour point by preventing the agglomeration of fuel crystals. The development of diesel fuel additives is likely to increase due to the increasing demand for diesel fuel and the consequent use of a wider variety of hydrocarbon constituents to meet the demand.

## 6.14 ALTERNATIVE FUELS

Alternative fuels are fuels which are alternative to conventional, petroleum-based gasoline and diesel fuels. Two factors have driven the search for alternative fuels. The first relates to concerns about the continuing availability of conventional fuels. At expected use rates, less than a century of world petroleum reserves remain, with the greatest remaining concentrations being in the Middle East and in the Commonwealth of Independent States (formerly the Union of Soviet Socialist Republics). The United States and other countries which must import a growing proportion of their petroleum needs have a strong incentive to seek alternatives. A second factor promoting alternative fuels is the growing need to reduce environmental pollution from engine exhaust emissions. Some alternative fuels, especially those containing oxygen, are less polluting than conventional petroleum fuels.

Butane and propane, which are gases at normal temperatures and pressures, may be compressed and stored as liquids in heavy

TABLE 6.4. Summary of gasoline additives

| Additive | Type | Concentration (ppm)* | Function |
|---|---|---|---|
| Octane boosters | MTBE | 15% | Extend chemical delay |
| Deposit modifiers | Boron and phosphorus compounds | — | Alter chemistry of combustion chamber deposits to reduce surface ignition and spark plug fouling |
| Antioxidants | Amines (derivatives of ammonia) | 4 - 60 | Inhibit gum formation |
| Detergents | Akyl amine phosphates | 48 | Prevent deposits in carburetor and manifold |
| Metal deactivators | Amin derivatives | 4 | Destroy catalytic effect of copper on gum formation |
| Rust inhibitors | Fatty-acid amines | 4 - 60 | Inhibit rust formation from water and air |
| Anti-icing additives | Alcohols and surfactants | 50 ppm - 1% | Prevent ice formation and adhesion in fuel lines and carburetor |
| Lubricants | Light mineral oils | 0.1 - 0.5% | Lubricate valve guides and upper cylinder regions |
| Dye | None | 1 - 12 | Identification |

*Parts per million

tanks as LPG (Liquified Petroleum Gas). As discussed in Section 9.10, LPG is burned in spark-ignition engines equipped with special fuel handling equipment for vaporizing the fuel before it enters the carburetor. LPG engines are clean burning. They are used in industrial vehicles and for stationary work but are no longer used in farm tractors.

Compressed natural gas is being considered as a replacement fuel for vehicles because it is clean burning. It is a high-octane fuel (approximately 120 research octane number) and is thus best suited for use in spark-ignition engines. Its low energy density (about one quarter that of gasoline) is a major disadvantage, that is, a very large tank on the vehicle and/or frequent refilling would be required. Thus, use of compressed natural gas is best suited for use in urban vehicles where the vehicles need never be far from refueling stations.

Carbon monoxide and hydrogen can be obtained through pyrolysis of coal and then reacted together using the Fischer-Tropsch process to form liquid hydrocarbons. The process is used in South Africa, where coal is abundant but petroleum supplies are limited, to produce a majority of the gasoline and diesel fuel requirements of that country. The process has a low efficiency and is used only where crude oil supplies are limited and coal is plentiful.

Ethanol derived from corn starch has come into widespread use in the United States. The ethanol is blended with gasoline in a blend that contains 10% anhydrous ethanol by volume. The federal government provides financial incentives for use of such blends. The stoichiometric air-fuel ratio for the blend is 14.4:1, that is, somewhat lower than for gasoline alone. Consequently, the blends can be burned in unmodified gasoline engines and help to reduce the CO emissions from the exhaust. In addition, the ethanol boosts the octane rating of the blend by approximately three octane numbers. Use of ethanol-gasoline blends is expected to increase as the United States strives to reduce exhaust emissions in large cities that have air-quality problems. Other countries are using ethanol in even greater quantities; many automobiles in Brazil are designed to run on 100% ethanol.

Vegetable oils (soybean oil, sunflower oil, rapeseeed oil, and others) are being considered for use as a fuel for compression-ignition engines. The cetane rating of most vegetable oils is near 40 and the oils will ignite in an unmodified, compression-ignition engine. However, the vegetable oils are at least 10 times more viscous than typical diesel fuel. The high viscosity leads to poor spray atomization, incomplete combustion and rapid carbon buildup in diesel engines. Fortunately, as explained in Section 6.3, the vegetable oils can be reacted with simple alcohols in the presence of a suitable catalyst to form esters. For example, reacting soybean oil with methanol forms methyl soyate, the methyl ester of soybean oil. The viscosity of methyl soyate is only a little higher than that of diesel fuel and the cetane rating of the ester is approximately 50. Ester fuels have been used experimentally in various countries and, in Europe, the methyl ester of rapeseed oil is being used commercially for farm tractors. An important advantage of the vegetable oils and the simple alcohols is that they are virtually free of sulphur.

## 6.15 FUEL STORAGE

There are local, state, and federal regulations concerning the storage of vehicle fuels. The regulations address two principal concerns, minimizing the danger of fire and reducing the risk of environmental damage due to spills.

Governmental agencies classify fuels according to their flammability. Minimum flash point limits are specified for diesel fuel to reduce the danger of fire. Because of its very low flash point (typically -40° C or -40° F), gasoline is classified into a category that requires more careful handling and storage procedures than diesel fuel. The governmental regulations typically relate to design of storage facilities and procedures for minimizing fire hazards. One usual requirement is the prohibition of smoking near fuel storage areas.

In the United States, federal regulations specify storage requirements to reduce environmental damage from spills. Secondary containment is required, so that the fuel will still be contained if the primary containment fails. In the case of underground tanks, double-walled tanks are used to provide secondary containment. In some cases, earthen berms are required to surround above-ground storage tanks to provide secondary containment.

## 6.16 SUMMARY

All of the petroleum fuels listed in Table 6.5 have been used for farm tractors. Butane and propane are gases at normal temperatures and pressures, but they may be compressed and stored as liquids in heavy tanks. Combined butane and propane stored in liquid form is known as LPG (liquified petroleum gas). LPG is burned in spark-ignition engines equipped with special fuel handling systems for vaporizing the fuel before it enters the carburetor. LPG engines are being used in industrial vehicles and for stationary work, but they are no longer being used in new farm tractors.

Gasolines in the United States are blended primarily for automotive use. Gasoline properties are changed to suit the season and geographic area. The octane rating and volatility can be lower for gasolines used at higher elevations, and gasoline volatility must be increased for cold weather starting. Various grades of gasoline have been developed to suit automotive needs, and some have been discontinued as need diminished. For example, except for aircraft fuels, use of regular leaded gasoline has been discontinued in the United States. Many fuel suppliers are selling gasoline, which contains 10% ethanol to increase the octane rating and to meet governmental regulations concerning carbon monoxide emissions. The early 1960s marked the beginning of a strong trend toward the use of diesel engines in farm tractors. Since about 1977, virtually all

TABLE 6.5. Comparison of properties of several fuels

| Fuel | API Gravity Degrees | Density kg/L (Lb/gal) | Higher Heating Value kJ/kg (BTU/Lb) | Research Octane No. | Boiling Range °C (°F) | Stoich Air-Fuel Ratio |
|---|---|---|---|---|---|---|
| Butane | 112 | 0.580 (4.835) | 49,500 (21,280) | 98 | 0 (32) | 15.5 |
| Propane | 146 | 0.509 (4.244) | 50,300 (21,625) | 111 | -44 (-42) | 15.7 |
| Gasoline | 61 | 0.735 (6.128) | 47,600 (20,464) | 93 | 30-230 (86-446) | 15.2 |
| No. 1 diesel | 40 | 0.823 (6.861) | 45,700 (19,647) | 40[a] | 160-260 (320-500) | 15.0 |
| No. 2 diesel | 38 | 0.834 (6.953) | 45,500 (19,560) | 40[a] | 200-370 (392-700) | 15.0 |
| Methyl soyate | - | 0.885 (7.378) | 38,379 (16,500) | 51[b] | | 12.5 |
| Methanol | - | 0.792 (6.603) | 22,700 (9,759) | 110 | 65 (149) | 6.49 |
| Ethanol | - | 0.785 (6.545) | 29,700 (12,769) | 110 | 78 (172) | 8.95 |
| Butanol | - | 0.805 (6.711) | 36,100 (15,520) | - | 118 (244) | 11.2 |

[a]Minimum cetane rating for diesel fuel
[b]Measured cetane rating for methyl soyate (methyl ester of soybean oil)

new farm tractors have been manufactured with diesel engines, and gasoline tractors are being phased out as older tractors are retired.

The preferred fuel for diesel farm tractors, busses, and heavy trucks is No. 2 diesel during most of the year. It is less expensive than No. 1 diesel fuel and has slightly greater energy per liter of fuel because of its greater density. In winter months, No. 1 diesel may be used as a fuel alone or in blends with No. 2 diesel. The low cloud and pour points of No. 1 diesel help to avoid filter blockage and fuel starvation during cold weather operations. New, low-sulphur grades of diesel fuel have been developed to meet future exhaust emissions requirements. The SAE has established limiting requirements for diesel fuels, and these are given in Table 6.3.

Alternative fuels are being used in various countries, including the United States. As was previously mentioned, ethanol is already being used to boost the octane rating of gasoline and to reduce CO emissions. Use of alcohol as a complete fuel is not an acceptable commercial practice in the United States yet, but ethanol is being used as a complete fuel in Brazil. The high octane ratings of alcohols indicate they are best suited for use in spark-ignition engines. Cetane ratings of the alcohols are so low that alcohols will not self-ignite in unmodified diesel engines without special additives. Vegetable oils will self ignite in compression ignition engines but are too viscous for unmodified use as engine fuels. Reacting the vegetable oils with simple alcohols in the presence of a suitable catalyst forms esters which are promising fuels for compression-ignition engines. The methyl ester of rapeseed oil is already in commercial use in Europe.

# QUESTIONS

Q6.1 Petroleum is composed of what two atoms? In approximately what proportion do these atoms occur in petroleum?

Q6.2 What principle is used by refiners to separate crude oil into various hydrocarbon products?

Q6.3 What are the approximate boiling ranges for gasoline and for diesel fuel?

Q6.4 Water is created when any hydrogen-bearing fuel is burned in an engine. What is the fate of the water that is created?

Q6.5 Why does free oxygen appear in the exhaust of diesel engines?

Q6.6 What must be subtracted from the higher heating value of a fuel to obtain the lower heating value?

Q6.7 (a) To what does volatility refer?
(b) Why is the volatility of liquid fuels important?

Q6.8 (a) With what is the $T_{10}$ point of gasoline associated?
(b) With what is the $T_{50}$ point associated?
(c) With what is the $T_{90}$ point associated?

Q6.9 (a) With what is the $T_{10}$ point of diesel fuel associated?
(b) With what is the $T_{50}$ point associated?
(c) With what is the $T_{90}$ point associated?

Q6.10 (a) What is the flash point of a fuel?
(b) Why is the flash point important?

Fuels and Combustion

Q6.11   In what kind of engine is fuel viscosity important? Why?

Q6.12   (a) What are the cloud and pour points of a fuel?
(b) For what type of fuel are these points important?

Q6.13   Why is it important to remove sulphur from fuels during refining?

Q6.14   Can gasoline and diesel fuel be stored for equally long periods of time? Why?

Q6.15   (a) When does knock occur in a spark-ignition engine?
(b) What characteristics of high octane gasoline is responsible for knock resistance?
(c) Why is knocking more likely to occur with lean mixtures?

Q6.16   Would a high octane fuel have good knock resistance in a diesel engine? Briefly explain your answer.

Q6.17   (a) What are the minimum and maximum cetane numbers that permit satisfactory operation?
(b) What are the symptoms of an excessively low cetane number?
(c) What are the symptoms of a cetane number that is too high?

Q6.18   Nitrate additives are available to raise the cetane rating of diesel fuel. What do these additives do to raise the cetane number?

Q6.19   Gasolines are blended to suit the season and the geographic location.
(a) What changes are made in a gasoline intended for use in the winter?
(b) What changes are made if the gasoline is to be used at high elevations?

Q6.20   Why is No. 1 diesel fuel often substituted for No. 2 diesel fuel for winter operations?

Q6.21   (a) What is an ester, that is, how and from what is it made?
(b) In what type of engine is it used?

Q6.22   What are the two primary concerns that regulations concerning fuel storage are designed to address?

# PROBLEMS

P6.1   (a) Work out the equation for the ideal combustion of methane.
(b) Calculate the stoichiometric air to fuel ratio.
(c) How many kilograms (lb) of water are created for each kilogram (lb) of fuel burned?
(d) What percentage of the dry (excluding water) exhaust molecules are nitrogen?
(e) What percentage of the dry exhaust molecules are carbon dioxide?
(Note: The percentages in parts d and e are also equal to the percentage by volume of these gases in the dry exhaust.)

P6.2   Rework P6.1 using propane as the fuel.

P6.3   Rework P6.1 using kerosene as the fuel.

P6.4   Rework P6.1 using diesel fuel as the fuel.

P6.5   Rework P6.1 using methyl alcohol as the fuel.
(*Hint:* In calculating the number of oxygen atoms that must be supplied by the air, do not forget to subtract the oxygen atom that is supplied in the fuel.)

P6.6   Rework P6.1 using butyl alcohol as the fuel. Also, see hint for P6.5.

P6.7   Rework P6.1 using methyl soyate as the fuel. Also, see hint for P6.5.

P6.8   Rework part of P6.1 using diesel fuel as the fuel. Then, after balancing the equation for ideal combustion, assume the air supply is doubled (100% excess air), and rebalance the equation. Then, work parts b, c, d, and e as in P6.1, but use the equation with excess air included. Also, calculate the percentage by volume of free oxygen in the exhaust gases.

Fuels and Combustion

P6.9  The diesel fuel used in OECD Nebraska Test No. 1619 (see Table 5.1) had a specific gravity of 0.8301 at 15.6° C (60° F).
(a) Calculate the API degrees.
(b) Calculate the higher heating value.
(c) Calculate the lower heating value.

P6.10  An API hydrometer was used to measure the specific gravity of a fuel at 15.6° C (60° F), and the reading was 61° API.
(a) Calculate the higher heating value.
(b) Calculate the lower heating value.
(c) Using Table 6.5 as a guide, what kind of fuel was tested?

P6.11  Rework P6.10, but assume a hydrometer reading of 40.

P6.12  In combustion, conversions of $H_2$ to $H_2O$ and C to $CO_2$ each liberate definite amounts of heat. The following equations were derived for estimating heating values of hydrocarbon fuels when their formula, $C_xH_y$ is known:

$$LHV = \frac{[395 * x/y + 121] * K_c}{12 * x/y + 1}$$

$$HHV = \frac{[395 * x/y + 141] * K_c}{12 * x/y + 1}$$

where
LHV = lower heating value in MJ/kg (BTU/lb)
HHV = higher heating value in MJ/kg (BTU/lb)
x  = number of carbon atoms in the fuel molecule
y  = number of hydrogen atoms in the fuel molecule
$K_c$ = units constant = 1 (430)

(a) Assuming the average molecule in a sample of No. 2 diesel fuel has the formula $C_{16}H_{29.3}$, calculate the HHV.
(b) Compare your results with Table 6.5.
(c) Calculate the LHV of the No. 2 diesel fuel.

P6.13  Rework P6.11, but assume the fuel sample is regular gasoline with an average composition of $C_8H_{15.8}$.

P6.14    Rework P6.11, but assume the fuel sample is propane, $C_3H_8$.

P6.15    (a) Calculate values of HHV for ratios x/y from 0 to 4 and plot HHV versus x/y on a graph.
(b) What is the effect of increasing the carbon to hydrogen ratio of the fuel?

# 7
# Electrical Systems

## 7.1 INTRODUCTION

The first half of this chapter deals with the fundamentals of electricity, semi-conductors, and electromagnetism as they apply to mobile vehicles. It will by necessary for you to study these fundamentals to understand how they can be applied to the analysis of charging, starting, and accessory circuits in the latter half of this chapter. Some of the fundamentals will also be applied in the study of ignition circuits in Chapter 8.

## 7.2 ELECTRICAL FUNDAMENTALS

*Electricity* is the flow of electrons from atom to atom in a conductor. All matter is composed of chemical elements, and atoms are the smallest particles into which an element can be subdivided. Atoms of several elements are illustrated in Figure 7.1. Each atom has a central nucleus around which one or more electrons orbit. Each nucleus contains one or more positively charged protons and also may contain neutral particles called neutrons. Each electron has a negative charge equal to the positive charge on a proton, and each atom has an equal number of electrons and protons. Elements differ from one another in their atomic structure, that is, in the number of protons and neutrons in the nucleus and in the number of rings or shells in which the electrons orbit. Each shell has a fixed capacity for electrons: only 2 electrons can orbit in the first or innermost shell; only 8 orbit in the second shell; 18 orbit in the third; and 32 orbit in the fourth. The outermost shell in any atom is called the valence

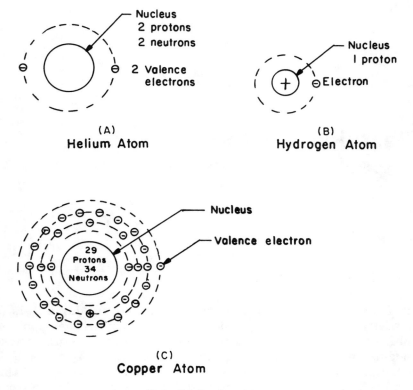

*Figure 7.1–Atomic structures.*

shell. If the valence shell is relatively full, valence electrons are shared with neighboring atoms; the atoms are then linked through covalent bonding.

### 7.2.1 Crystalline Structure and Conductivity

Many solids have their atoms arranged in a crystal lattice. If the valence shells in the atoms contain less than four electrons, neighboring valence shells tend to overlap and little energy is needed to free an electron from the attraction of the nucleus. As a result, free electrons can wander randomly through the lattice, and the solid is an *electrical conductor*. Copper has only one valence electron (Figure 7.1) and is, therefore, an excellent conductor. When an external voltage is applied across a conductor, the free electrons all begin to move through the lattice in the same direction, forming an electrical current. Vibration of the atoms in their lattice causes a resistance to current flow. The vibration of the atoms and thus the electrical resistance increases with temperature. At temperatures near absolute zero, resistance essentially disappears, and the

Electrical Systems

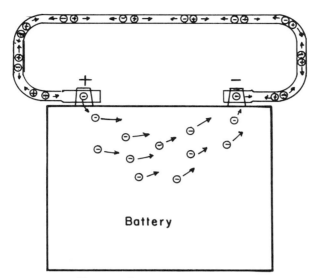

*Figure 7.2–Current flow in a conductor.*

material becomes a superconductor. Recently, new classes of materials have been discovered that are superconductors at temperatures far above absolute zero, although not as high as ordinary room temperatures. These new superconductors may be integrated into useful products in the future.

An *electrical insulator* also has its atoms arranged in a crystal lattice. However, the valence shells contain more than four electrons. These valence electrons are tightly bound to the nucleus and, thus, are not available as free electrons to create a current flow. Elements with four valence electrons are classified as *semiconductors* and will be discussed in Section 7.3.

### 7.2.2 Electron Flow and Current

Consider a copper wire connected across a battery as shown in Figure 7.2. A free electron in the left end of the wire is attracted to the plus terminal of the battery. It leaves its atom, and its departure leaves behind a positive charge. The positive charge attracts a free electron from a neighboring atom, which in turn is left with a positive charge, and so on. The net result is a flow of electrons toward the positively charged (+) end of the wire and an apparent flow of positive charges toward the negative end of the wire. Thus, although electric current is actually a flow of electrons through a conductor from the negative toward the positive end, it has become common practice to refer to a flow of positive electric current from the positive end of the conductor toward the negative end. Positive current is assumed to flow out of the positive (+) terminal of a battery, generator, or other electrical source, while electrons flow out of the negative (-) terminal.

### 7.2.3 Definitions and Units

Many definitions and units are needed to adequately describe electrical systems. The terms most commonly used with vehicle electrical systems will be defined here.

*Current* refers to the flow of electrons through a conductor, or the flow of positive charge in the opposite direction. Current is measured in amperes (A); very small currents are measured in milliamperes (mA). An ampere is equal to a current flow of $6.28 \times 10^{18}$ electrons/s past a given point in a conductor. In this book, current will be considered to be the flow of positive charge.

*Voltage* is the electrical pressure or force that causes current to flow in a conductor. Voltage is a potential force and can exist even when there is no current flow. For example, when a battery is removed from a vehicle, there is a voltage difference across the battery terminals, but no current flows until a circuit is connected to the battery. The basic unit of voltage is the volt (V); very small voltages are measured in millivolts (mV).

*Resistance* to current flow is present in all conductors except superconductors. The basic unit of resistance is the ohm ($\Omega$). One ohm of resistance will permit one ampere of current to flow when the potential across the conductor is one volt. Large resistances are measured in kilohms (k$\Omega$) or in megohms (M$\Omega$). A *resistor* is a device that is designed to have a given amount of resistance between its two terminals. The symbol for a resistor is shown in Figure 7.3.

*Ohm's Law* summarizes the relationship between electrical current, voltage, and resistance. The three different versions of Ohm's Law are as follows:

$$E = IR \tag{7.1}$$

$$I = \frac{E}{R} \tag{7.2}$$

$$R = \frac{E}{I} \tag{7.3}$$

where
    E = voltage across a resistor in volts (V)
    I = current through the resistor in amperes (A)
    R = resistance in ohms ($\Omega$)

Electrical Systems

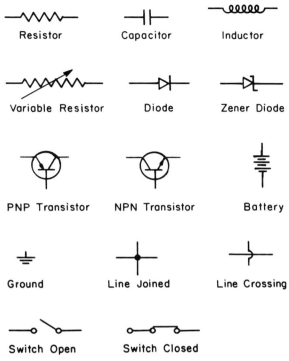

Figure 7.3–Electrical symbols.

A *circuit* consists of electrical devices connected in a continuous path through which current may flow. The circuit in Figure 7.4 includes a battery, a resistor, a switch, and wires to interconnect them all. When the switch is closed, the circuit is complete. Current can flow from the positive terminal of the battery, through the resistor and switch, and back into the negative terminal of the battery. No current can flow when the switch is open. Then, the circuit is called an open circuit.

A *series circuit* is a circuit in which there is only one path for current flow. The circuit in Figure 7.4 is a series circuit, because the same current flows through all parts of the circuit. A parallel circuit

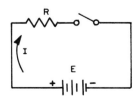

Figure 7.4–A series circuit.

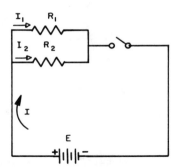

*Figure 7.5–A series-parallel circuit.*

provides more than one path for current flow. The two resistors $R_1$ and $R_2$ in Figure 7.5 are connected in parallel. The current $I_1$ flows through one resistor and, if the resistors are unequal, the current $I_2$ flows through the other resistor. The voltage across both resistors is the same, as is always the case for parallel circuits. The complete circuit in Figure 7.5 is an example of a series-parallel circuit. The resistors are connected in parallel with each other, but the pair of resistors is connected in series with the battery. The sum of the resistor currents $I_1 + I_2$ must therefore be equal to the battery current I.

A *capacitor* is a device for storing electrical charge. It consists of two large tinfoil plates separated and insulated from each other by waxed paper. The tinfoil plates and insulating layers are wrapped in a tight spiral to save space as shown in Figure 7.6. Capacitors used in ignition systems have one plate electrically connected to the metal case and the other plate connected to a lead wire. When the capacitor is connected across a battery (or other voltage source), electrons leave the negative terminal of the battery and flow to one plate of the capacitor. Electrons leave the other plate of the capacitor and flow to the positive terminal of the battery. Current cannot flow through the insulator between the plates and, as more and more electrons leave the positive plate, flow through the battery, and appear on the negative plate, a potential difference begins appearing across the plates. When this potential difference reaches the battery voltage, current flow stops, and the capacitor is fully charged. The capacitor will remain charged if it is disconnected from the battery, but it will discharge if a conducting circuit is connected between its terminals. During discharge, electrons flow from the negative plate through the conducting circuit to the positive plate. The electrical symbol for the capacitor is shown in Figure 7.3.

Electrical Systems

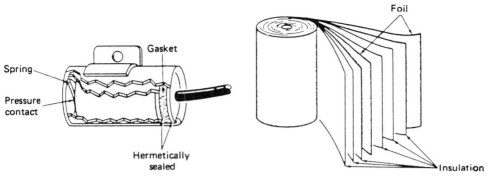

*Figure 7.6–The construction of a capacitor used in ignition systems. (Courtesy of Delco-Remy, Division of General Motors Corporation.)*

*Capacitance* is a rating that relates to the amount of charge that can be stored in a capacitor at a given voltage. The capacitance is equal to the amount of charge divided by the voltage. The basic unit of capacitance is the farad (F), but capacitance is more commonly measured in microfarads ($\mu$F).

*Electrical power* is measured in watts (W). Electrical power can be calculated by using Equation 7.4:

$$P = EI \qquad (7.4)$$

where
 $P$ = electrical power in W
 $E$ = electrical potential in V
 $I$ = electrical current in A

When Equations 7.1 and 7.4 are combined, we see that:

$$P = I^2 R \qquad (7.5)$$

Therefore, electrical power is lost and converted into heat whenever an electrical current flows through a resistance.

## 7.3 FUNDAMENTALS OF SEMICONDUCTORS

Many different combinations of materials can be used in making semiconductors. For simplicity, only those in widest use in engine electronic systems will be discussed here.

### 7.3.1 Intrinsic Semiconductors

Silicon atoms have four valence electrons; therefore, silicon crystals are intrinsically semiconductors. Silicon atoms are linked to neighboring atoms in the crystal lattice through covalent bonding. When a valence electron escapes by breaking a covalent bond, a mobile hole is said to remain in the lattice. A hole is an electron vacancy that has a strong localized attraction for other electrons. Thus, an electron may jump into the hole from an adjacent atom, filling the hole but creating a new hole in the adjacent atom. Therefore, current flow in a semiconductor can be visualized as an electron flow in one direction and a flow of holes, or apparent positive charges, in the opposite direction.

### 7.3.2 N-Type Semiconductors

Semiconductor conductivity can be radically altered by doping with impurities. If a silicon crystal is doped with phosphorus, for example, some of the silicon atoms will be displaced by phosphorus atoms. Each phosphorous atom has five valence electrons, and the fifth electron is relatively free for conduction. Silicon doped with phosphorus is called an *N-type semiconductor*, because there is an excess of negative charges. The excess electrons tend to fill holes in the lattice; so hole concentration is very low. In N-type material, therefore, free electrons are the majority carriers of current and holes are minority carriers.

### 7.3.3 P-Type Semiconductors

The silicon crystal also can be doped with boron, and boron has only three valence electrons. Therefore, when a boron atom displaces a silicon atom in the crystal, an electron deficiency, or hole, is created. The boron-doped silicon is called a *P-type semiconductor* because of the excess of positive charges. The extra holes tend to absorb free electrons in the lattice; so holes become the majority or current and electrons are the minority carriers. Unlike electrons, which can move through the entire circuit, holes can only move within the semiconductor material.

## 7.4 DIODES

A diode is a device that permits current to flow freely in one direction but prevents current flow in the reverse direction. A diode can be made by doping boron on one end of the crystal and phosphorous on the other to form a PN junction (Figure 7.7). When the junction is formed, electrons near the junction in the N-type material begin diffusing across the junction into the P-type material.

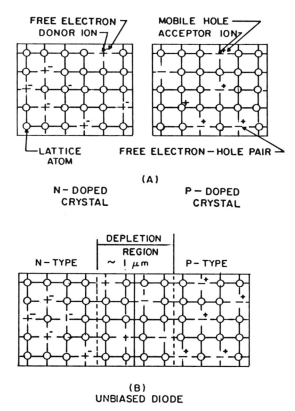

*Figure 7.7–Doping an N-type and P-type on the same crystal to form a diode.*

Simultaneously, holes begin diffusing from the P-side to the N-side of the junction. Soon, the accumulating positive charges on the N-side prevent further diffusion of electrons, and accumulating negative charges on the P-side prevent further diffusion of holes. The net result is an equilibrium condition with a depletion region, that is, a deficiency of free electrons and holes near the junction.

### 7.4.1 Reverse Biasing

A diode can be *reverse biased* by connecting a battery as shown in Figure 7.8. The + terminal of the battery is connected to the cathode or the N-type crystal. The - battery terminal is connected to the anode or the P-type crystal. Reverse biasing pulls majority carriers away from the PN junction. That is, free electrons are drawn away in the P-type material. The depletion region widens and, with so few majority carriers available, almost no current can flow across the

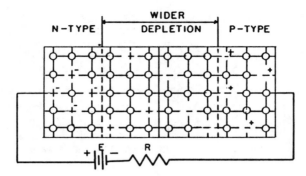

*Figure 7.8–Reverse biasing to widen the depletion region and stop current flow.*

junction. Reverse biasing the diode therefore allows almost no current to flow.

### 7.4.2 Forward Biasing

A diode can be *forward biased* by reversing the battery connections. A resistor must also be connected in the circuit, as shown in Figure 7.9, to prevent damage from excess current. Forward biasing injects electrons from the battery into the cathode. These electrons move toward the PN junction and begin to reduce the width of the depletion region as electrons and holes flow toward the junction and combine. With sufficient forward biasing, the depletion region disappears and the diode conducts current.

### 7.4.3 Zener Diodes

Raising the reverse biasing voltage beyond a critical level ruptures the covalent bonds in the crystals. Then, a large increase in reverse current flow occurs with almost no further increase in voltage. The

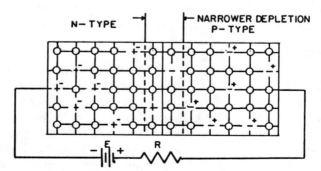

*Figure 7.9–Forward biasing to narrow the depletion region and permit current flow.*

Electrical Systems

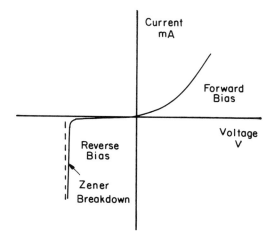

Figure 7.10–Voltage-current characteristics of a diode.

heavy reverse current will damage ordinary diodes, but *zener diodes* are constructed to survive the large current and recover. Zener diodes are often used in circuits to protect against excessive voltage and to maintain a constant voltage. Figure 7.10 shows current flow through a diode with forward and reverse biasing.

## 7.5 TRANSISTORS

A *transistor* is a device that uses a small electrical current to control the flow of a much larger current. A PNP transistor has boron doped on both ends of the crystal and phosphorous doped on the center section as shown in Figure 7.11. The boron-doped crystal on the left is called the *emitter*, the phosphorous-doped crystal is called the *base*, and the boron-doped crystal on the right is called the collector. Although NPN transistors can also be made, PNP types are more common in farm and industrial equipment. The base of the transistor

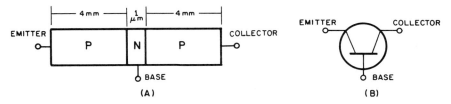

Figure 7.11–A PNP transistor showing (a) approximate dimensions and (b) a circuit symbol.

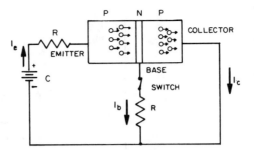

*Figure 7.12–A PNP transistor in a switching circuit.*

is very thin; it has a thickness comparable to the distance that holes and free electrons can diffuse in a diode.

Figure 7.12 shows the PNP transistor connected in a circuit. The emitter-to-base junction is forward biased; so holes flow toward that junction from the emitter, and free electrons flow toward the same junction from the base. The small size of the base greatly limits the number of free electrons it can furnish. Thus, the base current $I_b$ is far less than the emitter current $I_e$. The collector-to-base junction is reverse biased; so holes are attracted away from that junction in the collector. Because of the narrowness of the base, most of the holes from the emitter pass directly across the base to the collector. The collector current $I_c$, therefore, is much larger than the base current.

For example, if the emitter current was 1.0 A, the collector current might be 0.95 A. The base current would then be only 0.05 A. In this case, collector current would be 19 times larger than the base current. If the switch in the base circuit was opened, virtually all current flow in the transistor would stop, because stopping electron flow into the base would prevent the emitter from injecting holes across the junction into the base. Thus, in this example, by switching only 0.05 A of a base current, a collector current that is 19 times larger than the base current can be controlled.

## 7.6 MAGNETISM

The first experiments with *magnetism* occurred more than two thousand years ago, when iron ore fragments called lodestone were observed to attract other pieces of iron. When an elongated piece of lodestone was suspended in air on a string, it would align itself with one end pointed toward the North Pole of the earth. This end was called the N pole (north pole). The bar magnet, as the elongated

Electrical Systems 173

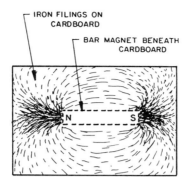

*Figure 7.13–A demonstration of the magnetic field surrounding a magnet.*

lodestone was called, became the basis for the magnetic compass used in navigation.

A magnetic field was found to exist around bar magnets. The magnetic field can be demonstrated by sprinkling iron filings on a sheet of cardboard and placing a bar magnet under the cardboard. The iron filings will arrange themselves as shown in Figure 7.13 when the cardboard is tapped lightly by hand. The filings form lines that coincide with magnetic lines of force. The magnetic lines leave the N pole, arch back in the space around the magnet, and reenter the S pole (south pole). The lines of force become crowded near the poles, and the magnetism is greatest in these areas of high concentration of lines of force.

When the N pole of one magnet is brought near the S pole of another magnet, the two magnets are strongly attracted to each other (Figure 7.14). However, when the N poles of two magnets are brought together, the two magnets strongly repel each other. Repulsion also occurs when two S poles are brought together. Thus, unlike magnetic poles attract while like magnetic poles repel each other.

Bars of ordinary soft iron or alloy steel can be converted into magnets by placing them in a magnetic field (Figure 7.15). The iron

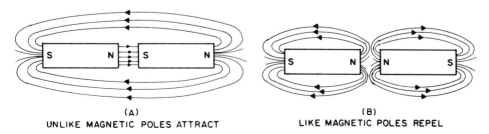

*Figure 7.14–Interactions of bar magnets.*

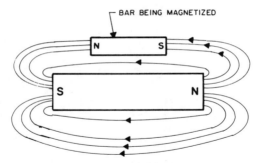

*Figure 7.15–Using one magnet to create another.*

or steel bar has an S pole, where the magnetic lines of force enter, and an N pole, where the magnetic lines leave. Soft iron bars quickly become magnetized, but they also quickly lose their magnetism when removed from the magnetic field. Alloy steel bars do not magnetize so readily, but tend to remain magnetic even when removed from the magnetic field. Thus, soft iron forms temporary magnets, while alloy

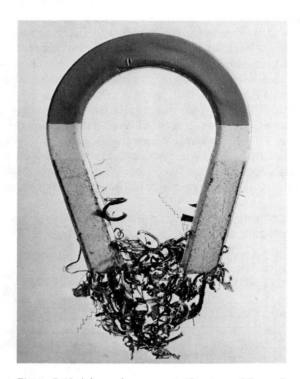

*Figure 7.16–A horseshoe magnet. (Courtesy of Deere & Company.)*

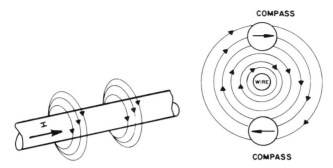

*Figure 7.17–A magnetic field forming around a current-carrying conductor.*

steel forms permanent magnets. Permanent magnets are often formed into a horseshoe shape to bring the N pole and the S pole into closer proximity and form a stronger magnetic field between them (Figure 7.16).

## 7.7  ELECTROMAGNETISM

Electromagnetism was unknown until 1819 when Hans Christian Oersted, a Danish scientist, discovered that a compass placed near a current-carrying conductor would align itself at right angles to the conductor (Figure 7.17). The compass needle aligns itself with magnetic lines of force and, thus, a magnetic field must exist around the wire. The magnetic field is strongest nearest the conducting wire and disappears as one moves far away from the wire. Both the strength and the size of the magnetic field increase as current in the conductor increases.

Imagine two parallel, adjacent conductors carrying current in opposite directions as shown in Figure 7.18. The magnetic lines of force between the wires are much more concentrated than would be the force for one wire alone, so the two wires try to move apart. As a general principle, current-carrying conductors tend to move out of strong magnetic fields into weaker magnetic fields. This principle is

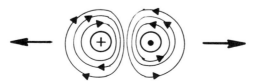

*Figure 7.18–Field crowding causes repulsion between conductors carrying currents in opposite directions.*

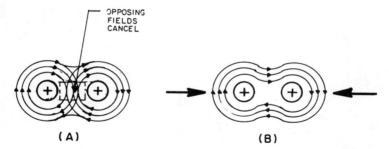

*Figure 7.19–Field linking causes attraction between conductors carrying currents in the same direction.*

the basis for the starting motors that will be discussed in Section 7.13.

Next, imagine two parallel, adjacent conductors carrying equal currents in the same direction, as shown in Figure 7.19. The magnetic fields between the two wires oppose each other and cancel out (Figure 7.19a). The two wires tend to move toward each other, and their magnetic fields join into one common, stronger field surrounding both wires (Figure 7.19b). Figure 7.20 shows current flowing through a wire formed into a *coil*. Here, the magnetic fields from each loop join together to form one concentrated field through the center of the coil. One end of the coil becomes a magnetic N pole, through which the lines of magnetic force leave. The magnetic lines arch back around the coil and enter the S pole of the coil. Reversing the direction of current flow through the coil would also reverse the position of the north and south poles.

An *electromagnet* is formed when a coil of wire is wrapped around a soft iron bar. The iron is a much better conductor of magnetic lines

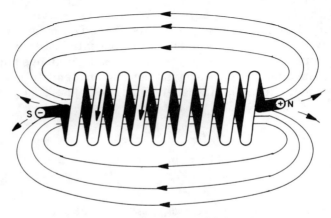

*Figure 7.20–The magnetic field of a coil.*

of force than is air. The iron core thus increases the magnetic strength of the coil several thousand times.

Magnetic lines of force form a closed circuit. That is, all the lines of force leaving the N pole of a magnet must reenter the S pole. Although the magnetic lines of force do not flow as does electric current, it is useful to form an analogy between magnetic and electric circuits. Ohm's Law of electrical circuits was discussed in Section 7.2. The magnetic equivalent of Equation 7.2 is as follows:

$$\Phi = \frac{\text{mmf}}{\mathfrak{R}} \qquad (7.6)$$

where
$\Phi$ = total magnetic flux in webers (Wb)
mmf = magnetomotive force in ampere-turns
$\mathfrak{R}$ = reluctance in ampere-turns/Wb

The *magnetomotive force* is the magnetic analog of voltage and is measured in ampere-turns. For example, a current of 1 A flowing in a 500 turn coil would provide an mmf of 500 ampere turns. Likewise, a current of 2 A through the same coil would produce an mmf of 1000 ampere-turns. *Magnetic flux* refers to the total number of lines of magnetic force leaving the magnet and is given in webers. *Reluctance* is analogous to electrical resistance. For a given mmf, an increase in reluctance reduces the magnetic flux. For example, removing the iron core from an electromagnet would greatly increase the reluctance and reduce the magnetic flux through the center of the coil.

## 7.8 ELECTROMAGNETIC INDUCTION

In Figure 7.21, a conductor is shown moving through a magnetic field at right angles to the lines of magnetic force. The conductor is said to be cutting the magnetic lines of force, and a voltage is induced in the conductor. Thus, one end of the conductor becomes electrically positive and the other end becomes electrically negative. The *right-hand rule for induced voltage* can be used to remember the polarity of the induced voltage. As illustrated in Figure 7.22, if the conductor is grasped with the right hand, with the fingers on the leading edge of the wire pointed in the direction of the magnetic lines of force, then the thumb will point in the direction that current would flow in the wire if the electrical circuit was completed. Thus, reversing either the direction of the magnetic field or the direction of motion of the

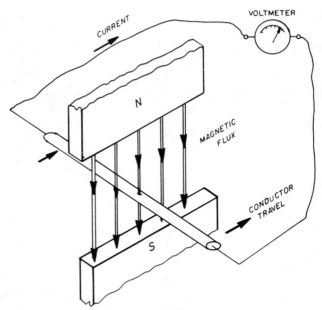

*Figure 7.21–Electromagnetic induction.*

conductor would reverse the polarity of the induced voltage. The magnitude of the *induced voltage* depends on the strength of the magnetic field and the speed with which the magnetic lines of force

*Figure 7.22–The right-hand rule for the polarity of induced voltage.*

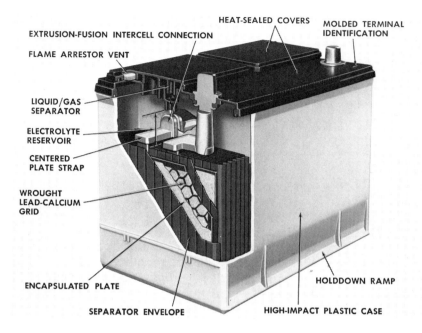

*Figure 7.23–The construction of a storage battery. (Courtesy of Delco-Remy, Division of General Motors Corporation.)*

are being cut. Induced voltages are created by generators and alternators (discussed in Section 7.10).

## 7.9 STORAGE BATTERIES

*Batteries* are used on mobile vehicles for storage of chemical energy. The chemical energy is converted to electrical energy to start the engine or when electrical demand exceeds the capacity of the charging system. The battery also serves to stabilize the voltage in the electrical system.

### 7.9.1 Battery Construction

The lead-acid storage batteries used in vehicles consist of individual storage cells in a hard rubber or plastic case (Figure 7.23). Each fully charged cell consists of a set of sponge lead (Pb) negative plates, a set of lead peroxide ($PbO_2$) positive plates, and an electrolyte of sulfuric acid ($H_2SO_4$) diluted with water ($H_2O$). The positive plates are interspersed between the negative plates but are separated from them by porous separators that allow free flow of electrolytes between the plates. Each cell produces a potential of approximately 2 V, but batteries of higher voltage are formed by connecting cells in

*TABLE 7.1. Characteristics of charged and discharged lead-acid batteries*

| Characteristics | Battery Charged | Battery Discharged |
|---|---|---|
| Positive plates | $PbO_2$ | $PbO_2 + PbSO_4$ |
| Negative plates | Pb | $Pb + PbSO_4$ |
| Electrolyte in % by volume | 32% $SO_4$ | 12% $H_2SO_4$ |
|  | 68% $H_2O$ | 88% $H_2O$ |
| Freezing point of electrolyte in °C (°F) | -60 (-76) | -8 (+18) |
| Cell voltage | 2.2 | 1.8 |

series. Thus, the typical 12 V battery has six cells connected in series.

### 7.9.2 Battery Discharging

Characteristics of fully charged and discharged batteries are summarized in Table 7.1. During discharge, electrical current flows from the positive terminal while chemical changes occur in the battery. The positive plates begin to change from lead peroxide to lead sulphate. Hydrogen released from the sulfuric acid links with oxygen from the lead peroxide to form water. The lead in the negative plates also begins to change to lead sulphate. Thus, lead sulphate forms at both the positive and negative plates and results in a gradual loss of cell voltage. The sulfuric acid becomes more diluted as water forms. Thus, the specific gravity of the electrolyte decreases, and its freezing point increases. Discharge eventually stops when the battery reaches the conditions in the right-handed column of Table 7.1.

### 7.9.3 Battery Charging

During charging, the battery is recharged by forcing current into the positive terminal. Chemical changes occur that essentially are the opposite of those occurring during discharge. The lead sulphate on the positive and negative plates begins to divide into lead and sulphate ($SO_4$). The water begins to split into hydrogen and oxygen. The oxygen links with lead to reform the positive plates, and sponge lead reforms on the negative plates. The cell voltage rises; the specific gravity of the electrolyte increases, and its freezing point decreases.

A *hydrometer* may be used to test the state of charge of a battery, as shown in Figure 7.24. Table 7.2 can be used to relate specific gravity to state of charge. If the electrolyte is not at 27° C (80° F) during the test, the reading must be corrected to account for the electrolyte's expansion at higher temperatures and contraction at lower temperatures. To make the correction, add 0.0007 (0.0004) to the reading for each degree Celsius (Fahrenheit) the electrolyte is

# Electrical Systems

*Figure 7.24–Checking the state of charge of a battery. (Courtesy of Deere & Company.)*

above 27° C (80° F) and subtract the same amount for each degree below 27° C (80° F). The procedure is illustrated in Example Problem 7.1.

## Example Problem 7.1
The specific gravity of the electrolyte is 1.220 at 20° C (68° F). What is the state of charge of the battery, and what is the freezing point of the electrolyte?

**Solution:** The correction factor is:

*TABLE 7.2. Changes in battery electrolyte with state of charge*

| State of Charge | Specific Gravity* | Freezing Point °C | °F |
|---|---|---|---|
| 100% charged | 1.260 | -60 | -76 |
| 75% charged | 1.230 | -41 | -42 |
| 50% charged | 1.200 | -28 | -18 |
| 25% charged | 1.170 | -19 | -2 |
| Discharged | 1.100 | -8 | 18 |

*Measured or corrected to 27 °C (80 °F)

or

$$(27 - 20)(0.0007) = 0.005$$

$$(80 - 68)(0.0004) = 0.005$$

The temperature of the electrolyte is below 27° C (80° F). Therefore, the correction factor must be subtracted from the measured specific gravity. The specific gravity (SG) at 27° C (80° F) would be:

$$1.220 - 0.005 = 1.215$$

Consulting Table 7.2 shows that, when the battery is between 50 and 75% charged, the freezing point of the electrolyte is between -28 and -41° C (-18 and -42° F).

### 7.9.4 Battery Sulfation

A battery should be stored in a fully charged condition to avoid *sulfation* of the plates. If a partially discharged battery is stored for a month or more, the lead sulphate on the plates can crystallize into hard deposits and reduce the ability of the plates to transfer current. Recharging of a sulfated battery can only be done at a slow rate and may be impossible if the deposits have hardened too much.

### 7.9.5 Maintenance-Free Batteries

Conventional batteries include a small amount of antimony in the plates for strengthening. The antimony promotes formation of hydrogen and oxygen gases during charging, and escape of these gases through the vented cell caps causes a gradual loss of water from the electrolyte. Thus, the caps must be removed to allow periodic replenishment with distilled water. Substitution of calcium for antimony greatly reduces gas formation and has permitted the development of *maintenance-free batteries*. Maintenance-free batteries are vented but do not have removable cell caps for water replenishment. Extra electrolyte capacity is designed into maintenance-free batteries to allow for the small amount of water that is lost through gas formation.

### 7.9.6 Battery Storage

Batteries will gradually discharge during high-temperature storage, even when no external circuit is connected. The self-discharge is caused by chemical reactions that can completely discharge the battery within three months of storage at 40° C (104° F). Therefore, a wet-charged battery (a charged battery filled with electrolyte) should be stored at temperatures of 0° C to 16° C (32° F to 60° F).

## 7.9.7 Dry-Charged Batteries

Many new batteries are now shipped from the factory as *dry-charged batteries*. The manufacturer charges the battery while the plates are immersed in an electrolytic solution of dilute sulfuric acid. The plates are then washed and dried before the battery is assembled, and the battery is shipped without electrolyte. Shipping without electrolyte reduces shipping weight and eliminates the self-discharge that occurs with wet-charged batteries. Dry-charged batteries are activated for use by filling with an electrolyte of 1.265 specific gravity and applying a slow charge for a few minutes to ensure that the battery is fully charged.

## 7.9.8 Battery Ratings

The SAE has developed several standard ratings for batteries. Cranking an engine in cold weather requires a high current when a battery is least able to supply it. The *cold cranking rating* is the number of amperes a battery can deliver continuously for 30 s while maintaining a cell voltage of at least 1.2 V or, for a 12 V battery, a battery voltage of at least 7.2 V. Two current ratings are given for the 30 s test: one for the battery tested at -18° C (0° F) and a lower rating for the battery tested at -29° C (-20° F). Similar cold cranking tests are performed on batteries for use in diesel engines, except that the battery must deliver the rated current continuously for 90 s while maintaining a cell voltage of at least 1.0 V/cell.

The SAE has also established a *reserve capacity rating* for batteries to measure the ability of a battery to supply current for ignition, lights, and accessories without recharging. The test is conducted with the battery at 27° C (80° F). The reserve capacity rating is the number of minutes the battery can deliver 25 A continuously before the cell voltage falls to 1.75 V/cell. Reserve capacity would allow a battery to keep a tractor operating for some time if the charging system should suddenly fail.

## 7.9.9 Battery Safety

Explosions and electrolyte burn are the two primary hazards to be avoided when working with batteries. As mentioned in Section 7.9.3, hydrogen and oxygen gases form when a battery is being charged; since hydrogen is highly flammable in the presence of oxygen, a spark can therefore set off an explosion. The electrolyte should be maintained at the recommended level so that less space will be available for gases to accumulate. A flashlight, never a lighter or match, should be used to check the electrolyte level since a flame can set off an explosion. To avoid creation of an electrical spark when installing a battery, the grounded terminal should be connected last.

When removing a battery, the grounded terminal should be disconnected first. When using a battery charger, the leads should be connected or disconnected to the battery when the charger is turned off.

The acid in the battery electrolyte can eat holes in clothing, burn the skin, and can cause blindness if splashed into the eyes. Therefore, when the electrolyte is being added to a new battery, rubber gloves and eye protection should be worn and the work should be done in a well-ventilated area. Contact with the electrolyte should also be avoided when using a hydrometer to check the specific gravity of the electrolyte. Electrolyte spilled on the skin should immediately be flushed off with water and baking soda or lime can be used to help neutralize the acid. If electrolyte gets into your eyes, flush immediately with large amounts of water and contact a doctor at once.

If discarded improperly, worn out batteries are an environmental hazard because of possible electrolyte spills. The most satisfactory means of disposal is to recycle worn out batteries. If the dealer will accept a worn-out battery when a replacement is being sold, the worn-out batteries can be collected for transport back to the manufacturer for recycling.

## 7.10 CHARGING CIRCUITS

A battery can supply the electrical needs of a tractor for only an hour or two before discharging. Therefore, vehicles have a generator or alternator to help the battery supply current during periods of high electrical demand. During periods of low demand, the generator or alternator supplies the entire demand and also recharges the battery. The charging circuit includes the battery, the generator or alternator, and a regulator. The regulator regulates voltage in the charging circuit, and some regulators also regulate current. Generators produce direct current. Alternators produce alternating current, which must be converted into direct current.

## 7.11 CHARGING WITH GENERATORS

The principle of the *generator* is illustrated in Figure 7.25. A coil of wire is spinning in a magnetic field. At the instant shown in Figure 7.25a, both sides of the coil are cutting through magnetic lines of force. By applying the right-hand rule for induced voltage (see Section 7.8), it is clear that current flows in the loop in the direction shown by the arrows. Each end of the loop is connected to a

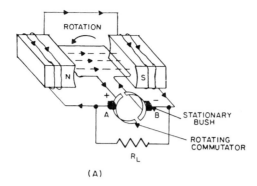

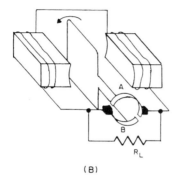

*Figure 7.25–A generator (a) cutting magnetic lines of force and (b) at static neutral.*

*commutator* segment which rotates with the loop. Stationary brushes ride against the commutator and transfer the generated current to the outside circuit. The outside circuit is symbolized by a load resistance, $R_L$. In Figure 7.25a, the brush nearest the S pole is contacting commutator segment B which is negative. The other brush is touching commutator segment A which is positive. After the rotating coil turns another half revolution, the right-hand rule shows that commutator segment B would be positive and commutator segment A would be negative. However, the commutator segments also would have switched positions. The brush nearest the S pole would still be negative, and the other brush would still be positive. The brushes are switching from one commutator segment to the other in Figure 7.25b. However, the coil is moving parallel to the lines of magnetic flux, and both commutator segments are neutral. Thus, current repeatedly reverses direction in the spinning loop of wire (alternating current), but the commutator converts it to current

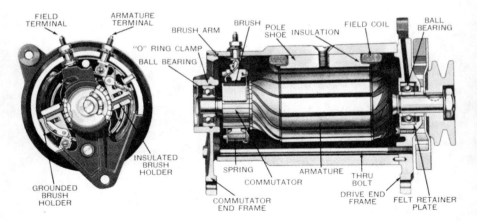

*Figure 7.26–A cutaway view of a generator. (Courtesy of Delco-Remy, Division of General Motors Corporation.)*

that always moves in one direction (direct current). For the simple generator of Figure 7.25, the direct current would not be constant; it would vary between the maximum (shown in Figure 7.25a) and zero (shown in Figure 7.25b).

The magnetic field in Figure 7.25 is created by stationary pole shoes which are weak permanent magnets. Current produced by the generator is fed to coils wrapped around the pole shoes to greatly strengthen the magnetic field.

A cutaway of a generator is shown in Figure 7.26. Many coils of wire are wrapped on the spinning *armature*. Each section of wire is connected to a different segment of the commutator. With many sections in the commutator, the generator produces nearly constant direct current. The armature rides in ball bearings and is driven by a pulley and V-belt. The field coils are formed by wrapping many turns of wire around the two pole shoes.

A generator and complete charging circuit are shown in Figure 7.27. The generator is called a shunt generator, because the field coils are connected in parallel with the armature. It is a type A generator, because the regulator is connected *after* the field. Type B generators have the regulator connected *before* the field. The regulator in Figure 7.27 includes a voltage regulator to protect against excess voltage, a current regulator to protect against excess current, and a cutout relay to prevent battery drain through the generator armature. Terminals on the generator are labeled **A** for armature and **F** for field.

Electrical Systems

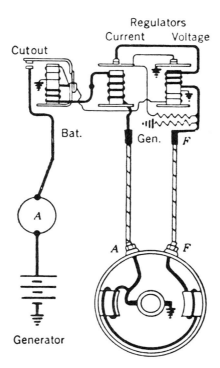

*Figure 7.27–A generator and complete charging circuit. (Courtesy of Deere & Company.)*

## 7.11.1 Voltage Regulation

The *voltage regulator* is a relay with two windings wrapped around an iron core. The series winding is connected in series with the generator field coils and in parallel with a resistor. Closing the voltage regulator points shorts out the resistor so that it is no longer in series with the generator field coils. The field current can then become stronger, and generator output can increase. When the generator voltage reaches a set limit, the voltage regulator windings are able to overcome a spring (not shown in Figure 7.27) and pull open the regulator points. Then, the field coils are in series with the resistor, the generator output falls, and the points close again. Thus, the voltage regulator points vibrate rapidly between open and closed in regulating the voltage at a constant value.

## 7.11.2 Current Regulation

All the current from the generator passes through the winding on the current regulator. When electrical demand is high and the battery is

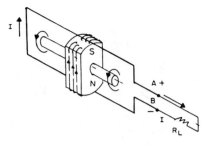

(A) TOP TERMINAL POSITIVE

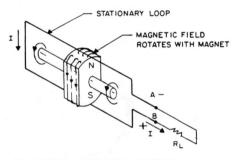

(B) BOTTOM TERMINAL POSITIVE

*Figure 7.28–A simple alternator.*

low — that is, when the battery is drained — the generator output increases until the current regulator points open. The generator field coils are then in series with the resistor, generator output falls, and the current regulator points close again. Thus, the *current regulator* points vibrate rapidly between open and closed to limit the generator current. The voltage and current regulators never operate simultaneously. The current regulator operates when battery voltage is low and the battery is being recharged. When the battery voltage is high, the voltage regulator works to regulate the voltage.

### 7.11.3 Reverse Current Cutout

Current flows from points of high voltage in a circuit to points of lower voltage. When generator voltage exceeds the battery voltage, the generator supplies current to recharge the battery. When generator voltage is low — that is, when the generator is not running — a *cutout relay* is needed to prevent the battery from discharging through the generator. The cutout relay has two windings that work in opposition when current flow is toward the generator. A spring pulls the points open to stop the current flow toward the generator.

Electrical Systems

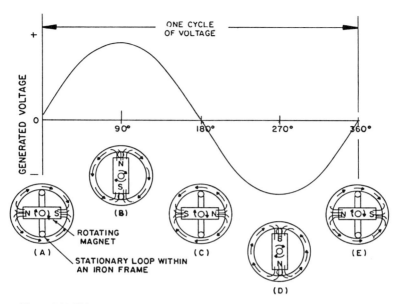

Figure 7.29–Voltage patterns produced during one revolution of a simple alternator.

When the generator voltage increases sufficiently, the shunt winding pulls the cutout points closed and, as current begins flowing toward the battery, the two windings work together to hold the points closed.

## 7.12 CHARGING WITH ALTERNATORS

A growing use of accessories on automobiles, trucks, and tractors led to an electrical demand that was difficult for generators to supply. Alternators are more compact than are generators and can supply more current at low speeds. Thus, alternators have largely replaced generators in recent years.

### 7.12.1 Basic Principles of Alternators

The basic principle of the *alternator* is illustrated in Figures 7.28 and 7.29. The alternator induces a voltage when the wire loop cuts magnetic lines of force. In contrast to the generator, however, the wire loop is stationary, and the magnetic field rotates with the rotating bar magnet. When the S pole is on top, as shown in Figure 7.28a, the right-hand rule for induced voltage shows that terminal A of the loop will be positive and terminal B will be negative. A half-turn later the N pole is on top, terminal A has become negative, and terminal B has become positive. The voltage alternates in polarity, and thus the device is called an alternator.

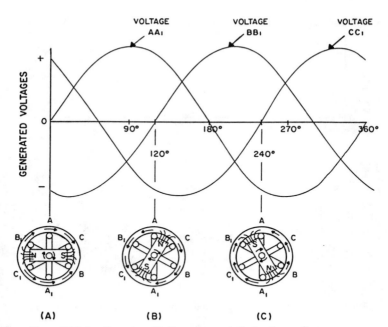

*Figure 7.30–An alternator with three phases producing three voltage waves.*

As was discussed in Section 7.7, the magnetic lines of force leave the N pole, arch back through space, and return to the S pole. By installing an iron frame around the alternator, the reluctance of the return path is greatly reduced, and the magnetic flux and alternator voltage are greatly increased. The stationary coil and the iron frame comprise the stator.

With the rotor turning at constant speed, as shown in Figure 7.29, magnetic lines of force leaving the N pole and crossing to the iron frame may be cut by the loop of wire. In Figure 7.29a, the loop is perpendicular to the rotating magnet, no magnetic lines of force are being cut, and the alternator voltage is zero. As parts b through e of Figure 7.29 show, the voltage is maximum positive 90° later, when the magnet poles are passing the wire loop. The voltage is zero again at 180°, maximum negative at 270°, and back to zero again at 360°. Thus, the alternator produces alternating voltage and, if a closed circuit is connected, alternating current flows in it.

If the rotor was turning at 3,600 rev/min, or 60 rev/s, the voltage curve of Figure 7.29 would be repeated 60 times/s. We would then say that one voltage frequency was 60 cycles/s. The magnitude of the voltage depends on three factors: the strength of the magnetic field produced by the rotor, the speed of the rotor, and the number of loops of wire in the stator winding. Only one loop is shown in Figure 7.28,

Electrical Systems

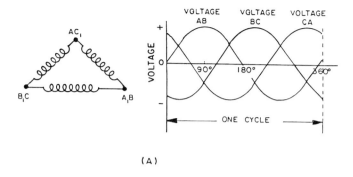

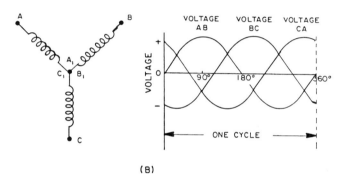

*Figure 7.31–The three phases of an alternator connected (a) in a delta connection and (b) in a y connection.*

but a long insulated wire could be wrapped into many adjacent loops. A 10-loop coil, for example, would produce 10 times as much voltage as a single loop. Also, the magnitude of the voltage increases in direct proportion to the rotor speed.

### 7.12.2 Three-Phase Alternators

Regardless of the rotor speed or number of turns in the stator coil, the alternator in Figure 7.29 would always produce zero voltage at 180° and 360°. However, alternators are actually built with three stator coils, as shown in Figure 7.30. The coils are equally spaced 120° apart. Now, when the rotor spins, the alternator produces three voltage curves, which are never all zero at the same time. The alternator is said to be producing *three-phase voltage.*

One of two arrangements is used to interconnect the three separate coils of an alternator. Figure 7.31a shows a delta-connected stator. The coil with terminals $AA_1$ (see Figure 7.30) has terminal A connected to adjacent coil terminal $C_1$ and terminal $A_1$ connected to

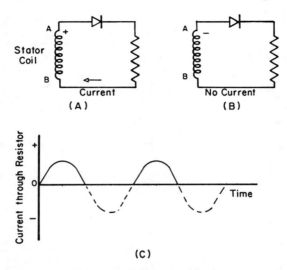

*Figure 7.32–Half-wave rectification.*

adjacent coil terminal B, and so on. The voltage across each side, or leg, of the delta is equal to the voltage produced by one independent coil. A y-connected stator is shown in Figure 7.31b. Here, one terminal of each of the three stator coils is joined in a common point, $A_1B_1C_1$. The voltage across any leg (for example, AB) of the y will be 1.732 times larger than the voltage across a delta leg.

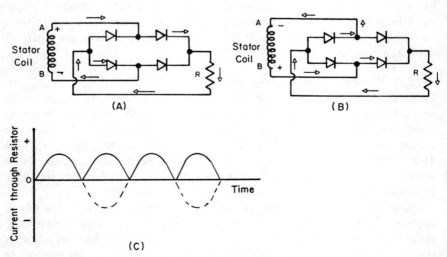

*Figure 7.33–Full-wave rectification.*

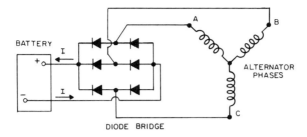

*Figure 7.34–A full-wave rectifier for a y-connected, three-phase alternator.*

## 7.12.3 Voltage Rectification

A diode can be used to convert alternating current to direct current. As explained in Section 7.4, a diode allows current to flow in one direction but not in the opposite direction. Figure 7.32 shows a diode and resistor connected in series with one stator winding on an alternator. When terminal A is positive (Figure 7.32a), the diode is forward biased; current flows from terminal A, through the diode and resistor, and back to terminal B. When terminal A is negative (Figure 7.32b), the diode is reverse biased; no current can flow through it. Figure 7.32c shows two cycles of alternating current. The dashed line shows the reverse current that is blocked by the diode. Thus, only positive or direct current flows through the resistor, but the current is zero half of the time. The circuit in Figure 7.32 is called a half-wave rectifier, because half of the current is lost.

A diode bridge is being used to provide full-wave rectification in Figure 7.33. Stator terminal A is positive in Figure 7.33a, the upper-right and lower-left diodes in the bridge are forward biased, and current flows through the circuit (as shown by the arrows). Terminals A and B have reversed in polarity in Figure 7.33b, and the lower-right and upper-left diodes in the bridge are now forward biased. Current flows as indicated by the arrows in Figure 7.33b. Notice that the current flows through the resistor in the same direction, regardless of the polarity of terminals A and B. Thus,

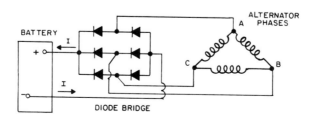

*Figure 7.35–A full-wave rectifier for a delta-connected, three-phase alternator.*

*Figure 7.36–A disassembled alternator. (Courtesy of Deere & Company.)*

instead of blocking the negative current from the resistor, the diode bridge reroutes it so that it flows through the resistor in the positive direction. The full-wave rectifier produces direct current, as Figure 7.33c shows.

Six diodes are required to provide full-wave rectification of the three phases of alternator current into direct current. Figure 7.34 shows a rectifier for a y-connected stator. Each of the terminals A, B, and C of the stator is connected to two diodes; one of the diodes will be forward biased when the other is reverse biased. When terminal A is positive, for example, the front diode conducts and connects terminal A to the positive terminal of the battery. When terminal A is negative, the other diode conducts and connects terminal A to the negative terminal of the battery. The rectification of all three phases produces a relatively smooth direct current, without the points of zero current shown in Figure 7.33c. Rectification of a delta-connected stator produces similarly smooth direct current. The rectification circuit for a delta-connected stator is shown on Figure 7.35.

A disassembled alternator is shown in Figure 7.36. The rotor is wrapped with many turns in a light winding called a field coil. The soft iron pieces enclosing the field coil provide alternating north and south magnetic poles. Current from the battery is fed to the field coil through slip rings. Thus, the electromagnets created produce much more magnetic flux than does the permanent bar magnet of Figure 7.28. Moreover, the voltage output of the alternator can be controlled by regulating the current in the field coil.

### 7.12.4 Regulators for Alternators

Regulators for alternators can be simpler than those for generators. No cutout relay is needed, because the rectifying diodes prevent the battery from discharging through the stator windings. The alternator is current self-limiting. Inductive reactance combines with resistance in the stator windings to limit alternating current flow. The alternator voltage and inductive reactance both increase with rotor speed. As the resistance is overshadowed above a certain speed, further increases in voltage are matched by increases in reactance to

# Electrical Systems

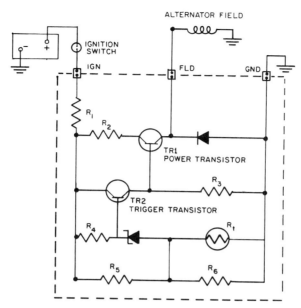

*Figure 7.37–A typical voltage regulator circuit for an alternator.*

keep the current constant. Thus, current output from alternators becomes self-limiting above a certain rotor speed. However, a voltage regulator is required to regulate the alternator voltage. Many different types of voltage regulators have been designed for use with alternators. Early models were adaptations of generator voltage regulators and used vibrating points. Later models included a transistor to extend point life by reducing current flow through the points; the transistor transmitted the field current, and the points handled a small current to control the transistor. Many of the mechanical and transistor-assisted regulators are still in use. However, now, the trend is toward the use of fully *transistorized regulators,* and these are the only regulators that will be discussed here. The fully transistorized regulators can be very small and are sometimes mounted within the alternator.

Regulator circuits include A circuits, in which the regulator is located *after* the field coil and B circuits, in which the regulator is located *before* the field. Also, some regulators use NPN transistors, and others use PNP transistors. The PNP transistorized regulators in a B circuit are more common and will be discussed here. The circuit diagram is shown in Figure 7.37. Turning on the switch allows battery current to flow through resistor $R_1$ to the regulator circuit. The zener diode is not conducting and current cannot flow through $R_4$. As Ohm's Law (Equation 7.1) states, there is no voltage

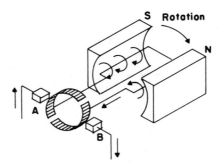

*Figure 7.38–Principle of a starter motor.*

drop across $R_4$, and with the base and emitter of transistor $TR_2$ at the same voltage, $TR_2$ is turned off. The emitter of $TR_1$ is at a higher voltage than is the base; so $TR_1$ turns on. Then, battery current flows through the emitter-collector circuit of $TR_1$ to the alternator field coils. Alternator voltage begins to increase. The higher voltage results in a greater current flow through $R_1$ to the regulator circuit. At a certain alternator voltage, the voltage drop across $R_5$ (Equation 7.1) becomes large enough to break down the zener diode. Current passing through $R_4$ and the zener diode biases the base of $TR_2$ negative with respect to the emitter, and $TR_2$ turns on. Emitter-collector current through $TR_2$ passes through $R_3$ and raises the base voltage of $TR_1$ to or above that of the emitter of $TR_1$. Then, $TR_1$ turns off and stops current flow to the field coil. System voltage begins to fall, the zener diode stops conducting, $TR_2$ turns off, and $TR_1$ turns back on. Thus, the transistors alternate in turning on and off many times each second in controlling the alternator voltage.

## 7.13 STARTER SYSTEMS

A *starting motor* cranks the engine by converting electrical energy into rotational mechanical energy. It is amazing that electric starting is possible, given that the engine is many times larger than the starter motor. Cranking is possible only because the starter motor delivers the required large amounts of energy in short bursts. Extended cranking must be avoided to prevent overheating of the starter motor.

### 7.13.1 Basic Principles of Starter Motors

The principle of the starting motor is illustrated in Figure 7.38. The loop of wire, or armature, of the starter is positioned between two magnets. A magnetic field is directed through the armature from the

Electrical Systems

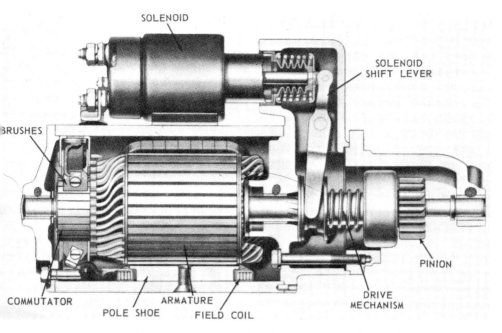

Figure 7.39–A cutaway view of a starter. (Courtesy of Deere & Company.)

N pole to the S pole. The armature carries current that enters through brush A and a commutator segment and flows through the wire loop in the direction shown. The current in the armature coil creates a new magnetic field around the wire in the direction shown by the arrows. Observe that in the wire segment nearest the S pole, the new magnetic field adds to the existing field below the wire but opposes it above the wire. Thus, the magnetic field becomes stronger below the wire and weaker above it, and the wire moves upward toward the weaker magnetic field. Meanwhile, the wire segment nearest the N pole creates a weaker field below itself and moves downward. The net result is that the current flow through the armature forces it to rotate clockwise. Reversing the direction of current flow through the armature would force it to rotate counterclockwise.

A cutaway view of a starter is shown in Figure 7.39. The armature has many segments. Each segment consists of a wire wrapped around the armature many times, with its two ends terminating at commutator segments. The stationary brushes continually shift from one pair of commutator segments to the next to keep the armature rotating in the same direction. The brushes are arranged to switch commutator segments at the neutral point, that is, when the armature coil is misaligned from the magnetic field as far as possible.

The permanent magnets in Figure 7.38 create only a weak magnetic field, and the starter could not produce nearly enough torque to crank an engine. Thus, the starter in Figure 7.39 uses field coils wrapped around pole shoes to create strong electromagnets. The armature coils are wrapped on an iron core to provide a low-reluctance path for the magnetic field through the armature. The pole shoes are mounted inside an iron housing to provide a low-reluctance return path between poles.

Typically, the field coils are connected in series with the armature coils in starter motors. Such motors are said to be series wound. The simple motor in Figure 7.38 has only two pole shoes and two brushes. It is a two-pole motor. Four- and six-pole starter motors are available to produce more armature torque for cranking larger engines.

### 7.13.2 Starter Solenoid

A starter motor produces very high cranking power considering its size. The motor is designed to run under heavy overloads for short times. The wire in the armature and field windings must be heavy enough to carry the high current demand of the starter. As Ohm's Law (Equation 7.1) indicates, the high current flowing through the resistance of the wires between the starter and battery can create a large voltage drop and, according to Equation 7.5, a considerable loss of electrical power. Therefore, a short, large-diameter electrical cable is used to connect the starter to the battery. The *solenoid*, in Figure 7.39, is a remote-controlled switch used to connect or disconnect the starter from the battery. A spring in the solenoid holds the switch contacts apart. A magnetic coil works against the spring to close the switch contacts. The driver uses a starter switch near the driver's seat to direct a small current to the coil in the solenoid, close the contacts, and thereby connects the starting motor to the battery.

### 7.13.3 Starter Pinions

A starter has a *pinion* (Figure 7.39) that engages with a ring gear on the flywheel to crank the engine. The pinion must be disengaged from the flywheel after the engine starts running. The starter in Figure 7.39 uses the solenoid and a lever mechanism to engage and disengage the pinion. The starter motor drives the pinion through an overrunning clutch. If the solenoid is not disengaged immediately after the engine starts, the overrunning clutch lets the pinion spin freely on the starter shaft. Several other starter drives have been designed for connecting and disconnecting the pinion from the ring gear on the flywheel.

Electrical Systems

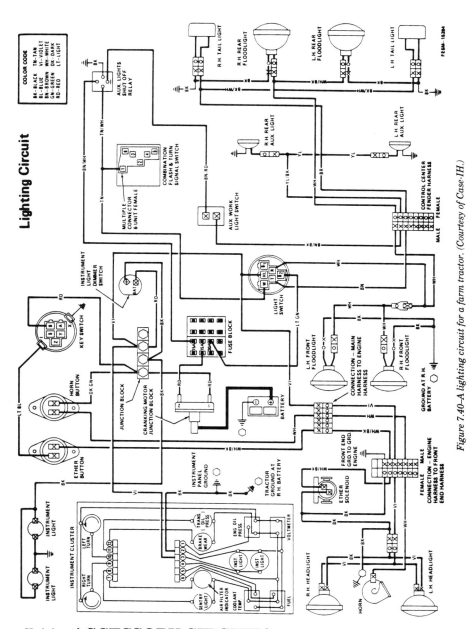

Figure 7.40-A lighting circuit for a farm tractor. (Courtesy of Case-IH.)

## 7.14 ACCESSORY CIRCUITS

Comfort and convenience have been increased on modern vehicles through the use of electrical accessories. Lighting circuits similar to the one shown in Figure 7.40 are a part of virtually all modern vehicles. Wires to the various lights are enclosed in a wiring harness. Fuses and/or circuit breakers protect the system against current overload. Excessive current causes the conductor in a fuse to melt, thereby opening the circuit and stopping the current. A circuit breaker opens when current is excessive. After the cause of the current overload is corrected, a circuit breaker resets automatically, or some must be reset by hand. A blown fuse, however, must be replaced with a new one. The new fuse should have the same amperage rating as the one it replaces.

Indicator lights for oil pressure, coolant temperature, and so forth have replaced gages on some engines. The circuits are designed so that the indicator lights glow when the key switch is turned on and not when the engine starts. Thus, the operator can verify that the indicator light bulbs are working properly. Sensors are designed to interrupt the circuits and turn the lights off when the engine is running with the correct oil pressure, coolant temperature, and so on. If oil pressure is too low, coolant temperature is too high, or some other malfunction occurs, however, sensors turn on an indicator light.

Microcomputer technology has been harnessed to provide electronic monitoring and control of farm tractors as well as automotive vehicles. On tractors, a radar unit delivers pulses to a microcomputer which uses the pulse frequency to compute and display travel speed. The same computer accepts pulses from magnetic pickups to compute and display engine speed, drive axle speed and wheel slip. Load-sensing pins in the three-point hitch allow the computer to determine the implement draft and, through electro-hydraulic valves, signal the hydraulic system to automatically raise or lower the hitch to control the draft. The latter system replaces mechanical sensing linkages that were used in earlier draft-control systems. Many other applications of microcomputer monitoring and control are expected in the future. The microcomputer and electronic devices must be designed to accommodate the often unfavorable environment (temperature, humidity, shock, and so forth) encountered on farm tractors.

Electrical circuits can operate many other accessories on farm tractors and other vehicles. Examples include horns, air conditioners, cigarette lighters, and other devices added to the vehicle to increase the operator's comfort and convenience.

## 7.15 SUMMARY

Many solids have their atoms arranged in a crystal lattice. The crystals are conductors, intrinsic semiconductors, or insulators depending, respectively, on whether the valence shells in the atoms contain less than four, exactly four, or more than four electrons. Electricity is the flow of electrons from atom to atom in a conductor. Conventional positive current is assumed to flow in the opposite direction of electron flow. Ohm's Law summarizes the relationship between current, voltage, and resistance in electrical circuits.

Intrinsic semiconductors, such as silicon, can be converted into N-type semiconductors by doping with phosphorus or into P-type by doping with boron. Doping with boron on one end of a crystal and phosphorous on the other produces a diode which normally permits current flow in only one direction. Zener diodes, however, can withstand the heavy reverse current that flows when the diode is reverse biased sufficiently to rupture the covalent bonds in the crystal. Zener diodes are used to maintain a constant voltage and to prevent excessive voltage in a circuit.

A PNP transistor is formed by doping a base of N-type crystal between an emitter and collector of P-type crystals. A small current in the emitter-base circuit can control a much larger current in the emitter-collector circuit. Transistors of the NPN type are also available, but they are less commonly used in mobile equipment.

Magnets were in use more than two thousand years ago, but it was not until 1819 that the presence of a magnetic field around a current-carrying conductor was discovered. Subsequently, electromagnetism has become the basis for electric motors. The magnetic equivalent of Ohm's Law summarizes the relationship between magnetic flux, magnetomotive force, and reluctance. Iron has much less reluctance than air and can be used to greatly increase the flux in a magnetic circuit. Electromagnetic induction produces a voltage across a conductor, which is moved at right angles to magnetic flux, and is the basis of electric generators.

Chemical energy stored in a battery is used to start the engine or supplement the electrical output of the charging system. Batteries should be stored fully charged to avoid sulfation of the plates and freezing of the electrolyte. A hydrometer is used to check the state of the charge. New batteries can be shipped dry charged to reduce weight and eliminate self-discharging. Maintenance-free batteries have such low loss of electrolyte that replenishment of water is unnecessary. Batteries have a cold cranking rating and a reserve capacity rating. Battery safety requires avoidance of explosion and of contact with the electrolyte. Recycling of worn-out batteries avoids the environmental hazard that could otherwise result from discarding them.

Vehicles have a generator or alternator to supply high electrical demands and to recharge the battery. Generators include a commutator and brushes to produce direct current from the heavy windings that rotate in a magnetic field. Alternators use a rotating field to produce three-phase electric current, which is rectified by diodes. The absence of a commutator and heavy rotating windings allows an alternator to rotate faster, be more compact, and produce more electrical current than a generator. Regulators for generators regulate current and voltage and prevent reverse current discharge. Alternators need only voltage regulation, and most regulators are fully transistorized. Regulators are connected after the field in A-type systems and before the field in B-type systems.

Starting motors crank engines by converting electrical energy into rotational mechanical energy. The energy is delivered in large quantities for short times; the starter must be connected to the battery through a short, large-diameter cable. The solenoid on a starter is a remote-controlled switch that is used to connect or disconnect the starter. A pinion on the starter shaft engages a ring gear on the flywheel for cranking and disengages when the engine starts.

Electrical accessories on modern vehicles include horns, radios, air conditioners, cigarette lighters, lights, and other accessories. Typically, wires to the various accessories are enclosed in a wiring harness. Circuit breakers or fuses are used to protect the wiring and accessories against excessive current. Microcomputers and electronic devices rugged enough to withstand the unfavorable environment near vehicles have been developed and are being used to provide many monitoring and control functions that were not previously possible.

## QUESTIONS

Q7.1     (a) What structural characteristic distinguishes an electrical conductor from an electrical insulator?
(b) Does the application of a voltage across a conductor affect the electron movement? Briefly explain your answer.

Q7.2     What is electrical current as used in common practice, and how does it relate to electron flow?

Q7.3     Why can voltage be called a potential force?

Q7.4     Suppose you had a 100 $\Omega$ resistor and a 200 $\Omega$ resistor.
(a) What could be said about the currents through each resistor and the voltage across each resistor if the resistors were connected in series?

Electrical Systems

(b) What would be the answer to part a if the resistors were connected in parallel?

Q7.5 (a) A capacitor will begin charging when it is connected across a battery or some other voltage source. How long will the capacitor continue charging if it remains connected to the voltage source?

(b) How long will the capacitor remain charged if it is disconnected from the voltage source?

(c) Suppose the capacitor had been charged by a 20,000 V source and then disconnected. Would it be safe to touch the terminals of the capacitor? Why or why not?

Q7.6 (a) What is a hole?
(b) How does hole flow relate to electron flow?

Q7.7 (a) Why is silicon doped with phosphorous called an N-type semiconductor?

(b) If silicon is doped with boron, why is it called a P-type semiconductor?

Q7.8 (a) What device is created when an N-type semiconductor is doped on the same crystal as a P-type semiconductor?

(b) How is the device reverse biased, and how does it respond to reverse biasing?

(c) How is the device forward biased, and how does it respond to forward biasing?

(d) What function does the device serve in a circuit?

Q7.9 (a) What would happen if you continued to increase the reverse biasing across a diode?

(b) How does a zenor diode differ from an ordinary diode?

(c) For what are zener diodes used?

Q7.10 (a) What are the three parts of a transistor called?
(b) What are the two types of transistors, and how do they differ from each other?

(c) What function does a transistor accomplish in a circuit?

Q7.11 (a) Of what is a magnetic field composed?
(b) Describe the shape of the magnetic field around a bar magnet.

Q7.12   What rule governs the attraction and/or repulsion of magnets?

Q7.13   (a) What phenomenon is demonstrated when a compass placed near a current carrying conductor aligns itself perpendicular to the conductor?
(b) With what is the compass needle aligned?

Q7.14   What is accomplished by placing a soft iron core in a coil?

Q7.15   (a) What phenomenon is demonstrated when a conductor is moved through a magnetic field at right angles to the magnetic lines of force?
(b) What changes occur in the conductor?
(c) On what does the magnitude of the effect depend?

Q7.16   (a) How many cells does a 12 V lead-acid storage battery have?
(b) What is sulfation, why is it bad, and how can it be avoided?
(c) Why should batteries be kept at or near full charge in the winter?

Q7.17   (a) What is the cold cranking rating of a battery intended for use in nondiesel engines?
(b) How does the cold cranking rating differ for batteries for diesel engines?
(c) What is the reserve capacity rating of a battery?

Q7.18   (a) What device causes a generator to produce direct current?
(b) How is the magnetic field of a generator created?
(c) What two devices control the generator field, and what is the purpose of each?

Q7.19   (a) What is the major difference between the armature coils that produce the electrical output from a generator and the stator coils that produce the electrical output from an alternator?
(b) What device in an alternator accomplishes the function of a commutator in a generator?
(c) Why is a current regulator not used with an alternator?
(d) Why is a cutout relay not used with an alternator?

Electrical Systems

Q7.20	(a) What are solenoids, and why are they used with electric starters?

(b) After an engine starts, what prevents the engine from driving the starter and keeping it spinning?

# PROBLEMS

P7.1	The filament of a certain light bulb has a resistance of 2 Ω.

(a) How much current will flow through the filaments when the bulb is connected across a 12 V battery?

(b) How much electrical power will be absorbed by the bulb?

P7.2	A tractor has a 12 V battery that delivers 100 A of current to the starter while cranking.

(a) What is the resistance of the starter circuit?

(b) How much power is delivered to the starting circuit?

(c) Suppose the electrical cable between the starter and battery has deteriorated so that the resistance of the cable is 0.05 Ω. What is the voltage drop across the cable when the current is 100 A?

(d) How much voltage is available to run the starter?

P7.3	The frame of tractors and other vehicles ordinarily serves as part of the electrical circuit. One terminal of the battery (called the grounded terminal) is connected to the frame. The nongrounded battery terminal is connected through wires, switches, and so forth to one terminal of lights, starters, and other electrical devices. The other terminal of such devices is connected to the frame to complete the circuit. A short is an unwanted conducting path between some part of the electrical circuit and the frame (or ground). Calculate the resistance that a short would have if it allowed 25 A of current to flow from a 12 V battery to ground. (*Note*: Such a short would completely drain a battery in the time specified as its reserve capacity rating.)

P7.4	The specific gravity of the electrolyte in a battery is 1.210 when measured at 15° C (59° F).

(a) What is the specific gravity corrected to 27° C (80° F)?

(b) According to Table 7.2, what is the state of charge of the battery?

(c) Again according to Table 7.2, what is the freezing point of the electrolyte?

P7.5  Rework P7.4, but assume the specific gravity is 1.230 when measured at 30° C (86° F).

P7.6  Rework P7.4, but assume the specific gravity is 1.100 when measured at 30° C (86° F).

P7.7  If it is read at 20° C (68° F), what should the specific gravity of a battery be when fully charged?

P7.8  (a) If a generator produces 10 V when spinning at 200 rev/min, how many volts would it produce at 3000 rev/min if the field current was not changed?

(b) If the field terminal was disconnected from the regulator and grounded instead, would the field current increase or decrease as the generator speed was increased to 3000 rev/min?

(c) Would the generator output voltage be greater than, equal to, or less that the answer you calculated in part a if the field terminal was grounded and the speed increased from 2000 to 3000 rev/min?

(d) How does the voltage regulator control generator output?

# 8
# Ignition Circuits

## 8.1 INTRODUCTION

Spark-ignited engines require a spark to initiate burning of the air-fuel mixture in the combustion chamber. The spark in each cylinder is provided by a spark plug and is actually a flow of electrical current through the air and fuel vapor between the closely spaced electrodes of the spark plug. The resistance of air is very high. Therefore, a 15,000 to 30,000 V potential across the gap is used to fire the plug. Typically, the ignition system must supply this high voltage from a 12 V storage battery. Moreover, the spark must begin at the proper point in the cycle and must be of sufficient duration.

Ignition systems of various designs have been developed for firing spark plugs. The SAE has developed the following classification for such systems:

1. The Kettering ignition system includes a battery, induction coil, breaker points, and capacitor.
2. The electronic ignition system uses semiconductors for switching.
3. The inductive system stores primary energy in a coil.
4. The capacitive discharge system stores primary energy in a capacitor.

The semiconductor systems have the following additional subclassifications: *breaker triggered*, *breakerless*, and *distributorless*.

Most ignition systems for multicylinder engines use a distributor to distribute secondary voltage for the spark plugs. Distributorless systems avoid the use of a distributor. Such systems will not be discussed in this book.

A magneto can also be used to fire spark plugs. The magneto uses electromagnetic induction as its source of electricity and does not require a battery. Although they have not been installed on new tractors for many years, they continue to be used on small engines.

In this chapter, the principles of mutual induction and the application of mutual induction to several ignition systems will be covered. Capacitive discharge systems will also be introduced.

## 8.2   MUTUAL INDUCTION

Most ignition systems include a coil to transform low voltage in a primary circuit to high voltage in a secondary circuit. The coil works on the principle of *mutual induction*. The principle of mutual induction is illustrated in the simple ignition circuit of Figure 8.1. Two windings are wrapped on the same soft iron core. The primary winding of heavy wire is connected to a battery through breaker points. The secondary winding consists of many turns of fine wire and is connected to a spark gap. When the breaker points are closed, a current flows through the primary winding and creates a magnetic field (as was discussed in Section 7.7). While the magnetic field is changing – that is, while it is increasing from zero to full strength – a voltage is induced in the secondary windings. Thus, mutual induction is the creation of a voltage in a secondary winding by a changing voltage in a primary winding. The magnitude of the voltage induced in the secondary winding depends upon the number of turns of wire in the secondary winding and the rate at which the magnetic field is changing.

Inductive reactance in the primary winding increases the time required for primary current to build from zero to a maximum after the points are closed. The slow increase in primary current causes a corresponding slow increase in the magnetic field, thereby inducing insufficient voltage in the secondary winding to cause a spark across the spark gap. Assuming the breaker points were closed long enough, however, the primary current would become fully established at a magnitude predicted by Ohm's Law (Equation 7.2) as the battery voltage divided by the primary coil resistance. The primary coil would establish a magnetic field, the strength of which would be proportional to the primary current and the number of turns in the primary winding (Equation 7.6).

Assume the breaker points in Figure 8.1 were suddenly opened after the magnetic field was fully established. The primary current would be interrupted suddenly, and the magnetic field would quickly

Ignition Circuits

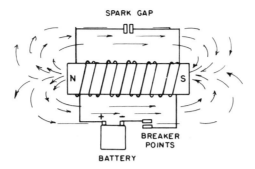

*Figure 8.1–A simple ignition circuit.*

collapse. The rapidly decaying magnetic field would induce a high voltage in the secondary coil. If the turns ratio was high – that is, if the number of turns in the secondary coil was much greater than that in the primary coil – the secondary voltage would be great enough to create a spark across the spark gap. Thus, the mutual inductance of a coil can be used to transform battery voltage into a voltage large enough to cause an arc across a spark gap.

## 8.3  KETTERING IGNITION SYSTEMS

*Kettering ignition systems* were the conventional ignition systems used on tractor and automotive engines for many years. Such systems were named in honor of Charles F. Kettering, a pioneer in the development of electrical systems.

### 8.3.1  System Components
A Kettering ignition system is illustrated in Figure 8.2. It includes a battery, switch, ballast resistor, coil, breaker points, capacitor (also called the condenser), distributor with cap and rotor, and spark plugs. Normally, the breaker points and capacitor are enclosed within the same housing with the rotor. Thus, the cam and the rotor can be driven by the same shaft. The distributor shaft must turn at one-half the crankshaft speed in a four-cycle engine or at the same speed as the crankshaft in a two-cycle engine.

### 8.3.2  System Operation
The Kettering system begins its operation when the ignition switch is closed and the engine is cranked. The cam profile is shaped to allow the points to be closed as long as possible to establish a strong magnetic field in the coil. At the instant when a cam lobe opens the points and the distributor is contacting one of the spark plug

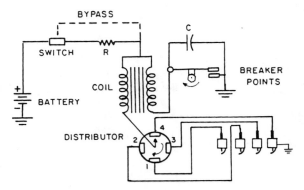

*Figure 8.2–A Kettering ignition system.*

connector towers, the magnetic field begins to collapse and induce a voltage in the secondary winding. The collapsing field also induces a voltage in the primary winding sufficient to cause an arc across the breaker points. However, the capacitor absorbs the induced current and prevents an arc from forming across the points. Thus, most of the energy from the collapsing magnetic field is converted to secondary voltage for firing a spark plug.

A typical cycle of *secondary voltage* is shown in Figure 8.3. A small oscillating voltage is created when the points close, and the points remain closed during the time known as the point dwell period. A very high secondary voltage is induced at the instant the points open, and an electrical current begins to arc across the spark plug gap. The current ionizes the air and reduces its resistance so that the arc can continue to form at a lower voltage. The arc ceases to form when the energy from the collapsing magnetic field has been expended.

The voltage required to fire a spark plug varies with the spark plug gap and with the temperature, pressure, and air to fuel ratio in

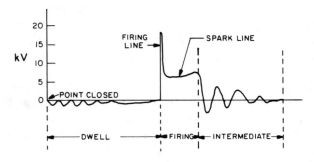

*Figure 8.3–A typical secondary voltage pattern.*

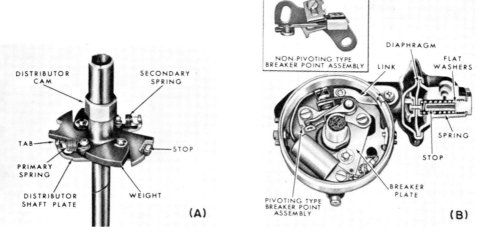

*Figure 8.4–Mechanisms for (a) centrifugal and (b) vacuum advance of the spark. (Courtesy of Ford Motor Company, Tractor Division.)*

the combustion chamber. As little as 3,000 V may be sufficient to fire the plug under ideal conditions, but reserve voltage must be provided to assure reliable firing under less than ideal conditions. A substantial primary current is required. The primary current is large enough to cause the surface of the points to melt and to transfer metal from the grounded to the positive contact. The ballast resistor in Figure 8.2 extends point life by reducing primary current when the engine is running. The switch causes the current to bypass the resistor and provides higher primary current while the engine is being started.

### 8.3.3 Ignition Timing

Correct timing of the spark varies with the engine speed and mixture richness, as was discussed in Section 4.2.2. A centrifugal advance causes the spark to advance to an earlier point in the cycle when the engine speed increases. Hinged weights on the *centrifugal advance* (Figure 8.4a) swing out against spring tension as speed increases. Movement of the weights rotates the cam follower assembly relative to the cam. The centrifugal advance mechanism may advance the timing as much as 30 crankshaft degrees as engine speed increases from low idle to maximum speed. Timing advance is also needed for the lean mixtures that occur when the throttle plate in the carburetor is partially or fully closed. Vacuum in the intake manifold is then high, and a *vacuum advance* (Figure 8.4b) is used to advance the timing. A diaphragm (Figure 8.4b) senses the vacuum transmitted by the vacuum line and works against a compression

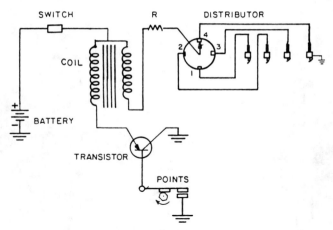

*Figure 8.5–A transistor-assisted Kettering ignition system.*

spring to rotate the rubbing block assembly. If the throttle plate is opened to supply a richer mixture, the vacuum diminishes, and the spring is able to retard the spark timing.

### 8.3.4 System Maintenance

Points in a Kettering ignition system must be replaced periodically. Usually, the capacitor is replaced at the same time. Then, the point gap must be set to the manufacturer's specifications. The point gap of new points can be checked with a feeler gage when the cam follower is riding on the nose of one of the cam lobes. After the point gap is set, the ignition must be timed to the manufacturer's specifications. The timing can be changed by loosening a clamp and rotating the entire distributor assembly. Some manufacturers require that the vacuum line be disconnected to disable the vacuum advance when the engine is being timed. Then, the engine is run at a specified speed to provide a specified amount of centrifugal advance. A timing light is used to illuminate the timing marks on the flywheel each time the spark plug fires in the No. 1 cylinder. The distributor is rotated until the spark plug fires at a specified number of degrees before HDC. The clamp is then tightened to prevent further rotation of the distributor.

## 8.4 TRANSISTOR-ASSISTED KETTERING IGNITION SYSTEMS

A transistor is able to react quickly in interrupting a circuit carrying a relatively high current. Thus, it is an ideal replacement for the points and condensor in a Kettering ignition system. Figure 8.5

# Ignition Circuits 213

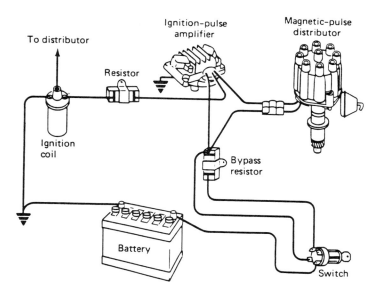

*Figure 8.6–An electronic ignition system. (Courtesy of Delco-Remy, Division of General Motors Corporation.)*

shows a transistor-assisted Kettering system. Breaker points are used to trigger the spark, but the points carry only the tiny base current of the transistor. Thus, point life is greatly extended. Since larger primary currents are used to increase secondary voltage, the coil must be designed to handle the larger primary current. Otherwise, the transistor-assisted system is just like the ordinary Kettering system.

## 8.5 INDUCTIVE-TYPE ELECTRONIC IGNITION SYSTEMS

Designs of *inductive-type electronic ignition systems* vary among manufacturers, but the principle of operation of all such systems is similar. A noncontacting rotating device is used to trigger one or more transistors to interrupt the primary current. One such system is shown in Figure 8.6. The distributor and coil are similar in outward appearance to those in the Kettering ignition system, but they differ in internal design. Coils for the electronic ignition systems are designed to handle higher primary current and secondary voltage than are those designed for the Kettering ignition system. Internal working parts of the distributor also differ considerably between the two systems.

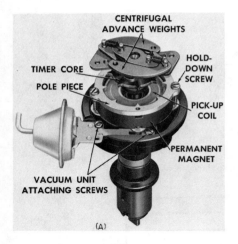 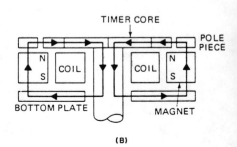

*Figure 8.7–A distributor (including a reluctor) for electronic ignition system. (Courtesy of Delco-Remy, Division of General Motors Corporation.)*

### 8.5.1 System Components

Figure 8.7a shows the internal working parts of the distributor in Figure 8.6. There are no breaker points; rather, an iron timer gear rotates with the distributor shaft. The timer gear has one tooth for every cylinder in the engine and rotates near a permanent magnet. Each time a tooth comes into close proximity to a pole piece on the magnet, the reluctance of the magnetic path decreases. A magnetic field is established through the pick-up coil surrounding the distributor shaft. As the teeth separate from the pole pieces with continued shaft rotation, the magnetic field collapses and induces a voltage pulse in the pick-up coil. The voltage pulse triggers the *ignition-pulse amplifier* to interrupt current flow in the primary winding of the ignition coil.

### 8.5.2 Pulse Amplifier Operation

Details of the ignition-pulse amplifier are shown in Figure 8.8. The pick-up coil is inactive in Figure 8.8a. Battery current is being delivered through ballast resistor $R_7$ and resistor $R_1$ to the emitter of transistor $TR_2$. Current flow continues through the emitter-base junction of $TR_2$ and through resistor $R_2$ to the ground. Thus, $TR_2$ turns on and conducts emitter-collector current through resistor $R_5$ to the ground. The increased current flow through $TR_2$ causes a voltage drop across resistor $R_1$ sufficient to bias the base of transistor $TR_1$ negative relative to its emitter. $TR_1$ then turns on and conducts primary current through resistor $R_8$ to the ignition coil. Thus, Figure 8.8a shows the part of the cycle when the magnetic field is being established in the ignition coil.

# Ignition Circuits

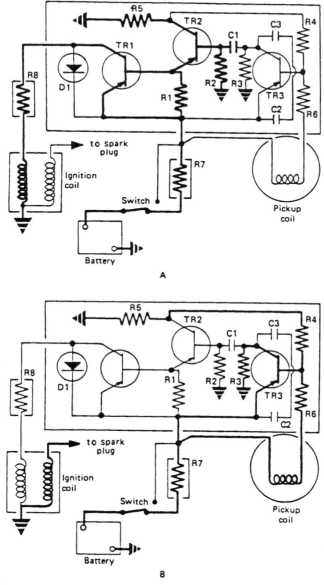

*Figure 8.8–A circuit diagram of a pulse amplifier in an electronic ignition system. (Courtesy of Delco-Remy, Division of General Motors Corporation.)*

Figure 8.8b shows the pick-up coil triggering a collapse of the magnetic field. The voltage pulse from the pick-up coil biases the base of transistor $TR_3$ negative relative to the emitter. When $TR_3$

conducts current through resistor $R_3$, transistor $TR_2$ turns off and, in turn, shuts off transistor $TR_1$. With primary current interrupted, the magnetic field in the ignition coil quickly collapses and induces a large secondary voltage in the ignition coil. The secondary voltage is directed to the magnetic-pulse distributor shown in Figure 8.6 and on to the proper spark plug.

### 8.5.3 Ignition Timing

The ignition system shown in Figures 8.6 and 8.7 has the conventional centrifugal advance and vacuum mechanisms. However, it has no breaker points to wear out and replace. The distributor must be correctly timed as explained in Section 8.3. The ignition-pulse amplifier is a sealed unit that cannot be repaired. If it fails, if must be replaced.

## 8.6 INTEGRATED ELECTRONIC IGNITION SYSTEMS

The use of semiconductors has permitted the miniaturization of ignition devices. The ignition system in Figure 8.9 has all components (including the coil) located inside the distributor housing. Thus, the only wires needed are a primary wire from the battery and spark plug wires to the individual cylinders. The system produces up to 35,000 V of secondary voltage and, thus, must use special spark plugs with extra-wide spark gaps.

## 8.7 MAGNETO IGNITION SYSTEMS

Magneto ignition systems do not require the use of a battery. They were used on early farm tractors that did not have an electrical system and are still used on small gasoline engines. The development of solid-state electronic devices has permitted the current magnetos to be simpler and more compact than the earlier magnetos used on farm tractors. The electronic devices have eliminated the need for the breaker points that were included in the earlier magnetos.

### 8.7.1 System Components

A modern magneto is shown in Figure 8.10. Two permanent magnets, a small one that works with the trigger coil and a larger one that works with the ignition coil, are cast into the flywheel. The trigger coil eliminates the need for the breaker-point assembly that was used in earlier, single-coil magneto systems. Two coils of insulated wire are wrapped on post B (the center post) of the ignition

Ignition Circuits

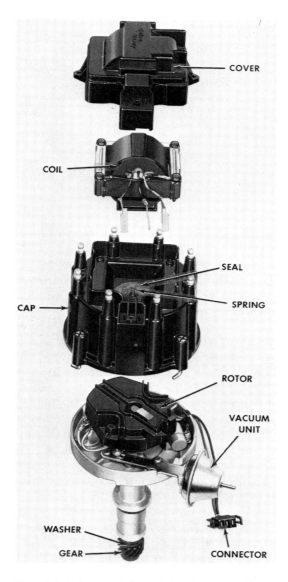

*Figure 8.9–An integrated electronic ignition system. (Courtesy of Delco-Remy, Division of General Motors Corporation.)*

coil assembly. The primary wire is grounded on one side of the coil; on the other side, the primary wire is connected to a condenser (capacitor), a diode, and an SCR (silicon-controlled rectifier) which serves as a GCS (gate-controlled switch). The secondary wire, which has many more turns than the primary, is grounded on one side of the coil; on the other side, the secondary wire is connected to the

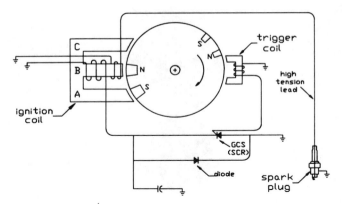

*Figure 8.10–A solid-state magneto ignition system for small engines.*

spark plug. One side of the trigger coil is connected to the GCS and the diode, while the other side is grounded. The trigger coil reacts to the small magnets in triggering an ignition pulse. The flywheel rotates clockwise in Figure 8.10.

## 8.7.2 System Operation

As the flywheel rotates, an ignition cycle begins when the larger magnet aligns with posts A and B of the ignition coil assembly. Magnetic flux "flows" out of the N pole, through posts B and A, and back into the S pole of the magnet. As the magnetic field is established, voltages are induced across the primary and secondary coils. The secondary voltage is not large enough to fire the spark plug. However, the primary voltage generates a primary current through the diode to ground. The primary current cannot flow through the GCS until it is triggered by the trigger coil.

The flywheel continues to turn until the larger magnet is aligned with posts B and C of the ignition coil assembly. Magnetic flux now "flows" out of the N pole, through posts C and B, and back into the S pole. Note that as the larger magnets leave posts A and B and move to B and C, the flux through the center post reverses in direction thus causing the primary current to reverse in direction. The reversed primary current is not able to flow through the diode. However, at the same instant that the larger magnet is aligned with posts B and C of the ignition coil assembly, the smaller magnet aligns with the trigger coil. The trigger coil induces a trigger current that opens the GCS, allowing the reversed primary current to flow through to ground.

With continued movement of the flywheel, the trigger magnet moves out of alignment. The trigger current falls, causing the GCS to close and interrupt the path of the reversed primary current to ground. The reversed primary current flows into the condenser until the condenser is fully charged and then stops abruptly. The sudden drop in primary current causes a rapid collapse of the magnetic field through the primary coil; at that instant, the condenser discharges through the primary coil to cause an even more rapid collapse of the magnetic field.

As the magnetic field in the primary coil collapses suddenly, a large voltage is induced in the secondary winding of the ignition coil, causing the spark plug to fire. The ignition cycle is then completed. The cycle repeats once for each revolution of the flywheel. Thus, in a single-cylinder, four-cycle engine, the spark plug fires twice per engine cycle. The unneeded firing occurs before HDC in the exhaust stroke and causes no difficulty.

### 8.7.3 System Performance

The simplicity of the system and the absence of breaker points allows the magneto system to function with little maintenance. The spark plug is subject to normal erosion and must be replaced when too badly eroded. The ignition module is hermetically sealed to exclude moisture and dust. The system produces a high voltage with rapid rise time, which provides easier starting, even when the spark plug is fouled or the engine is flooded.

## 8.8 CAPACITIVE DISCHARGE IGNITION SYSTEMS

All ignition systems store energy between spark plug firings and then release the energy quickly to fire a spark plug. A common feature of all previously discussed ignition systems was that the energy was stored in the magnetic field of an ignition coil. Interruption of the primary current provided rapid breakdown of the field and quick delivery of the stored energy to fire a spark plug. The *capacitive discharge system* differs from previous systems in that the energy accumulated between spark plug firings is stored in a capacitor. Battery-powered systems are used for large, multi-cylinder engines. Systems without batteries are used for small, single-cylinder engines.

### 8.8.1 Battery-Powered Systems

A diagram of a battery-powered capacitive discharge ignition system is shown in Figure 8.11. The power circuit consists of a transistorized oscillator that increases battery voltage to 250 V to 350 V of direct current. Between spark plug firings, the power circuit charges the storage capacitor. The timing circuit in Figure 8.11 could

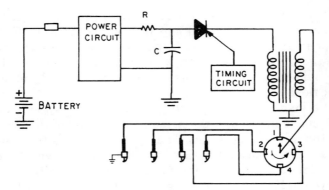

*Figure 8.11–A capacitive-discharge ignition system.*

be either mechanical breaker points or a pick-up coil. When a spark plug is to be fired, the timing circuit turns on a SCS (silicon control switch), and the capacitor quickly discharges into the primary winding of a pulse transformer. The large burst of current from the capacitor creates a strong, fast-rising voltage in the secondary winding. The spark plug fires when the magnetic field is rising, not when it is collapsing, as in other ignition systems. The capacitive discharge system permits the spark plug voltage to rise three to ten times faster than it can in inductive ignition systems. The fast rate of rise reduces charge leakage in the secondary circuit and therefore is beneficial in firing partially fouled spark plugs. Spark plug life also is increased because less total energy is needed to fire the plugs in fast-rise systems.

### 8.8.2  Capacitive Discharge Systems for Small Engines

The capacitive-discharge ignition system shown in Figure 8.12 is similar to the magneto system of Figure 8.10 in that it is intended for use on small engines. Neither system requires a battery. The same pattern of magnets is used on the flywheels of both systems. However, the wiring and the operation of the two systems differ considerably.

Unlike the ignition coil assembly of Figure 8.10, the charge coil assembly of Figure 8.12 contains only one coil. The charge coil works with the larger flywheel magnet to generate electrical current. The capacitor stores the electrical energy before it is discharged through the spark plug. A separate ignition coil increases the voltage before it is delivered to the spark plug. The capacitive-discharge system also includes four diodes arranged into a rectifier bridge to allow continued current flow to the capacitor when the charge coil current reverses in direction. The GCS permits primary current to flow to the

# Ignition Circuits

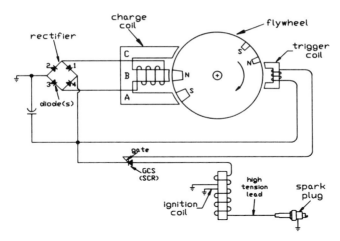

Figure 8.12–A capacitive-discharge ignition system for small engines.

ignition coil in response to signals from the trigger coil. The flywheel in Figure 8.12 rotates clockwise.

An ignition cycle begins as the larger magnet moves into alignment with posts A and B of the charge coil assembly. The magnetic flux through post B induces a voltage difference across the charge coil. With continued flywheel rotation, the larger magnet moves into alignment with posts B and C of the charge coil assembly reversing the flux direction and the voltage polarity across the coil. Although the voltage polarity reverses, the diode bridge always keeps the lower plate of the capacitor connected to the positive end of the charge coil. When the right end of the coil is positive, diodes 1 and 3 connect the coil across the capacitor while diodes 2 and 4 are blocked. When the left end of the charge coil is positive, diodes 2 and 4 are active while 1 and 3 are blocked. While the capacitor is being charged, the GCS prevents it from discharging through the primary winding on the ignition coil.

As the same time that the larger magnet aligns with posts B and C of the charge coil assembly, the smaller magnet aligns with the trigger coil. The voltage induced across the trigger coil causes the GCS to open, allowing the capacitor to discharge through the primary (top) winding of the ignition coil. The secondary winding on the ignition coil contains many more turns than the primary winding, thus greatly increasing the voltage from approximately 300 volts across the primary winding to approximately 30,000 V across the secondary winding. The large secondary voltage causes the spark plug to fire, thus completing the ignition cycle.

Note that the ignition cycle repeats each time the larger magnets approach the charge coil assembly, that is, once for each revolution of

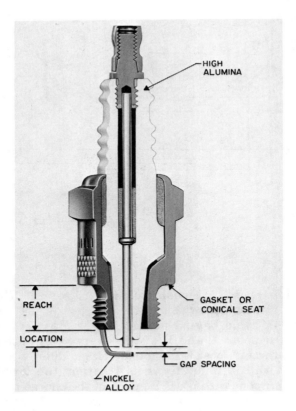

*Figure 8.13–Construction of a spark plug. (Courtesy of Champion Spark Plug Company.)*

the flywheel. Thus, in a single-cylinder, four-cycle engine, the spark plug fires twice as often as required. However, the unneeded firing occurs as the piston approaches HDC on the exhaust stroke and causes no difficulty.

## 8.9 SPARK PLUGS

A *spark plug* converts the secondary voltage from an ignition system into an arc across the electrode gap. Construction of a spark plug is illustrated in Figure 8.13. The steel outer shell of the spark plug is threaded so that it can be screwed into a tapped hole in the head of the engine. A metal gasket is used to seal in the combustion gases. Some spark plugs are designed with a conical seat for sealing and do not require a gasket. A ground electrode is attached to the lower part of the shell. The ground electrode is bent to form a parallel gap with the center electrode.

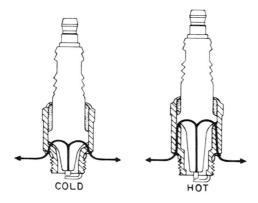

Figure 8.14–Heat ranges of a spark plug. (Courtesy of Champion Spark Plug Company.)

The center electrode is made of a nickel, chromium, or tungsten alloy to provide the required electrical and thermal conductivity and to withstand extremely high temperatures and erosive current discharges. The center electrode is insulated from the shell and therefore runs much hotter than the ground electrode. High temperature facilitates electron ejection, and therefore the ignition system is designed to produce negative polarity at the center electrode. Reversing the primary leads at the coil to produce positive voltage at the spark plug would increase the voltage requirement at the plug by about 30%.

A porcelain insulator separates the center electrode from the steel shell. The insulator must prevent leakage of the high secondary voltage to the steel shell and must also withstand the high pressures and temperatures from the combustion chamber.

The *reach* of the spark plug (Figure 8.13) must be compatible with the design of the cylinder head. The electrodes must extend into the combustion chamber, but spark plugs with excessive reach would be hit and damaged by the piston. Reaches vary from approximately 10 to 20 mm (0.4 to 0.8 in.). The diameter of the threaded end of the shell determines the size of a spark plug. Typical metric sizes are 10, 12, 14, 16, and 18 mm.

The *heat range* of a spark plug is determined by the distance heat must travel before escaping to the spark plug shell. Figure 8.14 illustrates a cold plug and a hot plug, but there are other spark plugs available with intermediate heat ranges. Manufacturers specify spark plugs that have heat ranges appropriate for their engines. Use of excessively cold plugs promotes sluggish combustion and spark plug fouling. Use of excessively hot plugs leads to preignition and rapid erosion of the electrodes. The heat range is affected by the reach of a spark plug; long-reach spark plugs run hotter, and short-reach plugs run colder.

Spark plugs must be replaced periodically. The electrodes erode with continued use, and the porcelain insulator can become glazed and allow shorting to the steel shell. When new spark plugs are installed, the *electrode gap* must be adjusted to the specifications of the engine manufacturer. If the gap is too narrow, the spark will be weak and cause fouling and misfiring. If the gap is too wide, the secondary voltage may not be high enough to produce a spark at high speeds and the engine will misfire. Typical spark gaps are in the range 0.5 to 1.0 mm (0.020 to 0.040 in.). The gap can be measured with a feeler gage.

## 8.10 MICROPROCESSOR-CONTROLLED SPARK-IGNITION SYSTEMS

Semiconductors have brought great improvement to spark-ignition systems. Microprocessors integrated into ignition systems have brought even greater improvements. A variety of sensors are used to feed information into a microprocessor. For example, an oxygen sensor sensing oxygen in the exhaust provides information about the air to fuel ratio of the engine. Other sensors can measure engine speed and pressure and temperature in the combustion chamber. A microprocessor is programmed to use the relevant information to calculate and set the optimum timing of the spark. Centrifugal and vacuum advances provided only two sources of information for regulating an ignition system. A microprocessor allows regulation to be based on much more information.

## 8.11 SUMMARY

A 15,000 to 30,000 V potential is needed to produce an arc across a spark-plug gap and ignite the air to fuel mixture of spark-ignited engines. Most ignition systems are inductive. That is, they use mutual induction and a collapsing magnetic field to supply the required voltage from a 12 V storage battery.

Conventional Kettering ignition systems are inductive. They store energy by establishing a magnetic field in the primary windings of a coil while the points are closed. Opening the points collapses the field, thereby inducing a sufficiently high voltage in the secondary winding of the coil to fire a spark plug. A capacitor is connected across the points to prevent an arc from forming across the points when they open.

# Ignition Circuits

A transistor-assisted Kettering system increases point life by using a transistor to interrupt primary current. The points switch only the tiny base current when triggering the transistor. The inductive-type electronic ignition system goes one step further by eliminating the points completely. A pulse amplifier switches the primary current when triggered by a rotating timer gear and pick-up coil.

Magneto ignition systems do not require a battery and are therefore the preferred spark-ignition system on small engines. Modern magneto systems do not require breaker points. One magnet imbedded in the flywheel works with an ignition coil assembly to generate the required secondary voltage. A smaller magnet works with a trigger coil to control the timing of the spark.

The capacitive discharge system differs from inductive systems in that energy is stored by charging a capacitor between spark plug firings. When triggered by a timing circuit, the capacitor quickly discharges into a pulse amplifier and fires the spark plug while the magnetic field is rising. The capacitive discharge system produces three to ten times greater spark plug voltage than do inductive systems.

A capacitive-discharge system that does not require a battery is available for use on small engines. It is similar to the magneto system in employing two magnets imbedded in the flywheel. However, the circuitry and operation differs considerably from the magneto system.

Most ignition systems for multicylinder engines include a distributor to deliver the high secondary voltage to the spark plugs in the proper order. The set of points or the breakless timing mechanism is housed within the distributor. In integrated electronic ignition systems, all components, including the coil, are housed in the distributor.

The spark must be timed properly for all engine speeds and loads. A centrifugal advance mechanism rotates the cam follower assembly relative to the cam to increase spark advance with engine speed. When the mixture is lean and more spark advance is needed, a diaphragm uses the increased vacuum in the intake manifold to advance the spark. Mechanics time the spark by rotating the distributor housing while using a timing light to illuminate timing marks on the flywheel, typically when the no. 1 spark plug fires. The housing is clamped in place when the timing is correct. Microprocessors permit automatic optimum spark timing in response to many measured engine variables.

Spark plugs are specially constructed to provide a spark at high voltages and temperatures. Misfiring can occur if the electrode gap is either too wide or too narrow. Spark plug heat range is determined by the distance heat must travel before escaping to the metal shell. Preignition and rapid electrode erosion occur if the spark plugs are too hot. Sluggish combustion and electrode firing are the result if the spark plugs are too cold.

## QUESTIONS

Q8.1 (a) In a Kettering system, does the spark occur at the instant the points begin closing or when they begin opening?
(b) What is the reason for this design choice?
(c) Why doesn't the current arc across the points as well as across the spark plug?

Q8.2 (a) What is the purpose of a ballast resistor?
(b) Is the ballast resistor always active in the ignition circuit? Briefly explain your answer.

Q8.3 (a) Why do ignition systems have a centrifugal advance?
(b) Why do they have a vacuum advance?

Q8.4 (a) At what part of the cam must the rubbing block be positioned when the point gap is being set?
(b) Why is it necessary to run the engine at a specified speed when setting the timing?

Q8.5 (a) Why is a capacitor not needed in a transistor-assisted Kettering ignition system?
(b) Can the same type of coil be used for both transistor-assisted Kettering systems and ordinary Kettering systems? Briefly explain your answer.

Q8.6 (a) What parts of a Kettering ignition system are not used in an inductive-type electronic ignition system?
(b) What parts of the latter system replace those missing parts?
(c) How do the coils for the two systems compare?

Q8.7 (a) Why is a magneto ignition system used on small engines rather than a conventional Kettering system?
(b) What is the purpose of the diode bridge in a magneto ignition system?

# Ignition Circuits

(c) What is a GCS and what is its purpose in the magneto?

Q8.8 What are the three major differences between a capacitor discharge ignition system and a Kettering system?

Q8.9 What part of an ignition system is used in multicylinder engines but is not needed in single-cylinder engines?

Q8.10 In a capactive-discharge system for small engines, how does the function of the capacitor differ from that of the capacitor in a magneto system?

Q8.11 Does it matter whether the center electrode of a spark plug has negative or positive polarity? Briefly explain your answer.

Q8.12 (a) What are typical spark plug sizes?
(b) To what dimension on a spark plug does the size refer?

Q8.13 (a) What determines the heat range of a spark plug?
(b) Why is it important to use spark plugs with the correct heat range?

Q8.14 Why is it important to set the gap to the correct distance when new spark plugs are installed?

## PROBLEMS

P8.1 Assume the voltage pattern in Figure 8.3 is for a four-cycle six-cylinder engine. That is, that pattern repeats six times during each revolution of the distributor shaft. Notice that the dwell time (when the points are closed) is about half the time for one full pattern. Assume the engine is running at 2400 rev/min.
(a) Calculate the speed of the distributor shaft.
(b) Calculate the length of time the points are closed.

P8.2 Rework P8.1, but assume the speed is 4000 rev/min.

P8.3 Rework P8.1, but assume the engine has four cylinders

P8.4 Rework P8.1, but assume the engine has eight cylinders

P8.5　　Spark advance usually is specified in crankshaft degrees. If the spark advance on a four-cycle engine is set a 15° before HDC and you wish to change it to 20° before HDC, how far must the distributor be rotated?

P8.6　　Rework P8.5, but assume the engine is a two-cycle engine.

# 9
# Fuel Systems and Carburetion

## 9.1 INTRODUCTION

All liquid-fueled engines have a tank for storing fuel, a method for transferring the fuel to the engine, and one or more filters to remove contaminants from the fuel. The remaining parts of the fuel system vary according to engine type. The fuel-injector systems used on diesel engines are discussed in Chapter 10. In this chapter, you will study the mixture requirements of a carbureted engine, the basic principles of carburetion, and the various types of carburetors. You will also learn about the electronic fuel injection (EFI) systems that have replaced carburetors on multicylinder gasoline engines.

## 9.2 FUEL TANKS, PUMPS, AND FILTERS

A *fuel tank* usually is made of sheet metal and is shaped to store as much volume as possible without being obtrusive. Typically, the filler cap is ventilated to allow air to enter when fuel is withdrawn. A blocked vent cap can cause the tank to collapse under atmospheric pressure as fuel is withdrawn. The inlet of the fuel draw-off tube is positioned a short distance above the bottom of the tank to avoid water and sediment that may be at the bottom. A drain cock usually is located at the bottom of the tank to allow water and sediment to be drained periodically.

In many early tractors, automobiles and trucks, the fuel tank was mounted above the engine so that fuel could flow to the carburetor by gravity. With the introduction of large engines and fuel tanks, it became inconvenient to mount the tank above the engine.

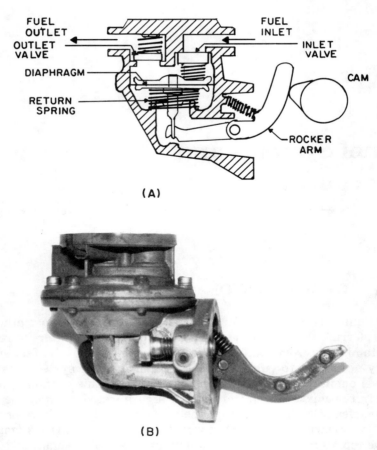

Figure 9.1–A fuel transfer pump, shown in (a) a schematic diagram and (b) a photograph.

Part or all of the fuel tank may be mounted at a lower elevation than the engine on modern vehicles, and a fuel pump is needed to transfer the fuel to the engine. A cam-driven *fuel transfer pump* is shown in Figure 9.1. The pump is mounted with the rocker arm protruding into the engine so that it can be operated by a lobe on the camshaft. A diaphragm in the pump is pulled down against spring pressure when the cam pushes the rocker arm. The spring-loaded outlet valve closes as the diaphragm descends, and a partial vacuum is created in the pump. Atmospheric pressure then pushes fuel from the tank through the fuel lines and inlet valve and into the pump to relieve the vacuum. As the cam rotates farther and releases the rocker arm, the spring is free to push the diaphragm upward. The inlet valve then closes, and the outlet valve opens to allow fuel to flow toward

Fuel Systems and Carburetion

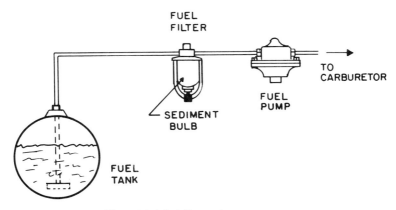

*Figure 9.2–A fuel filter with sediment bulb.*

the engine. The diaphragm pump automatically matches its delivery to the demand of the engine. If the engine is not accepting fuel, the spring cannot force the diaphragm upward, and pumping ceases.

Two different types of electrical fuel pumps are available. In the plunger type, an electromagnet moves the plunger against spring pressure to force fuel through an outlet valve into the outlet line. During the pumping stroke, an inlet valve prevents the fuel from returning to the inlet line. When the electromagnet is turned off at the end of the stroke, the spring returns the plunger to its original position. As the spring moves the plunger, fuel flows from the supply line into the pump through the inlet valve. During the return stroke, the spring-loaded outlet valve prevents fuel in the outlet line from returning to the pump. The plunger-type electrical pump includes a transistor to turn the electromagnet on at the beginning of each pumping stroke and off at the end of each pumping stroke. The plunger-type electrical fuel pump is used in situations in which it is inconvenient to use a cam-operated fuel pump.

A rotary fuel pump driven by an DC electric motor is used with electronic fuel injection systems. The rotary pump can produce the higher pressures that are needed for the injection nozzles and cannot be supplied by the cam-operated or plunger-type fuel pumps.

*Fuel filters* are used to remove particles that could harm the fuel system. Figure 9.2 shows a fuel filter mounted between the fuel tank and the fuel pump. Particles settle to the bottom of the sediment bulb. The sediment bulb is transparent and can be removed for periodic cleaning when sediment has accumulated. A fine porous filter may be located between the fuel pump and carburetor to provide final cleaning of the fuel.

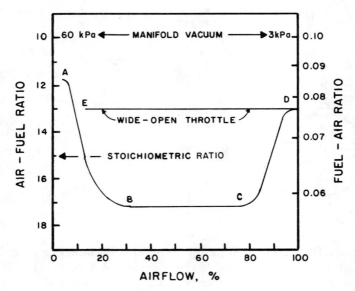

*Figure 9.3–Mixture requirements of a carbureted gasoline engine.*

## 9.3  MIXTURE REQUIREMENTS OF A SPARK-IGNITION ENGINE

The stoichiometric air to fuel ratio for gasoline is approximately 15:1, as was discussed in Chapter 6. The actual mixture requirements of an engine may vary above or below a 15:1 air to fuel ratio, as Figure 9.3 shows. The engine is idling at point A; it has no load, and the throttle is nearly closed to control the engine speed. Not much air or fuel is entering the engine, and residual exhaust gases (see Section 4.2.1) can dilute the mixture enough to cause poor combustion and rough idling. Therefore, the mixture should be enriched about 25% at point A to offset the effects of exhaust gas dilution. The mixture can become increasingly leaner from point A to point B as the throttle is opened and more air-fuel mixture is delivered to provide more power.

The effects of exhaust gas dilution have been overcome at point B in Figure 9.3. The mixture is kept lean between points B and C; excess air is supplied to ensure more complete combustion of the fuel. Maximum power is not needed from the engine, and maximum fuel economy is the goal.

The engine is approaching maximum power between points C and D in Figure 9.3. The throttle is nearly wide open to provide maximum airflow, and excess fuel is supplied to assure full use of the air. If the engine has a governor, point D would be the governor's maximum (see Section 5.8.2). The engine speed is controlled by the

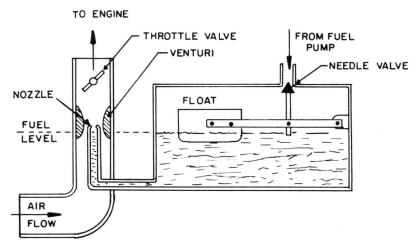

*Figure 9.4–A simple carburetor.*

load between points D and E; the throttle is wide open, and excess fuel is provided to produce as much torque as possible.

The air-fuel mixture requirements in Figure 9.3 are a goal that carburetor designers try to achieve. Several systems, (for example, idle, economizer, and load systems) are used in float-type carburetors to try to achieve a mixture pattern similar to the one represented in this figure.

## 9.4  PRINCIPLES OF A SIMPLE FLOAT-TYPE CARBURETOR

A simple float-type carburetor is shown in Figure 9.4. Fuel is supplied to the *float chamber* by gravity or by a fuel pump. The float operates a valve and regulates fuel delivery at a rate sufficient to maintain the proper depth of fuel in the float chamber. Airflow through the carburetor is initiated when a piston descends on the intake stroke and creates a partial vacuum in the combustion chamber. Atmospheric pressure pushes air through the air cleaner, carburetor, and intake manifold to relieve the vacuum in the combustion chamber. The *venturi* works on the Bernoulli principle which, in the absence of energy losses, states that the sum of the elevation, pressure and kinetic energies is constant. Elevation differences are negligible in the carburetor, and so the sum of the pressure and kinetic energies is the same in the venturi as in the area ahead of the venturi. As the venturi constricts the air flowing through the carburetor and forces it to flow faster, the air gains kinetic energy at the expense of pressure (potential) energy. Thus, constricting the airflow causes a low-pressure area to form at the center of the venturi. Because pressure is higher in the float chamber than in the venturi, fuel flows through the nozzle and sprays into the venturi. The *throttle plate* can be used to control the airflow rate through the carburetor and, at the same time, control the rate at which fuel is sprayed into the venturi. The throttle position is controlled by a flyweight governor (see Section 5.8) in tractor engines. In an ungoverned engine, it is controlled by the operator pressing on an accelerator pedal or by the cruise control if the vehicle is so equipped.

The bowl (float chamber) must be vented to allow air to escape as more fuel is pumped into the bowl and to allow air to enter as fuel is withdrawn. Venting to the atmosphere is undesirable because the fuel delivery rate through the nozzle depends on the pressure difference between the bowl and the venturi. For example, if the bowl was vented to the atmosphere and the air cleaner became partially blocked, a stronger vacuum would occur in the venturi, and the mixture would become too rich. Therefore, the bowl is vented to the air inlet of the carburetor so that pressure changes in the incoming air will be transmitted to both the venturi and the bowl.

A simple carburetor has limitations that would prevent it from giving satisfactory performance in an engine. These limitations, and the systems that overcome them, are discussed in Section 9.6.

## 9.5  CARBURETOR DRAFT

*Carburetor draft* refers to the direction the air is flowing when it passes through the venturi. All carburetors are designed with one of the three possible draft arrangements: *updraft*, *downdraft*, or *side draft*.

The carburetor in Figure 9.4 is an updraft carburetor and would be mounted below the intake manifold. The downdraft carburetor shown in Figure 9.5 would be mounted above the intake manifold. Small, single-cylinder engines do not need an intake manifold, and a side draft carburetor can discharge directly into the intake port on the head.

Selection of updraft or downdraft design relates to the type of engine enclosure. Automotive engines are serviced by opening a hood above the engine, and the use of the downdraft design makes the carburetor very accessible. Tractor engine enclosures are open at the sides, making the updraft carburetor more accessible. No one of the carburetor draft arrangements provides inherently better

Fuel Systems and Carburetion

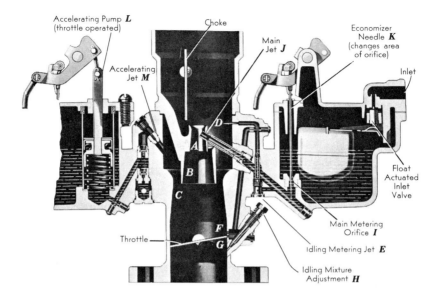

Figure 9.5–A downdraft carburetor. (Courtesy of General Motors Corporation.)

performance than the others. However, throats of updraft carburetors are made smaller so that the air velocity through the carburetor will be great enough to lift the fuel droplets into the intake manifold against the force of gravity. Downdraft carburetors are therefore preferred for high-performance engines so that the carburetor throat can be larger and provide less restriction to airflow.

## 9.6 CARBURETORS FOR MULTICYLINDER ENGINES

A carburetor for multicylinder engines includes a starting, idling, load, economizer, and accelerating system.

### 9.6.1 Starting System
An engine will start during cranking only if a combustible mixture of air and fuel vapor is present in the combustion chamber. If the engine is cold, too little fuel may vaporize to form a combustible mixture. The function of the *choke* (Figure 9.6) is to temporarily enrich the mixture until the engine is started and warm. The curves in Figure 6.8 and the top curve in Figure 9.7 were produced by using the standard ASTM test for the distillation of fuels. A curve of the *equilibrium air distillation* (EAD) shows the temperatures at

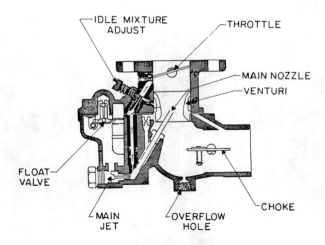

*Figure 9.6–An updraft carburetor.*

which fuel evaporates when mixed with air and is more representative of conditions in an intake manifold. For the gasoline whose EAD curve is shown in Figure 9.7, only 20% is vaporized at a temperature of -20° C (-4° F) and choking is required.

The choke enriches the mixture by reducing air delivery to the engine and by creating a strong vacuum in the venturi so that the nozzle sprays fuel at a higher rate. Some chokes (see Figure 9.6) have a spring-loaded relief valve that can open when the engine starts and pass enough air to prevent an over-rich mixture. The operation of a choke is illustrated in Example Problem 9.1.

## Example Problem 9.1

The leanest and richest combustible mixtures have air to fuel ratios of approximately 20:1 and 8:1, respectively. If the ambient temperature allows only 10% of the fuel to vaporize in the manifold, what air to fuel ratio must the carburetor deliver to start the engine? If the choke is not opened, will the engine continue to run after it is warm?

**Solution:** Solving this problem requires use of fuel to air ratios, which are just the inverse of air to fuel ratios. Since the leanest combustible mixture has an air to fuel ratio of 20:1, the fuel to air (F/A) ratio is as follows:

Fuel Systems and Carburetion

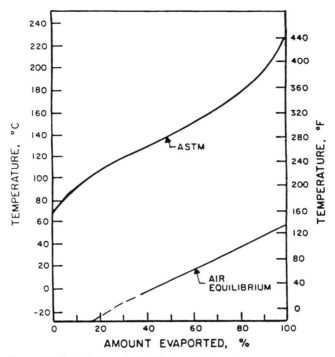

*Figure 9.7–Equilibrium air distillation (EAD) and ASTM distillation curves for gasoline. (Data from T. S. Sligh, Jr., Volatility tests for automotive fuels, SAE Journal 19(2):151-61. August 1926.)*

Let X be the fuel to air ratio supplied by the carburetor. Then, because only 10% of the fuel evaporates:

$$F/A = \frac{0.1X}{1} = \frac{0.05}{1}$$

and

$$X = 0.5$$

Therefore, the carburetor must supply a fuel to air ratio of 0.5, or an air to fuel ratio of 2:1, to start the engine. As the engine becomes warm enough to vaporize nearly all of the fuel, notice that the air to fuel ratio of 2:1 would be much richer than the richest combustible mixture of 8:1. Therefore, the choke must be opened as the engine warms up, or the engine will stall.

Chokes on most tractor engines are operated manually, but carbureted automotive and truck engines have *automatic chokes* (Figure 9.8). The linkage closes the choke when the driver fully depresses and then releases the accelerator pedal (not shown). The

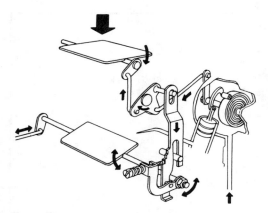

*Figure 9.8–An automatic choke. (Courtesy of Deere & Company.)*

choke is held closed by the thermostatic coil spring. When the engine starts, vacuum from the intake manifold acts on the small vacuum piston and partially opens the choke. Air heated by the exhaust manifold is transmitted through a small tube to the thermostatic spring. As the engine warms up, the spring gradually unwinds and opens the choke.

### 9.6.2 Idling System

At engine low idle, the throttle is nearly closed to control the idling speed and not enough vacuum forms in the venturi for fuel to be forced from the bowl through the nozzle. Therefore, a separate *idling system* must be provided. In the idling system of Figure 9.6, fuel can travel upward through the idle fuel pickup passage and the idle jet to a small hole near the throttle plate. A strong vacuum from the engine is exerted on the *idle jet* when the throttle is closed, and fuel flows through the jet and the small hole to supply the engine. The idle *adjusting needle* controls the vacuum on the idle jet, and therefore the richness of the idle mixture, by regulating the amount of air coming from behind the venturi. The idling system for a downdraft carburetor (lower part of Figure 9.5) operates on the same principle as the idling system in an updraft carburetor.

### 9.6.3 Load System

The throttle plate is opened to supply more air when engine torque load increases. As the throttle plate is opened, vacuum diminishes at the idle jet and it stops delivering fuel. However, the main fuel nozzle begins spraying fuel as the vacuum in the venturi increases. The fuel delivery rate is controlled by a *load jet*, or main jet, between the float chamber and the nozzle (see Figure 9.6). The mixture for full-load operation can be made richer by installing a load jet with a larger hole.

### 9.6.4 Economizer System
A venturi causes fuel delivery to increases faster than airflow as the throttle opens. An *economizer system* saves fuel at moderate loads by preventing the resultant increase in mixture richness. Economizer systems gradually reduce the pressure difference between the float chamber and venturi as the throttle is opened. All economizer systems are designed to cease functioning and allow the mixture to become richer when the throttle approaches the wide-open position.

### 9.6.5 Acceleration System
When the throttle opens suddenly, airflow increases almost instantaneously but friction in the nozzle causes fuel flow to lag. Without an accelerating system, the momentarily lean mixture would then cause the engine to falter or stall. Placing the fuel nozzle in an acceleration well (Figure 9.6) helps to overcome fuel lag. Fuel in the well flows through holes in the side of the nozzle to enter the airstream during engine acceleration. The acceleration well is the only accelerating system needed on tractor engines, but is insufficient for the sustained accelerations of automotive engines. An accelerator pump (Figure 9.5) is used on automotive engines to overcome fuel lag. When the throttle opens, the throttle linkage compresses the spring in the accelerator pump. The plunger begins moving downward under spring pressure to force fuel through the accelerating jet. By the time the plunger reaches the end of its stroke, the main nozzle has passed through the lag and is able to supply fuel for continued acceleration. Moving the throttle to a closed or partially closed position allows the plunger to move up in readiness for another acceleration.

### 9.6.6 Carburetor Adjustments
Most carburetors have an *idle speed adjustment* and an *idling mixture adjustment*. The idling speed, or throttle stop, screw (not visible in Figures 9.5 or 9.6) prevents the throttle from closing completely. It should be set at the idle speed specified by the manufacturer. The specific speed usually is the minimum engine speed at which the engine will run without running rough or stalling. The idling mixture is adjusted by turning the idle mixture needle (Figures 9.5 and 9.6) in for a richer idle mixture or out for a leaner idle mixture. After the idling speed has been set, the idle mixture

*Figure 9.9–Close proximity of the manifolds to promote heat transfer from exhaust to intake manifold. (Photo by Laurie Goering.)*

needle should be turned in until the engine begins to stall and then out enough so that the engine runs smoothly. Some older tractor carburetors also have a load needle valve that can be adjusted to set the mixture when the engine is operating under load. This adjustment was eliminated on later carburetors and the load mixture could only be changed by installing a load jet of a different size.

## 9.7 MANIFOLD HEAT

Cold weather starting and warm-up of a carbureted engine requires heat to vaporize the fuel in the intake manifold. Liquid fuel creeps along the walls of the intake manifold, providing nonuniform distribution among the cylinders. Complete vaporization of the fuel would provide more uniform distribution, but is impractical. Heating the intake manifold reduces the air density (see Equation 2.5) and therefore reduces the engine volumetric efficiency. Just enough manifold heat is needed to assure adequate vaporization of the fuel without excessively reducing the volumetric efficiency.

Fuel Systems and Carburetion 241

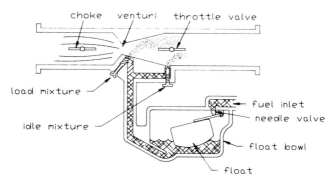

Figure 9.10–Float-type carburetor for small engines.

Several techniques can be used to supply heat to an intake manifold. Most often, heat is transferred from the exhaust manifold to the intake manifold through a hot spot in the wall between them (Figure 9.9). The hot exhaust gas impinges directly on the *hot spot* when the engine is cold, but it is deflected away from the hot spot by a thermostatically-controlled deflector plate when the engine is warm.

The intake and exhaust manifolds are on the opposite sides of some engines, so a hot spot cannot be used to vaporize the fuel. The intake manifold of such an engine may be designed as a heat exchanger. Hot engine coolant exiting from the engine head circulates through passages in the intake manifold and heats the air-fuel mixture before returning to the radiator.

## 9.8  CARBURETORS FOR SMALL ENGINES

The three types of carburetors available for use on small engines are the float type, the suction-lift type, and the diaphragm type. Two versions of the suction-lift carburetor are available, the vacuum type and the pulsating type.

### 9.8.1  Float-Type Carburetors

A float-type carburetor for small engines is shown in Figure 9.10. Notice that it is a side draft carburetor, but its principles of operation are similar to the carburetors discussed in Sections 9.4 and 9.6. At idle, when the throttle valve is nearly closed, all fuel is supplied through the idle jet. The idle mixture is made leaner by turning the idle valve (shown below the throttle valve in Figure 9.10) inward or richer by backing the idle screw out. As the throttle valve opens with increasing speed, air flow through the venturi increases enough to

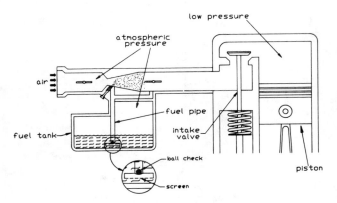

*Figure 9.11–Suction-lift carburetor for small engines.*

pull fuel through the main nozzle. At intermediate speeds, fuel is supplied through both the idle jet and the main jet, but the mixture richness is still adjusted by the idle valve. At high speeds, all of the fuel is supplied by the main jet and the mixture richness is adjusted by the high-speed mixture-adjustment valve (shown near the venturi in Figure 9.10).

### 9.8.2  Suction-Lift Carburetors

The suction-lift, vacuum-type carburetor shown in Figure 9.11 has no need for a fuel transfer pump, even though the carburetor is mounted above the fuel tank. A fuel pipe containing a ball-check valve and a filtering screen (not shown in Figure 9.11) extends from the carburetor into the fuel tank. When the piston moves downward on the intake stroke, the resulting vacuum in the carburetor allows atmospheric pressure in the fuel tank to open the check valve and push fuel into the carburetor. The entering fuel atomizes, mixes with air in the carburetor, and enters the combustion chamber. When the intake stroke ends, the carburetor pressure rises to atmospheric, the check valve closes and fuel remaining in the fuel pipe is trapped until the next intake stroke. Closing the choke (shown on the left of Figure 9.11) increases the carburetor vacuum during the intake stroke and forces extra fuel through the fuel pipe to aid starting a cold engine. Operation of the suction-lift carburetor is similar to that of the float-type carburetor of Figure 9.10 in that fuel is supplied through a main jet to the venturi at high speeds. A valve is provided to adjust the richness of the high-speed mixture. At idle, fuel is supplied through idle discharge holes below the throttle plate, but no valve is provided to adjust the idle mixture richness.

The suction-lift, pulsating carburetor is also mounted above the fuel tank (Figure 9.12) but requires no separate fuel transfer pump.

Fuel Systems and Carburetion

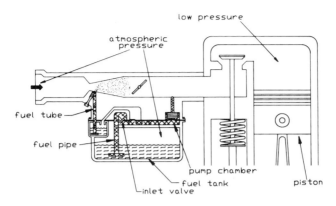

*Figure 9.12–Pulsating, suction-lift carburetor for small engines.*

Instead, a diaphragm pump is built into the carburetor. During an intake stroke, the vacuum draws fuel from the tank, through the fuel tube and into the pump chamber and also moves the diaphragm upward against spring pressure. When the intake stoke ends, the spring pushes the diaphragm downward to pump fuel to the fuel reservoir. A constant level of fuel is maintained in the reservoir and is supplied to the main jet through a fuel pipe. The remaining operation of the pulsating carburetor is identical to that of the vacuum-type, suction-lift carburetor.

### 9.8.3 Diaphragm-Type Carburetors

The diaphragm-type carburetor (Figure 9.13) contains a flexible diaphragm to transfer fuel from the tank into the carburetor. As the piston moves downward on the intake stroke, the resulting vacuum is transmitted to the upper side of the diaphragm, causing it to move upward. As the diaphragm flexes in moving upward, it opens the fuel inlet valve and allows fuel to enter the venturi through a ball-check

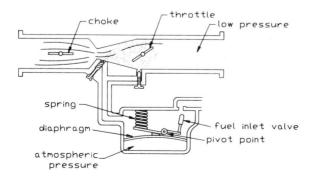

*Figure 9.13–Diaphragm-type carburetor for small engines.*

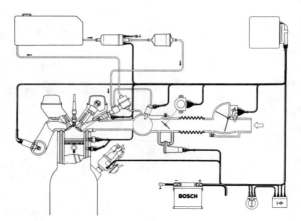

*Figure 9.14–An electronic fuel injection system for spark-ignition engines. (Courtesy of Robert Bosch, GmbH.)*

valve. At the end of the intake stroke, the diaphragm returns to its original position, closing the fuel inlet valve. The ball-check valve also reseats, trapping fuel in the line above it. The remaining operation of the diaphragm-type carburetor is identical to that of the vacuum-type, suction-lift carburetor. A major advantage of the diaphragm-type carburetor is that it will function properly in any orientation, including upside down. It is therefore the preferred carburetor for chainsaw engines.

## 9.9 FUEL INJECTION SYSTEMS FOR SPARK-IGNITION ENGINES

On most new automotive engines, the carburetor has been supplanted by a *fuel-injection system*. A wide variety of fuel injection systems have been developed. In the least-expensive systems, pressurized fuel is sprayed through a nozzle and mixed with air in a throttle body. Then, the intake manifold apportions the fuel and air to the various cylinders as in a conventional carbureted engine. *Electronic fuel injection* (EFI), in which a nozzle is positioned to spray fuel pulses into each intake valve port, is gaining in popularity and will be the only fuel injection system discussed in this section.

A diagram of an EFI system is shown in Figure 9.14. The principal parts of the system are the fuel-supply system, the air-supply system and the control system. The numbers on the various components in Figure 9.14 will be used in describing the operation of the system.

Fuel Systems and Carburetion    245

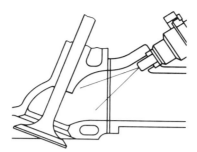

Figure 9.15–Positioning of the nozzle in an electronic fuel injection system. (Courtesy of Robert Bosch, GmbH.)

## 9.9.1 Fuel Supply System

In the fuel supply system, fuel is pumped from the tank (1) by an electrically-driven roller pump (2) and passes through a 10 µm filter (3) to reach the fuel manifold or *rail* (6). A *pressure regulator* in the end of the rail (6) recirculates a portion of the fuel back to the tank for cooling and to maintain a constant pressure, typically 250 kPa (36 psi), in the rail. The fuel injection nozzles (one for each engine cylinder) are all connected to the rail and are positioned to spray fuel on the upper side of the intake valves (Figure 9.15). The rail has sufficient internal volume to ensure equal pressure at all of the fuel injector nozzles. Therefore, the quantity of fuel injected is determined solely by the duration of nozzle opening. The *electronic control unit* or ECU (4) causes every nozzle to spray simultaneously once for each crankshaft revolution; the spray pulses are not coordinated to the piston or valve movement. Any fuel sprayed while the intake valve is closed begins to evaporate and mix with air and enters the combustion chamber when the valve opens. The ECU uses a solenoid built into each nozzle to lift a needle in 1.5 ms or less in starting the spray. The duration of the spray is controlled to meet the fuel requirements of the engine, and then the nozzle closes in 1.5 ms or less.

## 9.9.2 Air Supply System

Air from the air cleaner (not shown in Figure 9.14) passes through an *airflow sensor* (10) and the throttle plate area before entering the intake manifold (7) for distribution to the cylinders. The operator (or the cruise control if the vehicle is so equipped) controls the throttle plate to regulate engine speed, as in a carbureted engine. *Throttle-valve switch* (9) senses the position of the throttle plate to enable the ECU to coordinate the fuel pulse durations to the air flow rate.

### 9.9.3 The Electronic Control Unit

The ECU (No. 4 in Figure 9.14) uses data from sensors and its own internal program to regulate the duration of the fuel spray pulses. A sensor in the distributor (14) measures the engine speed. The angle of a spring-load plate in the airflow sensor (10) is measured as an indication of the airflow rate. The ECU uses the engine speed and airflow rate to calculate the amount of air per intake stroke and thus the amount of fuel needed to provide the desired air-fuel ratio. Further refinement of the calculations are required to meet the needs of cold starting, post-starting, warmup, idling, part-load economy, and acceleration.

### 9.9.4 Cold-Starting Features

The *cold-start valve* (8) is a solenoid-operated valve and nozzle that sprays fuel into the intake manifold to enrich the mixture for cold starts. The nozzle sprays a fine, swirling mist that mixes with the air in the manifold. A *thermo-time switch* (12) limits the duration of spray to prevent flooding. The duration is approximately 7.5 s when the ambient temperature is -20° C (-4° F). A heater in the thermo-time switch causes the switch to open and terminate fuel spray into the manifold. The switch also opens if the engine coolant is warm enough to indicate that extra fuel is not needed in the manifold.

After the cold-start valve closes, the engine continues to need extra fuel for warmup because some of the fuel condenses on the cold cylinder walls and is not available for combustion. At a temperature of -20° C (-4° F), for example, the engine speed would drop substantially unless extra fuel was supplied. Depending on the ambient temperature, 30 to 60% extra fuel must be provided during a 30 s, post-start enrichment. The ECU uses a signal from the *engine-temperature sensor* (13) and its internal program to regulate the pulse duration in providing the extra fuel needed for post-start. A small amount of extra fuel is also supplied for warmup after the 30 s post-start period.

### 9.9.5 Control of Engine Idling

A bypass in the airflow sensor (10) allows some air to bypass the sensor flap. An *idle-mixture-adjusting screw* in the bypass permits setting the idle mixture and thus the idle speed. Note that changing the airflow through the bypass does not change the fuel delivery and thus does change the air to fuel ratio at idle. Further control of the idle mixture is provided by an *auxiliary-air device* (15) below the throttle plate. Air bypassing the throttle plate is measured by the airflow sensor (10) and thus causes the ECU to increase the fuel delivery. The ECU uses a heater and bimetallic strip in the auxiliary-air device to regulate the airflow through the throttle bypass passage. The opening is steadily closed as the engine warms and less fuel is needed to maintain the desired idle speed. The ECU also uses the auxiliary-air device to compensate for changes in ambient air temperature, which therefore affect the density of the incoming air (see Equation 2.5) and the air-consumption rate of the engine. A temperature sensor in the airflow sensor (10) measures the temperature of the incoming air.

### 9.9.6 Part-Load Operation, Full-Load Operation, and Acceleration

The throttle plate switch (9) provides an indication to the ECU of the load on the engine. The ECU uses this information and its internal program to regulate fuel delivery for good fuel economy at part load and for high power output at full load. The ECU also provides the extra fuel needed for acceleration. When the throttle plate is opened abruptly, the airflow sensor plate (10) momentarily swings past the "wide-open" position, which signals the ECU to deliver extra fuel for acceleration.

### 9.9.7 Exhaust Sensing

The *lambda sensor* (11) is used for precise control of the mixture richness. Lambda is an excess air factor, that is, it is the actual air consumption rate divided by the theoretical air consumption rate needed for a stoichiometric mixture (see Section 6.3). Note that the lambda sensor is positioned to measure the concentration of oxygen in the engine exhaust. Small amounts of oxygen should be present; if too little oxygen is present, the ECU will lean the mixture or the mixture will be enriched if too much oxygen is present. The lambda sensor allows the ECU to adjust the mixture in response to fuel characteristics; for example, the mixture would automatically be enriched to compensate for the extra oxygen in an ethanol-gasoline blend.

### 9.9.8 Supplementary Functions

Overrun refers to situations in which the engine is serving as a brake, as when the vehicle is moving downhill and the throttle is closed. The ECU uses the throttle-valve switch (9) to sense overrun and cut off fuel delivery.

The ECU prevents excessive engine speeds. When the speed pickup in the distributor (14) indicates that maximum allowable engine speed has been reached, the ECU limits the fuel delivery to prevent further speed increases.

To reduce the possibility of fire, a safety circuit prevents the fuel pump from continuing to supply fuel after an accident. Electrical power to the fuel pump is supplied through the ignition switch and a

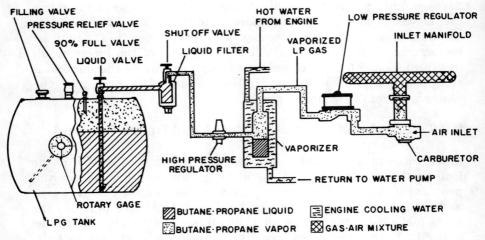

*Figure 9.16–A butane-propane fuel system.*

switch in the airflow sensor (10). Thus, the switch must be on and air must be flowing through the airflow sensor before the fuel pump will supply fuel. If the engine stops after an accident but the switch remains on, the switch in the airflow sensor will open to cut off power to the fuel pump.

The battery supplies the power used to lift the needles in the fuel injector nozzles. If the voltage supplied to the injectors is low, the injectors will not be held open long enough. Therefore, the battery voltage is continually measured and the ECU compensates for low voltage by extending the duration of the injection pulses.

### 9.9.9 Advantages of Electronic Fuel Injection

Several advantages justify the additional cost of EFI compared to carburetors. EFI delivers equal quantities of fuel to all cylinders and, through use of various sensors and the ECU, the mixture richness can be tailored precisely to the instantaneous requirements of the engine. Thus, with EFI, fuel economy is improved and exhaust emissions are reduced. Engines with EFI are easier to start than carbureted engines and also can produce higher power output from an engine of given displacement.

## 9.10 FUEL SYSTEMS FOR LIQUEFIED PETROLEUM GAS

Liquefied petroleum gas (LPG) is a blend of propane and butane, both of which are gases at ordinary temperatures. The gases are

Fuel Systems and Carburetion

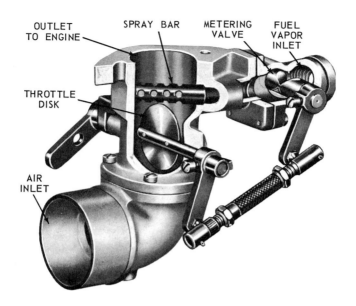

*Figure 9.17–An LPG carburetor. (Courtesy of Deere & Company.)*

liquefied by compressing and storing them under high pressure – thus, the term *liquefied petroleum gas*. LPG is no longer used as a fuel in tractor engines, but it is used in fork lifts and other industrial vehicles in which clean burning is especially important.

An LPG system is shown schematically in Figure 9.16. A heavy tank is needed to store the fuel because the vapor pressure of the fuel is very high. The vapor pressure forces the liquid fuel through the filter and regulator to the *vaporizer*. Hot water from the engine cooling system passes through the vaporizer and provides the heat needed to convert the liquid into vapor. The vapor passes through a low-pressure regulator and into the carburetor.

An *LPG carburetor* is shown in Figure 9.17. No venturi is needed because vapor pressure forces the fuel to flow into the carburetor. The throttle linkage controls a metering valve, which regulates the rate of fuel delivery. After passing through the metering valve, the fuel vapor enters a spray bar and is sprayed into the air.

No heat is available to vaporize the fuel in the vaporizer when a cold engine is being started. Therefore, provisions may be made to draw vapor from the top of the fuel tank for starting. The vapor passes through the same lines that are used to convey liquid fuel when the engine is warm. The intake manifold should not be heated on LPG engines because the fuel already is vaporized when it enters the manifold.

## 9.11 SUMMARY

All liquid-fueled engines have a tank for storage, a method (usually a diaphragm pump) for transferring fuel to the engine, and filters to remove contaminants. The remaining parts of the fuel system vary with engine type.

A carburetor supplied the fuel-air mixture to most spark-ignition engines in the past. Mixture requirements vary considerably with engine load. Several carburetor subsystems are used to supply the needed mixture. The basic carburetor for multi-cylinder engines includes a float chamber for fuel storage, a nozzle to deliver fuel to the venturi in the carburetor throat, and a throttle plate to regulate the flow of air-fuel mixture. The venturi increases the kinetic energy of the air at the expense of pressure energy, thereby creating the pressure difference that forces fuel through the nozzle. An economizer system reduces the pressure difference to conserve fuel when engine load is light. A separate idling system must supply fuel when the throttle plate is closed. An accelerating well supplies extra fuel to the nozzle to prevent the inherent fuel lag that occurs when engines accelerate. Automotive engines also have an accelerating pump to supply fuel for more sustained accelerations. A choke plate in the carburetor enriches the mixture to offset the poor fuel vaporization encountered in a cold engine. Chokes can be operated either manually or automatically.

Carburetor draft refers to the direction of air movement through a carburetor. Downdraft carburetors are mounted above the intake manifold, but updraft carburetors are mounted below it. In either case, heat must be supplied to the intake manifold to vaporize the fuel.

Carburetors for small engines include the float-type, the suction-lift type, and the diaphragm type. Since all three types attach directly to the intake port in the head without the need for an intake manifold, all three types use side draft. The diaphragm-type carburetor can operate in any orientation and is therefore the preferred carburetor for chainsaw engines.

Fuel injection systems are rapidly replacing carburetors on new spark-ignition engines. While there are several types of fuel injection systems, electronic fuel injection (EFI) is rapidly becoming the preferred system. With EFI, one injection nozzle injects fuel into the intake valve port of each cylinder. An electronic control unit (ECU) controls the duration of the injection pulses to maintain the correct mixture richness under all engine operating conditions. Use of EFI can improve fuel economy, reduce exhaust emissions, provide easier starting, and increase the power output for an engine of given

Fuel Systems and Carburetion

displacement. These advantages help to offset the higher cost of EFI compared to carburetors.

Liquefied petroleum gas is a mixture of gases that have been liquefied by compression and stored in a heavy-walled tank. LPG carburetors need no venturi because vapor pressure forces the fuel from the tank to the carburetor. A metering valve in the throttle shaft regulates fuel delivery to a spray bar. A pressure regulator regulates gas pressure. Hot water is supplied to the vaporizer to vaporize the fuel.

# QUESTIONS

Q9.1 Why is it necessary for a vehicle fuel tank to have a vented cap?

Q9.2 Suppose that an engine is running at high speed but with light load. Since the pump speed is high, but the demand for fuel is low, what prevents the fuel transfer pump from supplying too much fuel to the carburetor?

Q9.3 Should a carburetor or fuel injection system be designed to provide a constant air to fuel ratio at all loads and speeds? Briefly explain your answer.

Q9.4 Why does a low-pressure zone form in the venturi when air flows through it?

Q9.5 (a) What are the three types of carburetor draft?
(b) On what kind of engine is each type used?

Q9.6 (a) What does a choke do to help start an engine in cold weather?
(b) Why is it necessary to open the choke while the engine is warming up?

Q9.7 (a) Why is an accelerating system needed on carburetors for multi-cylinder engines?
(b) What provision does a tractor engine's carburetor have for acceleration?
(c) What additional provision does an automotive engine have for acceleration?

Q9.8 Most carburetors for multi-cylinder engines have two idle adjustments.

(a) What are the two adjustments?
(b) What does each adjustment accomplish?

**Q9.9** (a) Why is it necessary to heat the intake manifold of a multi-cylinder, carbureted engine?
(b) What are two common methods for supplying heat to the intake manifold?

**Q9.10** (a) What are the three types of carburetors used on small engines?
(b) Which type is used on chain saws? Why?

**Q9.11** What are the two types of suction-lift carburetors?

**Q9.12** (a) What is meaning of the letters, ECU in an EFI system?
(b) Recalling that constant pressure is maintained in the rail, how can the ECU vary the fuel delivery to the cylinders?
(c) What two primary variables does the ECU use in determining the quantity of fuel to inject?

**Q9.13** Is a choke used in EFI systems? If not, how is the engine started in cold weather?

**Q9.14** What is a lambda sensor and how is it used in an EFI system?

**Q9.15** Why is it unnecessary for an LPG carburetor to have a venturi?

# PROBLEMS

**P9.1** A gasoline engine produces 100 kW (134 hp) of brake power while it is running at 2000 rev/min rated speed and consuming 37 kg/h (81 lb/h) of gasoline. According to Figure 9.3, the air to fuel ratio would be approximately 13:1 at maximum power.
(a) Calculate the specific fuel consumption in kg/kW-h (lb/hp-h).
(b) Calculate the air consumption in kg/h (lb/h).

**P9.2** Assume in P9.1 that the load on the engine is reduced and the governor closes the throttle until the airflow is 50% of

Fuel Systems and Carburetion 253

that at rated speed and power. According to Figure 9.3, the air to fuel ratio would then be approximately 17:1.
(a) Calculate the air consumption in kg/h (lb/h).
(b) Calculate the fuel consumption in kg/h (lb/h).

P9.3 Assume in P9.1 that the load on the engine is increased so that the throttle remains wide open but the engine speed is pulled down until the airflow is 50% of that at rated speed and power. According to Figure 9.3, the air to fuel ratio would then be approximately 13:1.
(a) Calculate the air consumption in kg/h (lb/h).
(b) Calculate the fuel consumption in kg/h (lb/h).

P9.4 Suppose that the choke was closed to start a gasoline engine on a cold morning and the carburetor supplied a fuel to air ratio of 0.5, as calculated in Example Problem 9.1. Suppose further that the driver forgot to open the choke, and the gasoline vaporized according to the EAD curve in Figure 9.7. What temperature would the air in the intake manifold have to reach before the mixture became too rich to burn?

# 10
# Diesel Engines

## 10.1 INTRODUCTION

Rudolph Diesel intended his engine to burn the coal dust that was a useless byproduct of manufacturing in the 1880s. Although coal dust was unsuccessful as a fuel, Diesel was able to develop a compression-ignition engine that ran successfully on oil. Early diesel engines were large and slow and were used in stationary applications or to propel ships. The heavy distillate petroleum that was used as fuel was forced into the engines by means of compressed air.

Further development of the diesel engine awaited the development of improved fuel-injection systems in the 1920s. Robert Bosch began mass producing fuel-injection systems in 1927. The development of injector pumps was paralleled by the development of smaller diesel engines suitable for mobile applications. Diesel engines began appearing in industrial tractors and in some large farm tractors in the 1930s. Large-scale use of diesels in farm tractors began in the 1960s and today, almost all new tractors have diesel engines. Diesel engines are also used in large trucks and city busses. Some automobiles and pickup trucks also are equipped with diesel engines.

In Chapter 10, you will learn the major differences that distinguish diesel engines from spark-ignition engines. A major part of the chapter deals with the injection system because it is primarily this system that controls the operation of a diesel engine.

## 10.2 COMPARISON OF DIESEL AND GASOLINE ENGINES

Diesel and gasoline engine have many similarities, and there is little difference in their external appearance. There are differences in their construction, however, which are made necessary by the following fundamental differences in operation:

1. Fuel is injected into the cylinders of a diesel engine, but it is metered and mixed with air outside the cylinders of a gasoline engine.

2. The speed control of a gasoline engine is achieved by throttling the air-fuel mixture. In a diesel engine, only the fuel flow is controlled; the air is not throttled.

3. Air-fuel mixtures are ignited by an electrical spark in gasoline engines, but compression temperatures must be high enough to self-ignite the air-fuel mixture in a diesel engine.

The diesel cycle can be carried out in either two or four strokes of the piston, as was discussed in Chapter 4. The four-cycle diesel is more widely used and, in Chapter 10, four-cycle operation will be assumed unless two-cycle diesels are specifically mentioned. Differences between the four strokes in diesel and gasoline engines are illustrated in Figure 10.1.

The fuel injected into a diesel engine at 20° bHDC (before head dead center) has very little time to mix with air. Therefore, the mixture in the combustion chamber is very rich near the fuel spray and lean in other places. In contrast, the air-fuel mixture of a gasoline engine has much more time to mix and is nearly homogeneous by the time of ignition in the combustion chamber. The air to fuel ratio of the homogeneous mixture in a spark-ignition engine must be close to stoichiometric. Because the mixture in a diesel engine is heterogeneous, small pockets of combustible mixture can form in the combustion chamber and the overall air-to-fuel ratio can be far leaner than stoichiometric.

The compression ratio of a diesel engine must be high enough to cause autoignition of the air-fuel mixture. The compression ratio of a spark-ignition engine must be low enough to prevent autoignition. Therefore, the compression ratio of the diesel engine is much higher than that of a spark-ignition engine.

A spark ignites the mixture in a gasoline engine, and a flame front sweeps smoothly across the combustion chamber. Initial combustion in a diesel engine is rough and uncontrolled because the

# Diesel Engines

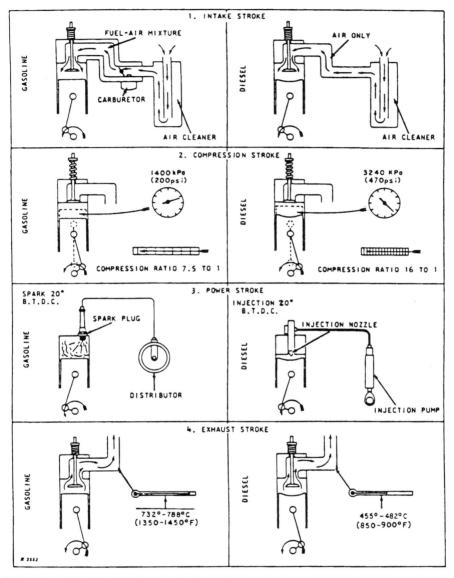

*Figure 10.1–Comparison of spark-ignition and compression-ignition engines. (Adapted from a drawing courtesy of Deere & Company.)*

mixture may ignite spontaneously at more than one place in the combustion chamber. Because their mixtures are nonuniform, diesels must be supplied with excess air to reduce the richness of the fuel-rich regions in the chamber. Typically, the overall air-to-fuel ratio of a diesel engine is 20:1 or higher at full load and can be much higher

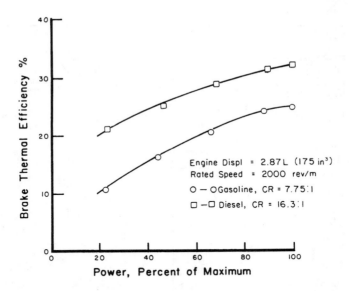

*Figure 10.2–The brake thermal efficiencies of spark-ignition and compression-ignition engines. (Courtesy of Deere & Company.)*

at part load. Since the power output of an engine is limited by its air-handling ability, a diesel cannot develop as much power as can an equal-size spark-ignition engine running at the same speed. However, the excess air and greater expansion ratio allows the diesel to run cooler. Thus, its exhaust temperature is lower than that of a gasoline engine.

Diesel engines are more efficient than are gasoline engines at both full load and part load. The excess air supplied to the diesel and its higher compression ratio both help to increase thermal efficiency. Also, the cycle efficiency of a diesel engine improves at part load because fuel injection is ended sooner (see Section 2.10). The gasoline engine has no corresponding improvement in cycle efficiency at part load. Figure 10.2 is a comparison of the brake thermal efficiencies of two engines from the same manufacturer. The brake thermal efficiencies for the gasoline and diesel engines at full load are, respectively, 24.9% and 32.0%. Thus, this diesel provides 28.5% better fuel economy at full load. The efficiency of the diesel engine declines at part load, but the efficiency of the gasoline engine declines faster. At 30% load, for example, the diesel engine provides 73% better fuel economy than does the gasoline engine.

Diesel engines must be constructed stronger than gasoline engines in order to withstand the higher pressures in the combustion chamber. Figure 10.3 shows how a four-cylinder engine was modified to adapt it for use as a diesel engine. Only three main bearings were

# Diesel Engines

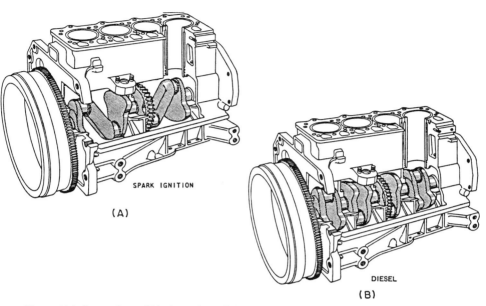

*Figure 10.3–Comparison of blocks and crankshafts of spark-ignition and compression-ignition engines. (Courtesy of Deere & Company.)*

used in the gasoline engine, but five were used in the diesel to reduce stress and deformation in the crankshaft. The connecting rods also must be heavier in the diesel, as Figure 10.4 shows. Usually, the block and head are made stronger and heavier in a diesel than in a gasoline engine of similar size.

## 10.3 COMBUSTION CHAMBER DESIGNS

Manufacturers have designed a number of different types of combustion chambers for diesel engines. The principal types are illustrated in Figure 10.5. Figures 10.5b, c, and d are variations of *indirect injection* (IDI) diesel engines. In all IDI designs, an extra chamber for starting the combustion process is provided, and combustion is continued in the main chamber. Ignition delay (see Section 6.12) is shorter with the IDI designs; only a small amount of fuel needs to accumulate in the small extra chamber before a combustible mixture is formed. Thus, IDI diesels are quieter than *direct injection* (DI) diesels and/or can be run on fuel with a lower cetane number. Also, IDI diesels can use fuels with higher viscosity because the fuel does not need to be atomized as finely as in a DI diesel. Finally, because of the shorter ignition delay and reduced

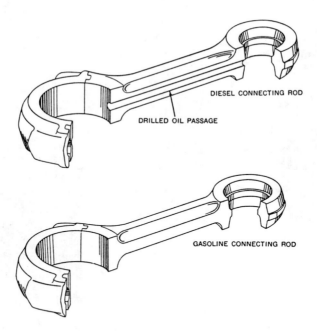

Figure 10.4–Differences between connecting rods of spark-ignition and compression-ignition engines. (Courtesy of Deere & Company.)

premixed combustion (see Section 6.12.1), there is less stress on IDI diesels so they can be lighter in weight. Because of their lighter weight and quieter operation, IDI diesels have been used in automotive applications instead of the heavier DI diesels. Advantages of DI diesels are discussed in Section 10.3.4.

### 10.3.1 Precombustion Chambers

A *precombustion chamber* is illustrated in Figure 10.5b. The precombustion chamber, or prechamber, contains about 20 to 30% of the total clearance volume of the cylinder and 70 to 80% of the clearance volume that is in the main chamber. The prechamber may be insulated from the remainder of the head by an airspace and thereby be kept very hot (600 to 750° C or 1100 to 1400° F). Mild turbulence is created in the prechamber as air flows in during the compression stroke. Fuel is injected into the hot prechamber and ignites. As the flaming fuel rushes into the main chamber through the restricted throat, considerable turbulence is generated to mix the unburned fuel vapors with the air in the main chamber.

### 10.3.2 Swirl Chambers

The extra chamber in Figure 10.5c is called either a *swirl chamber* or a *turbulence chamber*. It contains 50 to 90% of the total clearance

# Diesel Engines

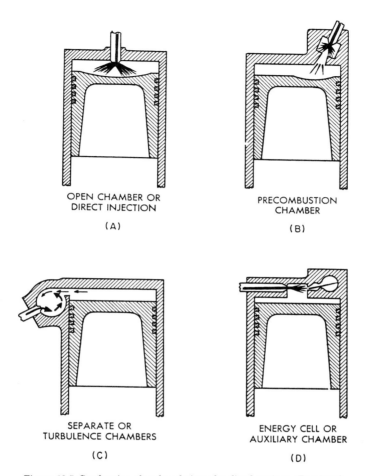

*Figure 10.5–Combustion chamber designs for diesel engines. (Reprinted with permission from Amoco.)*

volume and is connected to the main chamber by a tangential throat. A counterclockwise flow is established in the swirl chamber when air enters during the compression stroke. Fuel is injected into the hot swirl chamber and ignites. Since the flow must reverse in direction as the burning fuel and unburned vapors rush into the main chamber, considerable turbulent mixing occurs. The swirl chamber diesel is clean burning and is able to achieve low levels of smoke, $NO_x$, and unburned hydrocarbons in the exhaust. Typically, emissions of CO are low in all diesel engines.

### 10.3.3 Energy Cells

The auxiliary chamber in Figure 10.5d is called either an *air cell* or an *energy cell*. It contains 5 to 15% of the total clearance volume and is connected to the main chamber through a very restricted orifice. The injector nozzle is located directly across the chamber and directs a narrow spray plume toward the auxiliary chamber. Ignition occurs in the main chamber, and the pressure rise from combustion forces about 60% of the unburned fuel into the auxiliary chamber. The fuel ignites in the hot cell and creates strong turbulence as it reenters the main chamber and meets the remainder of the fuel being sprayed by the nozzle. The combustion is of longer duration in the engine in Figure 10.5d. Thus, although peak pressures in the combustion chamber are lower, thermal efficiency is also lower.

### 10.3.4 Direct Injection

Since around 1960, there has been a continuing trend toward the use of direct injection diesels in large trucks, busses, construction equipment and, farm tractors so that now DI engines are used almost exclusively in these vehicles. The combustion chambers of DI engines have less surface area per unit of displacement volume than do the combined combustion and precombustion chambers of IDI engines. Also, compared to an IDI diesel, more of the combustion of a DI diesel occurs in the premixed mode (see Section 6.12.1). Therefore, the DI diesels offer significantly better (typically 8 to 10% better) fuel economy than do IDI diesels.

The air must swirl in the combustion chamber of a DI diesel if adequate mixing of fuel and air is to be achieved. A multihole nozzle sprays the fuel out in several distinct plumes as shown in Figure 10.6. The swirling air moves perpendicular to the spray to achieve mixing. The intake valve and port are designed to start the air swirling when it enters the combustion chamber during the intake stroke. Swirl continues during the compression stroke, and it intensifies as air is forced into a cup on the top of the piston as the piston approaches HDC. The amount of swirl is a design compromise. Increased swirl improves mixing of fuel with air, but also tends to narrow the boundary layer and increase heat loss through the walls of the combustion chamber. The swirl speed increases with engine speed. Thus, direct injection diesels are classified according to their swirl ratio. Swirl ratio is defined as follows:

$$\text{swirl ratio} = \frac{\text{swirl speed}}{\text{engine speed}} \qquad (10.1)$$

# Diesel Engines

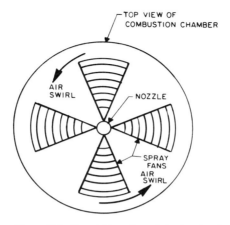

Figure 10.6–Air swirl in a direct injection diesel engine.

where
    swirl speed   = rotational speed of air in chamber in rev/min
    engine speed = rotation speed of crankshaft in rev/min

The concept of air swirl is illustrated in Example Problem 10.1.

## Example Problem 10.1

The injector nozzles in a certain DI diesel engine each have four holes. If the engine runs at 2,400 rev/min and the ignition delay is 18°, what is the theoretical swirl ratio that is needed to fan one spray plume halfway to the next plume during the ignition delay? (The ignition delay is the period between fuel injection and fuel ignition.)

**Solution:** The spray plumes from a four-hole nozzle are 90° apart. Theoretically, then, the air must move 45° during the delay period. The time available for this movement is:

    time = 18°*60 s/min/(2400 rev/min*360°/rev) = 0.00125 s

Therefore, the theoretical air rotational speed must be:

    speed = 45°*60 s/min/(0.00125 s * 360°/rev) = 6000 rev/min

The required swirl ratio is:

    swirl ratio = [6000 rev/min]/[2400 rev/min] = 2.5

The actual swirl ratio must be higher than the theoretical ratio because, if the air is to drag the spray droplets to a new location, the air must move faster than the spray droplets.

The DI engines used in large trucks, busses, construction equipment and farm tractors typically use injector nozzles with four holes and are medium-swirl engines. Medium swirl includes swirl ratios of 4 to 8 at the time of injection. Very large diesel engines use low swirl because their high fuel delivery rates permit the use of injector nozzles with six or more holes. High-swirl engines with single-hole nozzles have been designed, but these are less popular because of their higher heat loss.

## 10.4 FUEL SYSTEMS FOR DIESEL ENGINES

The fuel system shown in Figure 10.7 is typical of those used for diesel engines. The fuel tank is the same as those in gasoline engines (described in Section 9.2). Fuel is transferred from the tank by a pump identical to those described in Section 9.2. The transfer pump is omitted in some systems; the diesel fuel is transferred by a charge pump located in the same housing as the injector pump.

Fuel filters on diesel engines are more critical than those on gasoline engines because dirt or other small particles can ruin the expensive injector pump. Usually, two fuel filters are used on diesel engines. The fuel first passes through a primary filter, which removes the coarser particles, and then passes through a secondary filter, where finer particles are removed. It usually is necessary to change the primary filter more often than the secondary filter because the primary filter collects more foreign material.

The filtered fuel flows to the *injector pump*. At the proper times, the injector pump sends bursts of high-pressure fuel to the *injector nozzles* through *injector lines*. The injector lines must be of heavy-wall construction to resist the high pressure. All the injector lines on an engine are made the same length to ensure uniform injection timing in all cylinders.

A portion of the fuel going into each injector nozzle leaks out of the top end of the nozzle. The leakage fuel provides for lubrication of the injector needle and for cooling the injector. Since the leakage flow is hot, a low-pressure *return line* is provided to return the hot fuel to the tank for cooling. The injector pump in Figure 10.7 has a case drain to allow air and fuel vapor to escape from the pump. Discharge from the case drain is returned to the tank through the same line used to convey injector leakage.

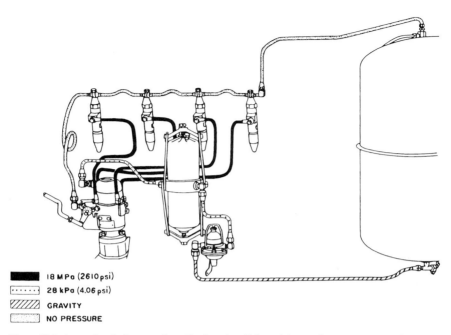

■ 18 MPa (2610 psi)
⋯ 28 kPa (4.06 psi)
▨ GRAVITY
☐ NO PRESSURE

*Figure 10.7–A complete fuel system for a diesel engine. (Adapted from a drawing courtesy of Deere & Company.)*

Injector pumps have a difficult task to accomplish. They must meter an amount of fuel that is appropriate for the engine speed and load to each cylinder. The fuel must be metered equally to all cylinders at the proper time and at the correct rate. The injection line pressure must rise sharply to a level high enough to produce a fine spray and must fall sharply enough to cause an abrupt end to each injection. Injector pumps of widely varying design are in use in diesel engines. The common rail system was one of the first systems used for injection; a variation of it is still being used on some modern diesel engines. However, jerk pumps are in much wider use. A jerk pump uses one or more plungers to deliver bursts of high-pressure fuel to the injectors. *In-line jerk* pumps have a separate pump for each cylinder in the engine. *Distributing pumps* have only one pump, but they have a distributor to direct the pump discharge to the proper injector. Jerk pumps are discussed in more detail in Sections 10.5 and 10.6.

Fuel injection nozzles of widely varying design are used on diesel engines. Fuel injectors are discussed in Sections 10.7 and 10.8.

## 10.5　IN-LINE INJECTOR PUMPS

In-line injector pumps have one individual pump for each cylinder, but the individual pumps are grouped together in a common housing. There are two principal types of in-line pumps. Each uses a different metering principle. One type uses pump plungers with a helical scroll; the other uses sleeve metering.

### 10.5.1 Scroll-Metering Systems

Details of one individual pump are shown in Figure 10.8. A reservoir of fuel surrounds the pump. The fuel can flow in through ports A and A' when the plunger is at the bottom of its stroke. The plunger is driven by a cam (not shown). When the plunger begins to rise, fuel flows back into the reservoir until the top of the plunger covers ports A and A'. As the plunger continues to rise, the fuel trapped in the pump is forced out through the delivery valve at the top and flows through an injector line to the injector nozzle. Notice that the lower part of the plunger is smaller in diameter and the reduced section is bound at top by a helical edge called a *scroll*. When the scroll reaches spill port A', fuel above the plunger can escape through a slot in the plunger, flow into the reduced section, and then flow out of spill port A' to the reservoir. Thus, the delivery valve closes, and injection ceases when spill port A' is uncovered by the scroll. By a slight modification in design, some pumps can work with only one port and port A is omitted.

The amount of fuel delivered per injection can be controlled by rotating the plunger. For example, rotating the plunger clockwise (as viewed from the top) would cause spill port A' to be uncovered later in the stroke and therefore would increase the size of the injection. Moving the *rack* forward or backward rotates a gear attached to the plunger and thus controls the size of fuel injections.

A cutaway of an in-line injector pump is shown in Figure 10.9. Three of the individual pumps can be seen near the center of the picture. A cam is located below each pump, and the cam lobes are arranged to provide the proper timing between cylinders. The entire pump is timed to the crankshaft through a set of gears at the front of the engine.

Gear teeth on the control rack can be seen in the lower-half of Figure 10.8. The rack is perpendicular to the pumping plungers so that one rack can control the rotation of all plungers simultaneously. A flyweight governor is located at the left end of Figure 10.9. The governor works on the principle that was discussed in Section 5.8 and controls the fuel delivery by moving the rack.

Engines with in-line pumps can be stopped by rotating the plungers (Figure 10.8) until the slot is aligned with inlet port A.

Diesel Engines

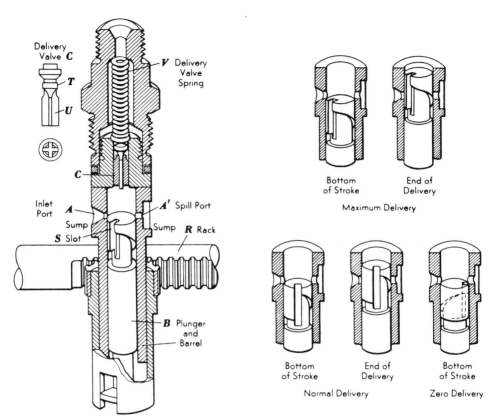

*Figure 10.8–A plunger from an in-line injector pump. (Courtesy of United Technologies Diesel Systems, Incorporated.)*

Since fuel can then escape to the sump at all times, the delivery valves never open, and no fuel is delivered to the engine.

### 10.5.2 Injection Timing with Scroll Metering

The in-line pump has the advantage of starting the injection at a fixed point in the cycle. Fuel delivery always starts when the top of the plunger covers ports A and A' in the pump in Figure 10.8. Thus, injection can be timed to start at the optimum point in the cycle. The rate of fuel delivery is determined by the shape of the cams in the injector pump. The end of delivery varies with the load on the engine. Delivery ends later, when the load is heavy and the engine needs more fuel.

Some in-line pumps have a *retard notch* at the top of each plunger. The notch aligns with the inlet port A (Figure 10.8) and delays the beginning of injection when the engine is being started.

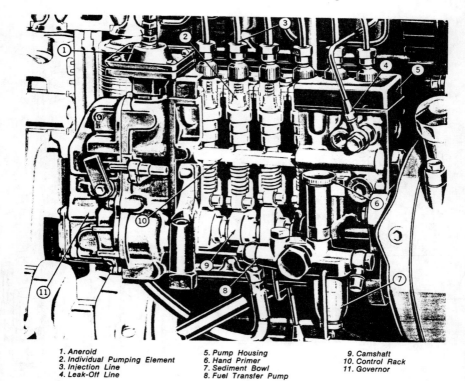

1. Aneroid
2. Individual Pumping Element
3. Injection Line
4. Leak-Off Line
5. Pump Housing
6. Hand Primer
7. Sediment Bowl
8. Fuel Transfer Pump
9. Camshaft
10. Control Rack
11. Governor

*Figure 10.9–A cutaway view of an in-line injector pump. (Courtesy of United Technologies Diesel Systems, Incorporated.)*

The piston rises further, the air is hotter when fuel injection begins, and starting is easier. The scroll can be shaped to uncover the *spill port* a little later, when the engine is being started. Thus, excess fuel can be injected to help start the engine.

### 10.5.3 Delivery Valve Action

Diesel fuel will compress to some extent when subjected to high pressure. If the injection line pressure were permitted to fall back to zero between injections, the compressibility of the fuel would cause the line pressure to increase too slowly at the start of injection and fall too slowly at the end of injection. As a result, large fuel droplets would dribble into the combustion chamber at the start and end of injection. The dribbled fuel would burn poorly, and engine performance would suffer. The purpose of the *delivery valve* in Figure 10.8 is to prevent fuel dribble. When the scroll uncovers the spill port at the end of injection, the spring forces the delivery valve downward. Initial downward movement closes the delivery valve, and continued movement creates a clearance space where the top of the delivery valve was previously located. Since fuel rushes back from the injection line to fill this clearance space, the line pressure falls abruptly. However, the total movement of the delivery valve is limited in order to trap some residual pressure in the injection line. Therefore, the trapped fuel cannot fully expand, pressure can rise sharply at the beginning of the next injection, and fuel dribble can be avoided. In-line injector pumps have a delivery valve above each plunger (see Figure 10.9).

### 10.5.4 Sleeve Metering In-Line Pumps

It is expensive to machine helical scrolls on each pumping plunger. Caterpillar, Incorporated produces in-line injector pumps in which *sleeve metering* eliminates the need for the helical scrolls. The sleeve-metering principle is illustrated in Figure 10.10, which shows the movement of one of the plungers in the in-line pump. A cylindrical passage is drilled from the top through most of the length of each plunger. The plungers are immersed in a reservoir of fuel inside the pump housing. A charge pump supplies fuel to the reservoir of fuel at $205 \pm 35$ kPa ($30 \pm 5$ psi) of pressure. In Figure 10.10b, the fill port is below the stationary upper sleeve, and fuel can flow into the cylindrical passage through the fill port. Upward movement of the plunger causes the fill port to be covered by the stationary sleeve (see Figure 10.10c). Then, the trapped fuel is forced out though a delivery valve (not shown) at the top of the stationary sleeve, and injection begins. Injection continues until the spill port is high enough to be uncovered by the metering sleeve (Figure 10.10e). Injection ends as the fuel pressure in the cylindrical passage immediately drops to the pressure in the reservoir. Thus, the effective stroke is controlled by moving the metering sleeve up or down, as shown in Figure 10.10a. The sleeve is moved upward for greater delivery per stroke or downward for less delivery. The engine is stopped by moving the sleeve all the way down so that the spill port is never covered.

The sleeve-metering system has some features in common with scroll metering. For example, injection begins at a fixed point in the combustion cycle and ends at a variable point. However, the sleeve system provides a less expensive means for metering the fuel.

## 10.6 DISTRIBUTING INJECTOR PUMPS

It is expensive to manufacture a separate pump for each cylinder in a diesel engine. Use of distributing injector pumps reduces costs by providing only one pump for the entire engine. A special distributor connects the pump to each injector line at the proper time.

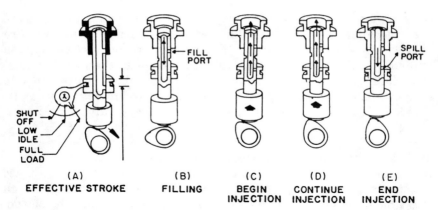

Figure 10.10–Sleeve metering in an in-line injector pump. (Adapted from drawing courtesy of Caterpillar Tractor Company.)

## 10.6.1 Charging Cycle

A cutaway view of a distributing pump is shown in Figure 10.11. Fuel enters through the port at the right end and flows to a vane-type charge pump. Since the flow rate and pressure from a vane pump increase with speed, a pressure regulator valve is provided. The regulator valve opens further as pressure increases and releases part of the flow from the charge pump back to the inlet.

Fuel from the charge pump flows through internal passages to the *rotary metering valve*, shown near the top of Figure 10.11. A flyweight governor (near the left end of Figure 10.11) works through a linkage to operate the metering valve. The metering valve is gradually opened as the engine slows down under increasing load.

Fuel passing the metering valve flows to an annular passage surrounding the central rotor of the pump. Holes in the side of the passage align with radial holes in the rotor (see Figure 10.11) when the main injector pump is ready to receive fuel. Fuel flows into the main pump and forces its rollers apart. An end view of the main pump is shown in Figure 10.12. An internal cam surrounds the pump, but fuel can force the rollers apart when the rollers are aligned with the low part of the cam. The rollers may or may not contact the cam when the pump is filling. That is, the metering valve allows only enough fuel into the pump to satisfy the load on the engine.

## 10.6.2 Discharge Cycle

Discharge from the main pump begins when the rollers reach a point where the cam begins to force them inward. At this time, since the radial inlet passages in the rotor are no longer aligned with openings in the annual passage, fuel cannot flow back to the metering valve.

Diesel Engines

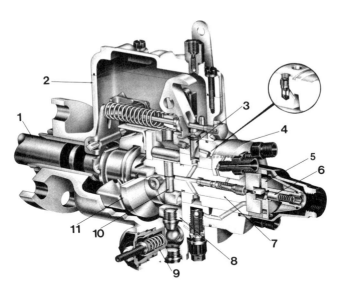

1. DRIVE SHAFT
2. HOUSING
3. METERING VALVE
4. HYDRAULIC HEAD
5. TRANSFER PUMP BLADES
6. PRESURE REGULATOR ASSEMBLY
7. ROTOR
8. INTERNAL CAM RING
9. AUTOMATIC ADVANCE (OPTIONAL)
10. PUMPING PLUNGERS
11. GOVERNOR FLYWEIGHT ASSEMBLY

*Figure 10.11–A cutaway view of a distributing-type injector pump. (Courtesy of Stanadyne Corporation.)*

Instead, fuel is forced to flow through the center of the rotor and through a delivery valve. After passing through the delivery valve, fuel flows into a radial outlet passage in the distributor rotor. The rotor is timed to have the outlet passage aligned with a passage to one of the injector lines when fuel is being discharged. The delivery valve in the rotor serves the same purpose as those in in-line pumps. That is, it prevents fuel dribble. In some pumps, a delivery valve is placed in each line connector.

### 10.6.3 Injection Advance
If the cam in Figure 10.12 was fixed in position, injections would always end at the same point in the cycle. The end of injections would occur at the point shown in Figure 10.12, that is, when the rollers are on the high point of the cam. The start of injection would then vary according to the load on the engine. With light load, the metering valve would not allow the plungers to move very far apart; therefore, the rollers would contact the cam later, and injection would be retarded. An *automatic advance mechanism* is sometimes provided to offset the inherent light-load retard.

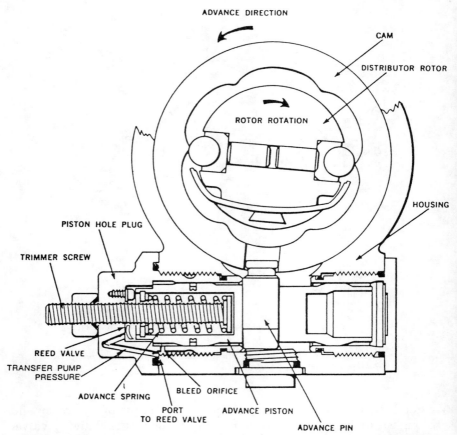

*Figure 10.12–The advance mechanism of a distributing-type injector pump. (Courtesy of Stanadyne Corporation.)*

In Figure 10.12, notice that the entire cam is free to rotate to any position dictated by the advance pin. Fuel is pumped into a small piston on the left and can rotate the cam to a more advanced position when fuel pressure is high. The metering valve in Figure 10.11 is a two-sided valve. When engine load is light and the front side of the valve is closing to reduce fuel delivery to the main pump, the back side of the valve is opening to increase fuel pressure in the advance piston. When fuel pressure declines, the spring in the piston expands and rotates the cam to retard the injection timing.

The mechanism in Figure 10.12 also advances the timing when engine speed is high. Recall that pressure from the charge pump increases with pump speed. Therefore, when the engine and pump speeds increase, the increased fuel pressure compresses the spring in the advance piston and rotates the cam to advance the timing.

The advance mechanism also influences engine torque reserve. As the cam rotates toward the retard position with heavily increased engine load, pump fill time increases and torque reserve increases.

The delivery of a vane pump increases with fuel viscosity. Therefore, distributing pumps usually have a special valve that, when fuel viscosity is high, opens and passes part of the charge pump delivery back to the inlet.

## 10.7 FUEL-INJECTION NOZZLES

The two principal types of injection nozzles are the *single-hole* type and the *multihole type* (Figure 10.13). Single-hole nozzles nearly always have a pintle at the lower end of the plunger. The pintle blocks the orifice when the nozzle is not injecting and partially blocks it when the needle is lifting to open the valve or falling to close it. The partial blocking helps to prevent a weak spray from entering the combustion chamber. Single-hole nozzles are used in IDI diesel engines. DI diesel engines require the use of multihole nozzles. As previously mentioned, four-hole nozzles are used in the medium-swirl DI diesels in farm tractors.

### 10.7.1 Nozzle Operation

A cutaway view of a multihole nozzle is shown in Figure 10.14. A *pintle-type* nozzle would be similar to the one in Figure 10.14, except for the details of the nozzle tip. A spring-loaded needle valve blocks flow to the orifices when fuel is not being injected. When the pump delivers a surge of fuel, fuel pressure acts on the lower part of the needle and forces the needle back against spring pressure. Fuel is injected until the pressure is insufficient to hold back the spring; then, the needle closes to stop the injection. An adjusting screw is provided for setting the pressure at which the needle valve opens. Another adjustment is provided for controlling the maximum needle lift. Both adjustments should be set in accordance with the manufacturer's specifications. A portion of the fuel leaks past the valve guide to provide lubrication of the guide. The escaped fuel passes through the threads of the opening pressure adjustment and into the fuel return line.

Maintenance of correct orifice size and opening pressure is especially important for multihole nozzles. The fuel spray from the nozzle must seek out and mix with the air in the combustion chamber, while avoiding excessive impingement on the chamber walls. Spray droplets that are too large will penetrate to the chamber wall, while droplets that are too small will not penetrate far enough into the air in the chamber. Opening pressures for multihole nozzles

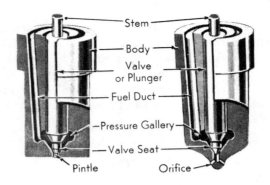

*Figure 10.13–Types of injector nozzles. (Courtesy of United Technologies Diesel Systems, Incorporated.)*

are typically 20 MPa (2900 psi) or higher. Typical orifice diameters are in the range from 150 to 320 μm (0.006 to 0.013 in.). On some injector nozzles, the entire tip can be replaced if the orifices become excessively large or become blocked with carbon.

### 10.7.2 Nozzle Testing

*Nozzle testers* are available for testing the performance of injection nozzles (Figure 10.15). The tester includes a fuel reservoir, hand pump, pressure gage, and valves. It can be used to measure the pressure at which the needle valve pops open and to observe whether a satisfactory spray pattern is produced. A properly functioning nozzle also should produce a characteristic chattering sound when the nozzle pops open. The tester can be used to verify that the nozzle tip does not leak when the nozzle pressure is slightly below the opening pressure. Finally, the tester can be used to determine whether fuel leaks past the valve guide at the proper rate. Because of the emphasis on proper opening of the nozzle, the tester is often called a *pop tester*.

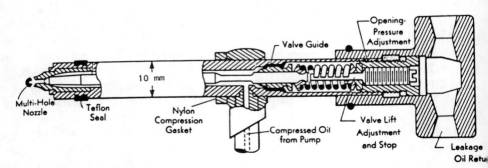

*Figure 10.14–A cutaway view of an injector nozzle. (Adapted from a drawing courtesy of Stanadyne Corporation.)*

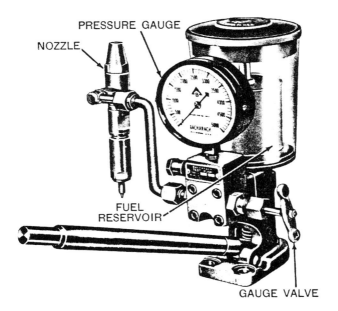

*Figure 10.15–Pop testing a nozzle.*

## 10.8 UNIT INJECTORS

Jerk pumps generate large transient pressures in the injector lines. Closing the needle valve in an injector causes a pressure wave to travel back and forth in the injection line. Under some conditions, the reflected pressure wave can be strong enough to lift the needle and cause a secondary injection. Secondary injections are bad because the fuel is injected too late to be used properly by the cylinder. Thus, there would be benefits if injection lines could be eliminated.

The injection system shown in Figure 10.16 eliminates the high-pressure injection lines. An individual pump and injector are combined into the same unit, and the device is therefore called a *unit injector*. The pump is operated by a cam, as Figure 10.17 shows. The spill port principle and scroll metering are used to control the size of injections, and a rack and gear is provided to rotate the plunger. Injection ceases when the scroll uncovers the spill port. The pump discharges directly into a passageway to the bottom of the needle. When pressure is sufficiently high, the needle lifts against spring pressure and opens to release fuel to the spray orifices. The unit injector principle eliminates the injection line but brings new problems. A more complicated camshaft and extra rocker arms are needed to operate the unit injectors. Also, a linkage is needed to

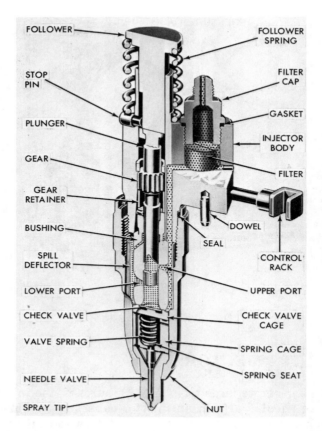

*Figure 10.16–A unit injector. (Courtesy of Detroit Diesel Allison, Division of General Motors Corporation.)*

permit the governor to operate all of the control racks simultaneously.

## 10.9 PRESSURE TIME INJECTION SYSTEM

The *pressure time injection system*, or PT system, was introduced by Cummins Engine Company in 1954 for use on their largest diesel engines. The conventional jerk-pump system is used on smaller diesel engines. The PT system, which is used only on direct-injected, four-cycle engines, consists of a low-pressure gear pump with a built-in pressure regulator, a throttle, a governor, a common rail connecting all injectors, and a manifold for return fuel (see Figure 10.18). The injectors are similar to unit injectors in that their plungers are driven down by a cam and raised by a spring. A plunger

Diesel Engines

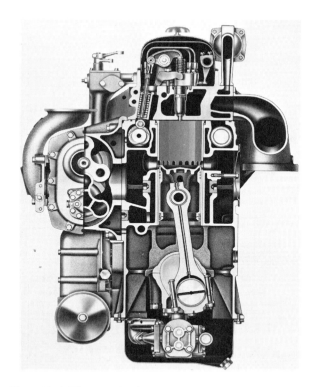

Figure 10.17–The mounting for a unit injector. (Courtesy of Detroit Diesel Allison, Division of General Motors Corporation.)

is raised during approximately half of each engine cycle. Fuel from the common rail enters orifice A when the plunger is raised and flows down to the cavity surrounding the base of the plunger. Approximately 80% of the fuel passes through orifice B to the return manifold and cools the injector by carrying heat back to the fuel tank. Fuel not returning to the tank is metered by orifice C into cavity D, the injector cup. The amount of fuel metered into the cup depends on the pressure of the fuel entering the injector at port A. As the piston is coming up on compression, the cam forces the injector plunger downward. Initial movement blocks orifice C, and then extremely high pressures are generated to force the fuel out through the eight tiny holes (177 μm or 0.007 in. diameter) in the nozzle tip. Thus, eight cones of very fine spray are created in the combustion chamber.

The fuel pump in Figure 10.18 contains a governor and a throttle. The throttle is a shaft with a cross-hole drilled through it. The governor controls fuel pressure at the injectors by rotating the shaft to vary the alignment of the cross hole with the connecting fuel

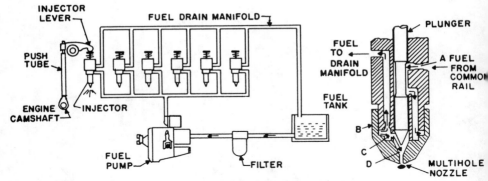

*Figure 10.18–A pressure time injection system. (Courtesy of Cummins Engine Company.)*

passage. When the cross hole is in perfect alignment, pressure at the nozzle and the size of fuel injections are both at a maximum. Thus, the governor controls the size of fuel injections, but the timing of injections is controlled by the camshaft.

## 10.10 ELECTRONIC FUEL INJECTION SYSTEMS

The development of fast, compact, inexpensive microprocessors has made it possible to electronically control individual fuel injections to a diesel engine. Both the quantity and the timing of individual injections can be controlled by the microprocessor.

The electronic injection system illustrated in Figure 10.19 was developed by the Cummins Engine Company. A simple, gear-type pump pumps fuel from the tank through a cooling plate and filter to a common rail and then back to the tank. Continuous circulation of fuel through the cooling plate provides a surface to which the ECU (Electronic Control Unit) can be mounted and be protected from engine heat. The ECU uses information from the cab interface panel, a throttle-position sensor and several other sensors to compute the optimum amount and timing of fuel injections. The EPS (Engine Position Sensor) senses the position and speed of the crankshaft to permit the ECU to control the injection timing.

The system illustrated in Figure 10.19 is for a six-cylinder engine, so six injectors are connected in parallel on the common rail. The timing plunger on each injector is driven by a cam and rocker arm; only one of the six rocker arms is shown in Figure 10.19. The ECU operates a solenoid valve on each injector to control the quantity and timing of each injection. A simplified diagram of one

Diesel Engines 279

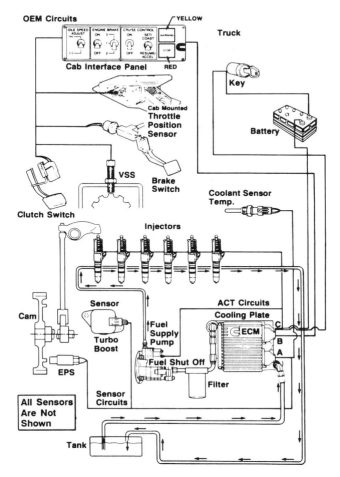

*Figure 10.19–An electronic fuel injection system for diesel engines. (Courtesy of Cummins Engine Company.)*

injector is shown in Figure 10.20 to illustrate the operation of each injector.

In Step 1 of Figure 10.20, the rocker arm is driving the timing plunger downward. Fuel in the metering chamber below the metering plunger is trapped by the closed check valve and because a cross port in the metering plunger is not aligned with the spill port. The solenoid valve is open, allowing fuel between the timing and metering plungers to escape to the fuel rail. In Step 2, the ECU starts the injection by signaling the solenoid valve to close, stopping the escape of fuel from between the timing and metering plungers. Since the trapped fuel is virtually incompressible, the metering plunger begins to move downward at the same speed as the timing

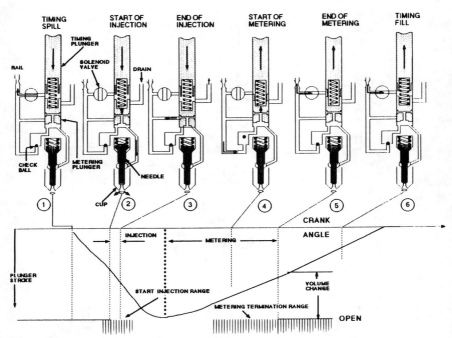

*Figure 10.20–Operation of the nozzles in an electronic fuel injection system for diesel engines. (Courtesy of Cummins Engine Company.)*

plunger. Fuel below the metering plunger flows through a passage to the lower part of the needle, forcing the needle to rise against spring pressure to open the valve and allow fuel to flow through the orifices into the combustion chamber.

In Step 3, injection ends when the cross port in the metering plunger aligns with its spill port on the left side of the injector, releasing the pressure in the metering chamber; the spring-loaded needle valve then closes. At the same time, the cavity between the timing and metering plungers is exposed to a spill port on the right side of the injector. Fuel trapped between the two plungers begins to escape through this spill port.

Step 4 is the start of metering for the next injection. As the cam retreats, fuel flowing through the check valve, into the metering chamber and to the lower edge of the metering plunger forces the metering plunger to move upward. As the timing plunger remains pressed against its rocker arm, the spring between the two plungers is compressed. The spill port on the right side of the injector allows fuel trapped between the two plungers to continue to escape until the plungers have come into solid contact.

Diesel Engines

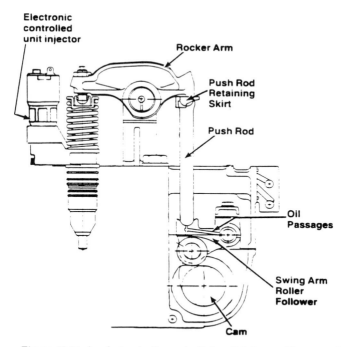

*Figure 10.21–An electronically controlled unit injector. (Courtesy of Caterpillar, Inc.)*

The cavity between the timing and metering plungers has moved out of register with the spill port on the right in Step 5. When the appropriate amount of fuel is in the metering chamber, the ECU signals the solenoid valve to open. When both the top and bottom edges of the metering plunger are exposed to fuel pressure, the spring begins forcing the timing and metering plungers apart. Closing of the check valve prevents the metering plunger from moving downward, so the spring keeps the timing plunger in contact with its rocker arm as fuel flows into the cavity between the two plungers.

In Step 6, as the timing plunger continues to move upward, fuel continues to flow through the solenoid valve to fill the expanding cavity between the two plungers. The cavity remains filled with fuel until, in Step 1, the timing plunger begins its downward movement in the next cycle.

The electronically controlled unit injectors illustrated in Figure 10.21 are used in some models of engines manufactured by Caterpillar. Internal operation of the unit injectors is illustrated in Figure 10.22. Between injections, fuel from a low-pressure fuel pump

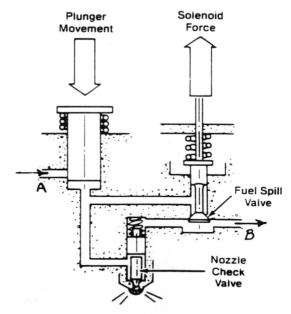

*Figure 10.22–Operation of the unit injector. (Courtesy of Caterpillar, Inc.)*

enters through inlet port A, flows through a cross passage past the normally-open spill valve and out of spill port B before returning to the fuel tank. A spring holds the spill valve open until the Electronic control module (ECM) signals the solenoid valve to pull the valve upward against spring pressure and close the spill port. An injection cycle is initiated when the rocker arm begins forcing the plunger downward. Fuel inlet is cut off when the plunger blocks port A but, with continued downward movement of the plunger, fuel can continue to flow out of the spill port. At a signal from the ECM, the solenoid closes the spill valve to begin an injection. With the spill valve closed, continued movement of the plunger forces fuel into the nozzle check valve chamber, forcing the check valve to lift and fuel begins spraying into the combustion chamber. Injection ends when the ECM turns off the solenoid, thus permitting the spill valve to open. The resulting drop in fuel pressure allows the nozzle check valve to close. The ECM is thus able to control both the timing and the duration of individual fuel injections.

The control circuit for the electronically-controlled unit injector is not shown, but it has many similarities to the circuit of Figure 10.19. As in the case of EFI for spark-ignition engines (see Section 9.9), the ECU or ECM is able to use information from many sensors in setting the quantity and timing of each injection. The program for the ECU or ECM can be changed easily to suit the needs of each type of vehicle. The system can provide electronic governing of engine speed or, alternatively, cruise control. The injection timing and duration can be controlled to meet alternative goals, such as maximizing power output, maximizing fuel economy, minimizing exhaust emissions, or some combination of the above.

## 10.11 BLEEDING INJECTION SYSTEMS

The presence of air or fuel vapor in the high-pressure lines of a diesel engine will prevent the engine from running. Both air and fuel vapor are far more compressible than is liquid fuel. Thus, air or vapor bubbles in the high-pressure injection lines will compress when the pump delivers a surge of fuel, and pressure will not rise enough to lift the needle in the injector nozzle. The bubbles will expand when the delivery valve closes and thus be ready to prevent the next injection. Air or fuel vapor bubbles can form when the filters are changed, when the high-pressure lines are opened or removed or when the engine runs out of fuel. Any air or vapor in the low-pressure portions of the system should be bled from the system before the high-pressure lines are bled. Usually, a plug can be removed from the top of each filter to allow air to escape when the engine is being cranked. Some injector pumps have one or more bleed plugs for bleeding air or vapor from the pump housing. All of the bleed plugs must be retightened when the air has been removed.

Air or fuel vapor is removed by *bleeding the injection system*. Fuel is forced into the high-pressure lines by cranking the engine or, on some engines, by means of a hand pump. The collars joining the high-pressure lines to the injectors are loosened enough to allow air and vapor to escape through the connections while fuel is being forced into the lines. The collars are retightened when all of the air and vapor have escaped.

## 10.12 TIMING FUEL INJECTIONS

Fuel injections must begin at the proper point in the cycle if engine performance is to be satisfactory. In contrast to spark-ignition engines, most diesel engines must be timed when they are not running. The timing operation is carried out when the No. 1 cylinder is at HDC at the end of the compression stroke. Typically, injector pumps are driven by the crankshaft through timing gears located inside the front cover of the engine. Generally, the timing gears have timing marks that must be aligned when the pump is in time.

However, the timing gears allow timing to be changed in increments of one or more teeth. For finer adjustments, the pump usually is mounted to the engine by means of a flange with slotted holes (see Figure 10.11). Thus, the entire pump can be rotated slightly (relative to the engine) to advance or retard the timing. An inspection window with a removable cover usually is provided for viewing timing marks on the pump shaft. For proper timing, the marks on the timing gears must be aligned as specified by the manufacturer. The bolts in the mounting collar must be tightened when the timing mark on the pump shaft aligns with a mark on the housing, as specified by the manufacturer. It is not possible to rotate the pump housing on some diesel engines. Instead, the gear on the pump is mounted to the pump shaft with a slotted flange. The gear can be rotated relative to the shaft by loosening bolts in the slotted flange.

## 10.13 DIESEL COMBUSTION AND SMOKE

Uniform mixing of air and fuel is not fully achieved in a diesel engine, and smoke may therefore appear in the exhaust. Generally, smoke is classified as cold smoke or hot smoke (see Figure 10.23).

*Cold smoke* is white in color and consists of a fog of unburned fuel particles. It is most likely to appear when a cold engine is being started. Low air temperatures, light loads, low-cetane fuels, and high air-to-fuel ratios also are conducive to white smoke formation.

*Hot smoke* is black or grey in color and consists of carbon particles (soot). Hot smoke is a product of incomplete combustion and occurs when the air supply is insufficient. Thus, hot smoke is most likely to occur under heavy engine load when the air to fuel ratio is lowest. Hot smoke often is negligible when the engine is idling, but it increases in intensity as more load is placed on the engine and greater quantities of fuel are consumed.

## 10.14 STARTING DIESEL ENGINES

The temperature in the combustion chamber of a diesel engine must be raised above the SIT (self-ignition temperature) of the fuel if the engine is to start and run (see Section 2.5). Usually, an electric starter is used to crank the engine. On some larger diesel engines, batteries may be connected in series to provide 24 V for starting. However, 12 V starters are more common on farm tractor engines.

The electric starter usually can start a diesel engine when air temperatures are 5 to 10° C (40 to 50° F) or above. Starting aids may be required when air temperatures are lower. *Electric glow*

# Diesel Engines

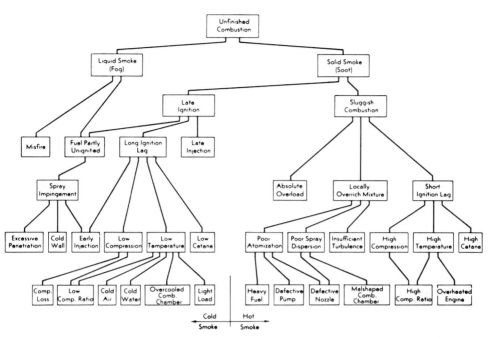

*Figure 10.23–A chart of diesel smoke and its causes. (Reprinted from Schweitzer, P. H., Must diesels smoke? SAE Transactions 1(3):476. 1947.)*

*plugs* are typically used for cold weather starting of IDI engines. A glow plug is placed in each precombustion chamber. A switch is used to electrically energize the glow plug and heat the small prechamber prior to cranking the engine. However, glow plugs usually are not used with direct injection diesels. Instead, ether is sprayed into the combustion chamber while the engine is being cranked. The ether has an extremely low SIT and thus can start an engine in cold weather. After the engine starts, combustion quickly generates enough heat to keep the engine running on diesel fuel. Often, provision is made to mount the ether spray can near the operator. A tube is provided to convey the ether to the intake manifold. Some diesel engines have a heater installed in the intake manifold to heat the incoming air. An ether starting air should never be used when a heater is used in the intake manifold. Block heaters are also used to improve starting. They can provide some warming of the combustion chamber and also allow the starter to crank faster in cold weather.

## 10.15 SUMMARY

Although diesel and gasoline engines have many similarities, they have fundamental differences in their means of fuel metering, speed control, and ignition which require differences in their engine construction. Because of these differences, diesel engines run leaner, have better full- and part-load fuel economy, and must be of stronger construction than gasoline engines.

Several types of indirect injection (IDI) chambers have been developed for starting the combustion process with compression ignition. The IDI diesels are quieter and can run on fuels of higher viscosity and lower cetane number than direct injection (DI) diesels. Direct injection yields greater fuel economy, however, and DI diesels are used in most construction equipment, farm tractors, large trucks, and busses. The DI diesels are classified by swirl ratio because air swirl is needed in the combustion chamber to mix fuel droplets with air, but too much swirl increases heat loss to the combustion chamber walls.

The fuel-injection system dominates the operation of diesel engines; it includes a fuel tank, transfer pump, filters, injection pump, and injectors. Lines of heavy-walled construction convey high-pressure bursts of fuel from the injector pump to the injectors. Low-pressure return lines convey injector leakage fuel back to the tank.

Injector pumps must meter fuel equally to all cylinders at the proper time and at a rate appropriate for the engine speed and torque. The injection pressure must rise sharply, open the injectors, and create a fine spray; then, it must fall sharply to cause an abrupt end to each injection. The two most common types of injector pumps are in-line pumps and distributing pumps.

In-line injector pumps have a separate pump for each cylinder, and the pumps are immersed in a reservoir of fuel within the pump housing. The pump plungers are forced to reciprocate by a camshaft. In-line pumps are available with either scroll metering or sleeve metering. With either type of metering, injection starts at a fixed point in the combustion cycle, but the end of injection is increasingly delayed as the engine torque increases. The sleeve-metering system is simpler and less expensive than the scroll-metering system.

Distributing injector pumps have only one pump for the entire engine. However, they include rotating distributors for discharging to each cylinder at the appropriate time. A rotary metering valve meters fuel on the inlet side of the pump during charging. Distributing pumps inherently end injection at a fixed point in the combustion cycle, but the start of injection is increasingly retarded as engine torque decreases. An automatic advance system sometimes is used to offset the retard at light loads.

Delivery valves are used in injector pumps to prevent fuel dribble into the combustion chambers. Delivery valves are designed to rapidly decrease fuel line pressure below the nozzle's opening pressure at the end of each injection. The delivery valves also trap residual pressure in the lines to permit a more rapid start of the next injection.

Injection nozzles include a spring-loaded needle valve, which is forced open by each burst of fuel from the injector pump. The spring closes the needle valve and helps trap residual pressure in the fuel line at the end of each injection. An adjusting screw is provided for setting the nozzle's opening pressure. Some fuel leaks past the needle guide to provide lubrication and is conveyed back to the tank through low-pressure return lines. There are two principal types of injection nozzles: single-hole, pintle nozzles are used in IDI diesels; and multihole nozzles are used in DI diesels.

Unit injectors combine a pump plunger and fuel injector into a single unit, thereby eliminating the problems that are possible with high-pressure lines. Since the spill port principle and scroll metering are used, a rack and gear arrangement is provided to rotate the plungers. A camshaft at the top of the engine causes the plungers to reciprocate.

The PT injection system is used on the largest engines made by Cummins Engine Company. The system includes a low-pressure pump for metering fuel delivery to the injectors and a manifold to return fuel from the injectors to the fuel tank. A cam-operated plunger in each injector traps fuel on the downstroke and drives it into the combustion chamber through eight tiny holes. The small holes and very high pressure create a very fine spray.

Electronic fuel injection systems have been developed for diesel engines. The injectors are similar to unit injectors, that is, each injector is mounted over its combustion chamber and is cam operated. A solenoid valve on each injector allows the ECU (electronic control unit) or ECM (electronic control module) to control the quantity and timing of each injection. The internal operation of the injectors vary depending on the manufacturer. Through the flexible control of injection quantity and timing, the ECU or ECM can optimize the engine performance for specific requirements. For example, the ECU or ECM could be programmed to provide maximum power, minimum fuel consumption, minimum emissions, or to meet other specific goals.

The presence of air or fuel vapor bubbles in the high-pressure line of a diesel engine will prevent the engine from running or producing full power. Compression of the bubbles prevents the nozzle from opening when line pressure increases. The bubbles can enter the fuel system during engine disassembly or when the engine runs out of fuel. In either case, bubbles must be bled from each line through a loosened connection to the nozzle while fuel is being forced into the other end of the line.

Diesel injection pumps are timed when the engine is not running. Marks on the timing gear are provided to aid in timing the pump. Usually, a pump is flange-mounted to the engine with bolts through elongated slots. Thus, the pump body can be rotated so that fine adjustments in timing can be made.

Nonuniform mixing of fuel and air results in smoke appearing in diesel exhaust. Cold smoke consists of a fog of unburned fuel. It is white in color, and is most likely to appear when a cold engine is being started. Hot smoke is black or grey, consists of carbon particles, and is most likely to appear when fuel to air ratio is high.

A diesel engine will start only if the combustion air is compressed to a temperature above the SIT of the fuel. An electric starter usually can start a diesel engine when the temperature is above 5 to 10° C (40 to 50° F), but starting aids must be used with lower temperatures. Electric glow plugs are used in the prechambers of IDI engines and preheat the chamber before the engine is cranked. Ether, a volatile fuel with a very low SIT, is sprayed into the intake manifold to aid the starting of DI diesels.

# QUESTIONS

Q10.1    How does fuel delivery to a diesel differ from that to a gasoline engine?

Q10.2    How does speed control of a diesel differ from that of a gasoline engine?

Q10.3    How does ignition in a diesel engine differ from that in a gasoline engine?

Q10.4    (a) How does the air to fuel ratio for a diesel differ from that of a gasoline engine?
              (b) Why?

Q10.5    (a) How does the exhaust temperature of a diesel differ from that of a gasoline engine?
              (b) Why?

Q10.6    (a) Which maintains better efficiency at part loads; a diesel or a gasoline engine?
              (b) Why?

Diesel Engines

Q10.7 Compare IDI and DI engines.
(a) For what is IDI an abbreviation?
(b) For what is DI an abbreviation?
(c) Which type of engine runs quieter?
(d) Which can use lower cetane fuel?
(e) Which can use higher viscosity fuel?
(f) Which is more efficient?

Q10.8 (a) What is the purpose of the cup in the top of a piston in a diesel engine?
(b) Is the cup needed in either an IDI or a DI engine? Is it needed in both types?

Q10.9 (a) Is fuel filtering more critical in gasoline or diesel engines?
(b) Why?

Q10.10 What is the purpose of leak-off lines on diesel engines?

Q10.11 Compare in-line and a distributor-type injector pump with regard to:
(a) Number of pumping plungers,
(b) How the fuel is metered, and
(c) When injection begins.

Q10.12 (a) When does fuel injection begin with an in-line pump?
(b) When does it end?
(c) How is the size of fuel injections controlled?

Q10.13 What is the purpose of a retard notch on an in-line injector pump?

Q10.14 (a) On what type of pump is an automatic advance mechanism used?
(b) Why is it needed?
(c) How does it work? That is, how does it accomplish its function?

Q10.15 (a) What is a delivery valve?
(b) How many are used on in-line pumps?
(c) How many are used on distributor pumps?

Q10.16 (a) With what type of engine are pintle-type injectors used?

(b) With what type of engines are multihole injectors used?

Q10.17  What adjustments can be made on fuel-injection nozzles?

Q10.18  (a) What is the range of orifice diameters for multihole nozzles?
(b) Why is the maintenance of correct orifice size and opening pressure especially important for multihole nozzles?

Q10.19  What tests can be accomplished with a pop tester similar to the one shown in Figure 10.15?

Q10.20  (a) How does a unit injector differ from injectors discussed in Section 10.17?
(b) What is the principal advantage of unit injectors?
(c) What, if any, are the disadvantages of unit injectors?

Q10.21  Compare electronic fuel injection for diesel engines (Section 10.10) with electronic fuel injection for spark-ignition engines (Section 9.9) as to:
(a) The circulation of fuel to and from the injectors.
(b) How the pressure is generated to drive the fuel through the orifices as it enters the engine.
(c) The means for controlling the injectors.
(d) The timing of individual injections.

Q10.22  (a) On what type of engines is the PT injection system used?
(b) How does its spray pattern differ from those produced by nozzles used with medium-swirl DI diesel engines?

Q10.23  (a) When is it necessary to bleed a diesel injection system?
(b) What does bleeding accomplish?

Q10.24  (a) What is cold smoke, and when is it most likely to form?
(b) What is hot smoke, and when is it most likely to form?

Q10.25  (a) What conditions are necessary for a diesel engine to start and run in cold weather?

(b) What starting air usually is used for cold weather starting of IDI engines?

(c) What aid is used to start DI engines?

# PROBLEMS

P10.1 A rough estimate of cylinder pressure at the end of the compression stroke (at normal cranking speeds) can be made using the following equation:

$$p_c = p_{atm} * r^{1.28}$$

where

$p_c$ = compression pressure in kPa (psi)
$p_{atm}$ = 100 kPa (14.5 psi)
r = compression ratio

(a) Use the preceding equation with the compression ratio specified for the gasoline engine in Figure 10.1 and compare your answer to the compression pressure stated in Figure 10.1.

(b) Repeat part a, except use the diesel engine in Figure 10.1.

P10.2 In Nebraska Test No. 1449, an engine produced 144 kW (193 hp) of brake power at rated speed and load while consuming 33.9 kg/h (74.7 lb/h) of No. 2 diesel fuel (HHV = 45 417 kJ/kg or 19,526 BTU/lb). At part load, the engine produced 33.4 kW (44.8 hp) of brake power while consuming 15.2 kg/h (33.5 lb/h) of No. 2 diesel.

(a) Calculate the brake thermal efficiency at rated load.

(b) Calculate it at part load.

P10.3 Rework Example Problem 10.1, but assume the nozzle has eight holes, as in a PT injection system.

P10.4 Diesel injection systems must be capable of mixing a small amount of fuel with a much larger amount of air in a very short time. Consider the following typical situation: A V8 diesel engine with a displacement of 10.48 L (640 in.$^3$) and a compression ratio of 15:1 consumes 0.820 L/min (0.217 gal/min) of No. 2 diesel fuel while running at 2500 rev/min. Assume 20° of crankshaft rotation is available for mixing.

(a) Calculate the clearance volume of each cylinder.

(b) Calculate the average volume of fuel injection to each cylinder.

(c) Calculate the percentage of the clearance volume that is occupied by an individual injection.

(d) Calculate the available time for mixing.

P10.5  Rework Problem 10.4, but assume the engine has six cylinders, a displacement of 5.87 L (358 in.$^3$) and compression ratio of 14.8:1. It consumes 0.383 L/min (0.101 gal/min) of diesel fuel while running at 2400 rev/min.

# 11
# Intake and Exhaust Systems

## 11.1 INTRODUCTION

The maximum power of an engine is limited primarily by its air supply. Therefore, the intake system must be capable of supplying large quantities of air. The intake system must clean the air and distribute it to the individual cylinders. The exhaust gases from the engine contain both heat energy and kinetic energy of high velocity. The exhaust system must collect the exhaust gases from the individual cylinders, cool them to reduce fire hazards, and reduce their energy levels to provide a quieter engine. A turbocharger sometimes is utilized to extract energy from the exhaust gases and use it to increase the air delivery rate to the engine. In this chapter, you will learn about intake and exhaust systems and how manufacturers use turbocharging to increase the versatility of engines.

## 11.2 AIR CLEANERS

Early tractors were not equipped with air cleaners. The air inlet was located high enough to avoid great concentrations of dust near the ground. However, even the small quantities of fine dust that entered the intake caused very rapid wear inside the engine. Research, undertaken in the 1920s, led to the development of *air cleaners* for tractor engines.

A *precleaner* (Figure 11.1) may be used to remove large dirt particles from the air before it enters the air cleaner. Vanes in the inlet cause the air to swirl as it enters the precleaner. As the dirt-

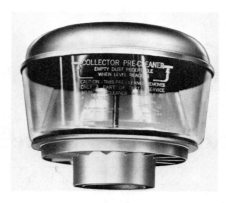

*Figure 11.1–A precleaner. (Courtesy of Donaldson Company, Incorporated.)*

laden air swirls around in the precleaner, the greater density of the dirt particles causes them to move to the outside and be trapped in the transparent container. The air exits through the central pipe. Since the accumulated dirt can be seen through the transparent container, the operator can periodically remove the container for cleaning when enough dirt has accumulated. Some precleaners are self-emptying.

*Oil bath air cleaners* were used almost exclusively for many years and still are used on some engines. An oil bath air cleaner is shown in Figure 11.2. Air enters through a central tube and moves downward into the oil in a cup at the bottom of the air cleaner. Then, the air turns and flows up through a wire mesh. Oil is carried upward with the air and deposits on the wire mesh. Fine dirt particles in the air are trapped on the oily wire mesh. When the engine is stopped, the oil drains back into the cup and carries the dirt with it. The cup must be removed periodically to wash out the layers of dirt that accumulate in the bottom. The cup is refilled with fresh oil before being reinstalled on the air cleaner.

A good oil bath air cleaner can remove approximately 98% of fine dust in the air while providing an initial restriction of 1 to 2 Pa (0.02 to 0.04 lb/ft$^2$) of pressure drop. Dry-type paper air cleaners can remove over 99% of the dust while providing an initial restriction of less than 0.5 Pa (0.01 lb/ft$^2$). Thus, nearly all new vehicle engines are equipped with dry-type air cleaners.

*Dry-type air cleaners* are produced in a wide variety of sizes and shapes, but they all work on the same principle. One style of dry-type air cleaner is shown in Figure 11.3. the dust-laden air is made to swirl as it enters the air cleaner; therefore, the outer shell serves as a precleaner. Large particles of dirt and dust move along the air

Intake and Exhaust Systems 295

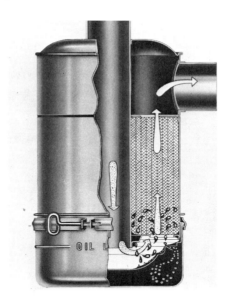

Figure 11.2–A cutaway view of an oil bath air cleaner. (Courtesy of Donaldson Company, Incorporated.)

cleaner shell, pass through the baffle, and are trapped in the dust cup. The dust cup must be emptied periodically when enough dirt has accumulated. Some dust cups are self-emptying. The swirling air moves inward, passes through the paper filter, and exits through the central tube. The paper cylinder has pleated walls to provide maximum surface area for trapping dust while offering minimum flow restriction to the air.

Dry-type air cleaners offer more and more restriction to airflow as dirt accumulates on the surface. If the flow restriction is permitted to become too great, the volumetric efficiency of the engine declines, and engine performance suffers. Therefore, an indicator (Figure 11.4) often is placed near the operator's seat to signal when the air cleaner needs servicing. The indicator is merely a vacuum gage that measures the air line vacuum after the air has passed through the cleaner. Often, the face of the gage is painted red to indicate at what level of vacuum is excessive and green to indicate at what level vacuum is acceptable.

When a paper air filter becomes dirty, it must be either cleaned or replaced with a new filter. Sometimes, the element can be cleaned sufficiently by tapping it on the heel of one's hand. Additional dirt can be removed with compressed air. The air pressure should not exceed 690 kPa (100 psi), and the air nozzle should be directed along each pleat, blowing from the inside toward the outside. If dirt still

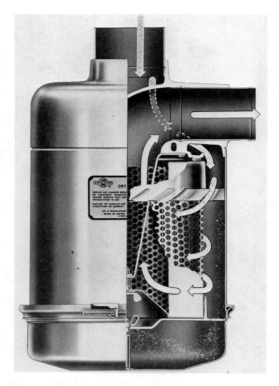

*Figure 11.3–A cutaway view of a dry-type air cleaner. (Courtesy of Donaldson Company, Incorporated.)*

remains, the element may be cleaned with water provided the element is a wettable type. A garden hose can be used to rinse the filters with the water being directed from the inside toward the outside. After washing, the element should be allowed to dry for 24 h before being reinstalled. It is important that the cleaning process does not create any holes through which dust may pass. The filter element should be replaced with a new one annually or at the manufacturer's recommended intervals.

## 11.3 MANIFOLDS

*Intake manifolds* for gasoline engines distribute both air and fuel to an engine. Therefore, a manifold must be designed to provide good engine performance. The inner surfaces of the manifold should be smooth to minimize the thickness of the film of liquid fuel moving along the manifold walls. the manifold is subdivided into branches

Intake and Exhaust Systems

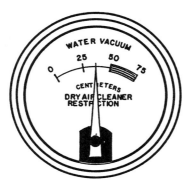

Figure 11.4–An air cleaner service indicator.

that carry air and fuel to individual cylinders or pairs of cylinders (Figure 11.5). Air movement in each branch must stop when the intake valve closes. Periodic opening and closing of the intake valve creates pressure waves that oscillate back and forth in the branch of the intake manifold. In normal manifolds, the pressure oscillations occur at a higher frequency than the frequency at which the intake valve opens and closes. By extending the length of the branch, the manifold can be tuned so that the pressure oscillations and the opening and closing of the intake valve occur at the same frequency. *Tuned manifolds* increase the volumetric efficiency of the engine, but the branch length in tuned manifolds is long and bulky.

Intake manifolds for diesel engines distribute only air and therefore can be much simpler than those for gasoline engines. Typically, the intake manifold on a diesel engine is not divided into branches. Instead, it is merely a box-like enclosure on the side of the engine (Figure 11.6). The enclosure covers the intake valve ports in the head and has a circular opening for connection to the line from the air cleaner.

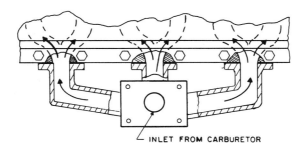

Figure 11.5–An intake manifold for a gasoline engine.

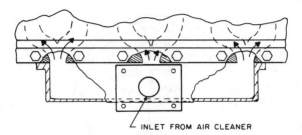

*Figure 11.6–An intake manifold for a diesel engine.*

*Exhaust manifolds* are subdivided into branches on both gasoline and diesel engines. The branches convey the exhaust gas from individual cylinders to the point where all branches join. As was discussed in Section 9.7, the exhaust manifold on gasoline engines may be located in close proximity to the intake manifold so that exhaust heat can be transferred for vaporizing the fuel. The intake and exhaust manifolds are separated on diesel engines and, on some engines, are located on opposite sides. Since the intake manifold carries no fuel in a diesel engine, it can be kept cool to improve volumetric efficiency.

## 11.4 MUFFLERS

Exhaust gases from an engine may carry sparks (hot carbon particles) which are capable of igniting dry vegetation. The exhaust gases also leave the exhaust manifold at high velocity and therefore are noisy. A *muffler* reduces the sound level of the exhaust gases and also serves as a spark arrester. Figure 11.7 shows the two common types of muffler construction. The outer chamber on the straight-through muffler is approximately three times larger in diameter than the central pipe. The space between the pipes may be packed with a sound-absorbing, heat-resistant material. The baffles in the reverse-flow muffler force the exhaust gases to reverse direction several times in passing through the muffler. Either type of muffler reduces the velocity and increases the pressure of the exhaust gases. The large surface area of the muffler shell also helps to dissipate heat and cool the exhaust gases. Mufflers must be designed to produce as little back pressure on the exhaust manifold as possible because the back pressure is subtracted from the indicated mean effective pressure of the engine.

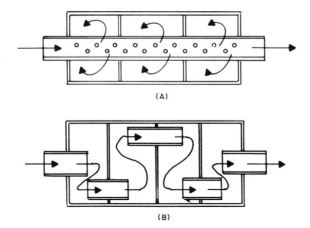

*Figure 11.7–The construction of (a) straight-through and (b) reverse-flow mufflers.*

## 11.5 SUPERCHARGING AN ENGINE WITH AIR

The maximum power output of an engine is limited primarily by its air supply. Therefore, maximum power can be increased by using some type of air pump to force extra air into the combustion chambers. Air pumps that are driven by exhaust gases are called *turbochargers*.

Superchargers have been used for many years on spark-ignition engines in racing cars and other high-performance vehicles. A more recent trend is to use turbochargers on SI engines in automobiles as will be discussed in Section 11.8. The cost of a mechanical drive is avoided because the turbocharger extracts its motive energy from the exhaust gases.

Turbochargers have been used on diesel engines for many years. The extra air supplied by a turbocharger can be used to increase engine power and/or to increase engine efficiency. Any boost in engine power is achieved through an increase in indicated mean effective pressure (see Sections 5.3 and 5.4) and, consequently, must increase engine stress. Therefore, the engine must be designed with sufficient strength to withstand the higher stress. Principles of turbocharging are discussed in Section 11.6.

The mechanically driven blower on two-cycle diesel engines (see Section 4.3.2) technically is a supercharger only if it forces extra air into the engine. Other engines will run without the blower. Therefore, the two-cycle diesel is not considered to be supercharged unless, as is sometimes done, a turbocharger is added in series with the blower.

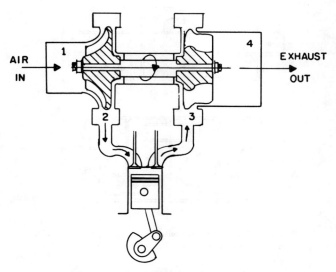

*Figure 11.8–The concept of a turbocharger.*

## 11.6  TURBOCHARGERS

The concept of a turbocharger is illustrated in Figure 11.8. A turbine wheel extracts energy from the hot exhaust gases and uses the energy to spin a compressor wheel. Air from the air cleaner is compressed by the compressor wheel before it goes into the engine. The turbine receives exhaust gases from the exhaust manifold, and the compressed air is fed into the intake manifold. A cutaway of an actual turbocharger is shown in Figure 11.9.

Air flows into a naturally aspirated engine only because the pistons create a vacuum on the intake stroke. Therefore, there is always a vacuum in the intake manifold, and the volumetric efficiency of the engine always is less than 100%. A turbocharger helps to move air into an engine by pressurizing and increasing the density of the air in the intake manifold (see Equation 2.5). Thus, the volumetric efficiency of a turbocharged engine can be much greater than 100% (see Equations 5.22 and 5.23). The turbocharger is said to provide *boost*, defined as the increase in air pressure provided by the *compressor*. With subscripts defined in Figure 11.8, boost may be expressed as follows:

$$\text{boost} = p_2 - p_1 \tag{11.1}$$

Intake and Exhaust Systems

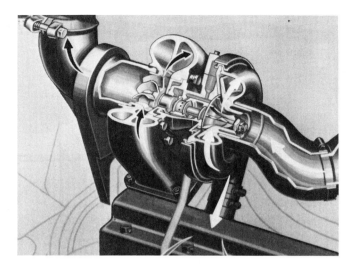

*Figure 11.9–A cutaway view of a turbocharger. (Courtesy of Deere & Company.)*

where
    boost = pressure increase in kPa (psi)
    $p_1$ = atmospheric pressure in kPa (psi)
    $p_2$ = absolute pressure in intake manifold in kPa (psi)

The *pressure ratio* across the compressor also is of interest. Pressure ratio ($p_r$) is defined as follows:

$$p_r = \frac{p_2}{p_1} \qquad (11.2)$$

The pressure ratio is related to boost by the following equation:

$$p_r = \frac{p_1 + \text{boost}}{p_1} \qquad (11.3)$$

The performance of a compressor can be displayed on a compressor map. A map for an example compressor is shown in Figure 11.10. Curves on the map relate compressor airflow, pressure ratio, efficiency, and speed. At a pressure ratio of 2.0 and an airflow of 18 kg/min (40 lb/min), for example, the compressor speed would be 46,000 rev/min, and the efficiency would be approximately 76%. The map demonstrates the high speeds at which turbochargers

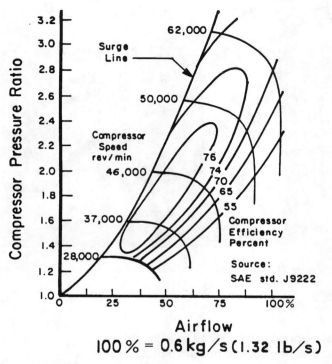

*Figure 11.10–Map of a turbocharger compressor. (Data from SAE Standard J922.)*

typically run. The shaft joining the *turbine* to the compressor runs in two bearings, which must be well-lubricated. Oil supplied by the engine oil pump passes over the bearings before returning to the crankcase.

Compressing a gas increases its temperature. The temperature of the air in the intake manifold can be calculated by using the following equation:

$$\frac{T_2}{T_1} = 1 + \frac{p_r^{0.286} - 1}{e_c} \tag{11.4}$$

where
 $T_2$ = absolute temperature of air in the intake manifold
 $T_1$ = absolute temperature of air in the atmosphere
 $p_r$ = pressure ratio as defined in Equation 11.2
 $e_c$ = decimal efficiency of the compressor

# Intake and Exhaust Systems

When the engine is operating at full load, the density of the air in the intake manifold is greater than the density of atmospheric air. Under such conditions, the volumetric efficiency of the engine can be estimated by using the following equation:

$$e_v = \frac{P_2}{P_1}\frac{T_1}{T_2} \quad (11.5)$$

where $e_v$ = decimal volumetric efficiency.

The pressures and temperatures are as previously defined. The benefit of a turbocharger in increasing volumetric efficiency is illustrated in Example Problem 11.1.

## Example Problem 11.1

A turbocharger is being installed on a diesel engine to provide a boost of 90 kPa (13 psi). Assuming the barometric pressure is 100 kPa (14.5 psi) and the air temperature is 20° C (68° F), calculate the pressure ratio across the compressor and the temperature of the air in the intake manifold for the turbocharged engine. Also, estimate the volumetric efficiency of the turbocharged engine when it is running at full load. Assume the compressor efficiency is 70%.

**Solution:** The pressure ratio can be calculated by using Equation 11.3:

$P_r$ = [100 kPa + 90 kPa] / [100 kPa] = 1.9

or

$P_r$ = [14.5 psi + 13 psi] / [14.5 psi] = 1.9

The compressor efficiency is 0.70. Therefore, by using Equation 11.4:

$T_2 / T_1 = 1 + (1.9^{0.286} - 1) / 0.70 = 1.288$

The air temperature is 20° C or 293° K (68° F or 528° R). Therefore, the temperature of the air in the intake manifold is:

$T_2 = 293 * 1.288 = 377°$ K (or 104° C)

or

$T_2 = 528 * 1.288 = 680°$ R (or 220° F)

Notice that the manifold air is very hot; that is, it is above the boiling point of water in this example. The estimated volumetric efficiency is:

$e_v = p_r * T_1 / T_2 = 1.9 / 1.288 = 1.48$

Thus, the volumetric efficiency of the turbocharged engine would be approximately 148%. Notice, however, the undesirable effects of the high temperature in the intake manifold. If $T_2$ would equal $T_1$, the volumetric efficiency would be 190%. Thus, the temperature rise takes away part of the benefits of pressurizing the air.

## 11.7 AFTERCOOLERS

*Aftercoolers*, or *intercoolers* as they are sometimes called, can be used to cool the air in the intake manifold. Aftercooling can increase the volumetric efficiency of the engine and can also extend engine life by reducing peak temperatures in the combustion chamber. The two types of aftercoolers are the *air-to-air* aftercooler and the *air-to-water* aftercooler.

In the first type, atmospheric air is blown through the aftercooler to transport heat from the air in the intake manifold. In the second type, water is pumped through the aftercooler to carry off the heat. An air-to-water aftercooler is shown in Figure 11.11. It consists of finned tubes located in the intake manifold. Water from the water pump goes though the tubes before passing into the engine block to cool the engine.

The aftercooler may be able to further increase the volumetric efficiency of the turbocharged engine. The following equation can be used to estimate the volumetric efficiency of a turbocharged, aftercooled engine:

$$e_v = p_r * \frac{T_1}{T_2} * \frac{T_2}{T_{2a}} \tag{11.6}$$

where $T_{2a}$ = absolute temperature of air exiting aftercooler

The other terms in Equation 11.6 are the same as defined in Equation 11.5. A comparison of the two equations shows that the ratio, $(T_2/T_{2a})$, gives the effect of the aftercooler. The pressure ratio across the aftercooler does not enter the equation because aftercooling is a constant-pressure process.

The aftercooler will not provide cooling unless the air temperature in the intake manifold is higher than the temperature of the fluid receiving the heat. Typically, a temperature difference of at least 15° C (27° F) is necessary for the efficient transfer of heat. In Example Problem 11.1, the air temperature in the intake manifold at

Intake and Exhaust Systems

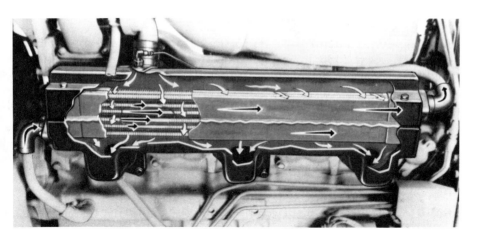

*Figure 11.11–An air-to-water aftercooler. (Courtesy of Deere & Company.)*

full engine load was 104° C (220° F). If the engine coolant temperature were 90° C (194° F), the temperature difference would be 14° C (26° F), and the air-to-water intercooler would be only marginally effective.

Since the atmospheric air temperature in the example problem was 20° C (68° F), an air-to-air intercooler would provide a temperature difference of 84° C (151° F). However, a liter (qt) of water can carry over three thousand times more heat than a liter (qt) of air. Therefore, air-to-air aftercoolers must pump large volumes of air in order to cool the intake manifold and, consequently, are quite bulky.

An entirely independent water supply is passed through the aftercooler on some engines. The water can be much cooler than the engine coolant and thus be very effective in cooling the air. the disadvantage of the system is that an extra pump is needed to pump the water and an extra radiator is needed to cool it.

## 11.8 ENGINE FAMILIES

It is common practice for engine manufacturers to supply a family of engines with several power levels from one basic engine. Airflow of the basic naturally aspirated (NA) engine is increased by turbocharging (TC) or turbocharging and intercooling (TC,IC), and the fueling rate is increased to take advantage of the additional air in producing additional power. The procedure is illustrated in Example Problem 11.2.

## Example Problem 11.2

An engine manufacturer wants to work from one basic six-cylinder engine of 7.64 L (466 in.$^3$) displacement in designing a family of four engines ranging in power from 75 to 120 kW (100 to 160 hp). All of the engines are to run at a rated speed of 2200 rev/min. Turbocharging and, where appropriate, aftercooling are to be used to increase airflow enough to permit the higher power outputs. The NA (naturally aspirated) version can a achieve a BSFC of 0.3 kg/kW·h (0.5 lb/hp-h). The compressor efficiency is 68%. If an aftercooler is used, heat will be rejected to the coolant whose temperature is 98° C (208° F). Show how the higher outputs can be obtained.

**Solution:** Typical ambient conditions of 20° C (68° F) temperature and 100 kPa (14.5 psi) barometric pressure will be assumed. The density of the ambient air under those conditions (see Example Problem 2.1) is 1.190 kg/m$^3$ (0.0743 lb/ft$^3$). From Equation 5.22, the theoretical air consumption of each of the engines will be:

$$\dot{M}_{at} = \frac{60 * 466 * 2200 * 0.0743}{2 * 1728} = 1322 \text{ Lb/h}$$

or

$$\dot{M}_{at} = \frac{60 * 7.64 * 2200 * 1.190}{2 * 1000} = 600 \text{ kg/h}$$

A typical volumetric efficiency of 0.85 will be assumed for the NA engine, giving its air consumption to be 510 kg/h (1124 lb/h). The required fuel consumption for the NA engine is obtained by multiplying the power output by the BSFC and is 22.5 kg/h (49.6 lb/h). Thus, the air to fuel ratio of the NA engine is 22.7:1. Diesel engines must run at an air to fuel ratio of at least 20:1 at full load to avoid excessive exhaust smoke.

The required fuel delivery to the 120 kW (160 hp) engine is obtained by multiplying the power output by the BSFC. Turbocharging and intercooling (TC, IC) will provide some improvement in BSFC. A 5% improvement will be assumed, giving the BSFC of the TC,IC engine to be 0.285 kg/kW·h (0.469 lb/hp-h). The fuel consumption rate will be 34.2 kg/h (75.4 lb/h). The turbocharger and aftercooler must boost the airflow enough to accommodate the increased fueling rate. By trial and error, a boost pressure of 100 kPa (14.5 psi) was selected, giving a pressure ratio,

$p_r = 2$, across the turbocharger compressor. The temperature ratio across the compressor is:

$$\frac{T_2}{T_1} = 1 + \frac{2^{0.286} - 1}{0.68} = 1.332$$

By multiplying by the absolute ambient temperature of 293° K (528° R), the temperature of the air leaving the compressor is 390° K or 117° C (703° R or 243° F). The aftercooler can bring the air temperature down to within 15° C (27° F) of the coolant which is at 98° C or 371° K (208° F or 668° R). Thus, the temperature of the air exiting the aftercooler is 386° K (695° R) and the temperature ratio across the aftercooler is 390/371 = 1.05 (703/668 = 1.05). From Equation 11.6, the estimated volumetric efficiency of the TC, IC engine is:

$e_v = (2) / 1.332 * 1.05 = 1.58$ or 158%.

Multiplying the volumetric efficiency times the theoretical air consumption gives the estimated air consumption of the TC, IC engine as 948 kg/h (2089 lb/h). The air to fuel ratio of the TC, IC engine is 27.8:1, giving a leaner mixture than the NA engine and more efficient combustion.

Two intermediate engines can be designed using similar calculations. The results are shown in Table 11.1. The engines have been designed to be equally spaced in power output. The boost of the intermediate engines is less than that of the 120 kW (160 hp) engine because, with less fuel delivery, the turbochargers of the

TABLE 11.1. A family of engines from one basic engine

| Engine Config. | Power kW (hp) | BSFC kg/kW.h (Lb/hp-h) | Fuel Delivery kg/h (Lb/h) | Boost Press. kPa (psi) | $T_2$ °C (°F) | $e_v$ | A/F Ratio |
|---|---|---|---|---|---|---|---|
| NA | 75 (100) | 0.300 (0.500) | 22.5 (49.6) | 0 (68) | 20 | 0.85 | 22.7 |
| TC | 90 (120) | 0.270 (0.444) | 24.3 (53.6) | 80 (11.6) | 99 (210) | 1.42 | 34.1 |
| TC | 105 (140) | 0.275 (0.452) | 28.9 (63.7) | 90 (13.1) | 107 (225) | 1.47 | 30.0 |
| TC, IC | 120 (160) | 0.285 (0.469) | 34.2 (75.4) | 100 (14.5) | 117 (243) | 1.58 | 27.8 |

intermediate engines receive less exhaust energy and thus provide less boost. Notice that, with less boost, the temperature of the air leaving the compressor of the intermediate engines was not high enough to justify use of an aftercooler.

There are advantages and disadvantages to supplying several engines from one basic engine, as in Example Problem 11.2. The obvious disadvantage is that the smaller engines are over-designed, because all of the engines must have enough strength to handle the power output of the largest engine. On the advantage side, the manufacturer must pay the costs of designing and tooling for only one engine rather than four. Even more importantly, only one basic parts inventory is needed instead of four, thus greatly reducing the costs of providing repair parts. Some parts would not be common to all engines. For example, only the largest engine has an aftercooler. Also, the fuel injection system for the NA engine might not have enough capacity to supply fuel to the TC, IC engine, and at least two different injection systems would have to be provided.

Engine manufacturers have found that the advantages of the technique of Example Problem 11.2 more than offset the disadvantages, and so it has become a commonly used technique.

## 11.9 AIR PRESSURE AND FLOW IN A TURBOCHARGED ENGINE

The effectiveness of a turbocharger varies greatly with engine speed and load. Figure 11.12 shows typical operating points of a diesel engine on a compressor map. The compressor efficiency and speed curves were omitted on Figure 11.12 to reduce clutter.

The engine is running at low idle at point A in Figure 11.12. The turbocharger is stopped or barely turning because there is very little energy in the exhaust gas for the turbine to extract. The pressure ratio is less than one, and the volumetric efficiency is essentially that of a naturally aspirated engine.

The engine speed is gradually increased between points A and B as the governor setting is changed from a low idle to high idle. The turbocharger still cannot extract much energy from the exhaust gas, but airflow increases as the faster-running engine pumps more air.

Load is gradually increased between points B and C as the engine moves from high idle to governor's maximum. Increasing amounts of fuel energy are delivered to the engine, and, as a greater percentage of the fuel energy is rejected into the exhaust, the turbocharger becomes increasingly effective in pumping more air into

Intake and Exhaust Systems

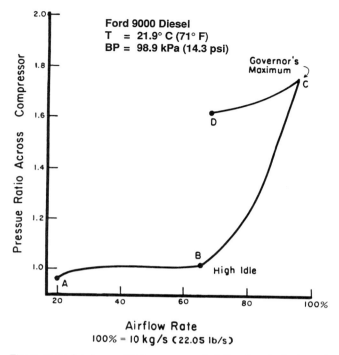

Figure 11.12–Intake manifold pressure and airflow in a turbocharged diesel engine.

the engine. The engine itself is slowing down and thus becoming less effective as an air pump.

The turbocharger is most effective at governor's maximum. As load is further increased and the engine moves into the load-controlled range, the injection pump begins slowing down and thus delivers less fuel to the engine. Consequently, there is less energy in the exhaust gases for the turbine to extract, and the turbocharger becomes less effective. Airflow falls rapidly as both the turbocharger and the engine become less effective in pumping air.

The drop-off in turbocharger effectiveness at low engine speeds is troublesome in SI automotive engines. Fuel economy is highest if the engine is just large enough to sustain cruising speed. Thus, a turbocharger is needed to accelerate the automobile engine from low speeds. Automotive turbochargers are therefore designed to provide high boost at low speeds. To keep the boost from becoming excessive at high speeds, automotive turbochargers include a waste gate. The gate opens and allows exhaust gases to bypass the turbine when the boost reaches the allowable limit. Most turbochargers for tractor engines do not have waste gates because tractors do not need to accelerate rapidly from low speeds.

The curves in Figure 11.12 can be used to design a good procedure for starting and stopping turbocharged diesel engines. If such engines are started and immediately put under heavy load, the turbocharger could begin spinning at high speed before the oil pump was able to deliver an adequate flow of oil to the turbocharger bearings. The bearing life would be reduced greatly if such a procedure was used for starting. A better procedure is to start the engine and let it run at low idle for 20 to 30 s. The oil pump could then build up pressure while the turbocharger was barely turning. Then, the engine could be brought to high idle and loaded without endangering the turbocharger.

## 11.10 ALTITUDE COMPENSATORS

Atmospheric pressure declines at higher altitudes, and air density declines with air pressure. Thus, the air-pumping capacity of a naturally aspirated engine declines as the engine is taken to higher elevations. Since power output of an engine is limited by its air supply, a naturally aspirated engine can produce less power at higher elevations. The engine is said to be derated for operation at higher elevations.

A turbocharger can compensate for changes in elevation. As atmospheric pressure declines at higher elevations, the pressure difference across the turbine increases. Therefore, the turbocharger spins faster and produces more boost. The increased boost helps to offset the pressure reduction in air entering the air cleaner. Thus, the pressure in the intake manifold is not greatly affected by changes in atmospheric pressure. Consequently, the power rating of turbocharged engines is not greatly affected by altitude.

When a turbocharger is added to a naturally aspirated engine, the injector pump is reset to provide a higher rate of fuel delivery in the load-controlled range. Adding more fuel to go with the extra air allows the turbocharged engine to produce more power. If the fuel delivery is not increased when the turbine and compressor are added, the device is called an *altitude compensator*. The altitude compensator usually increases the thermal efficiency of the engine and therefore produces a small gain in power. It also provides compensation for altitude. However, the altitude compensator does not provide the great increases in power that a turbocharger with increased fuel delivery can provide.

# 11.11 SUMMARY

Dry-type air cleaners have become the popular means for cleaning air entering an engine and can remove 99% of the dust. The filter element must be cleaned or replaced periodically to prevent excessive pressure drop across the filter. The muffler reduces sound level of the exhaust by reducing the gas velocity and also arrests any sparks.

The volumetric efficiency of an engine can be increased by tuning the intake manifold, by supercharging, or by turbocharging. The latter is the most common method. Turbocharging permits the use of smaller SI engines in automobiles because the turbocharger provides for acceleration. A waste gate is used to prevent excessive boost at high speeds.

Diesel engine manufacturers use turbochargers and intercoolers to provide several sizes of engines from one basic engine, adjusting fuel delivery to obtain the desired power from each engine. Aftercooling is used to moderate the high temperatures that result from turbocharging and added fueling. Turbocharging inherently compensates for the changes in air density that accompany changes in altitude. A turbocharger is called an altitude compensator if it is installed on an engine whose fuel delivery rate has not been changed to increase power.

# QUESTIONS

Q11.1 (a) In an oil bath air cleaner, how is the oil involved in the cleaning of the air?

(b) What happens to the dust that is removed from the air?

Q11.2 By what principle is a precleaner able to separate dirt from the air?

Q11.3 (a) Why have dry-type air cleaners replaced oil bath air cleaners on nearly all new tractors?

(b) Why do dry-type air cleaners have pleated walls?

Q11.4 Some tractors have an indicator gage near the driver's seat to warn the driver when the air cleaner needs servicing. On what principle does the indicator gage work?

Q11.5 Can a dirty air cleaner be cleaned for additional service? If so, how is it cleaned?

**Q11.6** (a) What is a tuned manifold?
(b) How does it affect engine operation?

**Q11.7** How does the intake manifold of a diesel engine differ from that of a gasoline engine?

**Q11.8** What are the two functions of a muffler?

**Q11.9** (a) What is boost?
(b) How does a turbocharger provide it?
(c) How does boost affect engine performance?

**Q11.10** (a) What does an aftercooler do?
(b) What are the two types of aftercoolers?
(c) Would an aftercooler be effective on a naturally aspirated engine? Briefly explain your answer.

**Q11.11** Why did the second engine in Table 11.1 have the leanest mixture, that is, the highest air to fuel ratio?

**Q11.12** (a) Under what conditions of engine load and speed is a turbocharger most effective?
(b) When is it least effective?
(c) Why is it desirable to allow a turbocharged engine to idle for 20 to 30 s before putting it under load?

**Q11.13** (a) How is a turbocharger able to compensate for changes in elevation?
(b) What is an altitude compensator and how does it differ from a turbocharger?

# PROBLEMS

**P11.1** A 6.89 L (420 in.$^3$) diesel engine has a bmep of 1045 kPa (150 psi) while running under full load at 2400 rev/min.
(a) Calculate the brake power of the engine.
(b) Assuming the back pressure on the exhaust manifold increases by 20 kPa (2.9 psi) due to an obstruction in the exhaust system, recalculate the brake power.
(c) By what percent did the power decrease?

**P11.2** Rework P11.1, but assume the back pressure was reduced 10 kPa (1.5 psi) through improved exhaust system design.

P11.3   Assume the ambient air entering a turbocharger compressor is at 20° C (68° F) and 100 kPa (14.5 psi) barometric pressure. Assume, too, that the boost pressure is 110 kPa (16 psi) and the compressor efficiency is 70%.

(a) Estimate the volumetric efficiency of the turbocharged engine.

(b) What is the pressure and temperature of air in the intake manifold?

(c) Would an intercooler be effective for increasing the volumetric efficiency if the engine coolant was used to receive the heat? Assume the coolant temperature is 97° C (207° F). Briefly explain your answer.

P11.4   Rework P11.3, but assume the boost pressure is 180 kPa (26 psi) and the compressor efficiency is 65%.

P11.5   A naturally aspirated six-cylinder, 6.128 L (374 in.$^3$) diesel engine consumes 21.9 kg/h (48 lb/h) of fuel and 440 kg/h (970 lb/h) of air while running at 2,400 rev/min and producing 93.8 kW (126 hp) of brake power. Assume the barometric pressure is 100 kPa (14.5 psi) and the ambient air temperature is 300° K (540° R).

(a) Calculate the theoretical air consumption of the engine.

(b) Calculate the volumetric efficiency.

(c) Calculate the air to fuel ratio.

Now, assume the engine is fitted with a turbocharger that provides 100 kPa (14.5 psi) of boost with a compressor efficiency of 70%.

(d) Estimate the volumetric efficiency.

(e) Estimate the air consumption of the turbocharged engine.

(f) Assuming the air to fuel ratio is kept constant by increasing the fuel delivery to the turbocharged engine and there is no change in the BSFC, what would be the brake power of the turbocharged engine? (Note: Usually, manufacturers increase the air to fuel ratio when adding a turbocharger. Thus, the power increase would not be as large as that calculated in part f).

P11.6   Rework P11.5, but assume the turbocharger provides 200 kPa (29 psi) of boost.

P11.7   Rework P11.5, but assume the compressor efficiency is 55%.

P11.8   Rework P11.5, but assume the compressor efficiency is 75% and the boost is 150 kPa (22 psi).

# 12
# Cooling Systems

## 12.1 INTRODUCTION

Peak combustion temperatures in an engine exceed the melting point of cast iron. Thus, some type of cooling system is needed to protect the engine from self-destruction. Although cooling is needed, overcooling is undesirable because corrosive compounds form in an engine that runs at low temperature. The cooling system must maintain the engine temperature within a desirable range.

## 12.2 HEAT TRANSFER IN AN ENGINE

Heat transfer in an engine is affected by engine type, size, efficiency, load, and speed. Figure 12.1 shows heat transfer in a typical turbocharged, water-cooled diesel engine. Only one-third of the fuel energy is converted to useful work at full load; two-thirds is lost as heat. Approximately 16% of the fuel energy is rejected into the cooling water. If the brake power for the engine of Figure 12.1 was at least 40 kW (54 hp), enough heat would be rejected to the coolant to heat a six-room house in midwinter. Thus, the cooling system must dispose of large quantities of heat.

Peak combustion temperatures in an engine can exceed 2700° C (4890° F), but the cooling system lowers temperatures substantially. Figure 12.2 shows a typical temperature profile for a section of a cylinder wall. The cooling system cools the wall, and a great temperature drop occurs in the boundary layer between the hot combustion gases and the chamber wall. Provided that it is not swept away by engine knock or by excessive turbulence, the boundary layer

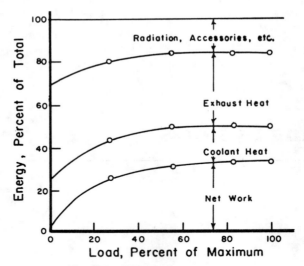

*Figure 12.1–Heat transfer in an engine.*

protects the cast-iron chamber wall from the high temperature of the combustion gas.

## 12.3 AIR COOLING

Air is used to cool most small engines, some larger stationary engines, and some large tractor engines. Heat cannot be transferred to air as readily as to water. Therefore, the hotter parts of *air-cooled engines* must have fins to provide more surface area for heat transfer. The fins can be seen on the head and surrounding the cylinders on the air-cooled engine in Figure 12.3. A cooling fan is provided to move large quantities of air past the fins. A sheet-metal enclosure and baffles direct the air over the hottest parts of the engine. The cooling fan is part of the flywheel of the engine in Figure 12.3.

Air cooling eliminates the need for a water pump, radiator, cooling jacket, thermostat, and antifreeze, but precise temperature control is more difficult in air-cooled engines than in water-cooled engines. Most vehicles are equipped with water-cooled engines.

## 12.4 WATER COOLING BY THERMOSIPHON

The earliest water-cooling systems were open-jacket systems. The cylinders were enclosed in a reservoir of water that was open to the

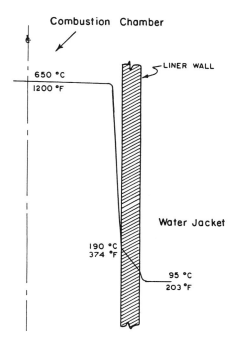

*Figure 12.2–Temperature profile in a combustion chamber. (Data from Kulhavy, J. T., Tractor engine cooling, ASAE Paper No. 64-637. 1964.)*

atmosphere. The system dissipated heat by evaporating water and allowing it to escape to the atmosphere as steam.

The *thermosiphon system* is a closed cooling system that was used on some early tractors (Figure 12.4). Cool water from the radiator enters the water jacket surrounding the cylinders. Heat transferred from the cylinders causes vapor bubbles to form in the water. The consequent reduction in density forces the water to rise and flow to the top of the engine and into the radiator. A fan pulls air through the radiator to cool the water. The cooled water at the bottom of the radiator reenters the engine to start another cycle. Thermosiphon action is present in modern cooling systems, but it is aided by a pump.

## 12.5 WATER PUMPS AND FANS

Modern water-cooling systems are similar to the thermosiphon system, except that a pump is added to create more positive circulation of the cooling water. The elements of a typical system are illustrated in Figure 12.5. The pump is mounted on the front of the

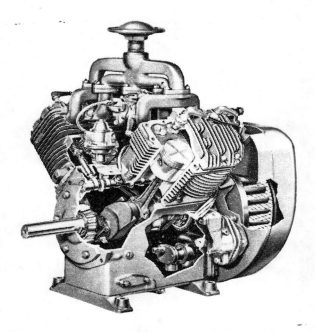

*Figure 12.3–An air-cooled engine. (Courtesy of Teledyne Total Power.)*

engine and is driven by the crankshaft through a V-belt. The *water pump* receives cool water from the lower part of the radiator and discharges it directly into the engine block. Thus, the pump assists the natural circulation that occurs in the thermosiphon system.

A centrifugal-type pump is used to circulate the water. A cutaway view of a typical pump is shown in Figure 12.6. The impeller shaft is supported on two ball or roller bearings, which are prelubricated and sealed to prevent water contact.

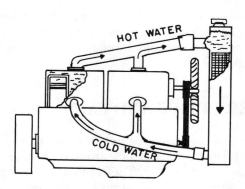

*Figure 12.4–A thermosiphon cooling system.*

Cooling Systems 319

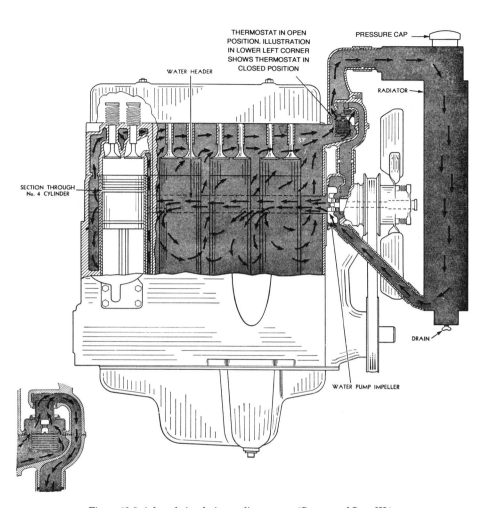

*Figure 12.5–A forced-circulation cooling system. (Courtesy of Case-IH.)*

It is common practice to mount the *fan* on the front of the water pump shaft so that the water pump and fan can be driven by the same V-belt. Early fans had only two blades, but now fans with up to six blades are common. The pitch of most fans is designed to pull air through the radiator and blow it across the engine. Some engines have pusher fans that push air through the radiator. A shroud is attached to the radiator and surrounds the fan to improve its efficiency in moving air. The fan is made to rotate much faster than the crankshaft for increased air-handling capacity. A fast-moving fan absorbs considerable power. Therefore, a thermostatically controlled clutch is sometimes used on engines to allow the fan to freewheel when the engine is cool.

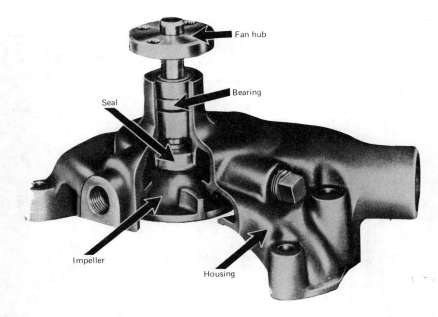

*Figure 12.6–A cutaway view of a water pump. (From Jones, F. R. and W. H. Aldred, Farm Power and Tractors, 5th Ed., 1980. Reprinted with permission from McGraw-Hill Book Company.)*

## 12.6 RADIATORS

A *radiator* is a water-to-air heat exchanger. Water flows through a set of finned tubes (Figure 12.7). The tubes are connected into tanks at the top and bottom of the radiator. The fins provide much surface area for the transfer of heat to the air that flows between the tubes. Since the radiator must have enough frontal area to dissipate the heat from the coolant, larger radiators are required for larger engines.

Water boils at 100° C (212° F) at one atmosphere of pressure. However, the boiling point of water is raised in modern cooling systems by maintaining the coolant pressure as much as 100 kPa (14.6 psi) above atmospheric pressure. The boiling point is raised approximately 1° C for each 4 kPa (3° F for each 1 psi) increase in pressure. Since excessive pressure could rupture the radiator, the radiator cap contains a pressure relief valve. The valve is normally closed, as shown in Figure 12.8a. The *pressure rating of the cap* is equal to the pressure at which the pressure relief valve opens to release coolant to the overflow tube (Figure 12.8b). The missing coolant causes a vacuum in the radiator when the system cools. Therefore, a vacuum relief valve is also included in the radiator cap (Figure 12.8c). The vacuum relief valve opens and admits air when

*Figure 12.7–A cutaway view of a radiator. (Courtesy of Young Radiator Company.)*

the radiator cools. The bottom of the overflow tube is immersed in an overflow tank on some engines (Figure 12.9). Thus, coolant that escapes through the pressure relief valve can return by suction through the vacuum relief valve when the radiator is cool.

## 12.7 TEMPERATURE CONTROL

Excessive temperature can cause severe damage in an engine. If the inside surface of the cylinder liner is not kept below approximately 200° C (390° F), the lubricating oil film can be destroyed with consequent scoring of the cylinder walls. Excessively high temperatures also can cause warping or fracture of valves, blocks, and other engine parts. Engines operate in a wide variety of air temperatures, and the cooling system must have enough capacity to protect the engine on the hottest day. Therefore, the cooling system has considerable excess capacity when the engine is operating under

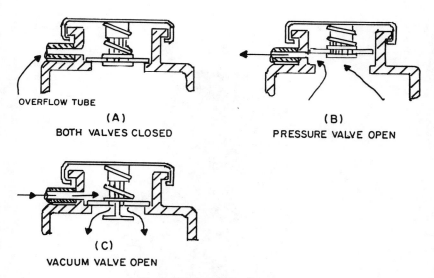

Figure 12.8–A typical radiator cap.

more normal conditions. Without some means to reduce cooling capacity, the engine would warm up very slowly and operate at too low a temperature. Then, water produced by combustion could condense and react with sulphur oxides in the exhaust gas to form corrosive compounds inside the engine. Operating an engine at too low a temperature increases wear rates, increases fuel consumption, and reduces power output (Figure 12.10).

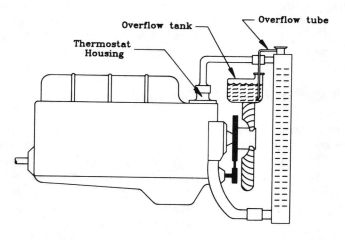

Figure 12.9–An overflow tank for capturing and returning radiator overflow.

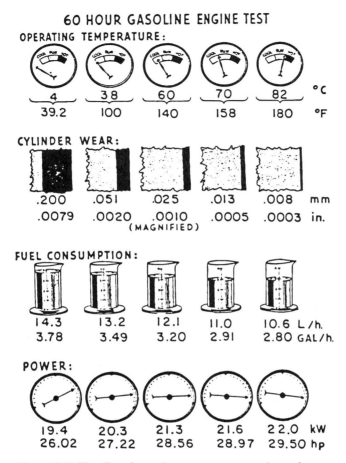

*Figure 12.10–The effect of operating temperature on engine performance and wear. (Reprinted with permission of Amoco.)*

The temperature of an engine can be regulated by covering or uncovering part of the frontal area of the radiator. On engines with thermosiphon systems, manually operated shutters are used to cover or uncover the radiator. However, *thermostats* provide the automatic regulation of engine temperature and are used almost exclusively to control the temperature of modern engines.

Two different styles of thermostats are shown in Figure 12.11. The bellows-type thermostat (Figure 12.11a) contains ether in a short, sealed tube. The elasticity of the bellows holds the thermostatic valve closed when the water is cold. The ether expands when the water is hot and opens the valve. The bimetal strip in Figure 12.11b consists of a strip of steel welded to a strip of bronze. When the water heats the bimetal strip, the bronze expands faster

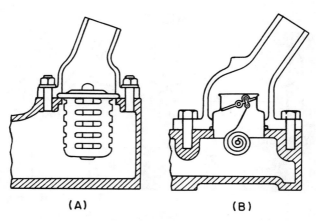

Figure 12.11–Thermostats. *(Courtesy of Deere & Company.)*

than the steel, causing the spiral strip to uncoil and open the valve. Manufacturers have designed thermostats to open at various temperatures. The temperature at which it opens is often stamped on a thermostat.

A thermostat is shown installed in an engine in Figure 12.5. When the engine is cold, the thermostat closes and prevents water from flowing through the radiator. A bypass passage of small diameter is provided to allow some coolant to flow from the head directly to the water pump. Thus, a small amount of coolant bypasses the radiator, but water continues to circulate through the engine. The engine warms up rapidly when the thermostat is closed, and the bypass provides for more uniform warm-up. When the coolant is warm enough, the thermostat opens and allows water to flow through the radiator. The bypass is so small that only a small fraction of the coolant flows through it when the thermostat is open. Some engines have the bypass arranged to be blocked by an extension when the thermostat is open.

## 12.8 COOLANTS

Water is effective in transferring heat, but it has serious limitations as an engine coolant. Water freezes at 0° C (32° F), and vehicles often are parked outdoors in colder temperatures. Thus, water alone could freeze in cooling systems, and the resulting expansion of water into ice could break the radiator or engine block. Water alone in contact with the iron inside an engine could cause severe rusting. Thus, a variety of other liquids have been used with water to overcome its limitations.

Methyl alcohol and denatured ethyl alcohol formerly were used as antifreeze agents. The alcohols provided good freezing point depression, but they were difficult to keep in the cooling system because of their low boiling points. Most antifreeze agents now are based on ethylene glycol ($C_2H_6O_2$). As Figure 12.12 shows, ethylene glycol lowers the freezing point of the coolant to a minimum of -69° C (-92° F) at a concentration of 68% by volume. Larger concentrations raise the freezing point. The ethylene glycol also increases the boiling point of the coolant. At a 50% concentration and at atmospheric pressure, ethylene glycol provides cooling performance over a temperature range from -37 to 109° C (-35 to 228° F). If the radiator was pressurized to 103 kPa (14.9 psi), the temperature range would extend up to 130° C (266° F).

Antifreeze containers usually contain a table relating the freezing point to the volume of antifreeze added into a cooling system of a given size. A hydrometer can also be used to check the concentration of ethylene glycol in the radiator since, as Figure 12.12 shows, the specific gravity of the solution increases with the concentration of ethylene glycol.

Several additives are included with ethylene glycol to improve its performance. Since solutions of ethylene glycol and water are corrosive to metals, chemical inhibitors are added to protect the metals in the cooling system. The inhibitors also contain an alkaline substance to neutralize any acids that may be enter the cooling system from exhaust gas leakage. Foam suppressors are added to the ethylene glycol. They lower the surface tension of the solution, thereby interfering with bubble formation. Rust inhibitors in the antifreeze form a chemical film over metal parts to retard rust formation. Finally, a dye is added to the antifreeze to give it a distinctive color.

As the preceding discussion indicates, antifreeze provides many more benefits than just freezing point depression. Therefore, it is good practice to keep an antifreeze solution in the cooling system even when temperatures are above freezing.

## 12.9 COOLING SYSTEM MAINTENANCE

Air-cooling systems require little maintenance. The screened inlet to the fan must be kept free of leaves, chaff, and other material to provide unrestricted airflow over the cooling fins.

Several types of maintenance are required to keep water-cooling systems in good working order. The coolant should be checked periodically to verify that the coolant level is above the finned tubes. Since additives in antifreeze gradually degrade, the cooling system

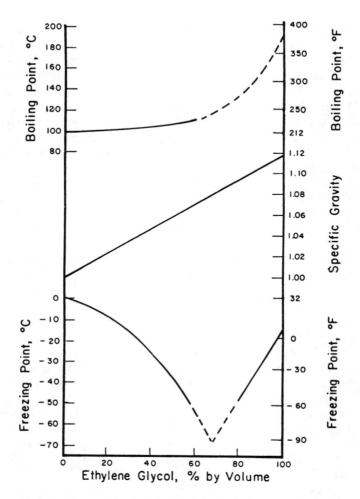

*Figure 12.12–Properties of ethylene and glycol solutions in water. (Data from Rueping, C. F., Antifreeze and coolant. Lubrication 65(3):26. 1979.)*

should be drained annually or biannually. After draining, the cooling system should be flushed with a solution of a cleansing agent and water. Typically, the cleaning solution contains oxalic acid and sodium bisulfate to aid in removing calcium and magnesium scale from the cooling system. After flushing, the cooling system is refilled with a solution of water and antifreeze. A good antifreeze will contain the additives that were discussed in Section 12.8.

Flexible rubber hoses are used to connect the radiator to the engine. The hoses gradually deteriorate with age. Figure 12.13 shows the type of hardening and cracking that can occur. The hoses

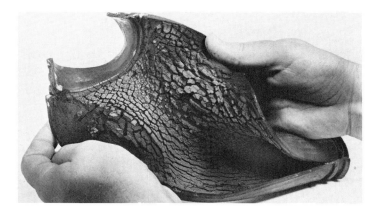

*Figure 12.13–A deteriorated radiator hose. (Courtesy of Deere & Company.)*

also may soften and swell. Therefore, hoses should be inspected periodically and should be replaced if they begin to deteriorate.

Thermostats may fail in service. Thermostats may become stuck in the closed position and cause the engine to overheat. Sticking in the open position causes the engine to warm up very slowly and run too cool. When a defective thermostat is replaced with a new one, it is essential that the sensing element face the engine as shown in Figure 12.5.

## 12.10 CERAMIC ENGINES

The purpose of the cooling system is to protect the metal parts of the engine against damage by overheating. If the vulnerable metals parts could be replaced by more heat-resistant materials, it would be possible to eliminate the cooling system. The ceramics developed for aerospace technology may be suitable replacement materials. Experimental diesel engines have been built in which parts exposed to high temperatures of combustion are coated with ceramics or are made wholly from ceramics. The term *adiabatic* means zero heat transfer and, because the ceramic diesels have no cooling system to receive heat, they sometimes are called adiabatic diesels. The much higher operating temperature of adiabatic diesels should permit them to operate more efficiently and produce more work from each liter (gal) of fuel.

## 12.11 SUMMARY

Since peak combustion temperatures exceed the melting point of cast iron, a cooling system is needed to protect an engine from self-destruction. Engines can be air cooled by directing air over finned surfaces on the hottest parts of the engine. However, most vehicle engines are water cooled.

Water-cooling systems include the internal passages in the engine block and head, a radiator to reject heat to the air, and a fan to move air through the radiator. A water pump is used on modern engines to supplement the natural thermosiphon circulation. A pressure relief valve in the radiator cap maintains pressure in the cooling system to increase the boiling point of the coolant. A vacuum relief valve in the cap prevents the formation of a vacuum, which could collapse the radiator.

Water alone is an unsatisfactory coolant. An antifreeze such as ethylene glycol is added to depress the freezing point below expected winter temperatures. The antifreeze contains rust inhibitors and other additives to protect the cooling system and should be used year-round.

A thermostat regulates the temperature by causing the coolant to bypass the radiator when the engine is cold. Thus, the thermostat overcomes the low engine temperatures that would cause corrosion, increase wear, and reduced power and efficiency. When the thermostat opens, the radiator prevents the oil film deterioration and engine damage that would result from excessively high temperatures.

Ceramic engines, although in the experimental stage, are expected to become available commercially. The ceramic parts in these engines eliminate the need for a cooling system and permit the engine to operate more efficiently.

## QUESTIONS

Q12.1  Peak combustion temperatures exceed the melting point of cast iron. Why don't the cast-iron cylinder liners melt?

Q12.2  Why are metal fins used on the exterior of air-cooled engines (Figure 12.13), but not on water-cooled engines?

Q12.3  What causes the water to circulate in a thermosiphon system?

Cooling Systems

Q12.4   (a) Does a water pump discharge into the engine block or into the radiator?
(b) Why?

Q12.5   Why is a thermostatically controlled clutch sometimes used to drive the fan? That is, why isn't the fan driven directly from the water pump shaft?

Q12.6   Will the engine coolant necessarily boil when its temperature exceeds 100° C (212° F)? Briefly explain your answer.

Q12.7   (a) What is the recommended maximum temperature of the inside of the cylinder liner?
(b) What is likely to occur if this maximum temperature is exceeded?

Q12.8   (a) What device is used to regulate the temperature of a water-cooled engine?
(b) Does the coolant circulate when this device is closed, and, if so, how does the circulation differ from when the device is open?
(c) Why is this device used? That is, why not design a cooling system with less capacity?

Q12.9   (a) What disadvantage caused the abandonment of alcohols as antifreeze in cooling systems?
(b) What type of antifreeze has replaced the alcohols?
(c) What principle can be used to test the freezing point of the solution in a cooling system?
(d) Do modern antifreezes have functions other than lowering the freezing point? Briefly explain your answer.

Q12.10   Is there any benefit to be gained from draining a cooling system periodically and replacing the antifreeze? Briefly explain your answer.

# PROBLEMS

P12.1  On a cold January day, 200 kW·h (270 hp-h) of energy are required to heat a seven-room house in central Illinois. Assuming that a tractor with 35 kW (47 hp) brake power has an energy balance similar to that shown in Figure 12.1 (32% of fuel energy goes to brake power and 16% goes into the coolant at full load), how many hours would the tractor have to run at full load if its radiator were used to heat the house?

P12.2  Rework P12.1, but assume the tractor has 100 kW (134 hp) of brake power.

P12.3  By combining Equations 5.6, 5.15, 5.16, and 5.19, the following equation for the fuel consumption of an engine can be derived:

$$\dot{M}_f = \frac{K_{fe}}{HV} * \frac{P_b + P_f}{e_{it}}$$

(a) Use the above equation to calculate the consumption of No. 2 diesel fuel by a 75 kW (100 hp) engine as the brake power is increased from zero to full load in increments of 7.5 kW (10 hp). Assume that the speed is held constant so that the friction power is constant at 13.2 kW (17.6 hp), and $e_{it}$ = 0.47 regardless of load. See Table 6.5 for the heating value of the fuel.

(b) At each load, use Equation 5.6 to calculate $P_{fe}$ and then multiply by $e_{it}$ to obtain the indicated power. Then, for each load, subtract $P_i$ from $P_{fe}$ to get an estimate of the power lost through the exhaust system; then divide by $P_{fe}$ and multiply by 100 to get an estimate of the percentage of the fuel energy lost through the exhaust.

(c) Next, for each load, subtract $P_b$ from $P_i$ to get an estimate of the power lost to friction and accessories in the engine; divide by $P_{fe}$ and multiply by 100 to get an estimate of the percentage of the fuel energy lost to engine friction and accessories.

(d) Finally, use your data to calculate a graph similar to Figure 12.1. Note that the curves are additive, that is, the second curve on Figure 12.1 is the sum of the energies for useful work and for coolant losses; you should also make your curves additive. You will have only three categories, that is, net work, exhaust heat and friction-accessories.

(e) Compare your graph with Figure 12.1. (Because of the numerous calculations required, consider using a spread sheet to work Problem 12.3.

P12.4 A tractor cooling system has a capacity of 12 L (12 qt). Refer to Figure 12.12.

(a) How much ethylene glycol would be required to protect the cooling system to -35° C (-31° F)?

(b) What would be the specific gravity of the solution of ethylene glycol and water?

(c) What would be the boiling point of the solution?

P12.5 Rework P12.4, but assume the cooling system is to be protected to -20° C (-4° F).

P12.6 Rework P12.4, but assume the capacity of the cooling system is 20 L (21 qt).

# 13
## Lubricants and Lubricating Systems

### 13.1 INTRODUCTION

The engine and power transmission systems in vehicles contain dozens of moving parts. Without proper lubrication, excessive friction would consume much of the engine power and the moving parts would wear at a rapid rate. In addition to reducing friction, a lubricant acts as a cushioning agent between the mating parts and can transport heat away from bearings. Lubricating oil serves as an effective seal to reduce the blowby of combustion gases past piston rings. Finally, lubricating oil acts as a cleansing agent inside an engine. Thus, lubrication is a vital part of engines and tractors.

### 13.2 THEORY OF LUBRICATION

Consider the contact between two mating parts in an engine. For example, Figure 13.1a shows a section of a piston ring in contact with the liner wall. Gas forces behind the ring and the tension in the ring itself cause the ring to press against the liner with a force $F_N$. If the piston is moving downward with velocity v, as shown in Figure 13.1a, a force $F_t$ appears in the contact area and is pointed in a direction to resist the movement of the rings. The two forces are related by the following equation:

$$f = \frac{F_t}{F_N} \qquad (13.1)$$

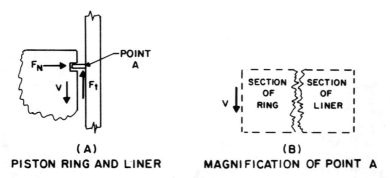

*Figure 13.1–An illustration of dry friction.*

where
    f    = coefficient of friction (dimensionless)
    $F_t$  = tangential force resisting motion
    $F_N$ = normal force pressing mating parts together

The tangential force arises from two primary sources:

1. One source is adhesion which occurs because of attraction between molecules in one part to those in the mating part. Adhesion may be augmented by chemical reactions and tends to bind the two parts together.

2. Mechanical friction, caused by the interlocking of irregularities on the two mating surfaces, is the second source.

    To initiate and maintain sliding, enough force must be applied to the ring by the piston to overcome the tangential force $F_t$. Adhesion increases when there is no relative motion and more force is, therefore, needed to initiate sliding than to maintain it after the piston is in motion. Equation 13.1 can be used to calculate a static *coefficient of friction* when sliding is being initiated, and a smaller, dynamic, coefficient of friction when sliding is underway.
    The mating surfaces on moving parts (for example, the liner wall and the face of the ring) may appear to be highly polished and smooth. Viewed under sufficient magnification, however, even highly polished surfaces have irregularities, as Figure 13.1b shows. Mechanical friction is the actual shearing of projections on one of the mating surfaces by those on the other. Thus, mechanical friction creates fine metal particles between the surfaces. Although Figure 13.1 depicts a ring and liner wall, the magnified surfaces in

Figure 13.1b also could represent sections of a crankshaft or camshaft journal and the mating bearings.

Mechanical friction can be reduced greatly if a film of oil is forced between the mating surfaces. If the film is very thin (approximately the thickness of a single layer of oil molecules), the lubrication is referred to as a *boundary lubrication*. *Full-film*, or *hydrodynamic*, *lubrication* occurs when the oil film is thick enough to prevent projections on one surface from contacting those on the mating surface. *Mixed-film lubrication* occurs when the film thickness is intermediate between boundary lubrication and hydrodynamic lubrication.

If an oil supply is available (for instance, if the liner wall in Figure 13.1a is coated with oil), motion of one part over the other tends to drag oil between the parts and increase the thickness of the oil film. The normal force between the parts tends to force oil out and decrease the film thickness. All bearings in an engine are in boundary lubrication when the engine is started from rest or when it is coasting to a stop. Hydrodynamic lubrication should develop when the engine is running at normal speed. Piston rings are in boundary lubrication when the piston stops at the HDC of each stroke. The rings are in hydrodynamic lubrication when the piston is moving rapidly.

## 13.3 TYPES OF LUBRICATING OILS

Before the discovery of petroleum, *fixed oils* were used to lubricate machine parts. The fixed oils included animal oils (such as lard or fish oils) and vegetable oils (such as castor oil). After the discovery of petroleum, the vast majority of lubricants were *mineral oils* derived from crude petroleum. The molecular structure of mineral oils varies with the source of crude oil. The two primary types of crude oil used in lubricating oils are naphthene-based crudes and paraffinic-based crudes (see Section 6.2).

In refining lubricants, the crude oil is first distilled to recover the lighter fuel fractions, such as gases, gasoline, kerosene, and so forth. The remaining stock is further fractionated to recover hydrocarbons in the proper viscosity range for lubricating oil base stocks. These base stocks are further treated to remove asphalt and aromatic hydrocarbons. Finally, paraffinic-based stocks must be dewaxed to provide an oil with a low pour point (see Section 6.9). Napthenic stocks are essentially wax free. The napthenic stocks are used to make lubricating oils with low to medium viscosity index (or VI, as discussed in Section 13.5). Paraffinic stocks are used to make oils with medium to high VI. Claims are sometimes made that lubricating oil from one type of crude oil is superior to others. However, modern refining methods can produce acceptable lubricating oil from a wide variety of crude oils, and it is difficult to prove that one source is superior to another.

The performance of a lubricating oil in hydrodynamic lubrication is determined primarily by the viscosity of the oil. Viscosity will be discussed in Section 13.5 Oiliness is a critical property in boundary lubrication. *Oiliness* refers to the ability of a lubricant to adhere to metal surfaces and is related to the polarity of the molecules. Molecules are electrically neutral as a whole, but the positive and negative charges within the molecule may not be arranged symmetrically. For example, $CO_2$ is nonpolar because the two oxygen atoms are arranged symmetrically on opposite sides of the carbon atom. However, $H_2O$ is a polar molecule because the two hydrogen atoms are not symmetrically arranged around the oxygen atom. A polar molecule tends to cling to metal surfaces. Polar lubricants contain long chains or rings, which are nonpolar, and are connected to a nonsymmetrical part of the molecule, which is polar. The polar part attaches the molecule to the metal surface, while the nonpolar portion extends outward to provide a lubricating film. Esters of fixed oils have great oiliness and are used as additives to supply this property to mineral oils.

## 13.4  LUBRICATION WITH GREASE

Sometimes, when it is impractical to provide a reservoir of oil for lubricating a bearing, grease is used as the lubricant. For example, grease is used to lubricate the wheel bearings of unpowered wheels on vehicles. *Grease* is an emulsion of mineral oil with soap. Typically, the liquid lubricant makes up 70 to 95% of the emulsion to provide the lubrication; the soap thickener provides a semisolid consistency that causes the grease to maintain its position in the mechanism. Greases do not continually flow through a bearing and thus do not perform the cooling and cleansing functions that are accomplished by oil. However, grease can reduce friction, serve as a cushion between mating parts, and act as a seal against the entry of dirt and water.

Grease may be placed in a bearing by hand packing or by means of a grease gun. The *grease gun* is a hand- or power-driven pump that pumps the grease into a bearing through a fitting. Several grease fittings are shown in Figure 13.2. The fitting actually is a check valve that is screwed into a tapped hole leading to the bearing. The grease gun can force grease through the fitting and into the bearing, but the check valve prevents return flow when the gun is removed.

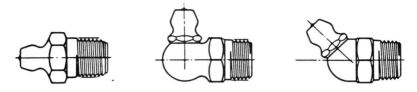

*Figure 13.2–Fittings for transmitting grease. (Reprinted with permission. © 1984 Handbook, Society of Automotive Engineers, Inc.)*

Grease fittings may be straight or have 45° or 90° elbows (Figure 13.2) to provide the grease gun with more convenient access.

The properties of a grease are dependent upon the type of soap used as an emulsifying agent. The three most common soaps used to make grease for farm equipment are lime- (or calcium-) based soap, soda- (sodium-) based soap, and lithium-based soap. *Lime-based greases* are water stabilized by adding approximately 2% water to aid the formation of soap fibers. Although they are water resistant, they melt at approximately 80° C (175° F). Therefore, they are used where water may be present but where temperatures are not too high. *Soda-based greases* can withstand temperatures up to 120° C (250° F) but will dissolve in water. *Lithium-based greases* have moderate water resistance and can withstand temperatures up to 160° C (325° F). They are used as general-purpose greases and have captured over 60% of the grease market in the United States.

Additives are used to improve certain properties of grease. Antioxidants are added to extend the service life at elevated temperatures. Rust and corrosion inhibitors prevent the grease from attacking copper, steel, and bronze and also prevent rusting in the presence of water. Extreme pressure (EP) additives increase the load-carrying capacity of the lubricant film. They are especially valuable in boundary lubrication. Antiwear agents reduce wear during boundary lubrication. Lubricity additives reduce friction at low sliding speeds. Tackifiers are added to allow the grease to adhere better to metal surfaces and improve water resistance. Solid fillers improve the performance of the grease when high loads or shock loads are present.

## 13.5 VISCOSITY OF MOTOR OILS

A section of piston ring is seen moving along a liner wall in Figure 13.3. The ring is separated from the liner wall by an oil film thick enough to provide hydrodynamic lubrication. Under such conditions, the tangential force $F_t$ is independent of the normal force

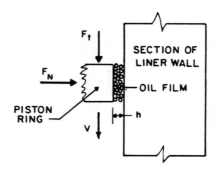

*Figure 13.3–An illustration of hydrodynamic lubrication.*

$F_N$ that presses the ring against the wall. The tangential force can be calculated with the following equation:

$$F_t = \frac{K_\mu * \mu * A * V}{h} \qquad (13.2)$$

where
- $F_t$ = tangential force (or shear force) in N (lb)
- $\mu$ = dynamic viscosity in Mpa·s (cP)
- $A$ = contact area between ring and liner wall in mm$^2$ (in.$^2$)
- $V$ = ring speed in m/s (ft/s)
- $h$ = film thickness in mm (in.)
- $K_\mu$ = units constant = $1.0 \times 10^{-6}$ ($1.74 \times 10^{-6}$)

The centipoise (cP) was the customary unit for dynamic viscosity before SI units were developed. Fortunately, 1 cP = 1 mPa·s exactly. In hydrodynamic lubrication, the oil film, and not the metal projections on the mating parts, is sheared. The shear force increases with speed and contact area and with an oil property called the *dynamic viscosity*.

A Cannon-Fenske viscometer (Figure 13.4) can be used to measure the viscosity of oil. After the lower part of the viscometer is filled with oil, the viscometer is placed in a constant-temperature bath. The test must be conducted at a specified temperature because oil viscosity changes with temperature. When the temperature has stabilized, suction is used on the small tube to pull the oil level above line A. The oil level begins to fall, and the lower part of the oil column must pass through capillary C when suction is released. A stopwatch is used to measure the time for the oil level to fall from line A to line B. Time in seconds is multiplied by a viscometer

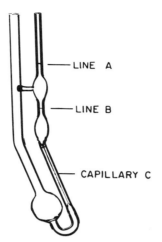

*Figure 13.4–A glass viscometer. (Adapted from a drawing by Cannon-Fenske Instrument Company.)*

constant to obtain the viscosity. Since oil density affects the time required for the oil to flow through the capillary, the measured viscosity is called kinematic viscosity. It is related to dynamic viscosity by the following equation:

$$\nu = \frac{K_v * \mu}{\rho} \quad (13.3)$$

where
- $\nu$ = kinematic viscosity in mm²/s (cSt)
- $\mu$ = dynamic viscosity as defined in Equation 13.2
- $\rho$ = density in kg/L (lb/ft³)
- $K_v$ = units constant = 1.0 (62.4)

The centistoke (cSt) was the customary unit for kinematic viscosity before SI units were developed. Again it is fortunate that 1 cSt = 1 mm²/s exactly.

A Saybolt universal viscometer (Figure 13.5) also can be used to measure the kinematic viscosity of oil. An oil sample is placed in the Saybolt tube and the temperature is allowed to stabilize. When the plug is removed, a stopwatch is used to measure the time the oil takes to flow out through the orifice. The viscosity is reported in Saybolt universal seconds (SUS).

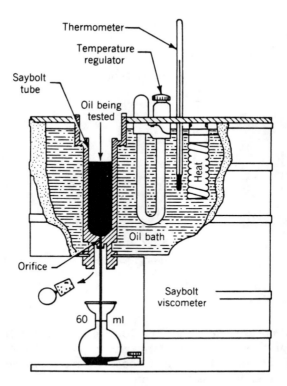

*Figure 13.5–The Sabolt universal viscometer. (Courtesy of Texaco's magazine Lubrication.)*

The apparent viscosity of engine oils at low temperatures is measured using a device called a cold-cranking simulator. It consists of a motor-driven cylindrical rotor immersed in oil in a stationary cylindrical container. The oil whose viscosity is to be determined fills the small space between the rotor and the container. The motor is a universal type electric motor whose speed varies with torque load. When the motor turns the rotor, its speed depends on the viscosity of the oil; the higher the viscosity, the lower the speed. Thus, through use of a suitable calibration curve, the oil viscosity can be determined by measuring the rotor speed.

The viscosity of oil declines as its temperature increases, as illustrated in Figure 13.6. Figure 13.6 shows curves for eight different oils. Each oil is identified by an SAE number. The numbers are part of a classification scheme for the viscosity of motor oils developed by the Society for Automotive Engineers (SAE).

The *SAE classification* scheme for viscosity is summarized in Table 13.1. An SAE number with a W indicates that the viscosity was determined at low temperature using the cold cranking simulator;

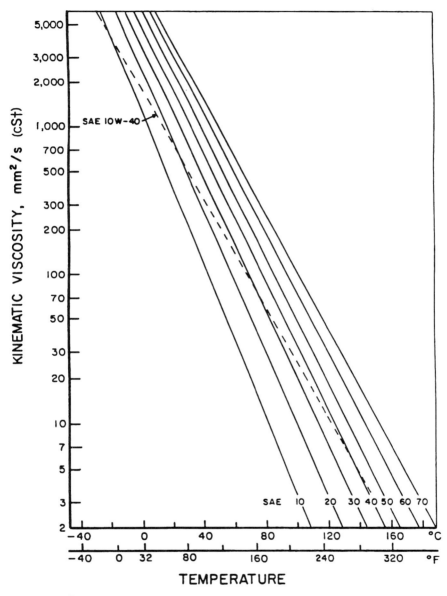

Figure 13.6–Variation of oil viscosity with temperature. (Data from ASTM Standard D341-37T.)

historically the specified low temperature was -18° C (0° F), but now a range of low temperatures are used depending on the viscosity class (see Table 13.1). SAE viscosity grades without the W are measured at 100° C (212° F) using a viscometer. The lower temperatures

TABLE 3.1. SAE classification of motor oils

| SAE Viscosity Grade | Max. Visc. mPa.s* | at Temp. °C (°F) | Borderline Pumping Temp. °C (°F) | Visc. at 100 °C (212 °F) Min. mm²/s** | Max mm²/s** |
|---|---|---|---|---|---|
| 0W | 3250 | -30 (-22) | -35 (-31) | 3.8 | --- |
| 5W | 3500 | -25 (-13) | -30 (-22) | 3.8 | --- |
| 10W | 3500 | -20 ( -4) | -25 (-13) | 4.1 | --- |
| 15W | 3500 | -15 ( 5) | -20 ( -4) | 5.6 | --- |
| 20W | 4500 | -10 ( 14) | -15 ( 5) | 5.6 | --- |
| 25W | 6000 | -5 ( 23) | -10 ( 14) | 9.3 | --- |
| 20 | --- | | --- | 5.6 | < 9.3 |
| 30 | --- | | --- | 9.3 | < 12.5 |
| 40 | --- | | --- | 12.5 | < 16.3 |
| 50 | --- | | --- | 16.3 | < 21.9 |
| 60 | --- | | --- | 21.9 | < 26.4 |

Source: SAE Standard J300
*1 mPa.s = 1 cP
**1 mm²/s = 1 cSt

approximate conditions in the engine during cold weather starting, while the higher temperature is typical of conditions in the crankcase of a fully warm engine operating under heavy load. The SAE viscosity system was first established in 1911 and has been revised several time since then. The "Borderline Pumping Temperature" indicates the lowest temperature at which the oil can be pumped by the lubricating system when the engine is being started in cold weather.

The oil in an engine sometimes must function over a wide range of temperatures. The change in oil viscosity with temperature (Figure 13.6) is undesirable. For example, an SAE 10 oil would have a viscosity of 3500 mPa·s (cP) when an engine is started at -20° C (-4° F). If the engine subsequently warms to 80° C (176° F) or higher under heavy load, the oil viscosity will decline below 10 mPa·s (cP). It is difficult for a lubrication system to function well over such a wide range of oil viscosities. Thus, motor oils with a high viscosity index are desirable.

*Viscosity index* refers to the ability of an oil to resist changes in viscosity as the temperature changes. An oil with a high viscosity index can serve as a multigrade oil because it can meet the viscosity limits of one grade of oil in the cold cranking simulator and also meet the requirements of an oil with a higher SAE number at 100° C (212° F). For example, the SAE 10W-30 oil has a high viscosity index. Oil refiners can produce motor oils with a high enough viscosity index to span two SAE grades (for example, SAE 10W-20 or SAE 20W-30), but additives to improve the viscosity index are used to increase the span of SAE grades. Typically, the additives are polymers which are added to oil of the lower SAE number. Rising temperature activates the polymer to cross-link oil molecules and moderate the usual thinning that would otherwise occur. Adding a polymer additive to an SAE 10W-20 oil, for example, might improve the viscosity index sufficiently to achieve that of an SAE 10W-40 motor oil.

## 13.6 OIL ADDITIVES

Straight mineral oil would not be an adequate lubricant for modern engines. Increasing demands on engines in the form of higher pressures and temperatures, higher speeds, and so forth have placed greater demands on the lubricating oil. Additives have helped to meet these greater demands. Viscosity index improvers were discussed in the previous section. Other oil additives are listed in Table 13.2.

Detergent-dispersant additives are especially important in motor oils for diesel engines. The nonhomogeneous combustion in diesel engines tends to produce carbon, which deposits in ring grooves. The detergent-dispersant additives help to keep the carbon in the oil in suspension so that it can be removed when the oil is changed. The motor oil should be black in color if the detergent-dispersant is working properly. Detergent-dispersants are used in modern gasoline engines as well as in diesel engines.

Nondetergent oils are commercially available. Problems can occur if detergent oil is used in an engine that has been run for long periods with nondetergent oil. The detergent can dislodge accumulated carbon deposits and sludge, which might block the strainer of the oil pump. In changing from a nondetergent to a detergent oil, it is well to drain the detergent oil after the first few hours of operation to remove the accumulated carbon and sludge.

Since motor oils contain some unsaturated hydrocarbons, the oil can oxidize in the presence of air and high temperatures. Oxidation rates increase rapidly when the oil temperature is above 100° C (212° F). Metals act as catalysts to increase the rate of oxidation. Oxidation causes the oil to thicken and also can cause the formation of corrosive acids. Oxidation inhibitors are added to oil to interfere with the oxidation reaction and thus decrease the rate of oxidation. A corrosion inhibitor may be included to neutralize any acids that form. The catalytic effect of metals can be reduced by the use of metal deactivators which form a protective film over metal surfaces.

An extreme pressure (EP) additive may be used to reduce the wear caused by metal-to-metal sliding at high speeds and loads. For example, an EP additive can reduce wear caused by valve tappets sliding on the cam lobes. The EP additives react chemically with the metal surface to form a film that prevents surface welding of mating parts.

TABLE 13.2. Common additives for motor oils (con't)

| Additive Type | Compounds Commonly Used | Reason for Use | Possible Mechanism |
|---|---|---|---|
| Dispersant | Alkylpolyamides, aklyl $P_2S_5$ products, nitrogen containing methacrylate polymers, metal sulfonates, organic boron compounds | To maintain engine cleanliness by keeping oil-insoluble material in suspension. | Primarily a physical process. Dispersant is attracted to sludge particle by polar forces; oil solubility keeps sludge suspended. |
| Detergent | Term often is used interchangeably with dispersant. Detergent, however, implies a cleaning action in addition to a dispersing action. Because these materials exhibit only a mild cleaning action, the term detergent is being replaced by dispersant. | | |
| Viscosity index (VI) improver | Methacrylate polymers, butylene polymers, polymerized olefins or isoolefins, alkylated styrene polymers, various selected copolymers | To lower the rate of change of viscosity with temperature. | VI improvers are less affected by temperature than is oil. They raise the viscosity at 99°C more in proportion than they do at 38°C due to changes in solubility. |
| Oxidation inhibitor | Zinc dithiophosphates, hindered phenols, aromatic amines | To retard oxidative decomposition of the oil, which can result in varnish, sludge, and corrosion. | Decomposition of peroxides, inhibition of free radical formation, and passivation of metal surfaces. |
| Corrosion inhibitor | Zinc dithiophosphates, metal phenolates, basic metal | To prevent attack of corrosive oil contaminants on bearings | Neutralization of acidic material by the formation of |

TABLE 13.2. Common additives for motor oils (con't)

| Additive Type | Compounds Commonly Used | Reason for Use | Possible Mechanism |
|---|---|---|---|
| Metal deactivator | Zinc dithiophosphates, organic sulfides, certain organic nitrogen compounds | To passivate catalytic metal surfaces to inhibit oxidation. | Formation of inactive protective film on metal surface. Formation of catalytically inactive complex with metal ions. |
| Antiwear extreme pressure (EP); oiliness film strength agents | Zinc dithiophosphates, organic phosphates; acid phosphates, organic sulfur and chlorine compounds, boron-nitrogen compounds | To reduce friction, prevent scoring and seizure; to reduce wear. | Formation of film by chemical reaction on metal-contacting surfaces that have lower shear strength than base metal, thereby reducing friction and preventing welding; seizure of contacting surfaces when oil film is ruptured. |
| Rust inhibitor | Metal sulfonates, fatty acids and amines | To prevent rusting of ferrous engine parts during storage and from acidic moisture accumulated during cold engine operation. This is a specific type of corrosion. | Preferential adsorption of polar-type surface-active material on metal surfaces to repel water. Neutralization of corrosive acids. |
| Pour point depressant | Methacrylate polymers, alkylated naphthalene or phenols | To lower pour point of lubricants. | Formation of wax crystals in oil to prevent growth and oil adsorption at reduced temperatures. |
| Foam inhibitor | Silicone polymers | To prevent the formation of stable foam. | Reduction of surface tension, which allows air bubbles to separate from the oil more readily. |

*Source:* Courtesy of Texaco's magazine *Lubrication.*

Rust-inhibitor additives prevent rusting by forming a protective film over iron and steel surfaces. The film repels the attack of water.

The pour point for motor oils has the same meaning as the pour point of fuels (see Section 6.9). The pour point of motor oils is high enough to interfere with lubrication when engines are started in winter conditions. A pour point depressant additive prevents the growth of wax crystals at low temperatures and thereby improves the flowability of the oil.

The splashing that can occur in a crankcase can entrap air in the oil and lead to the formation of foam. Foam-inhibitor additives reduce the surface tension of the oil and allow the air bubbles to escape from the oil.

## 13.7 SERVICE CLASSIFICATION FOR MOTOR OILS

The American Petroleum Institute (API) first adopted a *service classification* for motor oils in 1947. The early classification system did not recognize different requirements for motor oils for gasoline and diesel engines. In 1952, API developed a new classification system that established the following classifications:

ML – motor light for light-duty gasoline engines
MM – motor moderate for gasoline engines
MS – motor severe for severe duty in gasoline engines
DG – diesel general for light-duty diesel engines
DM – diesel moderate for diesel engines
DS – diesel severe for severe duty in diesel engines

The classifications were revised in 1955 and again in 1960 as engine requirements changed. However, because they lacked sufficiently precise definition of oil quality, engine manufacturers found it necessary to develop supplementary specifications. The API classification system developed in the 1950s is obsolete now, although the classification symbols are still found on some oil containers.

In 1969, the API, ASTM (American Society for Testing Materials), and SAE began a joint effort to establish a new service classification system for motor oils. The current classification system is shown in Table 13.3. The S-series of oils are considered to be service station oils for use in spark-ignition engines. The C-series oils are commercial-grade oils for use in compression-ignition engines. The second letter in each series designates the severity of service for which the oil is intended. For example, an SA oil may have no

TABLE 13.3. Service classification of motor oils

| Letter Designation | API Engine Service Description | ASTM Engine Oil Description |
|---|---|---|
| SA | Utility gasoline and diesel engine service: Service typical of engines operated under such mild conditions that the protection afforded by compound oils is not required. This classification has no performance requirement. | Oil without additives, except that it may contain pour and/or foam depressants. |
| SB | Minimum-duty gasoline engine service: Service typical of engines operated under such mild conditions that only minimum protection afforded by compounding is desired. Oils designed for this service have been used since the 1930s and provide only antiscuff capability and resistance to oil oxidation and bearing corrosion. | Provides some antioxidant and antiscuff capabilities. |
| SC | 1964 gasoline engine warranty service: Service typical of gasoline engines in 1964–1967 models of passenger cars and trucks operating under engine manufacturers' warranties in effect during those model years. Oils designed for this service provide control of high- and low-temperature deposits, wear, rust, and corrosion in gasoline engines. | Oil meeting the 1964–1967 requirements of the automobile manufacturers. Intended primarily for use in passenger cars. Provides low-temperature antisludge and antirust performance. |
| SD | 1968 gasoline engine warranty maintenance service: Service typical of gasoline engines in 1968–1970 models of passenger cars and some trucks operating under engine manufacturers' warranties in effect during those model years. Also may apply to certain 1971 and/or later models, as specified (or | Oil meeting the 1968–1971 requirements of the automobile manufacturers. Intended primarily for use in passenger cars. Provides low-temperature antisludge and antirust performance. |

TABLE 13.3. Service classification of motor oils (con't)

| Letter Designation | API Engine Service Description | ASTM Engine Oil Description |
|---|---|---|
| | recommended) in the owners' manuals. Oils designed for this service provide more protection against high- and low-temperature engine deposits, wear, rust, and corrosion in gasoline engines than do oils that are satisfactory for API engine service classification SC and may be used when API engine service classification SC is recommended. | |
| SE | 1972 gasoline engine warranty maintenance service: Service typical of gasoline engines in passenger cars and some trucks beginning with 1972 and certain 1971 models operating under engine manufacturers' warranties. Oils designed for this service provide more protection against oil oxidation, high-temperature engine deposits, rust, and corrosion in gasoline engines than do oils that are satisfactory for API gasoline engine warranty maintenance classifications SD or SC and may be used when either of these classifications are recommended. | Oil meeting the 1972 requirements of the automobile manufacturers. Intended primarily for use in passenger cars. Provides high-temperature antioxidation and low-temperature antisludge and antirust performance. |
| SF | 1980 gasoline engine warranty maintenance service: Service typical of gasoline engines in passenger cars and some trucks beginning with the 1980 model operating under engine manufacturers' recommended maintenance procedures. Oils developed for this service provide increased oxidation stability | Oil meeting the 1980 and later warranty requirements of automobile manufacturers. Intended primarily for use in gasoline engine passenger cars. Provides protection against sludge, varnish, rust, wear, and high-temperature oil thickening. |

(continued)

TABLE 13.3. Service classification of motor oils (con't)

| Letter Designation | API Engine Service Description | ASTM Engine Oil Description |
|---|---|---|
| | and improved antiwear performance relative to oils that meet the minimum requirements for API service category SE. The oils also provide protection against engine deposits, rust, and corrosion. Oils meetings API service classification SF may be used where API service categories SE, SD, or SC are recommended. | |
| SG | For service in passenger cars, vans and light trucks beginning with the 1989 model year; SG oils include performance properties of API grade CC. May be used where API categories SF, SE, SF/CC, or SE/CC are recommended. | Provides improved control of engine deposits, oil oxidation and engine wear relative to previous categories. Also provides protection against rust and corrosion. |
| CA (for diesel engine service) | Light-duty diesel engine service: Service typical of diesel engines operated in mild to moderate duty with high-quality fuels. Occasionally has included gasoline engines in mild service. Oils designed for this service were widely used in the late 1940s and 1950s. These oils provide protection from bearing corrosion and from high-temperature deposits in normally aspirated diesel engines when using fuels of such quality that they impose no unusual requirements for wear and deposit protection. | Oil meeting the requirements of MIL–L–2104A. For use in gasoline and naturally aspirated diesel engines operated on low-sulfur fuel. The MIL–L–2104A specification was issued in 1954. |
| CB (for diesel engine service) | Moderate-duty diesel engine service: Service typical of diesel engines operated in mild to moderate duty, but with low-quality fuels that necessitate more protection from wear and deposits. | Oil for use in gasoline and naturally aspirated diesel engines. Includes MIL–L–2104A oils for which the diesel engine test was run using high-sulfur fuel. |

TABLE 13.3. Service classification of motor oils (cont.)

| Letter Designation | API Engine Service Description | ASTM Engine Oil Description |
|---|---|---|
| | Occasionally has included gasoline engines in mild service. Oils designed for this service were introduced in 1949. Such oils provide necessary protection from bearing corrosion and from high-temperature deposits in normally aspirated diesel engines with high-sulfur fuels. | |
| CC (for diesel engine service) | Moderate duty diesel and gasoline engine service: Service typical of lightly supercharged diesel engines operated in moderate to severe duty and has included certain heavy-duty gasoline engines. Oils designed for this service were introduced in 1961 and used in many trucks, industrial and construction equipment, and farm tractors. These oils provide protection from high-temperature deposits in light supercharged diesels and also from rust, corrosion, and low-temperature deposits in gasoline engines. | Oil meeting requirements of MIL–L–2104B. Provides low-temperature antisludge, antirust, and light supercharged diesel engine performance. The MIL–L–2104B specification was issued in 1964. |
| CD (for diesel engine service) | Severe duty diesel engine service: Service typical of supercharged diesel engines in high-speed, high-output duty requiring highly effective control of wear and deposits. Oils designed for this service were introduced in 1955 and provide protection from bearing corrosion and from high-temperature deposits in supercharged diesel engines when using fuels of a wide quality range. | Oil meeting Caterpillar Tractor Company certification requirements for superior lubricants (Series 3) for Caterpillar diesel engines. Provides moderately supercharged diesel engine performance. The certification of Series 3 oil was established by Caterpillar Tractor Company in 1955. The related MIL–L–45199 specification was issued in 1958. |

TABLE 13.3. Service classification of motor oils (cont.)

| Letter Designation | API Engine Service Description | ASTM Engine Oil Description |
|---|---|---|
| CD II (for two-stroke diesel engines) | This category adopted in 1987 for severe duty service in supercharged diesel engines. | Requires evaluation in a a multicylinder, supercharged engine in addition to the performance requirements of the CD category. |
| CE (for diesel engine service) | This category adopted in 1987 service typical of turbocharged or supercharged heavy-duty diesel engines manufactured since 1983 and operated under both low-speed, high-load and high-speed, high-load conditions. May also be used where previous API categories for diesel engines are recommended. | |

*Source:* Reprinted with permission. © 1992 *Handbook*, Society of Automotive Engineers, Inc.

additives and is intended for very light duty. The system is open-ended. That is, as new engines that place more severe requirements on the motor oil are developed, new service classifications can be developed. A service classification defines the sequence of standardized engine tests that are used to evaluate oil samples as well as specifies the performance criteria that the oil samples must meet to be accepted into the class. The SAE is responsible for evaluating the need for new categories. The ASTM establishes test methods and performance limits that must accompany a new classification. The API communicates the classification system to oil consumers.

The service classification is reviewed annually. New classifications are added only when their need can be established. The SG and CE classifications were only recently established.

Oil refiners use additives to adapt their oils to fit the various classifications. Often, it is possible to produce a motor oil that will meet more than one service classification. For example, an oil package in a container marked CD-CC-SE-SF should be able to meet the requirements of any of the four service classifications listed.

## 13.8  ENGINE LUBRICATION SYSTEMS

The lubrication system must supply clean, filtered oil to all moving parts in an engine continuously while the engine is running. Engine lubrication systems are classified as *splash*, *pressure-feed and splash*, or *full-pressure* systems.

### 13.8.1  Splash Systems
Most small, single-cylinder engines do not have an oil pump and, therefore, are lubricated by splash lubrication. Typically, a small projection on the rod bearing cap dips into the oil pan during each crankshaft revolution and picks up oil that splashes inside the engine.

### 13.8.2  Pressure-Feed and Splash Systems
A pressure-feed and splash system is illustrated in Figure 13.7. The oil level in the crankcase is maintained just below the crankshaft. A screen-covered oil inlet near the bottom of the crankcase conveys oil to the oil pump. The pump usually is a gear pump (discussed in Section 14.4.1) and includes a spring-loaded relief valve to regulate the oil pressure. The valve opens and releases oil to the sump to prevent excessive pressures. The pump discharges into drilled oil galleries in the engine block. In most engines, the oil is first routed to a filter for removal of contaminants and then moves into other oil galleries for distribution throughout the engine. Parts that are oiled by pressurized oil include the main bearings, the connecting rod bearings, the cam bearings, and the rocker arm shaft. Oil forced from holes in the rocker arm shaft runs along the top of the rocker arms and drips onto the valve stems. Oil flows from the top of the head through the openings for the push rods and oils the cam and tappets before falling back into the crankcase. There are no galleries to transfer oil to the walls of the cylinders. Rather, oil escaping from the connecting rod bearings creates a spray mist that coats the cylinders. Oil control rings on the pistons wipe off most of the oil on each downstroke, and oil passes through the holes in the ring grooves to oil the piston pins before falling back into the crankcase.

### 13.8.3  Full-Pressure Systems
A full-pressure lubrication system is similar to the system shown in Figure 13.7, except that an oil passage is drilled through the center of each connecting rod. Pressurized oil leaving the connecting rod bearing flows inside the rod to oil the piston pin and then is sprayed through a nozzle in the top of the connecting rod. The oil spray on the underside of the piston transports heat to the crankcase, thereby

Lubricants and Lubricating Systems 353

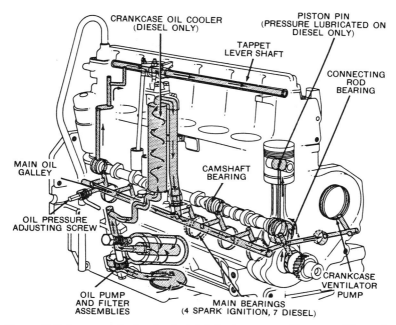

Figure 13.7–A pressure-feed and splash lubrication system. (Courtesy of Deere & Company.)

cooling the piston. Full-pressure systems are used on some high-output diesel engines.

### 13.8.4 Filtering Systems

Oil filtering systems can be classified as *full-flow* or *bypass* systems. A bypass system is illustrated in Figure 13.8a. In this system, approximately 5 to 10% of the oil from the pump is bypassed to the filter; the rest goes directly to the bearings. The bypass method permits filtering particles as small as 1 micrometer (0.00004 in.) from the oil, but not all of the oil is filtered at one time. The full-flow filter must be coarse to allow full flow. Particles several micrometers in size may pass through during normal operation. The full-flow filter must include a bypass valve to protect the engine. If the filter becomes blocked, the bypass valve can open to ensure a continuing supply of oil to the bearings.

Oil filters can be either surface filters or depth filters. Surface filters are made of accordion-pleated paper. Contaminants are trapped on the surface as oil flows through the paper. Depth filters are packed with cotton or other absorbent material, which traps contaminants as the oil flows through. Regardless of the filter medium, modern oil filters are enclosed in a metal housing

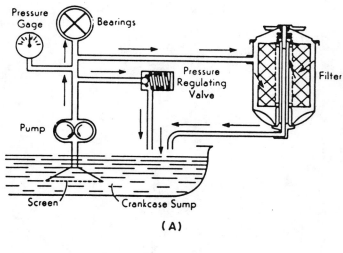

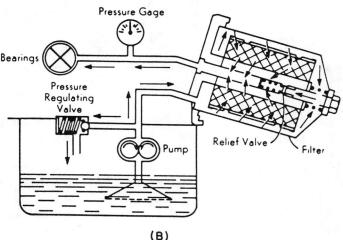

Figure 13.8–Oil filtering systems. (Courtesy of FRAM Division of Allied Automotive.)

(Figure 13.9). The end of the filter is threaded for attachment to the engine, and a rubber gasket is bonded to the end of the filter to prevent leakage. At periodic intervals, the entire filter is removed and discarded, and a new filter is installed.

Two indicators are provided for monitoring the operation of an engine lubrication system. A dipstick is mounted through a special opening in the block and extends down into the oil sump. Marks are placed on the dipstick to indicate the proper oil level. Engines

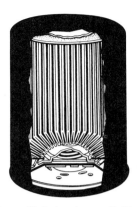

*Figure 13.9–A spin-on oil filter. (Courtesy of FRAM Division of Allied Automotive.)*

typically consume some oil during service, and the dipstick can be used to decide when more oil should be added. The lubrication system also includes a pressure gage (Figure 13.8) to indicate whether the oil pump is delivering pressurized oil to the oil galleries. The pressure gage is replaced with a pressure switch on some engines, which turns on a red light if the oil pressure falls below a safe level.

## 13.9 OIL COOLERS

One of the functions of motor oils is to absorb heat generated by friction and transport it to the crankcase. If the crankcase is sufficiently large, the oil will be able to remain in the crankcase and transfer heat out through the walls of the oil pan before being recirculated by the oil pump. Some heavy-duty engines have an auxiliary oil cooler to help dissipate the heat. Most oil coolers are oil-to-water heat exchangers. That is, the oil transfers heat to the engine coolant. An internal oil cooler is shown in Figure 13.10. A finned tube is mounted inside the crankcase. The water pump pumps water through the finned tube to receive heat from the oil. Then, the coolant passes through the engine block to pick up additional heat or goes directly to the radiator for cooling. On some engines, the oil cooler is mounted externally, and the oil pump must pump oil though the cooler.

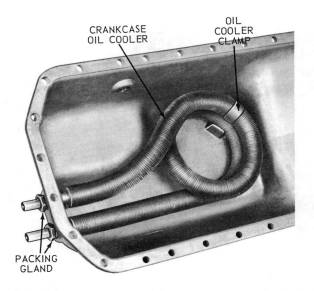

*Figure 13.10–An internal oil cooler. (Courtesy of Deere & Company.)*

## 13.10 LUBRICATION OF POWER TRANSMISSION SYSTEMS

Service requirements for gear oils differ from those for motor oil. Gear oils are not exposed to products of combustion but must withstand higher loads than motor oils. The API rates the load-carrying capacities of gear oils by comparing them to certain standard reference oils. Extreme pressure and/or antiscoring additives are used in gear oils that are subjected to moderate to severe service.

Several other factors in addition to load-carrying capacity are important for gear oils. Oxidation resistance is not critical in mild service, but can become important when ambient temperatures are very high and loading is heavy. Anti-foaming agents are included to prevent foaming. The oil must not attack the seals or other elastomers in the gear case. Finally, the viscosity of the oil must be in the proper range. The viscosity must be low enough to allow the oil to flow readily between contacting surfaces and, for manual transmissions, to allow easy gear shifting. Because increased viscosity reduces noise, wear and leakage, the viscosity must not be too low. The viscosity index must be high enough to keep the viscosity in the proper range over the range of expected operating temperatures.

The SAE has established a separate viscosity classification for gear oils, as Table 13.4 shows. The higher SAE numbers specify that

TABLE 3.4. SAE viscosity classifications for lubricants for axles and manual transmissions

| SAE No. | Temperature in °C (°F) for viscosity of 150,000 mPa.s (cP) | Viscosity Range at 100 °C (212 °F) in mm²/s (cSt) Min. | Max. |
|---|---|---|---|
| 70W | -55 (-67) | 4.1 | --- |
| 75W | -40 (-40) | 4.1 | --- |
| 80W | -26 (-15) | 7.0 | --- |
| 85W | -12 (-10) | 11.0 | --- |
| 90 | --- | 13.5 | <24.0 |
| 140 | --- | 24.0 | <41.0 |
| 250 | --- | 41.0 | --- |

Source: SAE Standard J306c

the oils are gear oils but do not indicate a viscosity higher than that for motor oils. A comparison of Tables 13.1 and 13.4 reveals that motor oils are as viscous or more viscous than gear oils.

Friction between gear teeth generates heat, which is transported by the lubricating oil as it returns to the oil sump. Heat is then conducted through the gear case where convective heat transfer carries it away. The temperature of the oil and gear case continue to rise until the heat transfer reaches equilibrium with heat generation. If its oil volume and surface area are large enough, the gear case will reach equilibrium at an acceptable temperature. If the equilibrium temperature is too high, an oil cooler (see Section 13.9) can be used to reduce the equilibrium temperature.

The transmission and differential case of a farm tractor generally is used as the reservoir for the hydraulic system. Thus, the same oil that lubricates the gears also serves as the hydraulic oil. For such applications, manufacturers supply special oils that meet the specifications of both gear oil and hydraulic oil.

## 13.11 MAINTENANCE OF LUBRICATING SYSTEMS

Some motor oil can enter the combustion chambers by moving past the piston rings or through the valve guides. Some oil consumption is normal, and the amount of oil consumption increases with engine load and speed. Oil consumption tends to increase as accumulated wear creates larger clearances around the valve stems and in the ring grooves. Therefore, the oil level should be checked daily in tractor engines, and oil should be added to the crankcase if necessary.

Oil does not wear out, but the oil can become contaminated with carbon, water, and other foreign material. Oil additives gradually become depleted with continued use. Therefore, the oil must be changed periodically. Typically, oil in tractor engines is changed after 100 h of operation, but manufacturers' recommended change intervals should be observed. The engine should be warm when the oil is drained to help keep sediment in suspension and to aid in more complete draining.

The oil filter is changed with each oil change or with every second oil change. Manufactures' recommendations should be followed as to the proper filter change interval.

## 13.12 SYNTHETIC AND LOW-FRICTION MOTOR OILS

Synthetic motor oils are produced from feedstocks other than naturally occurring petroleum. Many types of synthetic oils have been developed, but those used in motor oils are derived from petrochemicals or lipochemicals (animal and vegetable oils). Extensive work on synthetic lubricants began in the 1930s. Germany was forced to develop synthetic lubricants because of a shortage of crude petroleum. The synthetic lubricants helped solve operational problems with gas turbines and were adopted for jet engine use in the 1950s. After further development, synthetic motor oils were introduced for automotive use in the 1970s.

The most common base for synthetic motor oils for automotive use is polymerized alpha olefins (PAO). The PAO base is synthesized from olefinic hydrocarbons by controlled polymerization. Thus, the resulting fluid is composed entirely of hydrocarbons of similar molecular structure. The properties of the PAO can be controlled by careful selection of the correct olefins and careful control of the polymerization process. The resulting PAO is almost entirely paraffinic and contains no sulphur, nitrogen, or metallic impurities.

Esters are the second most common base for synthetic motor oils. An ester can be formed by chemically reacting an alcohol with a fatty acid. Fatty acids are obtained from animal fats or vegetable oils. Diesters, containing two fatty acids for each alcohol, appear to be more suitable than monoesters for use in synthetic motor oils.

Typically, a synthetic motor oil contains a mixture of base stocks, such as PAO and an ester fluid. Such an oil has a very high viscosity index. For example, a multigrade range of SAE 5W-20 can be obtained without adding a viscosity index improver. Typically, an additive package is specially formulated for use with a specific synthetic oil. An oxidation inhibitor generally is included in the additive package.

Usually, the synthetic motor oils cost two or three times more than conventional motor oils. With conventional motor oils in abundant supply, the synthetic motor oils must show clear advantages to gain acceptance. The following are among the possible advantages of synthetic motor oils:

Extended drain intervals (i.e., up to 32 000 km or
   20,000 miles between oil changes in automobiles).
Improved cold weather starting because of low oil viscosity.
Cleaner running engines.
Maintenance of higher oil pressure at hot idle because
   of high viscosity index.

Claims that synthetic oils reduce fuel and oil consumption and reduce engine wear also have been made, but tests have shown little, if any, benefit in these areas.

By definition, a synthetic oil contains essentially no mineral oil. Blends of synthetic-base stocks and mineral oil are, by definition, semisynthetic oils. The semisynthetic oils are less expensive than synthetic oils and are available commercially.

Certain commercially available motor oils contain a special additive to reduce friction. Typical friction-reducing additives include graphite and molybdenum disulphide. These additives must be in the form of very small particles in order to remain in suspension in the oil. The additives help to reduce friction in boundary lubrication but are of no benefit in hydrodynamic lubrication. Typically, use of oil with a friction-reducing additive might improve fuel economy by 1 to 2%.

In addition to synthetic motor oils, synthetic gear oils have also been developed. As in the case of synthetic motor oils, PAO and esters are two important components of synthetic gear oils. The synthetic gear oils require few additives, but an EP additive is included. The high VI of synthetic gear oils allows them to operate over a wider temperature range than conventional gear oils; one synthetic gear oil can span two SAE viscosity grades. Conventional gear oils can also span two SAE grades, but only if a substantial quantity of high grade polymer additive is used. The polymers are subject to temporary shear under high loads, thus reducing film thickness between mating parts and increasing wear. The synthetic gear oils do not require the polymer additive and thus can resist temporary shear.

## 13.13 SUMMARY

Lubrication of engines and power trains is essential to reduce friction and wear. Lubricants can also cushion mating parts, transport heat, serve as a cleanser, and seal piston rings.

Grease is an emulsion of mineral oil with soap and is used as a lubricant when it is impractical to provide a reservoir of oil. The grease is forced through a fitting into the bearing by a grease gun. Lime-based grease is water resistant, soda-based grease is heat resistant, and lithium-based grease is both water and heat resistant.

Hydrodynamic lubrication occurs when an oil film is thick enough to prevent the contact of metal projections on mating parts. Oil viscosity controls friction. Oiliness, the ability of oil molecules to adhere to metal surfaces, is important in boundary lubrication, that is, when the oil film is very thin. Both hydrodynamic and boundary lubrication occur in engines.

The SAE number of an oil is a viscosity classification. A separate range of numbers is provided for gear oils. Viscosity index is a measure of resistance to change in oil viscosity when the temperature changes. Multigrade oils have a sufficiently high viscosity index to qualify for two different SAE numbers.

An API service classification has been established for motor oils. Additives are used to adapt oils for specific types of service. For example, a dispersant is added to keep carbon and other insoluble material in suspension. The first letter of the API classification is either an S (for oils for spark-ignition engines) or a C (for compression-ignition engine oils). The second letter denotes severity of service. A given oil may qualify for more than one API service classification.

Synthetic oils are formulated from feedstocks other than petroleum. The synthetic oils are two to three times more costly than mineral oils, but they do have cost-offsetting advantages. Among these are a high viscosity index and extended drain intervals. Some motor oils contain graphite or other additives to reduce engine friction during boundary lubrication.

Engine lubrication systems are classified as splash, pressure-feed and splash, or full-pressure systems. Splash systems have no oil pump; they employ a projection on a rod bearing cap to splash oil on moving parts. Pressure-feed and splash systems employ an oil pump, pressure regulator valve, and filter to force a continuous supply of clean oil to all bearings. The cylinder walls and piston pin are oiled by oil splashing from rod bearings. Full-pressure systems are like pressure-feed and splash systems, except that each connecting rod is fitted with a nozzle for spraying oil against the underside of the piston.

Lubricants and Lubricating Systems 361

Oil carries heat from wear points to the oil sump, where heat must be rejected before the oil recirculates. Heavy-duty engines have an oil cooler to help reject the heat. Engine coolant circulates through the oil cooler, absorbs the heat, and transfers it to the radiator. Heavily-loaded transmissions may also be equipped with an oil cooler.

## QUESTIONS

Q13.1    What are the five principal functions of a lubricating oil?

Q13.2    (a) How does hydrodynamic lubrication differ from boundary lubrication?
(b) Can a given bearing be in boundary lubrication at some times and in hydrodynamic lubrication at other times? Briefly explain your answer.

Q13.3    (a) What is oiliness?
(b) Under what conditions is it important?

Q13.4    (a) What is grease?
(b) What functions of a lubricating oil cannot be performed by grease? Why?
(c) What are the three principal types of grease?

Q13.5    (a) What is dynamic viscosity?
(b) Under what conditions of lubrication is it important?
(c) Does temperature affect the viscosity of a mineral oil, and, if so, what is the effect?

Q13.6    (a) What does the presence or absence of the W in an SAE rating indicate?
(b) What does the number in an SAE rating indicate?

Q13.7    (a) Which oil would have the higher viscosity at 100° C (212° F): an SAE 40 oil or an SAE 10W-30 oil?
(b) Which oil would have the higher viscosity index?

Q13.8    What additive is absent or has failed if the lubricating oil in a diesel engine retains its original color after a number of hours of heavy engine operation? Briefly explain your answer.

Q13.9     The API service classification for motor oils includes two letters.
(a) What does the first letter indicate?
(b) What does the second letter indicate?

Q13.10    (a) What parts are oiled by pressurized oil in a splash system?
(b) What parts are oiled by pressurized oil in a pressure-feed and splash system?
(c) What parts are oiled by pressurized oil in a full-pressure system?

Q13.11    (a) How does a bypass filtering system differ from a full-flow system?
(b) How does a surface filter differ from a depth filter?

Q13.12    What two indicators are provided for monitoring the operation of a lubrication system, and what does each indicate?

Q13.13    (a) Which oil has the higher viscosity: an SAE 50 or an SAE 90 oil?
(b) What does the higher SAE number indicate in this case?

Q13.14    (a) Why is it necessary to change motor oil periodically?
(b) Why should the engine be warm when the oil is drained?

Q13.15    (a) By definition, how does a synthetic oil differ from the more common motor oils?
(b) What are the most common bases for synthetic oils?
(c) What is semisynthetic oil?

Q13.16    (a) How is an ordinary motor oil converted into a low-friction oil?
(b) Under what conditions can such an oil have truly reduced friction?

# PROBLEMS

P13.1 In a certain diesel engine with a bore of 96 mm (3.78 in.), the thickness of the top ring is 2.5 mm (0.1 in.). At 90° after HDC on the power stroke, the piston is moving downward at 11 m/s (36 ft/s) and the combustion gas pressure is 550 kPa (80 psi).

(a) Calculate the area of contact between the top ring and the cylinder liner.

(b) Assuming the gas pressure on the inside edge of the ring acts on an area essentially equal to that calculated in part a, calculate the normal force due to gas pressure.

(c) Also calculate the normal force due to ring tension, assuming ring tension is equivalent to 50 kPa (7.25 psi) of gas pressure, and the total normal force $F_N$ acting on the ring.

(d) Assuming the coefficient of sliding friction between the ring and liner is 0.42, calculate the shear force $F_t$ acting on the ring and the power absorbed by friction on the ring.

P13.2 Reconsider P13.1, but assume that an oil film of 0.1 mm (0.004 in.) thickness between the ring and liner has put the ring in fully hydrodynamic lubrication. Also, assume the dynamic viscosity of the SAE 30 oil is 10 mPa·s (cP)

(a) Calculate the shear force on the ring.

(b) Calculate the power absorbed by friction on the ring. (Note that fully hydrodynamic lubrication would not prevail at the ends of the piston stroke).

P13.3 Rework P13.2, but assume the SAE oil is cold so that the dynamic viscosity is 4000 mPa·s (cP) and the film thickness is 0.5 mm (0.02 in.).

P13.4 (a) In Table 13.1, calculate the minimum dynamic viscosity of SAE grade 10W at a temperature of 100° C (212° F). Assume the oil density is 0.92 kg/L (57.4 lb/ft$^3$).

(b) Calculate the ratio, maximum dynamic viscosity at the cold cranking temperature over minimum dynamic viscosity at 100° C (212° F). The ratio gives an indication of the need for multigrade motor oils.

P13.5 Rework P13.4, but use data for SAE 20W oil.

# 14
# Hydraulic Systems and Hitches

## 14.1 INTRODUCTION

Hydraulic systems became standard equipment on farm and industrial tractors following World War II. A tractor operator can raise or lower heavy implements or control implement depth with a minimum of physical effort when the tractor has a hydraulic system. Thus, hydraulic systems remove physical strength as a necessary qualification for tractor operators. Hydraulic systems also operate power steering, power brakes, front-end loaders, rear-mounted blades, backhoes, and other industrial implements. Also, tractors with hydraulic motors permit the transmission of power to remote locations more conveniently than do tractors with mechanical drives.

Gaining an understanding of hydraulic systems and being able to troubleshoot them may appear to be difficult tasks to the novice. Fortunately, there are a set of logical principles that govern the behavior of such systems. Learning the principles, equations, and Joint Industry Conference symbols presented in this chapter will enable you to understand and troubleshoot hydraulic systems.

## 14.2 BASIC PRINCIPLES

There are a number of basic principles that are important to the understanding of hydraulic systems. The first three of these principles are as follows.

> **Principle 1:** Liquids have no shape of their own, but they will flow to acquire the shape of a container.

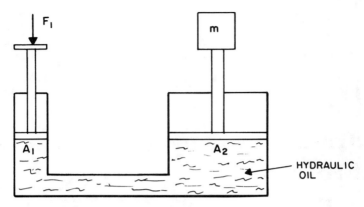

*Figure 14.1–A positive displacement hydraulic system providing mechanical advantage.*

**Principle 2:** Liquids can be considered to be incompressible at pressures used in hydraulic systems.
**Principle 3:** Liquids transmit pressure equally in all directions.

The preceding principles can be used to analyze the hydraulic jack shown in Figure 14.1. Suppose the mass resting on the large piston has a weight of 100 kN (22,500 lb). A fundamental relationship is that the force on a piston is the product of the piston area and the pressure acting on that area. Equations 14.1 and 14.2 below express the relationship with a constant inserted for more convenient units.

$$p = \frac{K_p * F}{A} \qquad (14.1)$$

or

$$F = \frac{p * A}{K_p} \qquad (14.2)$$

where
   $F$ = force on piston in kN (lb)
   $p$ = pressure in MPa (psi)
   $A$ = area of piston in cm$^2$ (in.$^2$)
   $K_p$ = units constant = 10 (1)

Suppose the small piston in Figure 14.1 has an area $A_1 = 5$ cm$^2$ (0.775 in.$^2$) and the large piston has an area $A_2 = 500$ cm$^2$ (77.5 in.$^2$). The pressure under the large piston would be:

$\quad$ p = 10*[100 kN] / [500 cm$^2$] = 2.0 MPa

or

$\quad$ p = 1*[22,500 lb] / [77.5 in.$^2$] = 290 psi

Principle 3 tells us that the pressure under the small piston also would be 2 MPa (290 psi). Therefore, the force $F_1$ on the small piston needed to support the heavy mass would be:

$\quad F_1$ = [2 MPa]*[5 cm$^2$] / 10 = 1.0 kN

or

$\quad F_1$ = [290 psi]*[0.775 in.$^2$] / 1 = 225 lb

In this example, the use of two pistons of differing areas permitted a gravitational load of 100 kN (22,500 lb) to be supported by a force of only 1 kN (225 lb). As long as the small piston was held in place, the heavy load could not sink because the oil has filled all the space below both pistons (Principle 1) and is incompressible (Principle 2).

Suppose the small piston in Figure 14.1 was pushed down a distance of 10 cm (4 in.) in 1 s. Oil would be forced into the large chamber, and the large piston would be forced to raise the heavy mass. How fast would the large piston move, and how far would the mass be raised? The fundamental relationship needed to answer the question is that flow is the product of velocity and area. Equations 14.3 and 14.4 show this relationship with a constant inserted for more convenient units:

$$Q = K_v * V * A \qquad (14.3)$$

$$V = \frac{Q}{K_v * A} \qquad (14.4)$$

where
$\quad Q$ = oil flow rate in L/min (gpm)
$\quad V$ = piston speed in m/s (ft/s)
$\quad A$ = piston area in cm$^2$ (in.$^2$)
$\quad K_v$ = units constant = 6 (3.12)

If the small piston was pushed downward a distance of 10 cm (4 in.) in 1 s, its speed would be:

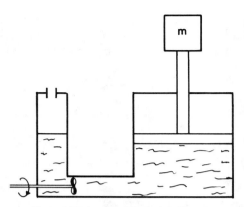

*Figure 14.2–A nonpositive hydraulic system.*

$$V = 10 \text{ cm}/1 \text{ s} = 10 \text{ cm/s} = 0.1 \text{ m/s}$$
or
$$V = 4 \text{ in.}/1 \text{ s} = 4 \text{ in./s} = 0.333 \text{ ft/s}$$

From Equation 14.3, the rate at which oil would flow out from the small piston can be calculated as:

$$Q = 6*[0.1 \text{ m/s}]*[5 \text{ cm}^2] = 3 \text{ L/min}$$
or
$$Q = 3.12*[0.333 \text{ ft/s}[*]0.775 \text{ in.}^2] = 0.8 \text{ gpm}$$

From Equation 14.4, the speed at which the large piston would rise can be calculated as:

$$V = [3 \text{ L/min}] / [6 * 500 \text{ cm}^2] = 0.001 \text{ m/s}$$
or
$$V = 0.8 \text{ gpm} / [3.12 * 77.5 \text{ in.}^2] = 0.0033 \text{ ft/s}$$

In the 1-s interval while the small piston was being pushed downward 10 cm (4 in.), the large piston would rise only 0.001 m (0.0033 ft) or 0.1 cm (0.04 in.). The smaller piston in this example must move 100 times faster and farther than the large piston.

The small piston in the hydraulic jack (Figure 14.1) has been replaced by a turbine in Figure 14.2. When the turbine is spinning, it might be able to generate enough pressure to lift a small mass on the large piston. The larger the mass, the slower it would be lifted by the turbine. The turbine in Figure 14.2 has *nonpositive displacement* because the amount of oil moved is greatly influenced by the pressure. In contrast, the small piston in Figure 14.1 is a simple,

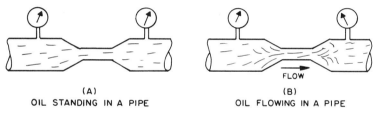

(A) OIL STANDING IN A PIPE  
(B) OIL FLOWING IN A PIPE

*Figure 14.3–Pressure drops occurring as oil flows through a pipe.*

*positive displacement pump*. The rate of oil delivery to the large piston depends only on the speed of movement of the small piston and not on the pressure. The preceding discussion is summarized in Principles 4 and 5:

**Principle 4:** The flow rate of oil from a nonpositive pump depends on the speed of the pump and on the system pressure.

**Principle 5:** The flow rate of oil from a positive displacement pump varies proportionally with the pump speed but is virtually independent of system pressure.

All hydraulic systems on farm and industrial tractors are positive displacement systems.

Two pipes containing pressurized oil are joined by a small orifice in Figure 14.3a. The oil is not flowing, and, according to Principle 3, the pressure must be equal in both pipes. The pressurized oil is flowing through the pipes in Figure 14.3b, and some pressure is lost as the oil passes through the orifice. The pressure drop represents a loss of hydraulic energy, which is converted to heat. Figure 14.3 is an illustration of a sixth principle of hydraulics:

**Principle 6:** Any flow of liquid through a pipe or orifice is accompanied by a reduction in liquid pressure.

## 14.3 JIC SYMBOLS

Hydraulic systems often are complex and include many components. It would be time-consuming to draw each component. Also, the completed drawing might not fully convey the logic of the hydraulic circuit. Thus, a Joint Industry Conference was sponsored by the hydraulics industry to devise symbols for hydraulic components. The resulting *JIC symbols* are presented in Appendix B. The JIC symbols simplify the drawing of hydraulic circuits in the same way that

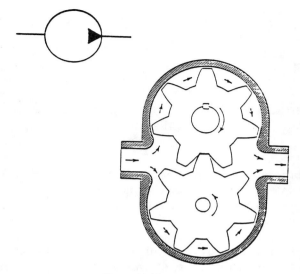

*Figure 14.4–A gear pump.*

electrical symbols simplify the drawing of electrical circuits. The shape of every JIC symbol was chosen to be as nearly self-explanatory as possible. Thus, you should be able to recognize and use the JIC symbols very quickly. Detailed drawings of some hydraulic components may be included in the remainder of this chapter, but all hydraulic circuits will be drawn with JIC symbols.

## 14.4 HYDRAULIC PUMPS

The pump is the heart of any hydraulic circuit. The pump converts mechanical power into hydraulic power. Only positive displacement pumps are used in tractor hydraulic systems. The three basic types of pumps used in hydraulic systems are *gear pumps*, *vane pumps*, and *piston pumps*.

### 14.4.1 Gear Pumps

A cutaway drawing of a typical gear pump is shown in Figure 14.4. One of the gears is forced to rotate by an external power source. The other gear is forced to rotate because the two gears are in mesh. Oil flowing into the inlet port is carried around the periphery in the spaces between the gear teeth. Not much oil can escape back to the inlet at the center of the pump because meshing of the gears fills most of the space between gear teeth. The gear pump is said to have *fixed displacement* because a fixed amount of oil is discharged from

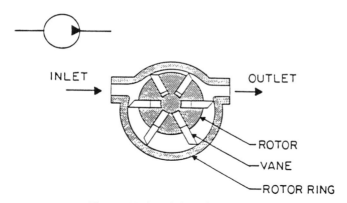

Figure 14.5–An unbalanced vane pump.

the pump during each revolution of the drive shaft. There are several variations of the gear pump, including internal gear pumps and rotor-type gear pumps, but all have fixed displacement.

## 14.4.2 Vane Pumps

A cutaway drawing of a vane pump is shown in Figure 14.5. The rotor is driven by an external power source. The rotor has slots in which vanes can move radially. Because of centrifugal force, the tips of the vanes ride against the housing of the pump. Since the shape of the housing creates an expanding volume between vanes moving past the inlet port, oil is drawn in. Conversely, when the volume between vanes passing the outlet port contracts, oil is forced out. The pump in Figure 14.5 is an *unbalanced vane pump* because pressures on the rotor are unbalanced. That is, pressure is high on the outlet side of the rotor and, therefore, the pump bearings are heavily loaded. *Balanced vane pumps* also are available. In these pumps, two outlets are used to balance pressure loads on the rotor. The two outlets are joined together into one outlet port.

## 14.4.3 Piston Pumps

A piston pump is shown in Figure 14.6. It is called an *axial piston pump* because the pistons move parallel to the axis of rotation. The pistons are carried in a rotating cylinder barrel. As the piston shoes slide along the cam plate, the pistons are forced to reciprocate in their bores. The stationary valving plate has two slots. Oil flows through the inlet slot and into the pistons, which are moving away from the valve plate. Pistons that are moving toward the valve plate force oil to flow out through the outlet slot. Some oil leaks past the pistons to provide lubrication and is allowed to escape from the pump through a case drain.

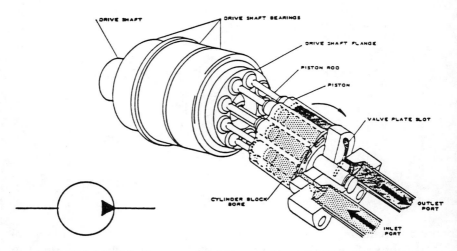

*Figure 14.6–A fixed displacement, axial piston pump. (Courtesy of Vickers, Incorporated.)*

### 14.4.4 Variable Displacement Pumps

The pump in Figure 14.6 is a fixed displacement pump because the cam plate has a fixed angle. A *variable displacement pump* is shown in Figure 14.7. Two small hydraulic cylinders within the pump housing are used to tilt a swash plate. Oil to operate the cylinders is supplied by a small charge pump and is controlled by a manually operated valve. When the swash plate is tilted, as shown in Figure 14.7, the bottom port of the axial piston pump is the discharge port. The top port becomes the outlet port when the swash plate is tilted in the opposite direction. The pump produces zero flow when the swash plate is perpendicular to the axis of rotation. Thus, the pump in Figure 14.7 has variable displacement. Note that variable displacement has a different meaning than nonpositive displacement. The pump in Figure 14.7 has positive displacement because the amount of oil delivered during each revolution of the pump is virtually independent of system pressure.

A cutaway of a *radial piston pump* is shown in Figure 14.8. The pistons are arranged radially to the axis of rotation and are forced to reciprocate by an eccentric on the pump shaft. The pump in Figure 14.8 is made to have variable displacement by means of a stroke control valve. When the pump outlet pressure is sufficiently high, the stroke control valve admits pressurized oil into the crankcase. When the pressurized oil pushes the pistons outward and out of contact with the eccentric, oil delivery ceases. The pump in Figure 14.8 is used in the pressure-compensated hydraulic system, which will be discussed in Section 14.10.2.

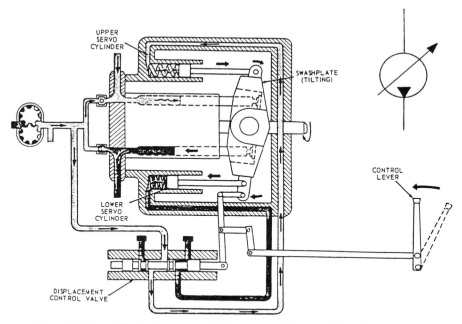

*Figure 14.7–A variable displacement, axial piston pump. (Courtesy of Deere & Company.)*

## 14.4.5 Pump Seal Protection

Mechanical power is supplied to a pump through a shaft which must protrude from the pump. A seal is used to prevent the leakage of oil through the shaft opening. The seals are incapable of preventing the escape of high-pressure oil and thus some means must be used to maintain low pressure at the seal. One means is to provide an internal passage from the seal housing to the low-pressure (inlet) port of the pump. Such pumps are unidirectional, that is, if the direction of rotation is reversed, high pressure oil would be routed to the seal, causing it to be blown out of the pump.

Pumps can be made bidirectional (capable of rotating in either direction) by providing a passage from the seal to each of the two ports. A check valve is placed in each passage to allow flow from the seal to the port but not the reverse. Thus, one of the check valves always isolates the seal from the high-pressure port while the other allows oil to escape from the seal to the low-pressure port.

A third method is available for protecting the seal. The seal area is vented to an external drain port; an external line must be connected from the drain port to the system reservoir to allow any oil reaching the seal area to be directed back to the reservoir at low pressure. If the pump is otherwise designed to be bidirectional, the

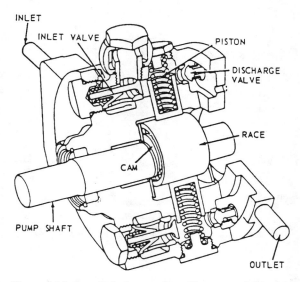

*Figure 14.8–A radial piston pump. (Courtesy of Deere & Company.)*

external drain will permit it to operate in either direction. The valve arrangement of the radial piston pump in Figure 14.8 prevents the pump from being bidirectional, even if the seal protection arrangement would allow bidirectional operation.

### 14.4.6 Pump Delivery

Pumps are rated in terms of the amount of oil they will move per revolution, that is, their displacement. The theoretical flow from a pump can be calculated by using Equation 14.5:

$$Q_T = \frac{D_p * N_p}{K_Q} \tag{14.5}$$

where

$Q_T$ = theoretical delivery in L/min (gpm)
$D_p$ = pump displacement in cm$^3$/rev (in.$^3$/rev)

$N_p$ = pump speed in rev/min
$K_Q$ = units constant = 1000 (231)

The theoretical delivery increases in direct proportion to pump size (displacement) and speed. Note that $D_p$ can be changed if the pump has variable displacement. Actual delivery is less than the theoretical delivery because of internal leakage from the pump outlet port to the pump inlet. Thus, the pump has a *volumetric efficiency*, defined as:

$$e_{vp} = \frac{Q_A}{Q_T} \qquad (14.6)$$

where
 $e_{vp}$ = volumetric efficiency in decimals
 $Q_A$ = actual delivery from pump in any units
 $Q_T$ = theoretical delivery from pump in same units as $Q_A$

If the volumetric efficiency is known or can be estimated, the actual delivery can be calculated from the following equation:

$$Q_A = \frac{Q * N_p * e_{vp}}{K_Q} \qquad (14.7)$$

Internal leakage increases somewhat as the pump works against higher pressures. Thus, volumetric efficiency declines. Except for the change in volumetric efficiency, however, the pump delivery is independent of system pressure.

## 14.4.7 Torque Requirement of a Pump

The theoretical torque needed to turn the pump shaft can be calculated from Equation 14.8:

$$T_T = \frac{\Delta p * D_p}{K_T * \pi} \qquad (14.8)$$

where
 $T_T$ = theoretical torque in N·m (lb-ft)
 $\Delta p$ = pressure rise across pump in MPa (psi)
 $D_p$ = pump displacement in cm$^3$/rev (in.$^3$/rev)
 $K_T$ = units constant = 2 (24)

If there is zero gage pressure at the pump inlet (the usual situation), Δp is equal to the gage pressure at the pump outlet. Note that the theoretical torque increases proportionally with pump size and pressure.

The actual torque needed to turn the pump shaft is higher than the theoretical torque because of friction in the pump. Thus, the pump has a *torque efficiency* defined as follows:

$$e_{Tp} = \frac{T_T}{T_A} \tag{14.9}$$

where
$e_{Tp}$ = torque efficiency in decimals
$T_T$ = theoretical torque in any units
$T_A$ = actual torque in the same units as $T_T$

If the torque efficiency is known or can be estimated, the actual torque can be calculated from the following equation:

$$T_A = \frac{\Delta p * D_p}{K_T * \pi * e_{Tp}} \tag{14.10}$$

## 14.4.8 Pump Power

The hydraulic power produced by a pump can be calculated by using Equation 14.11:

$$P_h = \frac{Q_A * \Delta p}{K_P} \tag{14.11}$$

where
$P_h$ = hydraulic power in kw (hp)
$Q_A$ = actual delivery in L/min (gpm)
$\Delta p$ = pressure rise across the pump in MPa (psi)
$K_P$ = units constant = 60 (1714)

The hydraulic power will be less than the mechanical power put into the pump shaft because of friction and leakage within the pump. The *pump power* (overall) *efficiency* can be calculated by using the following equation:

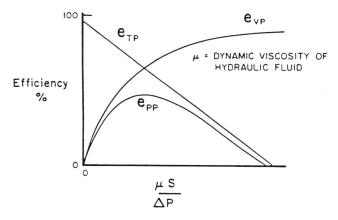

Figure 14.9–Torque, volumetric, and power efficiencies of a pump.

$$e_{pp} = \frac{P_h}{P_s} \quad (14.12)$$

where
  $e_{pp}$ = power efficiency in decimals
  $P_h$ = hydraulic power from pump in kW (hp)
  $P_s$ = shaft power into pump in kW (hp)

The power efficiency can also be calculated as follows:

$$e_{Pp} = e_{vp} * e_{Tp} \quad (14.13)$$

### 14.4.9 Pump Efficiency

Typical efficiency patterns for a pump are shown in Figure 14.9. Internal leakage is only a tiny fraction of theoretical pump delivery at high speeds. Consequently, the volumetric efficiency is high. Reducing the pressure rise across the pump also increases volumetric efficiency by reducing internal leakage. Conversely, when pump outlet pressure is high and pump speed is low, internal leakage can become as large as the theoretical delivery. Then, volumetric efficiency is zero. Similarly, all the shaft torque is used to overcome pump friction when the pressure rise across the pump is small. Then, the torque efficiency is zero. Friction losses also increase as the pump speed increases. The power efficiency is a product of the volumetric and torque efficiencies (Equation 14.13) and, thus, has the pattern shown in Figure 14.9. Figure 14.9 clearly indicates that pumps have an optimum operating point and operate very inefficiently when pump speed and pressure are either very low or very high.

The shaft power required to drive the pump can be calculated by using Equation 14.14:

$$P_s = \frac{Q_A * \Delta p}{K_P * e_{pp}} \tag{14.14}$$

Typical operation of a pump is illustrated in Example Problem 14.1.

## Example Problem 14.1

A gear pump has a displacement of 120 cm³/rev (7.32 in.³/rev). When it is driven at 1500 rev/min against a pressure of 18 MPa (2,600 psi), the volumetric efficiency is 0.85 and the torque efficiency is 0.90. Calculate the power efficiency, the delivery, and the torque and power needed to drive the pump. How much power does the pump convert into heat?

**Solution:** The power efficiency is:

$e_{Pp} = (e_{vp} * e_{Tp}) = 0.85 * 0.90 = 0.765$

The delivery is:

$Q_A = [120 \ cm^3/rev] * [1500 \ rev/min}] * [0.85] / 1000 = 153 \ L/min$

or

$Q_A = [7.32 \ in.^3/rev] * [1500 \ rev/min] * [0.85] / 231 = 40 \ gpm$

The required torque is:

$T_A = [18 \ MPa] * [120 \ cm^3/rev] / [2\pi * 0.90] = 380 \ N \cdot m$

or

$T_A = [2{,}600 \ psi] * [7.32 \ in.^3/rev] / [24\pi * 0.90] = 280 \ lb\text{-}ft$

The shaft power is:

$P_s = [153 \ L/min] * [18 \ MPa] / [60 * 0.765] = 60 \ kW$

or

$P_s = [40 \ gpm] * [2{,}600 \ psi] / [1{,}714 * 0.765] = 80 \ hp$

The hydraulic power from the pump is:

$P_h = e_{Pp} \ P_s = 0.765 * 60 = 46 \ kW$

or

$P_h = e_{Pp} P_s = 0.765 * 80 = 61$ hp

Therefore, the power lost in the pump and converted into heat is:

    power loss = 60 - 46 = 14 kW

or

    power loss = 80 - 61 = 19 hp

Early tractor hydraulic systems used inexpensive gear or vane pumps. Typically, system pressures were less than 14 MPa (2000 psi). The use of more expensive piston pumps in tractor hydraulic systems is more common now. The piston pumps work at higher pressures and at a higher volumetric efficiency than do gear or vane pumps. The piston pumps also permit design with variable displacement.

## 14.5 HYDRAULIC VALVES

Valves are used in hydraulic systems to control pressure, volume, and direction of flow. Accordingly, valves are classified as pressure control, volume control and directional control valves.

### 14.5.1 Relief Valves

A *relief valve* is the most common type of pressure control valve. Relief valves are used to limit the pressure in a hydraulic system to a safe level. A direct-operated relief valve is shown in Figure 14.10. The valve is closed during normal operation of a hydraulic system. When hydraulic pressure reaches a safe upper limit, the relief valve opens and allows oil to flow to the reservoir.

The pressure at which a relief valve opens is called the *cracking pressure*. The pressure across the valve increases as more flow is pushed through it. This increase in pressure is called *pressure override*. Direct-operated relief valves have a large pressure override, as shown in Figure 14.11. The pressure override can be reduced substantially by the use of a pilot-operated relief valve similar to the one shown in Figure 14.12. The small relief valve (3) opens at the cracking pressure and allows oil to flow out of the small drain at the top. The resulting flow through the passage (1) causes a pressure drop across the piston (see Principle 6, Section 14.2). The unbalanced pressure causes the piston to move upward against the spring (5) and open the large port at the bottom to the reservoir. Thus, the pressure override of the pilot-operated relief valve can be kept small.

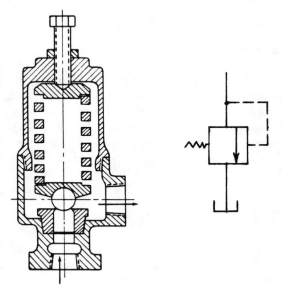

*Figure 14.10–A direct-acting relief valve.*

## 14.5.2 Unloading Valves

An *unloading valve* is illustrated in Figure 14.13. It is used to unload the pump when some point in a hydraulic circuit reaches a desired pressure level. When the pressure at the sensing port reaches a certain level, the plunger is pushed back against spring pressure

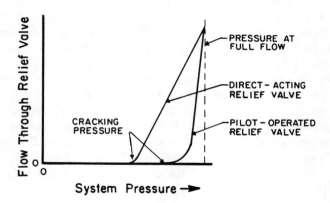

*Figure 14.11–Pressure override in a relief valve.*

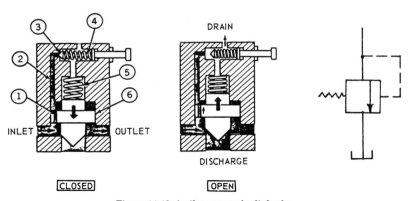

Figure 14.12–A pilot-operated relief valve.

until the groove in the plunger aligns with the pump and reservoir ports.

### 14.5.3 Volume-Control Valves

Two types of pressure-compensated volume-control valves are illustrated in Figures 14.14 and 14.15. The *throttling valve* in Figure 14.14 regulates flow to the outlet port regardless of downstream pressure. Flow through an orifice depends only on the size of the orifice and the pressure drop across it. The spring-loaded sliding spool in Figure 14.14 maintains a constant pressure drop across the orifice. If flow through the orifice increases beyond the correct rate, the pressure drop across the orifice increases and pressure on the spring side of the spool decreases. Thus, the spool moves to the right to partially block the outlet port, reduce the flow, and diminish the pressure drop across the orifice. The operator can use the hand knob to set the flow rate through the valve. The sliding spool then maintains that flow rate. The valve in Figure 14.14 is for

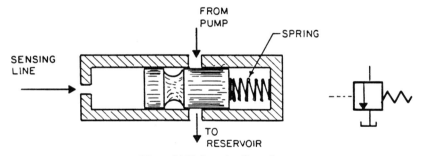

Figure 14.13–An unloading valve.

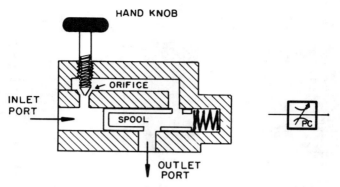

*Figure 14.14–A pressure-compensated, flow control valve.*

use with a variable displacement pump which can reduce its delivery when the throttling valve closes.

### 14.5.4 Flow-Divider Valves

The valve in Figure 14.15 is for use when the flow into the inlet port cannot be reduced. When flow to the outlet port is too high, the spool moves to the right against spring pressure, uncovers the bypass port, and allows part of the oil to divert to the reservoir.

The valve in Figure 14.15 also can be used as a *priority flow-divider valve*. The outlet port is connected to a hydraulic circuit that has first priority. Any excess flow diverts through the bypass port to a circuit that has lower priority. For example, a power steering circuit might be connected to the outlet port and a depth control cylinder might receive oil from the bypass port. The power steering system would have first priority for the oil flow, and only the excess would be available for the lift circuit.

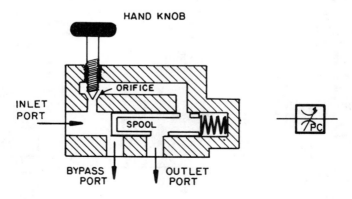

*Figure 14.15–A bypass-type, flow-divider valve.*

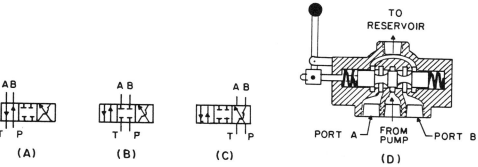

Figure 14.16–A closed-center, directional control valve.

## 14.5.5 Directional Control Valves

A *directional control valve* (DCV) is shown in Figure 14.16. The DCV has four hydraulic ports and is therefore classified as a *four-port* valve (in earlier terminology, it was called a four-way valve). The DCV has three possible positions of the sliding spool (left, centered, and right) and is therefore classified as a *three-position* valve. In Figure 14.16a, the pump is connected to port B, and port A is connected to the reservoir. In Figure 14.16c, the connections to port A and B are reversed. All ports are blocked in Figure 14.16b, and the valve is classified as a *closed-center* valve. Thus, the three-position, four-port, closed-center valve in Figure 14.16 could be used to cause a hydraulic cylinder to extend, hold in position, or retract.

Directional control valves with similar outward appearance can have greatly differing flow logic. JIC symbols, however, can convey the logic clearly. JIC symbols are shown for each position of the valve spool in Figure 14.16. For example, since the spool is shifted to the right in Figure 14.16a, the connections in the left-most rectangle are aligned with the external hydraulic lines. In practice, it is too time-consuming to show the JIC symbols for the DCV in all possible positions. Instead, it is always drawn in the spool-centered position. However, the reader can visualize the effect of shifting the spool to the left or to the right.

An *open-center* DCV is shown in Figure 14.17. The valve permits the pump to discharge freely to the tank or reservoir when the spool is centered. The open center also connects the two cylinder ports when the spool is centered. Therefore, a hydraulic cylinder controlled by an open-center DCV would not hold in position when the spool was centered.

Figure 14.18 shows dual *tandem-center* DCVs. The single-spool DCV in Figure 14.18c is similar to the previously mentioned DCVs except that, in the spool-centered position, the cylinder ports are

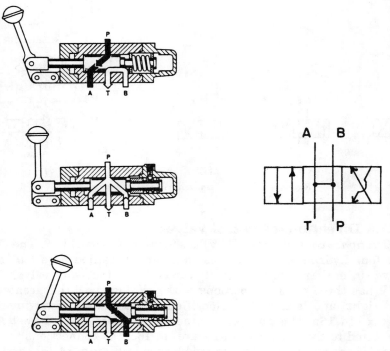

*Figure 14.17–An open-center, directional control valve.*

blocked while the pump is connected to the reservoir. Figure 14.18a shows the JIC symbol for the two-spool valve shown in Figure 14.18b. Because the valve has two spools, it can control two separate hydraulic devices. Each tandem-center spool blocks the cylinder ports when the spool is centered and thus could hold a hydraulic cylinder in position. Notice, however, that the tandem-center DCV permits free flow of oil from the pump to the reservoir when both spools are centered. Moving either spool off center blocks the open path between the pump and reservoir. Also, notice that the cylinders connected to the dual valve are in parallel so that oil returning from one cylinder flows to the reservoir and not to the other cylinder.

There are a wide variety of directional control valves for use in industry. Most DCVs used on farm tractors, however, are three-position, four-port valves and have either tandem centers or closed centers.

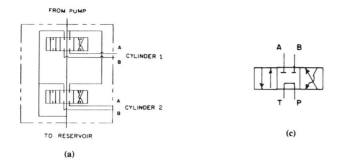

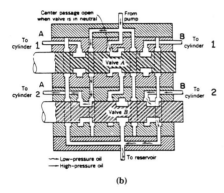

*Figure 14.18–Tandem center directional-control valves, including (a) schematic and (b) cutaway of a dual tandem center valve and (c) a single-spool tandem center valve.*

## 14.6 HYDRAULIC ACTUATORS

Hydraulic actuators convert hydraulic energy into mechanical energy. The two most common types of hydraulic actuators are cylinders and motors.

### 14.6.1 Hydraulic Cylinders

*Hydraulic cylinders* can be single-acting or double-acting. A cutaway of a *double-acting* cylinder is shown in Figure 14.19. Oil is pumped into the port on the left to make the cylinder extend. The movement of the piston forces oil out of the cylinder on the right. Conversely, oil can be pumped into the port on the right to make the cylinder retract. The cylinder in Figure 14.19 could be converted to a *single-acting* cylinder by emptying the oil to the right of the piston and by installing an air breather in the oil port on the right. A single-acting

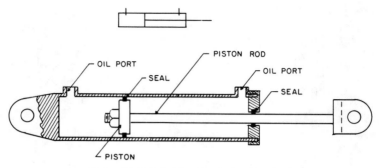

Figure 14.19–A double-acting hydraulic cylinder.

cylinder is used in situations when some external load – for example, the weight of an implement – is available to make the cylinder retract.

The load that can be moved by a hydraulic cylinder can be calculated from Equation 14.15:

$$F = \frac{p_1 * A_1 - p_2 * A_2}{K_p} \qquad (14.15)$$

where
- $F$ = force exerted by the cylinder rod in kN (lb)
- $A_1$ = area of piston in cm$^2$ (in.$^2$)
- $A_2$ = area of piston minus area of rod in cm$^2$ (in.$^2$)
- $p_1$ = pressure acting on area $A_1$ in MPa (psi)
- $p_2$ = pressure acting on area $A_2$ in MPa (psi)
- $K_p$ = units constant = 10 (1)

Equation 14.4 can be used to calculate the speed at which the cylinder extends or retracts. The speed of a typical cylinder and the load it can move are illustrated in Example Problem 14.2.

## Example Problem 14.2

A double-acting hydraulic cylinder has a bore diameter of 6.35 cm (2.5 in.) and a rod diameter of 2.54 cm (1 in.). Maximum pump pressure is 15 MPa (2175 psi). If one cylinder port is connected to the pump and the other is connected to the reservoir, what is the maximum load that can be moved when the cylinder is extending? When it is retracting? If the pump delivery is 75 L/min (20 gpm), how fast will the cylinder extend? How fast will it retract? What is the flow rate of oil from the cylinder while it is retracting?

**Solution:** The area of the piston is:

$$A_1 = \pi * \text{diameter}^2/4 = \pi[6.35]^2/4 = 31.7 \text{ cm}^2$$

or

$$A_1 = \pi * [2.5]^2/4 = 4.91 \text{ in.}^2$$

The area of the rod is:

$$\text{rod area} = \pi * [2.54]^2/4 = 5.07 \text{ cm}^2$$

or

$$\text{rod area} = \pi * [1.0]^2/4 = 0.785 \text{ in.}^2$$

Therefore, the area against which the oil can work when the cylinder is retracting is:

$$A_2 = 31.7 - 5.07 = 26.6 \text{ cm}^2$$

or

$$A_2 = 4.91 - 0.785 = 4.13 \text{ in.}^2$$

When the cylinder is extending, $p_1 = 15$ MPa (2175 psi) and $p_2 = 0$. Therefore, the maximum load on the cylinder rod can be:

$$F = [15 \text{ MPa} * 31.7 \text{ cm}^2 - 0 \text{ MPa} * 26.6 \text{ cm}^2] / 10 = 47.6 \text{ kN}$$

or

$$F = [2175 \text{ psi} * 4.91 \text{ in.}^2 - 0 \text{ MPa} * 4.13 \text{ in.}^2] / 1 = 10,680 \text{ lb}$$

The maximum load the cylinder can move while retracting is:

$$F = [0 \text{ MPa} * 31.7 \text{ cm}^2 - 15 \text{ MPa} * 26.6 \text{ cm}^2] / 10 = -39.9 \text{ kN}$$

or

$$F = [0 \text{ MPa} * 4.91 \text{ in.}^2 - 2175 \text{ psi} * 4.13 \text{ in.}^2] / 1 = -8980 \text{ lb}$$

The minus sign means that the cylinder is pulling the load instead of pushing it. Notice that the cylinder can move a higher load while extending. Typically, a hydraulic cylinder is used to raise an implement while it is extending. Since the extend-to-raise arrangement requires less pressure to hold an implement in the raised position, it is a safety feature.

The speed at which the cylinder extends can be calculated from Equation 14.4:

$$V = Q / [6 * A_1] = [75 \text{ L/min}] / [6 * 31.7 \text{ cm}^2] = 0.394 \text{ m/s}$$

or

$$V = Q / [3.12 * A_1] = [20 \text{ gpm}] / [3.12 * 4.91 \text{ in.}^2] = 1.30 \text{ ft/s}$$

The speed at which the cylinder retracts is calculated as follows:

$$V = Q / [6 * A_2] = [75 \text{ L/min}] / [6 * 26.6 \text{ cm}^2] = 0.470 \text{ m/s}$$

or

$$V = Q / [3.12 * A_2] = [20 \text{ gpm}] / [3.12 * 4.13 \text{ in.}^2] = 1.55 \text{ ft/s}$$

For equal oil delivery from the pump, the cylinder extends more slowly than it retracts.

When the cylinder is retracting, the oil returning to the reservoir is:

$$Q = 6 * V * A_1 = 6 * [0.470 \text{ m/s}] * [31.7 \text{ cm}^2] = 89.4 \text{ L/min}$$

or

$$Q = 3.12 * V * A_1 = 3.12 * [1.55 \text{ ft/s}] * [4.91 \text{ in.}^2] = 23.7 \text{ gpm}$$

Thus, the cylinder returns 89.4 L/min (23.7 gpm) to the reservoir during retraction, while the pump is supplying only 75 L/min (20 gpm). The reservoir must have enough space to accommodate the extra returning oil.

### 14.6.2 Hydraulic Motors

*Hydraulic motors* are used to supply rotary mechanical power. Motors are similar to pumps, and the pumps shown in Figures 14.4, 14.5, 14.6, and 14.7 also could be used as motors. Equations for calculations related to the performance of motors are similar to those related to the performance of pumps, except that efficiencies are reversed. Thus, the speed of a hydraulic motor is:

$$N_m = \frac{K_Q * Q_A * e_{vm}}{D_m} \qquad (14.16)$$

where
- $N$ = motor speed in rev/min
- $Q_A$ = oil delivery to motor in L/min (gpm)
- $D_m$ = motor displacement in cm$^3$/rev (in.$^3$/rev)
- $e_{vm}$ = volumetric efficiency of motor in decimals
- $K_Q$ = units constant = 1000 (231)

The motor torque can be calculated as follows:

$$T = \frac{\Delta p * D_m * e_{Tm}}{K_T * \pi} \qquad (14.17)$$

where
- T = shaft torque in N·m (lb-ft)
- $\Delta p$ = pressure drop across motor in MPa (psi)
- $D_m$ = motor displacement in cm³/rev (in.³/rev)
- $e_{Tm}$ = torque efficiency in decimals
- $K_{Tm}$ = units constant = 2 (24)

The power available from a hydraulic motor is calculated with Equation 14.18:

$$P_s = \frac{Q_A * \Delta p * e_{Pp}}{K_P} \quad (14.18)$$

where
- $P_s$ = shaft power available from motor in kW (hp)
- $Q_A$ = oil delivery to motor in L/min (gpm)
- $\Delta p$ = pressure drop across motor in MPa (psi)
- $e_{Pm}$ = power efficiency in decimals
- $K_P$ = units constant = 60 (1714)

Equation 14.13 for calculating pump efficiencies also calculates motor efficiencies. Furthermore, the trends in efficiencies for pumps (shown in Figure 14.9) also hold true for motors.

## 14.7 HYDRAULIC ACCUMULATORS

A *hydraulic accumulator* is a device for storing energy. An inert gas is compressed when oil is pumped into the accumulator and expands to force oil out of the accumulator. Either the oil and inert gas are separated by a flexible bladder, or, as shown in Figure 14.20, the inert gas is contained in a flexible diaphragm. The JIC symbol for an accumulator also is shown in Figure 14.20. The inert gas behaves in accordance with the ideal gas law (Equation 2.4). Since the compression and expansion of the gas are polytropic, Equation 2.7 can be used to determine an appropriate size for the accumulator. Volume $V_1$ is the internal volume of the accumulator, that is, the volume of the oil plus the compressed gas. Pressure $p_1$ is equal to the minimum oil pressure desired as the last oil is leaving the accumulator. Volume $V_2$ is the volume of the gas when the accumulator is fully charged with oil and the oil pressure is at $p_2$, the maximum system pressure. Essentially, the accumulator can deliver oil volume $V_1 - V_2$ in going from fully charged at pressure $p_2$ to fully

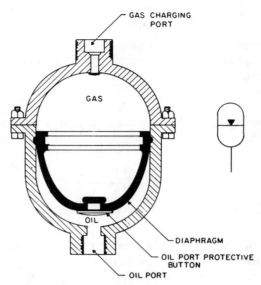

Figure 14.20–A hydraulic accumulator.

discharged at pressure $p_1$. The following equation can be used to calculate the required size ($V_1$) of an accumulator:

$$V_1 = \frac{\Delta V}{1 - [p_1/p_2]^{\frac{1}{n}}} \qquad (14.19)$$

where
 $V_1$ = total internal volume of the accumulator in L (gal)
 $\Delta V$ = $V_1 - V_2$ = oil capacity of accumulator in L (gal)
 $p_2$ = absolute oil pressure when fully charged in MPa (psi)
 $p_1$ = absolute pressure when fully discharged in MPa (psi)

A hydraulic system that includes an accumulator will be described in Section 14.10.4.

## 14.8 FILTERS, RESERVOIRS, AND COOLERS

*Filters* for cleaning hydraulic oil are similar to those for filtering engine oil (Section 13.8.4). Since hydraulic pumps often generate very high pressures, which could rupture a filter, it is common practice to filter the oil just before it returns to the reservoir. Then, the filter is not subjected to high pressures. A strainer or a filter with

*Figure 14.21–A hydraulic oil filter. (Courtesy of Deere & Company.)*

low pressure loss also can be placed in the suction line of the pump. A pleated paper filter is shown in Figure 14.21. The JIC symbol for a filter also is shown in the figure.

A *reservoir* supplies oil to the hydraulic pump and provides a place for oil to return after it passes through the hydraulic circuit. The reservoir must supply the extra oil needed when hydraulic cylinders are extending and provide for extra returning oil when cylinders are retracting. The reservoir also provides an opportunity for returning oil to cool before beginning the next cycle through the hydraulic system. A properly designed hydraulic reservoir has provision to present returning oil from immediately reentering the pump. This can be accomplished with baffles or by separating the pump inlet port from the return port. The return port should be below the oil level to prevent air entrainment and foaming as the oil returns to the reservoir. The reservoir must be vented to the atmosphere to accommodate changing oil levels. The air vent should have a filter to prevent dirt from entering with the air.

A considerable amount of heat can be generated in hydraulic systems. The oil passes through valves, hydraulic lines, and other devices that do no mechanical work. Each time oil passes through such a device, power is lost by conversion to heat. The power loss and heat generation rate can be calculated by using the following equation:

$$P_L = \frac{\Delta p * Q}{K_P} \qquad (14.20)$$

where

$P_L$ = power lost and converted to heat in kW (hp)
$\Delta p$ = pressure drop across the device in MPa (psi)
$Q$ = flow rate through nonworking device in L/min (gpm)
$K_P$ = units constant = 60 (1714)

If the reservoir is large enough, the oil may be able to remain in the reservoir long enough to dissipate sufficient heat before reentering the pump. If the reservoir is not large enough, the oil temperature will continue to rise until the oil can reject the heat to its surroundings. An *oil cooler* may be needed if the reservoir is not large enough to keep the oil sufficiently cool.

Two types of oil coolers are available for use in tractor hydraulic systems. An oil-to-air cooler is similar to the radiator used for cooling the engine. An oil-to-water cooler is similar to the units described in Section 13.9 for cooling engine oil.

## 14.9 HYDRAULIC LINES

Hydraulic lines are used to transmit the hydraulic oil from one component to another. The two most common types of hydraulic lines are steel tubing and hydraulic hoses. Both the steel tubing and the hydraulic hoses must be strong enough to withstand the highest pressure imposed by the hydraulic system. Also, both must be of large enough diameter to convey the hydraulic oil without excessive pressure loss (see Principle 6, Section 14.2). In addition, the tubing or hoses must be routed to avoid sharp bends.

The flow in a hydraulic line can be laminar or turbulent, depending on the value of a dimensionless parameter called the Reynold's number. The Reynold's number is calculated by multiplying the flow velocity times the inside diameter of the line and dividing by the kinematic viscosity (see Section 13.5) of the hydraulic fluid. Smooth, laminar flow occurs when the flow velocity is small enough to give a Reynold's number of 2000 or less. The flow is very turbulent when flow velocities are high enough to give a Reynold's number of 4000 or more. Transition from laminar to turbulent flow occurs at Reynold's numbers between 2000 and 4000. The inside diameter of a line can be calculated using the following equation:

$$d_i = \sqrt{\frac{K_d Q}{V}} \qquad (14.21)$$

TABLE 14.1. Selection of hydraulic hoses to meet pressure requirements

| Inside diameter | | Use single-wire braid for pressures up to: | | Use double-wire braid for pressures up to: | | Use spiral-wire hose for pressures to: | |
|---|---|---|---|---|---|---|---|
| mm | inches | MPa | psi | MPa | psi | MPa | psi |
| 6.35 | 0.250 | 20.7 | 3000 | 34.5 | 5000 | - | - |
| 9.53 | 0.375 | 15.5 | 2250 | 27.6 | 4000 | 34.5 | 5000 |
| 12.7 | 0.500 | 13.8 | 2000 | 24.1 | 3500 | 27.6 | 4000 |
| 15.9 | 0.625 | 12.1 | 1750 | 19.0 | 2750 | - | - |
| 19.1 | 0.750 | 10.3 | 1500 | 15.5 | 2250 | 20.7 | 3000 |
| 25.4 | 1.000 | 5.5 | 800 | 12.9 | 1875 | 20.7 | 3000 |
| 31.8 | 1.250 | 4.1 | 600 | 11.2 | 1625 | 20.7 | 3000 |
| 38.1 | 1.500 | 3.4 | 500 | 8.6 | 1250 | 20.7 | 3000 |
| 50.8 | 2.000 | 2.4 | 350 | 7.8 | 1125 | 17.2 | 2500 |

where
$d_i$ = inside diameter of tube or hose in mm (in.)
$Q$ = flow rate in L/min (gpm)
$V$ = flow velocity in m/s (ft/s)
$K_d$ = units constant = 21.2 (0.408)

The recommended flow velocity for suction lines is 0.6 to 1.2 m/s (2 to 4 ft/s), which provides laminar flow for typical flow rates used with farm tractors. For pressure lines, the recommended flow velocity is 2.0 to 4.5 m/s (6.5 to 15 ft/s). These velocities give laminar or transition flow but usually not fully turbulent flow in the pressure lines. Equation 14.21 can be used with flow velocities at both ends of the recommended range to find an allowable range of line diameters. Then Table 14.1, which lists most of the popular sizes, can be used to select a hose within the required range.

After a hose of the proper diameter is selected to transmit the flow, a hose design must be selected to withstand the system pressure. Table 14.1 can be used to select a hose design for various system pressures. Figure 14.22 illustrates the design of wire braid hose and of spiral wrap hose. In each case, the inner tube is formulated to withstand chemical attack from the hydraulic fluid and an outer layer is designed to resist abrasion and weathering. The intermediate layers differ depending upon strength requirements. Hose with a single wire braid is illustrated in the center of Figure 14.22. Layers B and C are repeated to obtain the higher strength of double-braid hose. The spiral-wrap hose at the bottom of Figure 14.22 provides the strongest construction. Special suction line hose is also available; it includes spring-steel spiral wire reinforcement to prevent collapse when the pressure in the hose is below atmospheric pressure.

# HOSE ASSEMBLIES

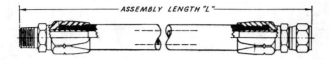

## WIRE BRAID HOSE

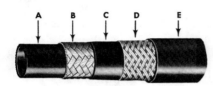

Construction Details:
A. Oil-resistant synthetic tube.
B. High-tensile wire reinforcing.
C. Synthetic rubber ply.
D. Braided cotton cord binder.
E. Synthetic rubber cover.

## SPIRAL WRAP HOSE

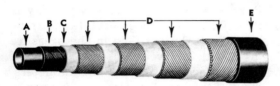

Construction Details:
A. Oil-resistant Neoprene tube.
B. Textile reinforcing braid.
C. Interply friction layers.
D. Spiral-wrapped reinforcement layers.
E. Synthetic rubber cover.

*Figure 14.22–Construction of hydraulic hoses.*

An appropriate fitting must be selected for each end of the hose. Figure 14.22 illustrates a hose with a male fitting on one end and a female fitting on the other. Several types of threads are available for either male or female fittings. They include:

1. American Standard Pipe Thread (NPTF)
2. SAE standard fitting with 45° flare
3. SAE standard fitting with 37° flare
4. Parker fitting with 30° seat
5. SAE straight thread O-ring boss

Manufacturers' catalogs can be used to select hoses with the proper fittings. Any of the above fittings can provide leak-free connections if the male and female parts of a given connection are the same type of fitting. Manufacturers also sell adapters that allow fittings of two different types to be joined.

## 14.10 HYDRAULIC FLUIDS

Viscosity is the most important property of a hydraulic fluid. Generally, pump manufacturers recommend fluid viscosities between 13 and 54 mm$^2$/s (cSt) at the operating temperature of the pump. A high viscosity index also is desirable when the hydraulic oil is subject to wide variations in temperature. As Figure 14.9 indicates, hydraulic pumps and motors become very inefficient when the oil viscosity is too high or too low.

The pour point becomes important when the hydraulic fluid is subjected to low temperatures. The pour point should be at least 11° C (20° F) below the lowest ambient temperature in which the hydraulic system is used.

Oxidation of a hydraulic fluid is accelerated by heat, by exposure to air, and by exposure to metal catalysts such as copper. The rate of oxidation approximately doubles for every 10° C (18° F) increase in temperature, but oxidation of hydrocarbons is slow when the oil temperature is below 60° C (140° F). Therefore, the oil temperature should be kept below 60° C (140° F) for long service life.

Foaming of a hydraulic fluid is undesirable because foam bubbles can collapse under pressure and give the system a spongy behavior. Antifoaming additives reduce foaming tendency by lowering the surface tension of the hydraulic fluid.

Antiwear additives may be used to reduce wear in gear or vane pumps operated at pressures above 7 MPa (1000 psi). The additives are most useful at wear points that are subject to boundary lubrication. Generally, a rust inhibitor also is added to hydraulic fluid.

The transmission case also serves as the hydraulic reservoir on modern farm tractors. Therefore, the hydraulic fluid also serves as the lubricant for the gears in the transmission and an EP additive is added. Each tractor manufacturer specifies a fluid that will meet the combined needs of the transmission and hydraulic fluid.

## 14.11 HYDRAULIC SYSTEMS

Hydraulic systems on farm and in industrial tractors include a pump that is driven by the tractor engine or power train. The hydraulic system is said to be in a standby condition when the pump is running

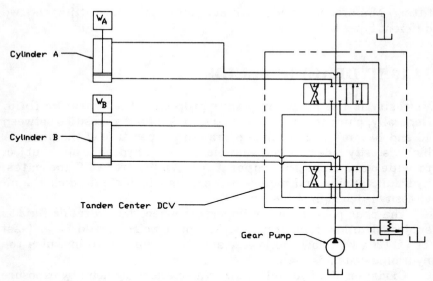

*Figure 14.23–An open-center hydraulic system.*

but no hydraulic power is needed. Any power delivered to the pump during standby is wasted and converted to heat. As Equation 14.14 shows, there are three possible ways to minimize standby power:

To minimize the pump pressure
To minimize the pump delivery
To minimize the pump delivery and pressure

These three methods for minimizing standby losses and increasing pump life have lead to three types of hydraulic systems in farm tractors.

### 14.11.1 Open-Center Systems

The first tractor hydraulic systems included an inexpensive, fixed displacement pump that continued to deliver oil during standby. Such systems were called *open-center systems* because the neutral position of the directional control valve provided an open passage for the pump to discharge freely to the reservoir (Figure 14.23). The system pressure was essentially zero at standby, and the standby power was almost zero. The term *open-center* was a misnomer because, as Figure 14.23 shows, such systems used tandem-center valves, not open-center valves. Nevertheless, the term still persists in the equipment industry.

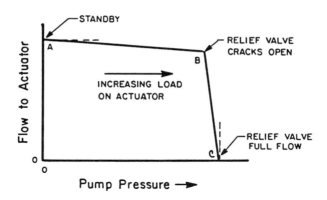

*Figure 14.24–A pressure-flow diagram of an open-center hydraulic system.*

System pressure in an open-center system is determined by the lightest load connected to the system. Suppose, for example, that 7 MPa (1000 psi) was needed to lift weight WA in Figure 14.23 but 10 MPa (2000 psi) was needed to lift weight WB. If the DCV spools were moved to try to lift both weights simultaneously, the pressure would rise to only 7 MPa (1000 psi). The heavier load could not be lifted until the cylinder with the lighter load reached the end of its stroke. The delayed movement of the heavier load is called *sequencing* and is the major disadvantage of open-center hydraulic systems.

A relief valve is needed to protect open-center hydraulic systems. Suppose, for example, that the operator held both DCV spools in the lift position after the cylinders reached the end of their strokes. Without a relief valve, the pressure would quickly increase until rupture occurred in the weakest part of the hydraulic system. The relief valve protects the system by allowing oil to escape to the reservoir before the pressure becomes high enough to rupture any components.

Figure 14.24 shows flow-pressure relationships for an open-center system when the pump is running at rated speed. The system is in the standby condition at point A. Except for a small loss in volumetric efficiency, pump delivery is nearly constant between points A and B as a DCV is opened and increasingly heavier loads are placed on an actuator. The relief valve cracks open at point B. With actuator load increasing, more and more oil diverts through the relief valve between points B and C. At point C, all the pump delivery is going through the relief valve; none is going to the actuator.

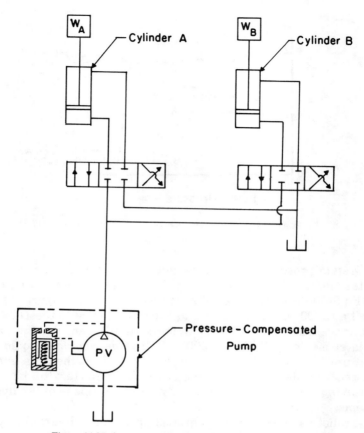

*Figure 14.25–A pressure-compensated hydraulic system.*

Extended operation at any point between B and C would cause overheating of the oil. The power converted into heat could be calculated from Equation 14.18 by using the pump delivery rate and the full-flow pressure across the relief valve.

## 14.11.2 Pressure-Compensated Systems

Early tractor hydraulic systems typically included only one actuator, and open-center systems worked very well. However, the sequencing action of open-center systems became a serious problem when more hydraulic actuators were added. The pressure-compensated system (Figure 14.25) provided a means for eliminating sequencing. The heart of the system is a pressure-compensated piston pump (see Figure 14.8) that automatically adjusts its delivery to maintain constant system pressure. A typical system pressure would be 14 MPa (2000 psi). When system pressure reaches 14 MPa (psi), the stroke control valve admits pressurized oil to the pump crankcase,

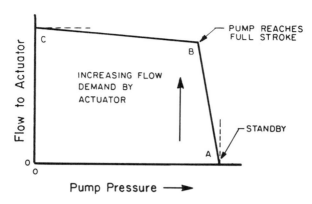

*Figure 14.26–A pressure-flow diagram of a pressure-compensated hydraulic system.*

holds the pistons away from the cam, and reduces pump delivery to near zero. If system pressure falls (for instance, when a DCV is opened), the pressure in the crankcase drops and the pump again begins delivering oil. The DCV spools have a closed-center design to block the pump flow during standby. Thus, according to Equation 14.14, standby power can be low because pump delivery is only large enough to make up for leakage.

Pressure-flow relationships for the pressure-compensated system are shown in Figure 14.26. The system is in standby at point A. System pressure drops slightly between points A and B as more and more oil is needed by the actuators. The pump is at full stroke at point B. If even more oil is needed by the actuators, system pressure begins to fall; between points B and C, the system behaves exactly like an open-center system. The pressure-compensated system is not well-suited for use with hydraulic motors. The motor speed would vary with motor load if the hydraulic system was operating between points A and B. If the motor load increased, the motor would slow down and vice versa. Constant motor speed could be achieved by selecting a motor so large that the system would operate between points B and C. However, if another actuator was used in addition to the motor, the system would then be subject to the sequencing action of open-center systems.

### 14.11.3 Pressure-Flow-Compensated Systems

*Pressure-flow-compensated hydraulic systems* (PFC systems) are a recent innovation on farm tractors. A PFC hydraulic system is illustrated in Figure 14.27. Closed-center DCVs are used to maintain near-zero flow when the system is in standby. Unlike pressure-compensated systems, however, the PFC system operates with the

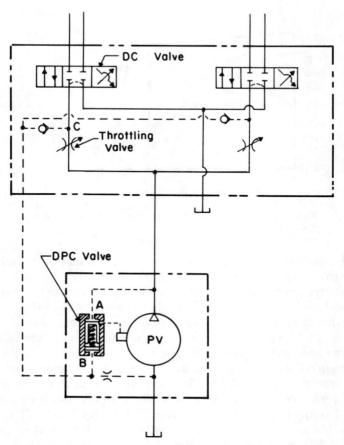

*Figure 14.27–A pressure-flow-compensated hydraulic system.*

lowest pressure needed to move the load on the actuator. The pump includes a *differential pressure compensator valve* (DPC valve), which is the key to operation of the system.

The DPC valve controls admission of oil to the stroke control mechanism of an axial piston pump. With port B of the DPC blocked, the system would behave like an ordinary pressure-compensated system with very low standby pressure (typically, 1.4 MPa or 200 psi). However, a sensing line transmits pressure from the DCV to port B of the DPC valve. When a DCV spool is opened, the actuator pressure is transmitted to port B and fortifies the spring in the DPC valve. Consequently, the pressure at port A of the DPC valve remains 1.4 MPa (200 psi) higher than the pressure needed by the actuator. The same 1.4 MPa (200 psi) pressure is maintained across a throttling valve near the DCV. The operator can set the throttling valve for the desired flow rate, and the DPC valve will maintain pump pressure at 1.4 MPa (psi) above the requirement of the actuator.

Several DCVs can be used simultaneously with the PFC system of Figure 14.27. When more than one actuator is used at the same time, the system maintains a 1.4 MPa (200 psi) drop across the throttling valve that is supplying oil to the actuator with the highest pressure demand. Pressure drops across the other throttling valves would be greater than 1.4 MPa (200 psi). The PFC system will prevent sequencing as long as the combined flow setting of the active throttling valves is less than the maximum flow capacity of the pump. It is common practice to design each throttling valve to accommodate the full flow capacity of the pump. Then, if two or more throttling valves are used in the wide open position simultaneously, the pump will operate at full stroke and the PFC system will be subject to sequencing.

If the pressure-flow relationship for a PFC system was shown on Figure 14.26, the standby pressure at point A would be only 1.4 MPa (200 psi), and the standby flow would be essentially zero. Depending upon actuator loads, the pump pressure could vary anywhere from standby pressure up to the rated pressure of the pump. When the rated pressure is reached, a pressure control valve admits oil to the stroke control mechanism and causes the pump delivery to cease. Pump delivery in Figure 14.26 could be anywhere between zero and the maximum delivery of the pump, depending on the setting of the throttling valves.

### 14.11.4 Accumulator Systems

A hydraulic system with an accumulator is shown in Figure 14.28. The system includes a small, fixed displacement pump that can be charging the accumulator during long periods when hydraulic power is not needed, for example, while a tractor is pulling a plow across a field. When the accumulator is charged to the desired working pressure, for example, 14 MPa (2000 psi), the unloading valve opens and allows the pump to discharge freely to the reservoir. By moving the spool on one or more DCVs, the operator can use the accumulated hydraulic energy to move one or more hydraulic cylinders. The DCVs must have closed centers to prevent the accumulator from discharging while the system is in standby. A unique feature of the system is that the hydraulic system can remain in standby and be ready to deliver pressurized oil even when the tractor engine is not running. The major advantage of the accumulator system is the lower power demand on the pump. The accumulator can be charged by a small pump over a relatively long period of time, and the stored energy can be withdrawn in short, intense bursts when needed.

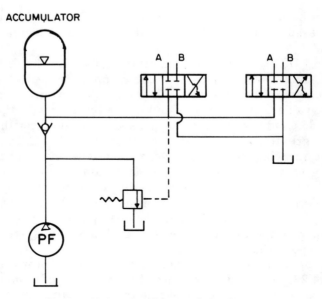

*Figure 14.28–An accumulator-type hydraulic system.*

Obviously, the system is not suited for use with hydraulic motors. A continuously running hydraulic motor would empty the accumulator quickly and the small pump would be unable to supply sufficient oil to the motor.

## 14.12 HYDRAULIC HITCHES

Early farm tractors were equipped with a drawbar for pulling trailed implements. In the 1930s, hydraulic hitches that permitted implements to be carried on the rear of the tractor were developed. Today, the *three-point hitch* has become standard on most farm and industrial tractors.

### 14.12.1 Three-Point Hitches

The three-point hitch (3ph) shown in Figure 14.29 attaches to an implement at the hitch points shown in Figure 14.30. Dimensions of the three-point hitch have been standardized by the American Society of Agricultural Engineers since 1959. Table 14.2 shows the four categories of hitches that have been developed to fit tractors of varying size. Hitch dimensions associated with the implement are shown in Table 14.3. Notice that the lower hitch studs and upper hitch pins have larger diameters for the higher category hitches. Special bushings can be slipped over the studs and upper hitch pins

Hydraulic Systems and Hitches 403

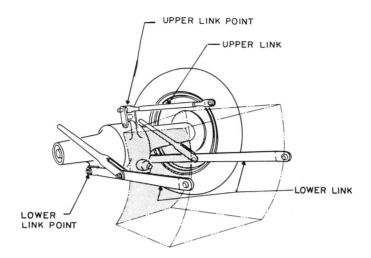

*Figure 14.29–A three-point hitch for a tractor. (Reprinted from ASAE Standard S217.10, Three-point free-link attachment for hitching implements to agricultural wheel tractors, reconfirmed December 1979.)*

to adapt, for example, a category II tractor to a category I implement.

Minimum lift capacities of the 3ph have been standardized by the ASAE. The lift capacities are measured at a distance 610 mm (24 in.) to the rear of the lower hitch points. For tractors with drawbar power up to 65 kW (85 hp), the lift capacity must be at least 310 N/drawbar kW (52 lb/drawbar hp). Above 65 kW (85 hp), the

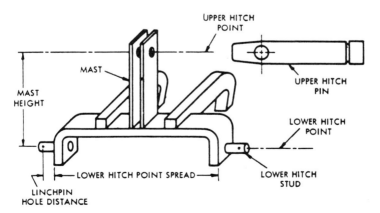

*Figure 14.30–Three-point hitch connections on an implement. (Reprinted from ASAE Standard S217.10, Three-point free-link attachment for hitching implements to agricultural wheel tractors, reconfirmed December 1979.)*

TABLE 14.2. Three-point hitch categories

| Category | Maximum Drawbar Power in kW (hp) |
|---|---|
| I | 15 to 35 (20 to 45 hp) |
| II | 30 to 75 (40 to 100 hp) |
| III and III–N | 60 to 168 (80 to 225 hp) |
| IV and IV–N | 135 to 300 (180 to 400 hp) |

*Source:* Reprinted from ASAE Standard S217.10, *Three-point free-link attachment for hitching implements to agricultural wheel tractors*, reconfirmed December 1979.

lift capacity must be at least 20.15 kN plus 155 N/drawbar kW (4420 lb plus 26 lb/drawbar hp).

### 14.12.2 Position Control

The three-point hitch can be raised hydraulically. Typically, a single-acting cylinder is used and the weight of the lower links and attached implement provides the only force for lowering the hitch. The essential elements of the hydraulic lift are illustrated in Figure 14.31. Movement of the control lever from point A to point A' shifts the valve spool to the lift position because point E is momentarily stationary. Then, point C is stationary so that, as the lift arms rotate clockwise, point E moves to the right and the valve spool is shifted back to the neutral position. Thus, the position or depth of the hitch mimics the position of the control lever. Therefore, the control system shown in Figure 14.31 is called a *position* or *depth control*.

### 14.12.3 Draft Control

One of the first uses of the three-point hitch was to connect a moldboard plow to the tractor. When draft on the plow became very heavy and overloaded the tractor, the operator could reduce the draft by raising the plow slightly. When soil conditions changed and the draft became light, the operator could again lower the plow and increase the draft. The draft control system in Figure 14.32 accomplishes the raising and lowering of the plow automatically. The upper link in Figure 14.32 is in compression when a two- or three-bottom plow is hitched to the tractor. As plow draft increases, the greater compressive force in the upper link compresses the load spring. Thus, point E in the linkage moves to the left, moves the valve spool to the lift position, and causes the plow to raise. As draft diminishes while the plow is raising, point E moves back toward the right and moves the valve spool back to the neutral position. The system in Figure 14.32 is called an *automatic draft* or *load control* because it tries to maintain the draft selected by the control lever.

TABLE 14.3. Dimensions for four categories of three-point hitches

| | Category I | | | | Category II | | | | Category III[ll] | | | | Category IV[ll] | | | |
|---|---|---|---|---|---|---|---|---|---|---|---|---|---|---|---|---|
| | Millimeter | | Inches | | Millimeter | | Inches | | Millimeter | | Inches | | Millimeter | | Inches | |
| | Min | Max | Min | Max | Min | Max | Min | Max | Min | Max | Min | Max | Min | Max | Min | Max |
| UPPER HITCH POINT | | | | | | | | | | | | | | | | |
| Width inside | 44.5 | — | 1.75 | — | 52.3 | — | 2.06 | — | 52.3 | — | 2.06 | — | 65 | — | 2.56 | — |
| Width outside | — | 85.9 | — | 3.38 | — | 95.3 | — | 3.75 | — | 95.3 | — | 3.75 | — | 132 | — | 5.20 |
| Clearance radius for upper link * (†) | 57.2 | — | 2.25 | — | 57.2 | — | 2.25 | — | 57.2 | — | 2.25 | — | 76.2 | — | 3.00 | — |
| Hitch pin hole diameter | 19.3 | 19.56 | 0.76 | 0.77 | 26.65 | 25.91 | 1.01 | 1.02 | 32.0 | 32.26 | 1.26 | 1.27 | 45.2 | 45.5 | 1.78 | 1.79 |
| LOWER HITCH POINT | | | | | | | | | | | | | | | | |
| Stud diameter | 21.84 | 22.10 | 0.86 | 0.87 | 28.19 | 28.45 | 1.11 | 1.12 | 36.32 | 36.58 | 1.43 | 1.44 | 49.7 | 50.8 | 1.96 | 2.00 |
| Linchpin hole distance† | 38.86 | — | 1.53 | — | 48.52 | — | 1.91 | — | 48.52 | — | 1.91 | — | 68 | — | 2.68 | — |
| Linchpin hole diameter | 11.68 | 12.19 | 0.46 | 0.48 | 11.68 | 12.19 | 0.46 | 0.48 | 11.68 | 12.19 | 0.46 | 0.48 | 17.5 | 18 | 0.69 | 0.71 |
| Lower hitch point spread | 681.0 | 684.3 | 26.81 | 26.94 | 822.5 | 825.5 | 32.38 | 32.50 | 963.7 | 966.7 | 37.94 | 38.06 | 1165 | 1168 | 45.87 | 45.99 |
| Clearance radius for lower link * (†) | 63.5 | — | 2.50 | — | 73.2 | — | 2.88 | — | 82.6 | — | 3.25 | — | 82.6 | — | 3.25 | — |
| Implement encroachment in front of lower hitch point if implement extends laterally behind tire | — | 12.7 | — | 0.5 | — | 12.7 | — | 0.5 | — | 12.7 | — | 0.5 | — | 12.7 | — | 0.5 |
| IMPLEMENT MAST HEIGHT ‡ § | 457 | | 18 | | 483 | | 19 | | 559 | | 22 | | 686 | | 27 | |

\* Some tractors with quick-attachable connectors require 140 mm (5.50 in.) space for clearance above the upper hitch point and below the lower hitch point.
† Refer to section for attachment of implements to agricultural wheel tractors equipped with quick-attaching coupler for three-point free link hitch.

Tractors equipped with a standard quick-attaching coupler for the three-point free-link hitch require an auxiliary attaching pin on the implement mast located 76 mm (3.0 in.) for categories I and III, and 102 mm (4.0 in.) for Category II, below the standard upper hitch point. To facilitate attachment and detachment of the implement, a clearance zone must be maintained 76 mm (3.0 in.) rearward from and extending 104 mm (4.10 in.) above and 216 mm (8.50 in.) below this pin. In addition, a clearance zone must be maintained 94 mm (3.70 in.) rearward from and extending 25 mm (1.0 in.) above and 211 mm (8.30 in.) below each lower hitch point.

To facilitate the attachment and detachment of the implement with tractors equipped with a standard Category IV-N or IV quick-attaching coupler for the three-point free-link hitch, a clearance zone must be maintained 85 mm (3.35 in.) rearward from and extending 120 mm (4.72 in.) above and 252 mm (9.92 in.) below the standard upper hitch point on the implement mast. In addition, a clearance zone must be maintained 94 mm (3.7 in.) rearward from and extending 32 mm (1.26 in.) above and 272 mm (10.71 in.) below each lower hitch point.

‡ The mast height is not necessarily a mechanical dimension on the implement itself. It is a figure used in design and if properly used for design of both implement and tractor, a well performing interchangeable implement and tractor combination will be achieved. This standard makes it possible to produce tractors and implements that will give good performance in any combination; therefore, consideration to hitch geometry is essential. This makes it desirable to establish a standard mast height and a standard mast adjustment within a working range, because these items influence the position of hitch points that are common to both the implement and the tractor.

Mast height is one of the essential factors in establishing the virtual hitch point of the free-link system, draft signal for the draft-responsive system, loads on the linkage and hitch points, changes in implement pitch corresponding to changes in working depth, implement pitch when the implement is in transport position, clearance of the implement with the tractor, especially in transport position and clearance of the hitch links with the implement or with the tractor, especially in the transport position.

When an implement mast height is made different than standard to accomplish some specific performance feature, care should be exercised to insure that the desired performance is secured with tractors likely to operate the implement.

§ Some Category II tractors are designed to accommodate a 559 mm (22 in.) mast height for optimum performance. In the design of implements for use on these tractors care should be taken to investigate the need for providing a 559 mm (22 in.) mast height. Tractors that are designed only for use with 559 mm (22 in.) mast height must be properly identified.

[ll] See Section 3 for Category IV-N or III-N, Narrow Hitch, dimensions.

*Source:* Reprinted from ASAE Standard S217.11, *Three-point free-link attachment for hitching implements to agricultural wheel tractors,* revised December 1991.

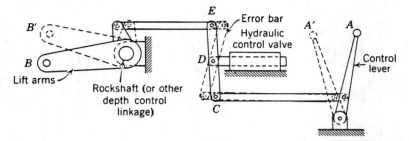

*Figure 14.31–A position control system for a tractor hitch. (Reprinted from Hockey, W. S., Tractor mounted implements and adaptations, Proceedings of the Automobile Division of the Institution of Mechanical Engineers, Symposium on Agricultural Tractors, 1961, London.)*

### 14.12.4 Position and Draft Control

Three-point hitches on modern tractors are designed to respond to a combination of draft and position. One such system is illustrated in Figure 14.33. Two control levers are used; one to set the desired position and the other to set the desired draft. As Figure 14.33 illustrates, the draft on modern three-point hitches is sensed at the lower links rather than at the upper link. With increased plow sizes, the weight of a plow can cause the upper link to be in tension rather than compression. The compression spring of Figure 14.32 would then be unsuitable for sensing draft.

The hitch in Figure 14.33 employs a mechanical linkage to sense hitch load and/or position and feed the information back to the control valve. Electronic systems are replacing the mechanical systems on some late-model tractors. In one such system, the pins in the lower link points (see Figure 14.29) are instrumented to sense shear and produce an electrical signal that is proportional to the load on the lower links. A potentiometer is used to sense the angular position of the lower links. Potentiometers also sense the position of

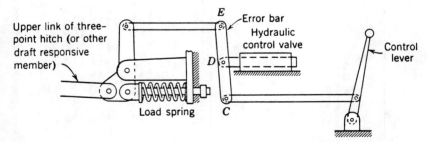

*Figure 14.32–A draft control system for a tractor hitch. (Reprinted from Hockey, W. S., Tractor mounted implements and adaptations, Proceedings of the Automobile Division of the Institution of Mechanical Engineers, Symposium on Agricultural Tractors, 1961, London.)*

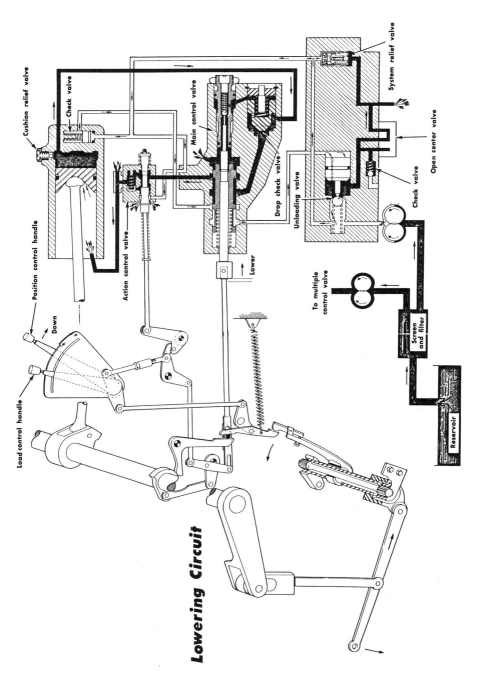

Figure 14.33–A combination draft and position control system for a tractor hitch. (Courtesy of Case-IH.)

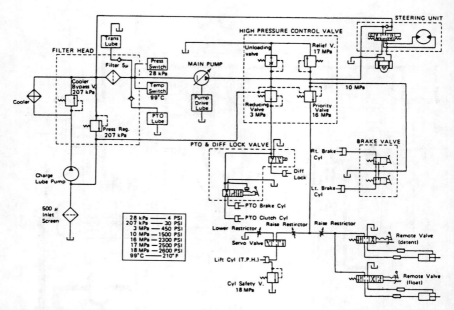

Figure 14.34–A complete tractor hydraulic system. (Reprinted from Liljedahl, J. B. et al., *Tractors and Their Power Units*, 3rd Ed., New York: John Wiley & Sons, 1979. Reprinted with permission of the authors.)

levers provided for the operator to set the desired load and position of the hitch. All of the signals are sent to a microprocessor, which compares the actual and desired hitch positions, and/or actual and desired hitch loads, and then signals an electrohydraulic control valve to raise or lower the hitch as needed.

## 14.13 A COMPLETE TRACTOR HYDRAULIC SYSTEM

The great convenience of the hydraulic system has resulted in its being used for many tasks that were accomplished manually on earlier tractors. A schematic diagram of one hydraulic system is shown in Figure 14.34. The system includes hydraulically assisted steering, hydraulically activated brakes, differential lock and pto clutch, and hydraulic lifting of the three-point hitch. The system includes outlets for a hydraulic cylinder that can be used remotely on trailed implements. The hydraulic oil provides forced lubrication of the transmission.

## 14.14 HYDRAULIC SYSTEM MAINTENANCE AND TROUBLESHOOTING

Maintenance of a hydraulic system is not difficult. Five key rules of proper maintenance are as follows:

1. Use a hydraulic oil recommended by the tractor manufacturer. (Use of unrecommended oils could damage seals or other hydraulic components and is therefore risky).
2. Maintain the correct amount of oil in the hydraulic system. Check the oil level in the reservoir at the intervals recommended in the operator's manual.
3. Keep the hydraulic oil clean. Change the filter and the hydraulic oil at the intervals recommended in the operator's manual. Be especially careful to prevent dirt from entering when the system is open.
4. Repair external leaks. (They look bad, waste oil, and may signal a more serious rupture at the point of leakage. Where oil leaks out, dirt can enter.)
5. Use the hydraulic system within its intended capabilities. (Operating the pump at speeds or pressures greater than those recommended by the manufacturer can greatly reduce the life of the hydraulic system.)

Typically, a tractor hydraulic system cannot be operated beyond its capabilities unless the user modifies the system. Increasing the system relief pressure is a modification that would be hazardous to the hydraulic system.

When a hydraulic system fails to perform correctly, the problem usually can be located by an intelligent system of troubleshooting. Logical thinking can be coupled with careful tests to isolate the source of the problem. A key step is to make a list of possible causes of the symptoms and then to perform tests that will eliminate as many of the causes as possible. The objective is to pinpoint the real cause, if possible, before starting any disassembly or repair of the system. Suppose, for example, that the three-point hitch in the system in Figure 14.33 failed to lift when the operator moved the control lever to the raise position. Some key questions could be asked before the list of possible causes was compiled. One question would be: Does the hitch fail to lift under all conditions or only when lifting a heavy load? This question indicates either an interruption of oil delivery to the lift cylinder or the failure of the system to generate full-system pressure. Assuming that the hitch failed to lift only when heavily loaded, we could then ask: Is the load on the hitch greater than the hitch was designed to lift? If not, we then would compile a list of possible causes for inadequate system pressure and conduct tests to eliminate some of them. One test would be to put a heavy load on one of the remote cylinders. If the cylinder was able to lift the load, many possible causes could be scratched from the list. The problem would be pinpointed to those few parts of the hydraulic system that served the three-point hitch but not the remote cylinders. A similar troubleshooting approach can be used to pinpoint the probable cause of virtually any hydraulic problem.

## 14.15 SUMMARY

Hydraulic systems have taken over the heavy work of controlling tractors and implements and have removed physical strength as a necessary qualification of tractor operators. Also, hydraulic motors allow power to be transmitted to remote locations.

A complete hydraulic system includes hydraulic oil, a pump, a reservoir, a filter, valves, one or more actuators, and, possibly, other components. Open-center systems were the first hydraulic systems used on tractors and are still used on some modern tractors. These systems minimize standby losses by permitting the free flow of oil from a fixed displacement pump to the reservoir through tandem-center valves. When more than one actuator is used, system pressure rises only high enough to move the lightest load. Sequential moving of loads can result.

Pressure-compensated systems include a pressure-compensated piston pump that automatically adjusts its stroke to maintain constant system pressure. Closed-center valves block all flow during standby so that standby losses are low. Unless the flow demand requires the pump to go to full stroke, pressure-compensated systems avoid the problem of sequencing. However, they are not well suited for use with hydraulic motors.

Pressure-flow-compensated (PFC) systems include a differential pressure compensator (DPC) valve to control the stroke of a piston pump. The DPC valve maintains a constant pressure drop across a flow control valve, thereby maintaining the flow rate selected by the operator. The DPC valve also maintains system pressure just high enough to move the heaviest load. Standby losses are low because both pressure and flow are low. Unless the flow demand causes the pump to go to full stroke, sequencing is not a problem in PFC systems and they are also well suited for use with hydraulic motors.

Some hydraulic systems use a small, fixed-displacement pump and unloading valve to charge an accumulator. Hydraulic cylinders are connected to the accumulator through closed-center directional control valves. The system is ideal when relatively long standby periods are available for recharging the accumulator and the stored energy is needed in short, intense bursts.

The three-point hitch was developed in the 1930s, standardized by ASAE in 1959, and now has become the standard hitch on tractors. On modern tractors, the operator can set the hitch at a desired position, for a desired implement draft, or for some combination of position and draft. Four categories of three-point hitches have been developed to fit tractors of varying size.

Although hydraulic systems appear complex, their operation is governed by a small set of logical principles. These principles and the JIC symbols for hydraulic circuits provide the basis for understanding and troubleshooting hydraulic systems.

## QUESTIONS

Q14.1 Assume the small piston in Figure 14.1 is held firmly in place while a heavy mass (m) rests on the large piston.
(a) Will the large piston sink? Briefly explain your answer.
(b) What will the oil pressure be just below the large piston? (Show the equation to calculate the pressure.)
(c) What will the oil pressure be just below the small piston?
Mention all appropriate basic principles when answering Q14.1.

Q14.2 (a) If the small piston in Figure 14.1 was moved downward at a speed of 1 mm/s (0.04 in./s), would the upward speed of the large piston depend on the amount of mass (m) resting on it? Briefly explain your answer.
(b) How fast would the large piston rise?

Q14.3 Rework part a of Q14.2, but assume the small piston has been replaced with a turbine pump as in Figure 14.2.

Q14.4 (a) What is the difference, if any, between the terms *fixed displacement* and *positive displacement*?
(b) Must a positive displacement pump also have fixed displacement?
(c) Must a fixed displacement pump also have positive displacement?

Q14.5    Does volumetric efficiency increase, decrease, or remain constant as pump speed increases? Why?

Q14.6    Assuming pump inlet pressure is constant at one atmosphere, does volumetric efficiency increase, decrease or remain constant as pressure on the pump outlet increases? Why?

Q14.7    (a) Would you expect volumetric efficiency to increase or decrease as the viscosity of the hydraulic oil in the pump increases?
(b) Is your answer to part a consistent with the trend shown in Figure 14.9 for volumetric efficiency? Briefly explain.

Q14.8    Rework Q14.6, but substitute torque efficiency for volumetric efficiency.

Q14.9    (a) What is the difference, if any, between a relief valve and an unloading valve?
(b) Could an unloading valve be used as a relief valve and, if so, how?

Q14.10   (a) Is the valve in Figure 14.17 a two-, three-, or four-port valve?
(b) Is it a two- or three-position valve? Briefly explain your answers.

Q14.11   Would the valve in Figure 14.17 be suitable for controlling the lift cylinder on a moldboard plow? Briefly explain your answer.

Q14.12   Assuming that a double-acting cylinder is used with a fixed displacement pump running at constant speed, will the cylinder extend and retract at the same speed? Why?

Q14.13   What causes a single-acting cylinder to retract?

Q14.14   Because torque efficiency is less than 1.0, actual pump torque must be greater than the theoretical torque. Is the same statement true for a hydraulic motor? Briefly explain your answer.

Q14.15   How is energy stored in the hydraulic accumulator shown in Figure 14.20?

Hydraulic Systems and Hitches 413

Q14.16   Why is a reservoir needed in a hydraulic system? That is, why not route the returning oil directly to the pump inlet?

Q14.17   Why is a hydraulic filter usually placed near the reservoir inlet rather than between the reservoir and pump inlet or just after the pump outlet?

Q14.18   What is a typical upper limit for the operating temperature of hydraulic oil? Why?

Q14.19   (a) In normal operations, what determines the pump outlet pressure in an open-center hydraulic system?
(b) What determines the flow rate from the pump?

Q14.20   Rework Q14.19, but assume the system is a pressure-compensated system.

Q14.21   Rework Q14.19, but assume the system is a pressure-flow-compensated system.

Q14.22   Is a hydraulic system with an accumulator best suited for continuous or intermittent use? Why?

Q14.23   Which valve is best suited for regulating flow in an open-center hydraulic system: The valve in Figure 14.14 or the valve in Figure 14.15? Why?

Q14.24   When blocks are placed under the lower hitch points of a three-point hitch and the control lever is used to lower the hitch, it is found that the rear wheels of some tractors will lift off the ground. On most tractors, however, the hitch points merely rest on the blocks with no further movement of the hitch or tractor. What difference in hitch design explains this difference in operation?

Q14.25   (a) In the hydraulic system of Figure 14.22, what happens if the operator continues to hold the DCV control levers in the extend position after the hydraulic cylinder reaches the end of its stroke?
(b) In the hydraulic system of Figure 14.30, does the same action as in part a result if the operator moves the control lever from point A to point A′ and then fails to return the lever to point A? Briefly explain your answer.

# PROBLEMS

P14.1  In Figure 14.1, A1 = 10 cm$^2$ (1.56 in.$^2$) and A$_2$ = 100 cm$^2$ (15.6 in.$^2$). Assume force F$_1$ is 50 kN (11,240 lb) and is pushing the small piston downward at a speed of 0.2 m/s (0.66 ft/s).

(a) How large a mass (m) could be raised by the large piston?
(b) How fast would the large piston rise?
(c) What would be the pressure of the hydraulic oil?

P14.2  The following specifications for a certain gear pump were listed in a catalog:

displacement = 29.5 cm$^3$/rev (1.80 in.$^3$/rev)
rated speed = 2500 rev/min
rated pressure = 20.7 MPa (3000 psi)
rated delivery = 68.13 L/min (18 gpm)
power input = 28.35 kW (38 hp) at rated speed and delivery

(a) Calculate the theoretical delivery.
(b) What is the volumetric efficiency?
(c) What is the actual torque?
    (*Hint*: See Equation 5.5 for rotary power.)
(d) What is the theoretical torque?
(e) Calculate the torque efficiency.
(f) Calculate the power efficiency.
(g) How much power is converted to heat under rated conditions?

P14.3  Rework P14.2, but assume the pump is a fixed displacement pump with the following specifications?

displacement = 35.1 cm$^3$/rev (2.14 in.$^3$/rev)
rated speed = 1800 rev/min
rated pressure = 34.5 MPa (5000 psi)
rated delivery = 58.3 L/min (15.4 gpm)
power input = 37.6 kW (50 hp)

P14.4  The following specifications for a certain double-acting hydraulic cylinder were listed in a catalog:

piston diameter = 7.62 cm (3 in.)
rod diameter = 2.54 cm (1 in.)

stroke length = 20.32 cm (8 in.)
maximum operating pressure = 17.2 MPa (2500 psi)
(a) Calculate the piston area, $A_1$.
(b) Calculate the area of piston minus rod, $A_2$.
(c) What is the maximum safe load the cylinder can move while extending?
(d) What is the maximum safe load the cylinder can move while retracting?
(e) If the pump supplies oil at 68.13 L/min (18 gpm), how fast will the cylinder move while extending?
(f) How fast will it move while retracting?
(g) How much oil will be returning to the reservoir when the cylinder is extending?
(h) How much oil will be returning when the cylinder is retracting?

P14.5   Rework P14.4, but assume the piston diameter is 5.08 cm (2 in.).

P14.6   Rework P14.4, but assume the piston diameter is 10.16 cm (4 in.).

P14.7   Rework P14.2, but assume the hydraulic component is a gear-type motor with the following specifications:

displacement = 65.5 cm$^3$/rev (4.0 in.$^3$/rev)
rated speed = 1800 rev/min
rated pressure = 20.7 MPa (3000 psi)
required delivery = 130 L/min (34.3 gpm)
power output = 35.8 kW (48 hp) at rated conditions

P14.8   Rework P14.2, but assume the hydraulic component is a piston-type motor with the following specifications:

displacement = 41.0 cm$^3$/rev (2.50 in.$^3$/rev)
rated speed = 3600 rev/min
rated pressure = 20.7 MPa (3000 psi)
required delivery = 148 L/min (39.1 gpm)
power output = 50.7 kW (68 hp) at rated conditions

P14.9   Suppose the motor of P14.7 was hydraulically coupled to the pump of P14.2.

(a) If the pump ran at 2500 rev/min and the volumetric efficiencies of pump and motor were the same as was calculated in P14.2 and P14.7, respectively, how fast would the motor turn?

(b) Assuming torque efficiencies of the pump and motor were the same as in P14.2 and P14.7, respectively, how much torque and how much pressure could the motor produce at rated pressure?

(c) How much power would the pump and motor combination convert to heat?

P14.10   In Figure 14.22, assume the open-center hydraulic system has the pump specified in P14.2 and the hydraulic cylinders specified in P14.4. The relief valve is set to open at 10 MPa (1450 psi). The weight WA is 40 kN (8990 lb) and the weight WB is 50 kN (11,240 lb). Assuming the operator moves both DCVs to the extend position and continues to hold them there, do calculations that will allow you to describe the resulting sequence of events.

(a) What system pressures will exist at each stage of operation?

(b) Where will the pump discharge be directed at each stage?

(c) How long will each stage last?

P14.11   Rework P14.10, but assume the relief pressure is 15 MPa (2175 psi).

P14.12   The pressure in the hydraulic system of Figure 14.27 can vary 10% above or below the average system pressure as the accumulator charges and discharges. Use Equation 14.19 (assume n = 1.2) to calculate and plot a curve of accumulator oil capacity ($\Delta V$) versus accumulator size ($V_1$).

P14.13   (a) Rework P14.12, but let the pressure vary by x% above and below the average system pressure. Calculate the ratio $\Delta V/V_1$ for values of x ranging from 0 to 25%.

(b) Plot the results on a graph with $\Delta V/V_1$ on the y-axis versus x on the x-axis.

P14.14   Starting with Equation 2.7, derive Equation 14.19.

P14.15 Two hoses are required to connect a double-acting hydraulic cylinder to the remote outlets of a tractor. If the maximum flow is 76 L/min (20 gpm) and the maximum system pressure is 20.7 MPa (3000 psi), select the size and type of hose required to transmit the oil.

P14.16 Rework P14.15, but assume the maximum flow is 19 L/min (5 gpm) and the maximum system pressure is 34.5 MPa (5000 psi).

# 15
# Power Trains

## 15.1 INTRODUCTION

The power train is the means for transmitting power from the engine to the point of use. The power train may include a traction clutch or other means for interrupting the flow of power to the drive wheels. One of several types of transmissions is included for changing travel speeds and for providing a means of reversing directions. At least one differential is included for dividing power between the drive wheels. One or more power-take-off drives may be included for supplying rotary power to tractor implements. A separate clutch may be provided to interrupt the flow of power to the power-take-off drive. Finally, brakes are provided to allow the operator to stop the vehicle when desired.

By selecting from relatively few types of transmission elements, vehicle manufacturers can design a wide variety of transmissions for their new tractors or other vehicles. For example, one manufacturer may choose to combine a six-speed synchromesh transmission with a two-speed power shift transmission to obtain a twelve-speed transmission. Another manufacturer may obtain a twelve-speed transmission using only power shift elements. Each introduction of new models of tractors brings new combinations. Consequently, a textbook that focussed on the transmissions in specific tractors or other vehicles would not prepare the students adequately in understanding the transmissions in recently introduced vehicles. Therefore, the approach taken in this chapter is to focus on the principles of operation, the advantages, and the limitations of the various types of transmission elements. A knowledge of these principles, advantages and limitations will enable you to analyze and understand the operation of transmissions in specific vehicles. You also may gain insights as to why a manufacturer chooses a particular combination of elements in any given transmission.

## 15.2 CLUTCHES AND BRAKES

A *clutch* provides a means for the tractor operator to start a smooth delivery of power to the transmission, to interrupt power while the transmission gear ratio is being changed, and to interrupt power when the tractor is to be stopped. The two most common types of clutches used with engines are over-centering clutches and spring-loaded clutches. Clutches may also be classified as wet or dry and as single- or multiple-disk clutches.

Brakes have many similarities to clutches, except that clutches are used to start a vehicle in motion, while brakes are used to stop the vehicle.

### 15.2.1 Over-Centering Clutches

A cutaway view of an *over-centering* clutch is shown in Figure 15.1. The clutch includes driving plates that are attached to the flywheel. Friction disks are bonded to the front and rear faces of the driving plates. The driving plates with attached friction disks are between driven plates, which are connected to the output shaft. The clutch is operated by a hand lever. When the hand lever is in the left-most position, as shown in Figure 15.1, the driven plates are squeezed tightly against the friction disks, and the clutch transmits torque. Pulling the clutch lever to the right causes the clutch linkage to move over center and separate the driven plates so that the driving plates spin freely between them. Then, power flow would be interrupted. The clutch in Figure 15.1 is a multiple-disk clutch (it has more than one driving plate), and it is a dry clutch (the clutch disks do not run in a liquid bath).

Stationary engines for operating irrigation pumps, electric generators, and so forth do not need a transmission for changing speeds. An over-centering clutch is used on such engines because it will remain in either the engaged or disengaged position without operator attention. Over-centering traction clutches also were used on some tractors in the past. Now, however, all new tractors have spring-loaded traction clutches. An over-centering clutch may be used on modern tractors to interrupt power flow to the power-take-off drive.

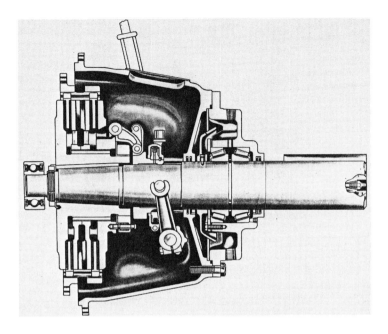

*Figure 15.1–An over-centering clutch. (Courtesy of Twin Disc, Incorporated.)*

## 15.2.2 Spring-Loaded Clutches

A cross-sectional drawing of a *spring-loaded*, dry, single-disk clutch is shown in Figure 15.2. A *clutch disk* and a *pressure plate* assembly with three release levers are shown in Figure 15.3. The pressure plate housing is bolted directly to the flywheel in Figure 15.2. The clutch disk is between the flywheel and pressure plate and is spline connected to the output shaft. The clutch is said to be engaged when the clutch springs press the pressure plate tightly against the clutch disk and torque can be transmitted from the flywheel to the drive shaft. The operator disengages the clutch by pressing a clutch pedal (not shown in Figure 15.2). The linkage moves the *release*, or *throwout, bearing* to the right against the tips of the clutch release levers. The release levers are forced to pivot and pull the pressure plate away from the clutch disk. Then, the disk can stop while the flywheel and pressure plate continue to spin. A *pilot bearing* in the center of the flywheel supports the end of the output shaft.

## 15.2.3 Brakes

There are two types of brakes used to stop vehicles. Originally, drum-type brakes were the most popular, but disk brakes have gained in popularity in recent years.

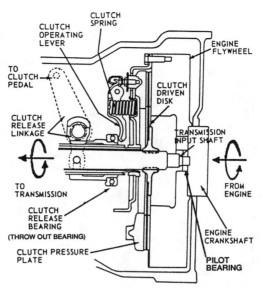

*Figure 15.2–A spring-loaded clutch. (Courtesy of Deere & Company.)*

With *drum brakes*, each wheel has a set of brake shoes that are anchored to the axle housing and ride inside a drum that is connected to the rotating axle. When actuated, the *brake shoes* are forced outward until their friction surfaces press firmly against the inner diameter of the drum. The friction force between the brake shoes and the drum provides the braking torque needed to bring the vehicle to a halt. The brakes convert the kinetic energy of the vehicle motion into heat that must be absorbed by the brake shoes and drums.

*Disk brakes* include a disk that is attached to the rotating axle of each wheel. A *caliper* that is anchored to the nonrotating axle housing contains a set of *brake pads* that straddle the brake disk. When the brakes are actuated, the caliper squeezes the brake pads together, forcing them to grip the rotating disk. As with drum brakes, the disk brakes convert the kinetic energy of vehicle motion into heat that must be absorbed by the disk and brake pads.

Either drum-type or disk brakes can be actuated mechanically or hydraulically. Hydraulic brakes are normally used to bring a vehicle to a stop. When the operator presses the brake pedal, the brake linkage pushes inward on the plunger of a small hydraulic cylinder called a master cylinder. The *master cylinder* generates high pressure which is transmitted through hydraulic brake lines to a *slave cylinder* at each wheel. The pressure forces each slave cylinder

Power Trains 423

*Figure 15.3–A clutch pressure plate and disc. (Courtesy of Borg-Warner Corporation.)*

to extend and actuate the brakes. Alternatively, with *power brakes*, pressing the brake pedal causes pressurized oil from the vehicle hydraulic system to be delivered to the slave cylinders to actuate the brakes with less pedal effort.

Brakes on the earliest vehicles are actuated through a mechanical linkage between the brake pedal and each set of brake shoes. Such braking systems have been succeeded by hydraulic brakes with one exception. A mechanical cable system between a parking brake pedal (or lever) and the rear wheel brakes is still used to engage the brakes for parking. The parking brake system thus removes the need to maintain high hydraulic pressure in the braking system during the long periods when the vehicle may remain parked.

### 15.2.4 Clutch or Brake Capacity
The torque-transmitting capacity of a clutch or brake can be calculated by using Equation 15.1:

$$T = F_c * f * r_m * n \qquad (15.1)$$

where
- $T$ = torque in N·m (lb-ft)
- $F_c$ = clamping force in kN (lb)
- $f$ = coefficient of friction

$r_m$ = mean radius of the clutch or brake in mm (ft)
n = number of torque-transmitting surfaces

In the case of drum brakes, $r_m$ is one half the inside diameter of the brake drum. For disk brakes, $r_m$ is the radius from the axle centerline to the center of the brake pads. For clutches, the following equation can be used to calculate the mean radius:

$$r_m = \frac{(d_o^3 - d_i^3)}{3(d_o^2 - d_i^2)} \tag{15.2}$$

where
$d_o$ = outside diameter of clutch disk in mm (ft)
$d_i$ = inside diameter of clutch disk in mm (ft)

A skillful operator can use the clutch to smoothly accelerate a vehicle from rest to full speed. Initially, the flywheel and pressure plate spin at high speed, but the clutch disk is at rest. By slowly releasing the clutch pedal, the operator causes a gradual increase in the clamping force and a gradual increase in the torque-transmitting ability of the clutch. Initially, clutch slippage is 100%, but it gradually decreases to less than 1% when the clutch is fully engaged.

With braking, the process is similar; that is, the slippage between the rotating brake drum and the stationary shoes (or moving brake disk and stationary calipers) is initially 100%, but decreases to zero as the vehicle is brought to a stop.

### 15.2.5 Dry and Wet Clutches or Brakes

With either clutches or brakes, slippage generates heat, and the temperature can increase to 500° C (932° F). The friction material in the clutch or brake must be capable of dissipating the heat and also must be capable of withstanding the high temperatures without glazing or scoring; otherwise, the coefficient of friction would change too much. Asbestos-based materials meet these requirements. However, ceramic materials have replaced the asbestos materials in more recent vehicles.

A *dry clutch* is incapable of handling the heat and high temperatures that are produced in very heavy-duty vehicles. In such cases, the clutch disks run in an oil bath and the clutch is called a *wet clutch*. Bimetal elements, such as steel plates running against bronze disks, often are used in wet clutches. Running a clutch in oil reduces the coefficient of friction. To obtain an adequate torque-transmitting capacity (see Equation 15.1), therefore, a wet clutch must have many disks in order to provide a large number of torque-transmitting surfaces.

Although dry brakes are the most common, brakes can also be designed to run in oil. Again, as in the case of wet clutches, multiple disks may be used in wet brakes to provide sufficient torque capacity.

### 15.2.6 Clutch and Brake Adjustments

The clutch linkage must be kept in proper adjustment. The clutch pedal should have a certain amount of *free travel*. That is, the pedal should move a certain distance before the release bearing contacts the release levers. The free travel should be in accordance with manufacturer's recommendations. Too little free travel may keep the release bearing in constant contact with the release levers and cause the bearing to wear out prematurely. Too much free travel may prevent complete disengagement of the clutch. The clutch would then drag and make the shifting of gears difficult.

Brakes may also require adjustment. The brakes should be adjusted so that the brakes are fully engaged while the brake pedal is still some distance from the floor. As with clutches, there should be some free travel of the brake pedal to assure that the brakes are fully released when braking is not desired.

## 15.3 BASIC PRINCIPLES OF TRANSMISSIONS

Generally, several sets of gears are used to transmit power from the engine to the drive wheels of a vehicle. The gears are used to reduce speed and increase torque as power flows toward the drive wheels. When two gears are in mesh, the rotation of either gear can be calculated from the rotation of the other by using the following equation:

$$n_1 * \Theta_1 = n_2 * \Theta_2 \tag{15.3}$$

where
    $n_1$ and $n_2$ = number of teeth on gears 1 and 2, respectively
    $\Theta_1$ and $\Theta_2$ = rotation of gears 1 and 2, respectively

Since the two rotations are accomplished within the same time-period, the speed of either gear can be calculated from the other by using the following equation:

$$n_1 * N_1 = n_2 * N_2 \tag{15.4}$$

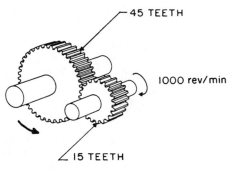

*Figure 15.4–Spur gears in mesh.*

where $N_1$ and $N_2$ = rotational speeds of gears 1 and 2, respectively.

The calculation of speed ratio is illustrated in Example Problem 15.1.

## Example Problem 15.1

A 15-tooth gear on the input shaft is in mesh with a 45-tooth gear on the output shaft, as shown in Figure 15.4. The input shaft is being driven at 1000 rev/min. How fast does the output shaft rotate? How many revolutions does the 15-tooth gear rotate for every revolution of the 45-tooth gear?

**Solution:** The speed of the 45-tooth gear can be calculated by using Equation 15.3. When $n_1$ = 15 teeth and $n_2$ = 45 teeth, then:

[15 teeth] * [1000 rev/min] = [45 teeth] * [$N_2$ rev/min]

$N_2$ = [15/45] * [1000] = 333 rev/min

Also, by using Equation 15.3, the rotations of the 15-tooth gear can be calculated:

[15 teeth] * [$\Theta_1$ rev] = [45 teeth] * [1 rev]

$\Theta_1$ = [45/15] * [1] = 3 rev

Thus, the output shaft rotates at 333 rev/min. The input shaft rotates three revolutions for every revolution of the output shaft. It is always true that, when two gears are in mesh, the smaller gear must turn through a greater rotation and therefore must rotate faster than the larger gear. Notice also that the meshed gears must turn in opposite directions. If the 15-tooth gear turns clockwise, for example, the 45-tooth gear must turn counterclockwise. The term, gear ratio,

Power Trains

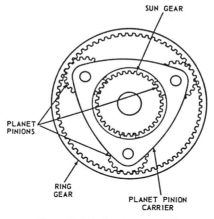

*Figure 15.5–A planetary gear set.*

is used to express the relationship between input and output speed. The *gear ratio*, R, for Example Problem 15.1 is calculated as follows:

R = input speed/output speed = 1000/333 = 3

Thus, the gear ratio of the drive is 3.0. The sliding friction between gear teeth causes some loss of power. A general rule is that a 1 to 2% power loss occurs in each well-lubricated gear mesh. Thus, if the gears of Example Problem 15.1 were well lubricated, the efficiency of the drive would be 98 to 99%.

One type of *planetary gear* set is shown in Figure 15.5. The name is taken from our solar system, in which planets rotate about the sun. In Figure 15.5, the planet gears are carried on a planet carrier and are in mesh with both the sun gear and the ring gear. The planetary gear set cannot transmit power unless two of the elements are locked together or one of the elements is held stationary. If any two elements are locked together, the entire assembly rotates as one unit and the speed ratio is 1:1. Equations 15.3 and 15.4 do not apply directly to the planetary gear set if the planet carrier is moving, because then the planet gears are moving as well as rotating. However, the following equation can be used to calculate speed ratios regardless of which element is held stationary:

$$N_s * n_s = N_{pc} * [n_s + n_r] - N_r * n_r \quad (15.5)$$

where
 $n_s$ = number of teeth on sun gear
 $n_r$ = number of teeth on ring gear

$N_s$ = rotational speed of sun gear in rev/min
$N_{pc}$ = rotational speed of planet carrier in rev/min
$N_r$ = rotational speed of the ring gear in rev/min

To use the equation, the speed of the stationary element is set to zero. The speed of the input element is inserted along with the numbers of gear teeth on each element, and then the speed of the remaining element can be calculated. Notice that, because the planet gears are idlers between the sun and ring gears, the number of teeth on the planet gears is not needed in the equation. If gear rotations are desired instead of gear speeds, the respective $\Theta$ is substituted for each N in Equation 15.5. Notice that Equations 15.3 and 15.4 were identical except that rotations were used in one and speeds were used in the other. Therefore, in the remainder of this chapter, only the equations for speeds will be shown because the equations for rotations will always be similar.

A popular application of the planetary gear set of Figure 15.5 is to achieve a speed reduction by connecting the input shaft to the sun gear, holding the ring gear stationary, and connecting the output shaft to the planet carrier. The reader may verify that Equation 15.5 then reduces to the following:

$$R = \frac{N_s}{N_{pc}} = 1 + \frac{n_r}{n_s} \qquad (15.6)$$

As in the case of Example Problem 15.1, the gear ratio of a planetary gear drive is calculated as the ratio of the input speed over the output speed. In Equation 15.6, for example, the sun gear was on the input shaft and the planet carrier drove the output shaft while the ring gear was held stationary. Thus, the gear ratio was equal to the speed of the sun gear divided by the speed of the planet carrier.

The efficiency of a well-lubricated planetary gear set varies with its configuration and speed ratio. In a typical application in which a planetary gear set is used as a final drive (see Section 15.11), the efficiency would typically be 97 to 98%.

## 15.4 THEORY AND TYPES OF TRANSMISSIONS

The torque-speed curve for an engine running at full governor setting is shown in Figure 15.6a. Figure 15.6b shows torque-speed curves at the drive wheels after the power has passed through the transmission, differential, and final drives. The eight-speed transmission has converted the torque-speed curve of the engine into

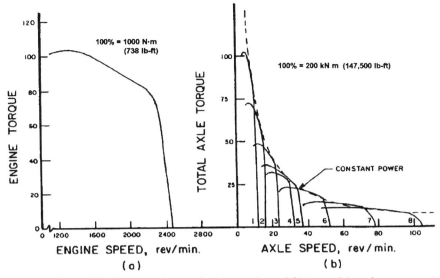

*Figure 15.6–Torque-speed curves for (a) an engine and (b) tractor drive axles.*

eight distinct torque-speed curves at the drive wheels. Notice that the axle speed is much less than the engine speed, but the axle torque is much greater than the engine torque. The following equations can be used to convert engine speed and torque to axle speed and torque:

$$N_A = \frac{N_E}{R_{PT}} \tag{15.7}$$

$$T_{CA} = R_{PT} * e_{PT} * T_E \tag{15.8}$$

where
- $N_E$ = engine speed in rev/min
- $N_A$ = axle speed in rev/min
- $T_E$ = engine torque in N·m (lb-ft)
- $T_{CA}$ = combined torque in the drive axles, in N·m (lb-ft)
- $R_{PT}$ = $(R_T)(R_D)(R_{FD})$ = gear ratio of power train
- $R_T$ = ratio of transmission input speed to output speed
- $R_D$ = ratio of differential input speed to output speed
- $R_{FD}$ = ratio of final drive input speed to output speed
- $e_{PT}$ = $(e_T)(e_D)(e_{FD})$ = efficiency of power train in decimals
- $e_T$ = efficiency of transmission in decimals
- $e_D$ = efficiency of differential in decimals
- $e_{FD}$ = efficiency of final drive in decimals

In Equation 15.8, $T_{CA}$ is the sum of the torques in all of the drive axles. For a rear-wheel drive, for example, $T_{CA}$ would be two times the torque carried in each axle extending from the differential. In a four-wheel-drive tractor with all wheels of equal size, the combined axle torque of all four axles would be used on the left side of Equation 15.8.

The dashed curve in Figure 15.6b shows the combination of torque and speed that would be available if the full engine power at governor's maximum could be used at the rear axles. The dashed curve touches the curve for each gear at the point where the engine is operating at governor's maximum.

It is desirable to operate an engine near governor's maximum. Operating with less torque gives inefficient engine operation, while operation in the load-controlled range provides poor speed control. The function of the transmission is to match the load to the engine. The more speed ratios in the transmission, the better the matching. Suppose, for example, that a tractor with the transmission characteristics of Figure 15.6b was loaded with axle torque of 40 kN·m (30,000 lb-ft). If the transmission was in sixth gear, the engine would be operating well into the load-controlled range, and speed control would be poor. If the transmission was operated in fifth gear, speed control would be good, but the engine would be operating at part load, that is, at a load less than governor's maximum. Load matching would be better if the transmission had another speed ratio between fifth and sixth gears.

There are at least five different types of transmissions in use on farm tractors. The five types – manual shift, synchromesh, power shift, hydrostatic, and hydrokinetic transmissions – are listed here in increasing order of load-matching capability. The five types of transmissions are discussed in Sections 15.5 through 15.9.

## 15.5 MANUAL SHIFT TRANSMISSIONS

The speed ratio of a *manual shift transmission* can be changed only when power is interrupted by disengagement of the traction clutch. The operator uses one or more shift levers to change the selection of transmission gears that transmit the power. After a new set of gears is selected, the traction clutch can be reengaged to resume power flow.

### 15.5.1 Classification by Shaft Arrangement

Manual shift transmissions are available in two basic designs; with input and output shafts *parallel* and with input and output shafts *in line*. A parallel shaft transmission is illustrated in Figure 15.7. Use of a parallel shaft transmission permits the output shaft to be placed at a different level than (usually below) the input shaft. In all forward gears, the output shaft of a parallel shaft transmission turns opposite in direction to the input shaft.

A manual shift transmission with in-line shafts is shown in Figure 15.8. The top shaft is split at the bearing so that the input shaft can rotate at a different speed than the output shaft. In Figure 15.8, power from the input shaft is being transmitted through a gear mesh to the countershaft, then through another gear mesh to the output shaft. Since each gear mesh produces a direction reversal, the two gear meshes cause the output shaft to turn in the same direction as the input shaft.

### 15.5.2 Classification by Shifting Means

In addition to classification by shaft arrangement, transmissions are classified as *sliding gear* or *sliding collar*. In sliding gear transmissions, internal splines permit each gear to slide along its shaft without rotating relative to the shaft. In contrast, the transmissions in Figures 15.7 and 15.8 are sliding collar (or sliding coupling, as they are also called) transmissions. The gears on the main countershaft in Figure 15.7 have bearings that permit the gears to rotate freely on the shaft while staying in continuous mesh with mating gears. Between each set of gears is a sliding coupling that is spline connected to the main countershaft. When the sliding coupling is locked to one of its adjacent gears, that gear can no longer rotate relative to the main countershaft. Only spur gears can be used in sliding gear transmissions, and the repeated making and breaking of tooth contacts on mating gears (see Figure 15.4) is noisy. Gears with spiral cut teeth can be used in collar shift transmissions because mating gears remain continuously meshed. Such transmissions operate more quietly because the contact of one set of mating teeth can be sustained until the following set of teeth begins to mesh.

Only one shift lever is usually provided for manual shifting in automotive vehicles. So many speed ratios are provided in tractor transmissions that it is often necessary to provide two or more shift levers. A shift lever and range lever are provided in the transmission of Figure 15.7. The range lever is used to move the no. 3 sliding coupling. All other sliding elements are moved by the shift lever.

### 15.5.3 Calculation of Speed Ratios

The speed ratios across a transmission can be calculated if the number of teeth on each transmission gear is known. The procedure is illustrated in Example Problem 15.2.

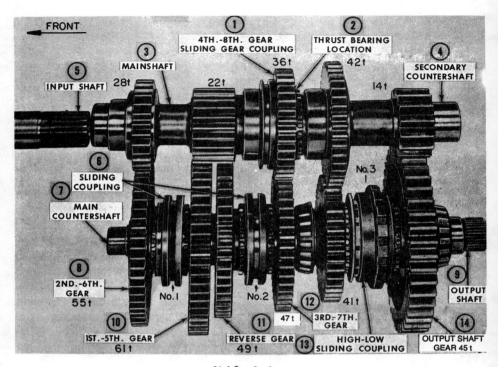

|       | Shift  | Range | Slider Positions | | | Sliding |     |
| Gear  | Lever  | Lever | No.1 | No.2 | No.3 | Gear | Key |
|-------|--------|-------|------|------|------|------|-----|
| $R_1$ | 1(F)   | F     | C    | F    | B    | F    |     |
| 1     | 2      | F     | B    | C    | B    | F    |     |
| 2     | 3      | F     | F    | C    | B    | F    |     |
| 3     | 4      | F     | C    | B    | B    | F    |     |
| 4     | 5(B)   | F     | C    | C    | B    | B    | SHIFT LEVER |
| $R_2$ | 1      | B     | C    | F    | F    | F    |     |
| 5     | 2      | B     | B    | C    | F    | F    |     |
| 6     | 3      | B     | F    | C    | F    | F    |     |
| 7     | 4      | B     | C    | B    | F    | F    |     |
| 8     | 5      | B     | C    | C    | F    | B    |     |
| N     | X      | C     | X    | X    | C    | X    | RANGE LEVER |

Key: F = forward position; C = centered position; B = back position; X = irrelevant position.

Note: Mainshaft does not continue through to secondary countershaft. 36t gear is spline connected to mainshaft; when back, it couples to secondary countershaft. Reverse gear is driven from 22t gear through an idler gear (not shown). Main countershaft does not continue through to output shaft. Output shaft gear (45t) rotates freely on output shaft. 41t gear is keyed to main countershaft. Four other gears rotate freely on main countershaft. High-low sliding coupling is spline connected to output shaft. Two sliding couplings are spline connected to main countershaft.

Figure 15.7–A manual shift transmission. (Adapted from a diagram provided by Ford Motor Company, Tractor Division.)

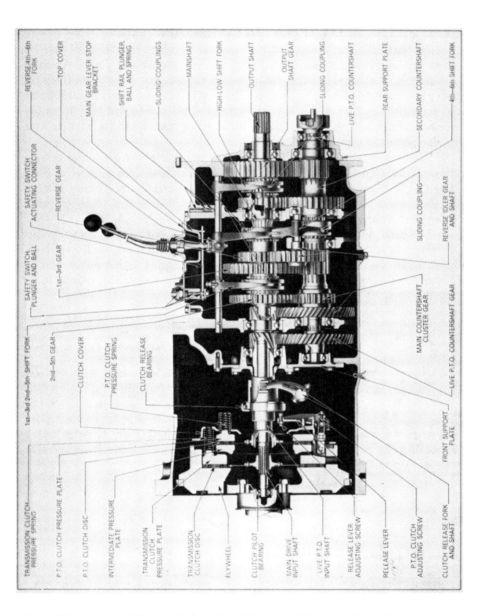

*Figure 15.8–A manual shift transmission with in-line shafts. (Courtesy of Ford Motor Company, Tractor Division.)*

## Example Problem 15.2
Calculate the ratio of input speed to output speed for the transmission of Figure 15.7 when it is running in third gear.

**Solution:** It is first necessary to trace the power flow through the transmission in third gear. Notice that all gears on the input mainshaft are permanently attached to that shaft and are in constant mesh with gears on the main countershaft. The first four gears can freewheel on the main countershaft, but the 41-tooth (41t) gear is keyed to the main countershaft. Shifting in this transmission is accomplished by couplings that are spline connected to the main countershaft, but that can be slid forward or backward to latch to one of the adjacent gears.

The secondary countershaft has two permanently attached gears. The output shaft has one freewheeling gear and one sliding collar. The No. 3 sliding coupling can be slid forward to latch the output shaft to the main countershaft or backward to latch the 45-tooth (45t) gear to the output shaft.

In third gear, the No. 2 sliding coupling is back. It latches the 47-tooth (47t) gear to the main countershaft. Thus, power flows from the input shaft to the main countershaft through the mesh of the 36-tooth (36t) gear with the 47-tooth gear. By using Equation 15.4, the speed ratio across the gear mesh can be calculated to be:

$$36\ N_{is} = 47\ N_{mcs}$$

where
$N_{is}$ = speed of the input shaft in rev/min
$N_{mcs}$ = speed of the main countershaft in rev/min

The No. 3 sliding coupling is back in third gear. Power cannot flow directly to the output shaft. Instead, it must flow through the secondary countershaft. The speed ratio across the mesh of the 41-tooth gear with the 42-tooth (42t) gear is:

$$41\ N_{mcs} = 42\ N_{scs}$$

where $N_{scs}$ is the speed of the secondary countershaft. The speed ratio across the final mesh is:

$$14\ N_{scs} = 45\ N_{os}$$

where $N_{os}$ is the speed of the output shaft. Now, the speed ratios for all three meshes can be combined:

$$N_{is} = [47/36] * N_{mcs} = [47/36] * [42/41] * N_{scs}$$

$$= [47/36] * [42/41] * [45/14] * N_{os}$$

or

$$R_{T3} = N_{is} / N_{os} = [47 / 36] * [42 / 41] * [45 / 14] = 4.30$$

Therefore, the input shaft turns 4.30 times faster than the output shaft in third gear and the gear ratio of the transmission is 4.30:1. With three meshes, the input shaft and output shaft must turn in opposite directions.

Although it cannot be seen in Figure 15.7, a reverse shaft with an idler gear is used when it is desirable to move the vehicle in reverse. The reverse idler is in mesh with the 22-tooth (22t) gear on the input shaft and the 49-tooth (49t) gear on the main countershaft. In the first reverse gear, the No. 2 sliding coupling is forward, and the No. 3 sliding coupling is back. Therefore, the power flows through the following meshes:

>22t gear with reverse idler
>Reverse idler with 49t gear
>41t gear with 42t gear
>14t gear with 45t gear

With four meshes, the output shaft rotates in the same direction as the input shaft. The differential is arranged to cause the vehicle to move backward when the transmission output shaft turns in the same direction as the input shaft or to move forward when the two shafts turn in opposite directions. The speed ratio in gear R1 can be calculated using a procedure similar to that used for third gear. The reader can verify that the input shaft turns 7.33 times faster than the output shaft when the transmission is in the first reverse gear.

## 15.6 SYNCHROMESH TRANSMISSIONS

*Synchromesh transmissions* are sliding collar transmissions with synchronizers added to aid the operator in manually shifting gears. Manual shifting of an unsynchronized transmission can be difficult and time-consuming. For example, imagine that the transmission of Figure 15.7 is operating in second gear and the operator wishes to shift to first gear. After disengaging the traction clutch, the operator would be able to slide the No. 1 sliding coupling out of contact with the 55-tooth gear. The gears on the input shaft and all gears in mesh with them would immediately begin slowing down and coasting toward a stop. However, the main countershaft would still be connected to the output shaft (through two gear meshes), and the momentum of the vehicle would keep the main countershaft and No. 1 sliding coupling rotating with little loss in speed. Therefore, the No. 1 sliding coupling would be turning faster than the 61-tooth

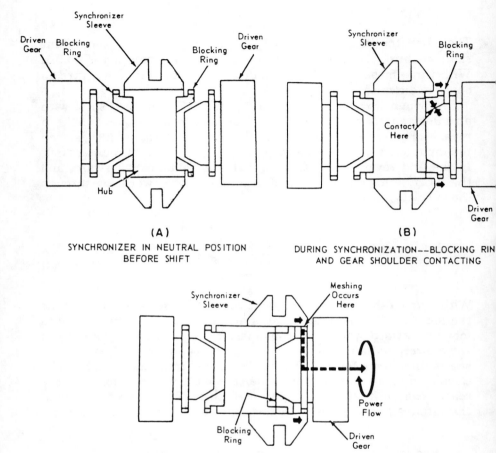

Figure 15.9–A block-type synchronizer. (Courtesy of Deere & Company.)

gear, and it might not be possible to latch them together until the vehicle came to a complete halt. Shifting between gears is considerably faster when a means to equalize the speed of the sliding coupling and mating gear prior to latching them together is used. A synchronizer accomplishes such speed equalization.

Several different types of synchronizers are available for equalizing speeds. The operation of one of these, the block-type synchronizer, is illustrated in Figure 15.9. The synchronizer sleeve is spline connected to the transmission shaft while two drive gears can freewheel on the shaft. In Figure 15.9a, the synchronizer sleeve has been moved out of contact with the drive gear on the left. The two drive gears are coasting to a stop while the vehicle momentum keeps the synchronizer spinning with little loss of speed. In Figure 15.9b, the synchronizer sleeve has been slid until a conical friction surface on the blocking ring contacts a mating surface on the drive gear. Friction between the two surfaces equalizes the speed of the drive gear and the synchronizer sleeve. The speed equalization occurs very quickly, and the operator can then move the sleeve further to latch it to the drive gear.

Synchromesh transmissions can be shifted quickly while the vehicle clutch is disengaged. They have been used for many years on automotive vehicles and are now standard equipment on manually shifted tractor transmissions. They increase tractor productivity compared to an unsychronized, manual shift transmission because less time in lost in shifting gears. A further productivity gain can be achieved if the transmission is shifted without disengaging the traction clutch to interrupt power flow. Such transmissions are available and are called power shift transmissions.

## 15.7 POWER SHIFT TRANSMISSIONS

The term power shift refers in part to the fact that hydraulic power assists in shifting between different speed ratios. More importantly, the term refers to the fact that shifting does not require the operator to disengage a traction clutch. Shifting occurs so quickly that there is no apparent interruption of power flow to the drive wheels. The two basic types of power shift transmissions are the countershaft type and the planetary type.

### 15.7.1 Countershaft Transmissions

A *countershaft transmission* is shown in Figure 15.10. The input shaft is permanently connected to the drum on the right and to gear G-1. Gear G-1 drives the countershaft and, through gears G-3 and G-4, also drives the drum on the left end of the transmission. Thus, the two drums rotate at different speeds. The left drum can rotate either faster (overdrive) or slower (underdrive) than the right drum, depending upon the numbers of teeth in gears G-1 through G-4. The output shaft of the transmission is permanently connected to a set of clutch disks in each drum. Either set of clutches can be engaged by supplying hydraulic pressure to the small hydraulic cylinders in each clutch. When the right clutch is engaged, the output shaft turns at the same speed as the input shaft. The left clutch is engaged in Figure 15.10. Therefore, the output shaft turns at a different speed than the input shaft. Usually, the number of teeth on gears G-1 through G-4 are designed so that the output shaft would turn slower

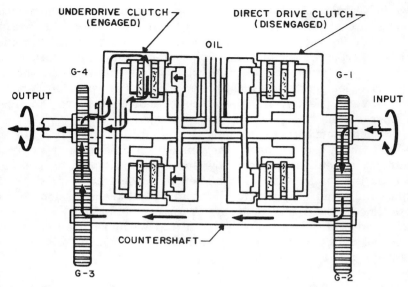

*Figure 15.10–A power shift transmission of the countershaft type. (Courtesy of Deere & Company.)*

than the input shaft when the left clutch was engaged. A procedure similar to that used in Example Problem 15.2 could be used to calculate the gear ratio of the drive. Notice that, with two gear meshes, the output shaft rotates in the same direction as the input shaft. With two gear meshes, the countershaft-type, power-shift transmission has an efficiency of 96 to 98% when power flows through the countershaft; the efficiency is nearly 100% in direct drive.

A reversing unit is shown in Figure 15.11. A reversing pinion, G-5, has been added to the countershaft transmission of Figure 15.10. When the left clutch is engaged, as in Figure 15.11, there are three gear meshes in the power train. Thus, the output shaft turns opposite to the direction of the input shaft. Both shafts turn in the same direction when the right clutch is engaged. The number of teeth on gear G-5 does not affect the speed ratio of the transmission, since gear G-5 is simply a reverse idler. The efficiency of the reversing unit is 94 to 97% in reverse and nearly 100% in direct drive.

### 15.7.2 Simple Planetary Transmissions

A *simple planetary transmission* is shown in Figure 15.12. This planetary transmission has no ring gears. The planet carrier can be locked to the input shaft by engaging the direct drive clutch on the

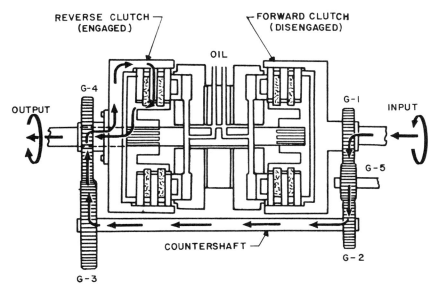

*Figure 15.11–A power shift reversing transmission. (Courtesy of Deere & Company.)*

right. It can be held stationary by engaging the underdrive brake on the left. When the clutch is engaged and the planet carrier rotates at the same speed as the input shaft, the speed ratio is 1:1. When the brake is engaged and the planet carrier is held stationary, the transmission becomes a countershaft transmission with the planets serving as parallel countershafts. The desired speed ratio is obtained by proper choice of the numbers of teeth on the two sun gears and the two sets of planets. The transmission can be placed in neutral by disengaging both the clutch and the brake.

### 15.7.3 Compound Planetary Transmissions

The planet carrier in a *compound planetary transmission* carries two sets of planets of differing size; one set meshes with a sun gear and the other meshes with a ring gear that is offset from the sun gear. The transmission illustrated in Figure 15.13 includes a compound planetary in the input section of Figure 15.13a, another in the center section of Figure 15.13b, and a third in the output section of Figure 15.13c. Taken together, the three sections form a complete power shift transmission.

The input section of Figure 15.13a has two concentric output shafts. The inner shaft is driven when clutch $C_1$ is engaged, while the outer shaft is driven when clutch $C_2$ is engaged. Connected to outer shaft $C_2$ are the disk portion of clutch $C_{Lo}$ and the planet carrier of a compound planetary gear set. The smaller planet gears roll in a ring

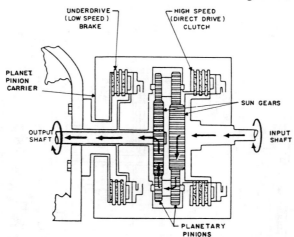

*Figure 15.12–A power shift transmission of the simple planetary type. (Courtesy of Deere & Company.)*

gear which drives the output shaft of the compound planetary gear set. The larger planets roll on a sun gear which is connected to the high-low drum. When clutch $C_{Lo}$ is engaged, the sun gear is forced to rotate at the same speed as the planet carrier; thus the planet gears cannot rotate on their axes, the ring gear must rotate at the same speed as the planet carrier, and output ring gear turns at the same speed as the engine. When brake $B_{Hi}$ is engaged, the sun gear is held stationary, the larger planet gears roll on the sun gear and the ring gear is driven by the smaller planet gears. Equation 15.5 is not sufficient to calculate the speed ratio of this compound planetary gear set, since it contains no reference to the numbers of teeth in the planet gears. The following more general equation is needed:

$$N_s * n_s = N_c * \left[ n_s + n_r \frac{n_{ps}}{n_{pr}} \right] - N_r * n_r \frac{n_{ps}}{n_{pr}} \qquad (15.9)$$

where
- $N_s$ = speed of the sun gear in rev/min
- $N_r$ = speed of the ring gear in rev/min
- $N_{pc}$ = speed of planet carrier in rev/min
- $n_r$ = number of teeth on the ring gear
- $n_s$ = number of teeth on the sun gear
- $n_{ps}$ = number of teeth on each planet gear that is in mesh with the sun gear
- $n_{pr}$ = number of teeth on each planet gear that is in mesh with the ring gear

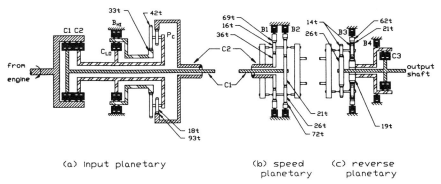

*Figure 15.13–A power-shift transmission of the compound planetary type.*

Notice that $N_s = 0$ in using Equation 15.9 to calculate the speed ratio of the compound planetary drive in this case, because the sun gear is held stationary by engaging brake $B_{Hi}$. Equation 15.9 then reduces to the following equation for the speed ratio between the input (planet carrier) and the output (ring gear):

$$R_i = \frac{N_{pc}}{N_r} = \frac{n_r}{n_r + n_s \frac{n_{pr}}{n_{ps}}} \qquad (15.10)$$

where $R_i$ = speed ratio of input section.

With clutch $C_2$ engaged, the outer shaft ($C_2$) is driven at engine speed when clutch $C_{Lo}$ is engaged but with speed ratio $R_i$ when brake $B_{Hi}$ is engaged. The inner shaft ($C_1$) is driven at engine speed when clutch $C_1$ is engaged.

The center section of the transmission (Figure 15.13b) also contains a compound planetary. Notice that this compound planetary contains two sun gears and two ring gears in addition to a planet carrier with two sets of planet gears. The input is through the sun gear on the right if clutch $C_1$ is engaged, or through the sun gear on the left if clutch $C_2$ is engaged. The ring gear on the right can be held stationary by engaging brake $B_2$, or the ring gear on the left can be held by engaging brake $B_1$. Output is always through the planet carrier. Five different speed ratios are possible from the center section of Figure 15.13b. They are:

I. Drive the right sun gear and hold the right ring gear.

II. Drive the left sun gear and hold the left ring gear.
III. Drive the right sun gear and hold the left ring gear.
IV. Drive the left sun gear and hold the right ring gear.
V. Drive the right and left sun gears at the same speed.
VI. Drive the right and left sun gears at different speeds.

In Cases I and II above, the planet gears only serve as idlers between the driven sun gear and the held ring gear, the planetary gear set is therefore not compound, and Equation 15.6 can be used to calculate the speed ratio. The unused sun and ring gear will rotate, but do not transmit any power. Cases III and IV involve compound planetary gear sets in which a ring gear is held stationary. Equation 15.9 can be adapted to calculate the speed ratios by setting $N_r = 0$ to obtain the following equation for speed ratio:

$$R_c = \frac{N_s}{N_{pc}} = 1 + \frac{n_r}{n_s}\frac{n_{ps}}{n_{pr}} \tag{15.11}$$

where $R_c$ = speed ratio of the center section of transmission

Cases V and VI involve driving both sun gears while both ring gears free wheel and the planet carrier is the output. Because the input and center sections must work together when both sun gears are driven, the combined ratio for the two sections is calculated using the following equation:

$$R_i * R_c = \frac{N_{ss}}{N_{pc}} = \frac{1 - \frac{n_{fs} n_{ps}}{n_{ss} n_{pf}}}{1 - R_{fs}\frac{n_{fs} n_{ps}}{n_{ss} n_{pf}}} \tag{15.12}$$

where
- $R_i * R_c$ = combined speed ratio
- $N_{ss}$ = speed of slower sun gear in rev/min
- $N_{pc}$ = speed of planet carrier in rev/min
- $R_{fs}$ = $N_{fs} / N_{ss}$ = speed ratio of faster sun to slower sun
- $n_{fs}$ = number of teeth on faster rotating sun gear
- $n_{ss}$ = number of teeth on slower rotating sun gear
- $n_{pf}$ = number of teeth on planet in mesh with faster sun gear
- $n_{ps}$ = number of teeth on planet in mesh with slower sun gear

If brake $B_{Hi}$ is engaged (Case VI), the left sun is driven faster than the sun on the right and $R_{fs}$ is greater than one. When clutch $C_{Lo}$ is engaged instead (Case V), $R_{fs} = 1$ and, as Equation 15.12 shows, the combined speed ratio is one and the planet carrier rotates at engine speed.

Combining the transmission sections of Figures 15.13a and 15.13b provides a total of eight possible speed ratios. They are two ratios each for Cases II and IV above (depending on whether clutch $C_{Lo}$ or brake $B_{Hi}$ is engaged) and one ratio for each of the other four cases. Up to this point, no reverse has been provided.

The output section in Figure 15.13c is always driven by the planet carrier. Unlike the previous compound planetary gear sets, the two sets of planet gears on the carrier are carried on separate shafts arranged such that one set of planet gears meshes with the other. The larger set of planet gears on the right roll in a ring gear and on the right sun gear, as in a standard planetary gear set. The smaller set of planet gears mesh with the larger planets and also with the sun gear on the left. The output shaft is connected to the sun gear on the left. The right sun gear is connected to a drum to which are attached clutch $C_3$ and brake $B_4$. In direct drive, when clutch $C_3$ is engaged, the two sun gears are forced to rotate at the same speed. Consequently, the output shaft is forced to rotate at the same speed as the planet carrier. Overdrive is achieved by engaging Brake $B_4$, thus, holding the right sun gear stationary. The planet carrier forces the larger planet gears to roll on the right sun gear, driving the smaller planet gears, which in turn drive the left sun gear in the same direction as the planet carrier. Equation 15.9 does not hold for the compound planetary in the output section because the paired planet gears run on separate shafts. However, the following equation can be used to calculate the speed ratio in overdrive:

$$R_o = \frac{N_{pc}}{N_{sl}} = \frac{n_{sl}}{n_{sl} + n_{sr}} \qquad (15.13)$$

where
   $R_o$ = speed ratio of output section
   $N_{pc}$ = speed of planet carrier in rev/min
   $N_{sl}$ = speed of sun gear on the left in rev/min
   $n_{sl}$ = number of teeth on sun gear on the left
   $n_{sr}$ = number of teeth on sun gear on the right

When brake $B_3$ is engaged, the ring gear is held stationary and the planet carrier forces the large planet gears to roll in the stationary ring gear. The larger planets drive the smaller planets which, in turn, drive the sun gear on the left. Again, Equation 15.9 does not

TABLE 15.1. Engagement of elements in a 15-speed power-shift transmission

| Gear | $C_1$ | $C_2$ | $C_{Lo}$ | $B_{Hi}$ | $B_1$ | $B_2$ | $B_3$ | $C_3$ | $B_4$ |
|---|---|---|---|---|---|---|---|---|---|
| 4R |   | X |   | X |   | X | X |   |   |
| 3R |   | X | X |   | X |   | X |   |   |
| 2R | X |   |   | X |   | X | X |   |   |
| 1R | X |   | X |   | X |   | X |   |   |
| NR |   |   |   |   |   |   |   |   |   |
| Park |   |   |   |   |   |   |   | X | X |
| NF |   |   |   |   |   |   |   |   |   |
| 1 | X |   |   | X* | X |   |   | X |   |
| 2 | X |   |   | X* |   | X |   | X |   |
| 3 | X |   | X* |   | X |   |   |   | X |
| 4 |   | X | X |   | X |   |   | X |   |
| 5 |   | X |   | X | X |   |   | X |   |
| 6 |   | X | X |   |   | X |   | X |   |
| 7 |   | X |   | X |   | X |   | X |   |
| 8 |   | X | X |   | X |   |   |   | X |
| 9 |   | X |   | X | X |   |   |   | X |
| 10 |   | X | X |   |   | X |   |   | X |
| 11 |   | X |   | X |   | X |   |   | X |
| 12 | X | X | X |   |   |   |   | X |   |
| 13 | X | X |   | X |   |   |   | X |   |
| 14 | X | X | X |   |   |   |   |   | X |
| 15 | X | X |   | X |   |   |   |   | X |

*Elements engaged for convenience, not needed to transmit power.

hold, but the following equation can be used to calculate the speed ratio:

$$R_o = \frac{N_{pc}}{N_{sl}} = \frac{n_{sl}}{n_{sl} - n_r} \tag{15.14}$$

Normally, $n_r$ is greater than $n_{sl}$, the ratio is therefore negative, and the left sun gear turns opposite in direction to the planet carrier.

Engaging brake $B_3$ provides eight possible reverse speeds, one for each of the eight possible speeds of the planet carrier of the output section. Depending on whether clutch $C_3$ or brake $B_4$ are engaged, two possible ratios are provided for each of the eight possible speeds of the planet carrier for a total of sixteen possible forward speeds for the entire transmission. A transmission manufacturer would not necessarily choose to use all of the possible combinations. For example, two possible speed ratios might be so close together that the manufacturer would not choose to use both. Also, few vehicles have need of eight different ratios in reverse. Table 15.1 summarizes the use of the transmission in Figure 15.13 to provide a power-shift transmission with 15 forward speeds and 4 reverse speeds. Example Problem 15.3 illustrates the calculation of one of these speed ratios.

The problems at the end of the chapter provide the reader with an opportunity to calculate the remaining ratios.

## Example Problem 15.3

Calculate the speed ratio of the power shift transmission in Figure 15.13 in 11th and 15th gears.

**Solution:** Clutch $C_2$ and brake $B_{Hi}$ are engaged in either 11th or 15th gears (see Table 15.1). Equation 15.10 can be used to calculate the speed ratio of the input section when those two elements are engaged and the input section drives only one of the sun gears in the center section. The ratio is:

$$R_i = N_{pc} / N_r = n_r / [n_r + n_s \, n_{pr} / n_{ps}]$$

$$= 93 / [93 + 33 * 18 / 42] = 0.868$$

The input section is an overdrive in this case, that is, the speed is increased in the input section.

In 11th gear, the ring gear of the input section (Figure 15.13a) drives the right sun of the center section (Figure 15.13b), while the left ring gear of the center section is held stationary. Equation 15.11 can be used to calculate the speed ratio of the center section:

$$R_c = N_s / N_{pc} = 1 + n_r * n_{ps} / [n_s * n_{pr}]$$

$$= 1 + 72 * 16 / [36 * 26] = 2.23$$

In 15th gear, the left sun gear in the center section is driven at a faster speed than the sun gear on the right. Equation 15.12 is used to calculate the combined speed ratio of the input and center sections. Notice that, when $B_{Hi}$ is engaged, $R_{fs} = 1/R_i = 1/0.868 = 1.152$. Also, $n_{fs} = 36$, $n_{ss} = 21$, $n_{pf} = 16$, and $n_{ps} = 26$. Grouping these tooth numbers in the combination needed in Equation 15.12 gives:

$$[36 * 26] / [21 * 16] = 2.788$$

Then the combined speed ratio of the input and center sections is:

$$R_i * R_c = [1 - 2.788] / [1 - 2.788 * 1.152] = 0.808$$

In the output section, the planet carrier is driven, the right sun gear is held stationary, and the left sun gear drives the output shaft. Equation 15.12 can be used to calculate the speed ratic, as follows:

$$R_o = N_{pc} / N_{sl} = n_{sl} / [n_{sl} + n_{sr}] = 26 / [26 + 19] = 0.578$$

The output section functions as an overdrive in this case – that is, the speed is increased in the output section.

The speed ratio for the entire transmission, $R_t$, is the product of the speed ratios of the three sections. In 11th gear, the ratio of the entire transmission is:

$$R_t = R_i * R_c * R_o = 0.868 * 2.23 * 0.578 = 1.12$$

In 15th gear, the transmission ratio is:

$$R_t = R_i * R_c * R_o = 0.808 * 0.578 = 0.467$$

The transmission is an overdrive in 15th gear – that is, the output shaft rotates faster than the input shaft.

### 15.7.4  Practical Power Shifting

A primary advantage of a full-range power-shift transmission is that speed ratios can be changed with essentially no interruption of power. A traction clutch, as described in Section 15.2, is not needed for a full-range power shift transmission. However, a clutch pedal is usually provided for safety reasons. In an emergency, an operator will instinctively reach for the clutch pedal to stop the vehicle. The clutch pedal need not operate a conventional clutch; it could rather shift the transmission into neutral, for example, by releasing both clutches $C_1$ and $C_2$ in Figure 15.13.

Full-range power-shift transmissions also have disadvantages. It is common practice for a power-shift transmission to include its own hydraulic system, including a pump and an accumulator. Considerable energy is used in the hydraulic shifting of the various clutches and brakes and because of friction in the numerous gear meshes in the transmission. The efficiency, $e_t$, of a full-range power-shift transmission is typically below 85%. Such transmissions also are expensive to manufacture.

Tractor manufacturers have recognized that full-range power shifting may not be essential. As an option, they may provide part-range power shifting by placing a manual shift transmission in series with a power shift element. The tractor clutch must be disengaged to shift the manual shift transmission. Power shifting within each manually selected gear can be accomplished without disengaging the tractor clutch. The part-range power shift transmission is less expensive and its efficiency approaches 90%.

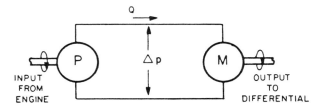

*Figure 15.14–A hydrostatic drive.*

## 15.8 CONTINUOUSLY-VARIABLE TRANSMISSIONS

One of the goals of modern transmission design is to permit the operator to keep the engine operating close to governor's maximum – that is, at the constant power line in Figure 15.6. Thus, transmissions are provided with many speed ratios and with quick shifting between ratios. A *continuously-variable transmission* (CVT) provides an infinite number of speed ratios. By observing the engine tachometer and controlling the transmission speed ratio, the operator theoretically can keep the engine running at governor's maximum while the tractor is pulling any heavy drawbar load.

Several different types of CVT have been developed. The variable-speed V-belt drives on self-propelled combines are one type of CVT, but these are too bulky and have insufficient capacity for use in tractors. Prototypes of mechanical CVT have also been developed, but are not yet reliable enough for commercial use. One type of CVT that has been in commercial use for many years is the hydrostatic transmission.

### 15.8.1 Classification and Theory of Hydrostatic Transmissions

A hydrostatic transmission consists of a pump hydraulically coupled to a hydraulic motor, as Figure 15.14 shows. Hydraulic pumps and motors are available in either fixed or variable displacement models. Therefore, the following four possibilities exist for a hydrostatic transmission:

**Type 1:** Fixed displacement pump and fixed displacement motor.
**Type 2:** Variable displacement pump and fixed displacement motor.
**Type 3:** Fixed displacement pump and variable displacement motor.
**Type 4:** Variable displacement pump and variable displacement motor.

The equations governing hydrostatic transmissions will help you to understand these transmissions. Combining Equations 14.7 and 14.16 gives the following equation for the speed output of a hydrostatic transmission:

$$N_m = [e_{vm} * e_{vp}] * \frac{D_p}{D_m} N_p \qquad (15.15)$$

where
- $N_m$ = motor speed in rev/min
- $N_p$ = pump speed in rev/min
- $D_p$ = pump displacement in cm³/rev (in.³/rev)
- $D_m$ = motor displacement in cm³/rev (in.³/rev)
- $e_{vm}$ = volumetric efficiency of motor in decimals
- $e_{vp}$ = volumetric efficiency of pump in decimals

Equation 14.17 for the torque output of a hydraulic motor is repeated here for convenience:

$$T_m = \frac{\Delta p * D_m * e_{Tm}}{K_T * \pi} \qquad (14.17)$$

where
- $T_m$ = torque output of motor in N·m (lb-ft)
- $e_{Tm}$ = torque efficiency of motor in decimals
- $\Delta_p$ = pressure drop across motor in MPa (psi)
- $D_m$ = motor displacement in cm³/rev (in.³/rev)
- $K_T$ = units constant = 2 (24)

Combining Equation 14.10 for calculating the actual torque needed to turn a pump shaft and Equation 14.17 for calculating motor torque gives the following alternative for motor torque:

$$T_m = [e_{Tp} * e_{Tm}] * \frac{D_m}{D_p} T_p \qquad (15.16)$$

where
- $T_p$ = pump torque in N·m (lb-ft)
- $e_{Tp}$ = torque efficiency of pump in decimals

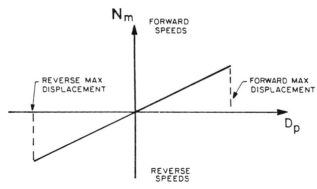

*Figure 15.15—Speed-changing characteristics of a hydrostatic transmission with variable displacement pump and fixed displacement motor.*

Other variables are as previously defined. The motor torque must be calculated using both Equations 15.16 and 14.17. The actual motor torque will be the smaller of the two numbers.

### 15.8.2 Type 1 Hydrostatic Transmissions
The first type of hydrostatic transmission – that is, with pump and motor both having fixed displacement – is the least expensive of the four types. However, it has no provision for changing speed ratios unless part of the pump flow is diverted from the motor and diverting flow sacrifices power capacity.

### 15.8.3 Type 2 Hydrostatic Transmissions
As Equation 15.15 indicates, the speed output of the second type of transmission changes in direct proportion to the pump displacement. Moreover, the direction of rotation of the motor shaft can be reversed by tipping the pump swash plate (Figure 14.7) far enough to reverse the direction of oil flow. Thus, the type 2 hydrostatic transmission provides a full range of speed control in both the forward and reverse directions, as shown in Figure 15.15. However, the motor torque cannot be increased with increasing system pressure (Equation 14.17). The pressure would be near its safe upper limit if the transmission was operating at full power, that is, at maximum motor speed and torque. If the motor speed was reduced by decreasing the pump displacement, it would not be possible to increase the motor torque by raising the system pressure. Thus, the type 2 transmission has the disadvantage of having less power-transmitting capability at lower speeds. It often is called a *constant torque transmission*. It is used in lawn and garden tractors and in

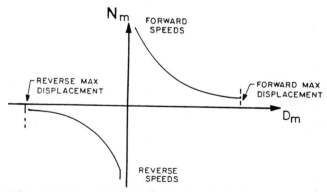

*Figure 15.16–Speed-changing characteristics of a hydrostatic transmission with fixed displacement pump and variable displacement motor.*

self-propelled combines, where high drawbar power at low speeds is not a consideration.

### 15.8.4 Type 3 Hydrostatic Transmissions
The type 3 hydrostatic transmission has a fixed displacement pump and a variable displacement motor. Motor speed can be increased by reducing the motor displacement (Equation 15.15) or, conversely, reduced by increasing the motor displacement. Increasing the motor displacement automatically raises the motor torque (Equation 15.16) without changing the system pressure. Thus, theoretically, the power-transmitting capability of the type 3 transmission is independent of the speed ratio, and it can be called a *constant power transmission*. Manual shift and power shift transmissions also have the constant power characteristic; it is a desirable characteristic in transmissions. However, the type 3 transmission cannot provide reversing in direction. Figure 15.16 shows the relationship of motor speed to motor displacement. If the motor displacement was changed from forward to reverse, the motor speed would instantly change from very high forward speed to very high negative speed. Such large speed changes cannot be tolerated, and variable displacement motors cannot provide reversing capabilities. Variable displacement motors are always designed so that zero displacement cannot be reached. Because it has no provision for reversing, the type 3 hydrostatic transmission is only of theoretical interest.

### 15.8.5 Type 4 Hydrostatic Transmissions
The type 4 hydrostatic transmission provides the excellent speed control and reversing capabilities of the type 2 transmission, but it

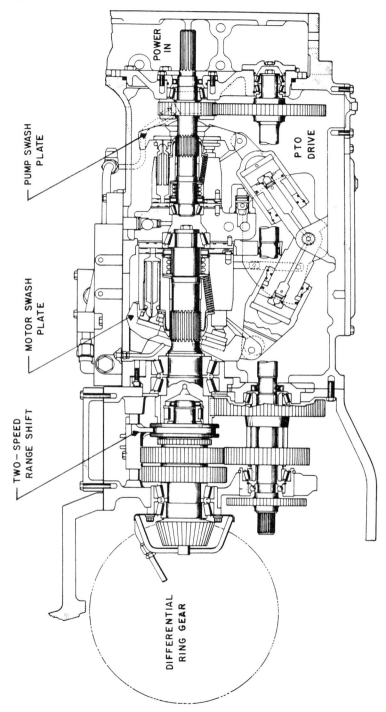

Figure 15.17–A heavy-duty hydrostatic transmission in series with a manual shift transmission. (Courtesy of Case-IH.)

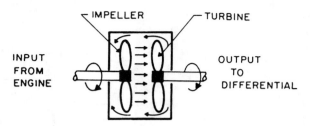

*Figure 15.18–A simplified schematic diagram of a fluid coupling.*

has better power-transmitting capabilities at lower speeds. Therefore, a variable displacement pump and a variable displacement motor usually are included in hydrostatic transmissions designed for farm tractors.

### 15.8.6 Practical Hydrostatic Transmissions

It is common practice to place a type 4 hydrostatic transmission in series with a manual shift transmission, as shown in Figure 15.17. Theoretically, the hydrostatic transmission alone can cover the entire speed range, but not at peak efficiency. Torque and volumetric efficiencies decline at extremes of speed and pressure, as was illustrated in Figure 14.9. The manual shift transmission can be used to select a general speed range; the hydrostatic transmission can provide infinitely small changes in speed ratio within that general speed range. The overall efficiency of such a transmission is higher than that of a full-range hydrostatic transmission. Even so, the efficiency of a practical hydrostatic transmission is typically below 80% but is generally above 70%.

## 15.9 HYDROKINETIC TRANSMISSIONS

Power is transmitted in a hydrostatic transmission by oil moving under high pressure at relatively low velocity. In contrast, power is transmitted in a *hydrokinetic transmission* by oil moving at high velocity with relatively low pressure. The fast-moving oil provides a fluid coupling between an impeller and a turbine.

### 15.9.1 Principle of Hydrokinetic Transmissions

The concept of a *fluid coupling* is illustrated in Figure 15.18. The engine is coupled to an impeller, which causes it to spin and generate a flow of oil toward the turbine. In passing over the curved blades of the turbine, the oil imposes a torque on the turbine and causes it to spin. However, the turbine torque cannot be greater than the torque input to the impeller. If the torque load on the turbine exceeds the

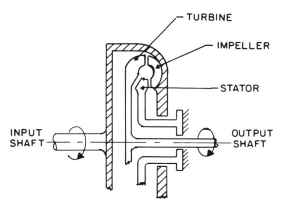

*Figure 15.19–A schematic diagram of a hydrokinetic transmission.*

input torque, the turbine stops, even though the impeller continues to spin.

A schematic diagram of a hydrokinetic transmission is shown in Figure 15.19. The addition of a stator permits the hydrokinetic transmission to increase torque. Oil enters the spinning impeller near the center, flows through its curved blades, and exits near the periphery. Then, the oil passes into the turbine and, in being forced to change directions by its curved blades, generates a torque in the turbine, causing it to spin. Oil leaving the turbine passes through the curved blades of the stator and is again forced to change directions. Thus, torque is exerted on the stator, but, because the stator is stationary, the torque is transferred effectively to the turbine. Thus, the stator permits the turbine torque to be much greater than the input torque.

## 15.9.2 Operation of Hydrokinetic Transmissions

The torque and speed of the turbine have some effect on the impeller, but the hydrokinetic transmission is more easily understood if we assume the effect is insignificant. Then, the impeller would have a definite torque-speed curve. Intersection of the impeller torque-speed curve with that of the engine locates the operating point, as shown in Figure 15.20. The engine and impeller would tend to run at torque $T_{in}$ and speed $N_{in}$ unless the operator changed the governor setting and made a new operating point. Thus, unless the governor setting was changed, the hydrokinetic transmission would tend to keep the engine operating at constant torque and speed. The speed output of the hydrokinetic transmission would depend on the output torque, as shown in Equation 15.17:

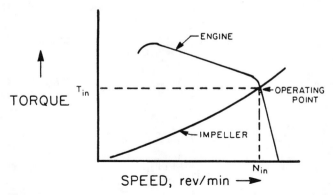

*Figure 15.20–Torque-speed curves for an engine and a hydrokinetic transmission.*

$$N_{out} = \frac{T_{in} * N_{in}}{T_{out} * e_t} \tag{15.17}$$

where
- $N_{out}$ = output speed of transmission in rev/min
- $N_{in}$ = input speed of transmission in rev/min
- $T_{in}$ = input torque in N·m (lb-ft)
- $T_{out}$ = output torque in N·m (lb-ft)
- $e_t$ = power efficiency of transmission in decimals

Thus, the hydrokinetic transmission automatically reduces output speed if the torque load on the output shaft increases and automatically increases output speed if the torque load declines. Consequently, the torque-speed curve at the drive axles is similar to the dashed constant power curve shown in Figure 15.6b. The hydrokinetic transmission tends to automatically keep the engine operating at optimum load.

### 15.9.3 Practical Hydrokinetic Transmissions

Performance curves for a typical hydrokinetic transmission are shown in Figure 15.21. The torque ratio is highest when the output shaft stalls, but then the efficiency is zero. The torque ratio falls and the efficiency increases as the output speed increases until the speed ratio approaches one; then both the output torque and the efficiency go to zero. The hydrokinetic transmission of Figure 15.21 can operate at 80 to 81% efficiency only if the output speed is from 50 to 90% of the input speed. To maintain efficiency while providing a wider speed range, a manual shift transmission usually is placed in series with hydrokinetic transmissions in a tractor. The manual shift

# Power Trains

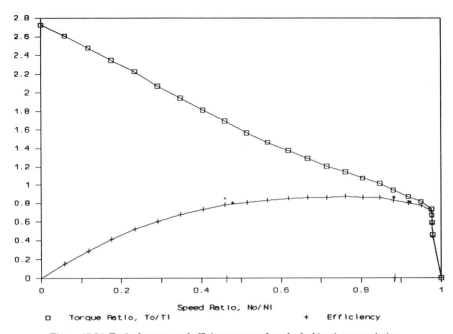

Figure 15.21–Typical torque and efficiency curves for a hydrokinetic transmission.

transmission can be used to select a general speed range. The hydrokinetic transmission can adjust speed automatically within that range. The combined transmission might have an efficiency of 70 to 75%.

Hydrokinetic transmissions automatically adjust the output speed in response to changing torque loads and thus are advantageous for many tillage operations. The transmissions are not advantageous when constant speed is needed (for example, in crop planting or spraying). Some tractors have provision to lock out the hydrokinetic transmission and prevent the automatic speed adjustment when constant speed operation is desired. Locking out the hydrokinetic unit also improves the transmission efficiency to that of the manual-shift unit.

### 15.9.4 Hydrokinetic Transmissions in Automobiles

The hydrokinetic transmission in series with a selective gear transmission is widely used in automatic transmissions in automobiles. The hydrokinetic transmission eliminates the need for a clutch. A mechanism is included to shift the selective gear transmission automatically to keep the hydrokinetic transmission operating at high efficiency. The driver can use a selector lever to prevent the transmission from shifting into high gears. When the

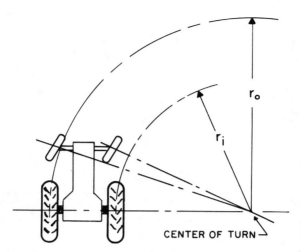

*Figure 15.22–Path of rear tractor wheels during a turn.*

transmission is kept in lower gear on steep downgrades, the engine acts as a brake because, while being driven by the automobile's travel down the slope, the engine absorbs power.

## 15.10 DIFFERENTIALS

A tractor is shown negotiating a turn in Figure 15.22. The rear wheel nearest the center of the turn is traveling on a shorter path than is the other rear wheel. That is, radius $r_i$ of the inner path is shorter than radius $r_o$ of the outer path. Therefore, one rear wheel must rotate faster than the other. The purpose of a *differential* in a vehicle is to permit the drive wheels to rotate at different speeds while the vehicle is making a turn.

### 15.10.1 Principles of Differentials

The principle of a differential is illustrated in Figure 15.23. The meshing of the small bevel pinion with the larger ring gear provides a speed reduction and also provides a 90° change in shaft direction. The carrier is attached to the ring gear and is forced to rotate with it. Each of the two axles is attached to a side gear, and both side gears mesh with one or more differential bevel pinions. When the tractor is traveling straight ahead on a uniform surface, the differential bevel pinions do not rotate on their carrier shafts; so both side gears rotate at the same speed. In a turn, however, the differential pinions rotate and allow one side gear to rotate faster than the other. Thus, the drive wheels can rotate at different speeds.

Power Trains

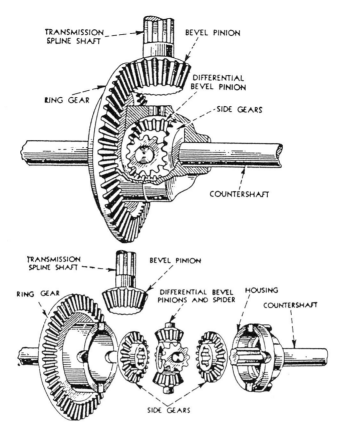

Figure 15.23–Exploded view of a differential. (Courtesy of Case-IH.)

The differential bevel pinions are not able to exert more torque on one side gear than on the other; therefore, the torque in both axles must be equal. The efficiency of the differential is:

$$e_D = \frac{\text{power out through both axles}}{\text{power in through bevel pinion}} \quad (15.18)$$

The torque and speed relationship for the differential is:

$$T_L * N_L + T_R * N_R = e_D * T_{in} * N_{in} \quad (15.19)$$

where
$N_L$ and $N_R$ = speed of left and right axles, respectively, in rev/min

$T_L$ and $T_R$ = torque in left and right axles, respectively, in N·m (lb-ft)
$T_{in}$ = torque input to bevel pinion in N·m (lb-ft)
$N_{in}$ = speed of bevel pinion in rev/min

The torque is equal in both axles. That is, the axle torque ($T_A$) is:

$$T_A = T_L = T_R \tag{15.20}$$

The average speed ($N_{ave}$) of the two rear axles is:

$$N_{ave} = \frac{N_L + N_R}{2} \tag{15.21}$$

Therefore, the rear axle torque is:

$$T_A = \frac{e_D * R_D * T_{in}}{2} \tag{15.22}$$

The gear ratio, $R_D$, of the differential is defined as:

$$R_D = \frac{N_{in}}{N_{ave}} = \frac{n_r}{n_{bp}} \tag{15.23}$$

where
$n_r$ = number of teeth on the ring gear
$n_{bp}$ = number of teeth on the meshing bevel pinion

Notice that this gear ratio reduces the axle speed but increases the axle torque. Also, notice the factor of 2 in the denominator of Equation 15.22; the total axle torque is divided, with half going to the left axle and half to the right axle.

The efficiency of a differential typically ranges from 96% when all of the power is being transmitted through one axle, to 98% when the power is divided equally between the axles.

## 15.10.2 Limitations of Differentials

The differential permits a vehicle to turn corners, but it has two disadvantages. The first is that the two axle torques must be equal so that neither axle can transmit more torque than is permitted by the wheel with the poorest traction. If one axle lost all traction, for example, if its attached wheel was on a sheet of ice, neither axle could transmit any torque and the vehicle would be unable to move. The second disadvantage is that the differential delivers more than half the power to the drive wheel with the poorest traction. The wheel with the poorest traction spins faster than the other drive wheel. Because both axle torques are equal, the fastest spinning wheel receives the most power. A differential lock can overcome both of the disadvantages of a differential.

### 15.10.3 Differential Locks

One type of *differential lock* is illustrated in Figure 15.24. The operator can use a pedal to hydraulically engage a clutch in the differential and lock the carrier to one side gear. Then, both axles are forced to rotate at the same speed. The two axle torques are not necessarily equal. Torque can be higher in the axle attached to the wheel with the best traction. Because axle speeds are equal, most of the power is transmitted to the drive wheel with the best traction. However, the differential must be unlocked each time the tractor must make a sharp turn. The tractor can make small changes in direction when the differential is locked.

Differential locks are not used in automotive vehicles. However, a limited-slip differential may be used. The limited-slip differential permits enough speed difference between the two axles to allow the vehicle to make normal turns but, if the speed difference becomes large, the differential automatically locks until the speed difference is again reduced. When only one of the drive wheels is on a surface which will not provide traction, the limited-slip differential allows the vehicle to get started.

## 15.11 FINAL DRIVES

The *final drive* permits the drive wheels to run at much slower speed and with much higher torque than the earlier parts of the drive train. Most of the drive train can be of lighter construction because it runs at high speed and with low torque.

One common type of final drive is shown in Figure 15.25. A planetary gear set is built into the axle of each drive wheel. The final drive shaft is attached to the sun gear on one end and is spline connected on the other end to one of the side gears in the differential. The ring gear is held stationary in the axle housing, and the rear axle shaft is driven by the planet carrier. The speed ratio across the final drive can be calculated using Equation 15.5. The rear axle shaft extends well beyond the axle housing. The drive wheels can be

*Figure 15.24–A differential lock. (Courtesy of Deere & Company.)*

attached at different points along the rear axles to change the drive wheel spacing.

The final drive in Figure 15.25 is called an *inboard* planetary drive. An *outboard* planetary drive is shown in Figure 15.26. The planetary drive is located within the wheel hub to eliminate bending stresses on the axle. This arrangement does not permit adjustable spacing of the drive wheels. The outboard planetary is used as the final drive for tractors with four-wheel drive.

*Figure 15.25–A final drive with an inboard planetary set. (Courtesy of Deere & Company.)*

Power Trains 461

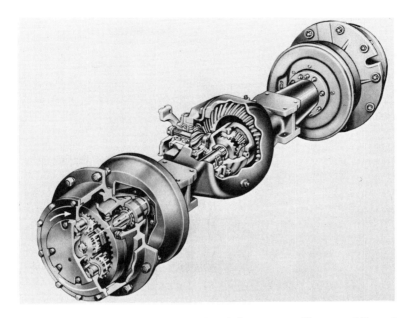

*Figure 15.26–A final drive with an outboard planetary set. (Courtesy of Deere & Company.)*

A final drive with drop housing is shown in Figure 15.27. This type of final drive was in more common use in earlier model tractors. The drop housing provided extra clearance under the housing of the final drive shaft. The extra clearance was useful when the tractor was used to cultivate tall crops. Notice that, in contrast to planetary-type final drives, the final drive shown in Figure 15.27 gives a speed reversal. The final drive shaft turns opposite to the direction of the drive wheel axle.

## 15.12 POWER-TAKE-OFF DRIVES

A *pto drive* provides a means for transmitting power to machines that are used with the tractor. The standard location of the pto shaft is at the rear of the tractor, as shown in Figure 15.28. In 1926, the American Society of Agricultural Engineers (ASAE) published a standard on pto drives, which has since been updated periodically. The direction of rotation, rotational speed, approximate location, and exact dimensions of the pto shaft are specified in the standard. The pto shaft must turn clockwise as viewed from the rear of the tractor. The standard rotational speed was 540 rev/min in the early standards. A 1000 rev/min pto of the same diameter was

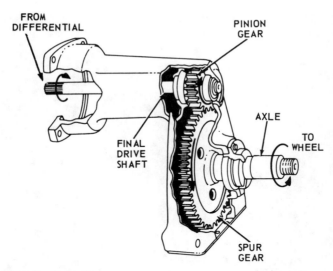

*Figure 15.27–A final drive with a drop axle housing (Courtesy of Deere & Company).*

subsequently developed to provide greater power-transmitting capability. Later, a 1000 rev/min pto drive of larger diameter was developed for even greater capacity. Three different shaft designs are used (Figure 15.29) to ensure compatibility between the tractor and the pto-driven machine. The 540 rev/min pto is used on tractors up to 65 kW (87 hp) pto power. The 1000 rev/min pto shaft of 35 mm (1.375 in.) diameter is used on tractors with 45 to 120 kW (60 to 160 hp). Tractors in the power range of approximately 45 to 65 kW (60 to 87 hp) often have provision for providing both pto speeds (Figure 15.30). The 1000 rev/min pto shaft of 45 mm (1.75 in.) diameter is used of 110 to 190 kW (147 to 255 hp). Larger 4WD tractors do not have a pto drive.

Three types of pto drives are defined in ASAE standards. They are as follows:

> Transmission-driven pto
> Continuous-running pto
> Independent pto

The *transmission-driven pto* is controlled by the same clutch that interrupts power to the transmission. Thus, the pto stops whenever the operator disengages the clutch to stop the tractor. Because it is often convenient to keep the pto shaft running when the tractor is stopped the *continuous-running pto* was developed. Both it and the transmission operate only when the master clutch is engaged, but

Power Trains 463

*Figure 15.28–A tractor pto (power take-off) drive.*

auxiliary means are provided for stopping the travel of the tractor without stopping the pto. In one form of the continuous-running pto, initial movement of a foot pedal disengages the traction clutch and further movement also disengages the pto clutch. In another version, a foot clutch disengages both the pto and the transmission, but a separate hand clutch is also provided to interrupt forward travel. *Independent ptos* have two separate clutches. A foot pedal controls

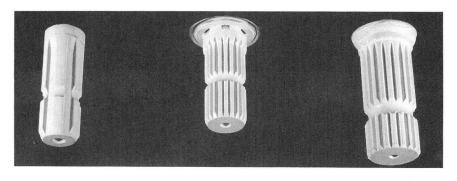

| (A) | (B) | (C) |
|---|---|---|
| 540 rev/min | 1000 rev/min | 1000 rev/min |
| 6 splines | 21 splines | 20 splines |
| 35 mm (1.375 in) diameter | 35 mm (1.375 in) diameter | 45 mm (1.75 in) diameter |

*Figure 15.29–Splines for 540 and 1000 rev/min pto shafts.*

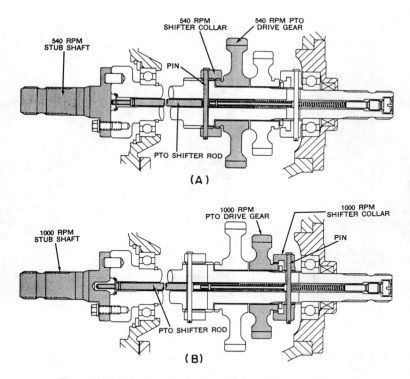

*Figure 15.30–A dual-speed pto drive. (Courtesy of Deere & Company.)*

the transmission and a hand clutch typically controls the pto. Current practice is to equip tractors with an independent pto.

The ASAE has developed standards for auxiliary pto drives. Thus, a pto shaft may extend from the side of the tractor to operate side-mounted machines, or extend forward from the lower midpoint of the tractor to drive front-mounted machines.

A rotating, unshielded pto shaft can catch the clothing of a bystander and, by wrapping up the clothing, pull the bystander into the shaft. Serious injury or death can result. Therefore, the ASAE has developed standards for the shielding of pto drives. The pto shields should be kept in place to avoid the severe consequences of their removal.

## 15.13 SUMMARY

The power train is the means for transmitting power from the engine to points of use. It includes one or more clutches, a transmission, differential, final drive, and pto drive. Brakes are also provided for stopping the vehicle.

Over-centering clutches are used on stationary engines. On modern vehicles equipped with a clutch, a spring-loaded traction clutch is used. A dry clutch is used in moderate-duty applications, and asbestos or ceramic materials are used in the friction disks. Wet clutches are used in heavy-duty applications. Because the bimetal friction elements run in an oil bath, wet clutches must have many friction disks to provide adequate torque capacity. Clutch linkages must have proper free travel to prevent premature failure of the release bearing but allow complete release when the clutch is disengaged.

Brake theory is similar to clutch theory, except that the clutch is used for starting a vehicle, while the brake is used for stopping. Drum brakes and disk brakes are available. Hydraulic actuation of brakes is used except for parking brakes, for which mechanical actuation is used.

A transmission converts the torque-speed curve of the engine into a multiplicity of torque-speed curves, one for each gear, at the drive wheels. The more gear ratios in the transmission, the more likely that the tractor operator can select a ratio that will load the engine close to governor's maximum. Load matching also is enhanced if the operator can shift gears quickly, because implement loads vary in the field. Five basic types of transmissions with different load-matching capabilities are available.

The manual shift transmission is the simplest transmission, but operators must disengage the traction clutch and interrupt power flow each time they shift. It may be necessary to stop the tractor before the new selection of gears will mesh. Synchromesh transmissions can be shifted more quickly; a synchronizer quickly equalizes the speed of the desired gear with an adjacent collar until they can be locked together. However, the traction clutch must still be disengaged to shift a synchromesh transmission.

Power shift transmissions make use of internal, hydraulically operated clutches and brakes for changing speed ratios and can be shifted so quickly that there is no apparent interruption of power flow to the drive wheels. Full-range power shifting is expensive and may not be essential. Therefore, tractor manufacturers provide part-range power shifting by placing a manual shift transmission in series with a power shift element.

Continuously variable transmissions (CVT) provide an infinite number of speed ratios and thus permits the operator to select a ratio for optimum loading of the engine. While several types of CVT are possible, the hydrostatic transmission is the only CVT currently used in tractors. Hydrostatic transmissions include a variable displacement pump to provide reversing capability. A fixed-displacement motor is usually used in hydrostatic drives for lawn and garden tractors, but a variable-displacement motor is included in large tractors to increase power-transmitting capacity at low speeds. A hydrostatic transmission cannot operate efficiently over the entire speed range. Therefore, it is used in series with a manual shift range transmission in large tractors.

A hydrokinetic transmission includes an impeller, a stator, and a turbine in an oil-filled case. The engine tends to run at constant speed and load when connected to the impeller. The turbine automatically adjusts its speed inversely with the torque load on the output shaft. Thus, the hydrokinetic transmission tends to automatically keep the engine operating at optimum load. However, a hydrokinetic transmission cannot operate efficiently over the entire speed range. Therefore, like the hydrostatic transmission, it is used in series with a manual shift range transmission.

Transmissions for new tractors are either one of the basic types of some combination of the basic types. Thus, the principles learned in Chapter 15 on the five basic types of transmissions should be sufficient bases for the analysis of a transmission of any tractor.

Differentials are necessary to permit drive wheels to run at different speeds in a turn, but they cause the pulling ability of a vehicle to be limited by the drive wheel with the poorest traction. Differential locks, when engaged, cause most of the power to be transmitted to the drive wheel with the best traction. The differential lock must be disengaged while turning.

Several types of final drives are available for tractors. The final drive permits the drive wheels to run at much lower speed and higher torque than the earlier parts of the drive train. Thus, the drive train can be of lighter construction because it runs at high speed and low torque.

A pto drive provides a means for transmitting power to machines that are used with tractors. The dimensions, speed, direction of rotation, and approximate location of pto shafts have been standardized by the ASAE. A 540 rev/min pto is available for tractors with up to 65 kW (87 hp) of pto power. Two 1000 rev/min ptos are available, one with a 35 mm (1.375 in.) diameter shaft for tractors up to 120 kW (160 hp) and the other with a 45 mm (1.75 in.) shaft for tractors up to 190 kW (255 hp). Tractors with more than 190 kW (255 hp) do not have a pto. Each of the three types of pto has different shaft dimensions to that the machine coupled to the pto shaft is compatible with the tractor. Early tractors had pto shafts that stopped whenever the operator disengaged the clutch to stop the tractor. Current practice is to equip tractors with an independent pto that is controlled by a separate clutch.

A rotating, unshielded pto shaft can catch the clothing of a bystander and pull the bystander into the shaft. Because serious injury or death can result, it is essential that pto shafts be shielded properly.

## QUESTIONS

Q15.1　According to Equation 15.1, the torque-transmitting ability of a clutch varies directly with the clamping force. What controls the clamping force in a spring-loaded clutch, and how could the maximum clamping force be increased?

Q15.2　(a) In a spring-loaded clutch, under what conditions is there relative motion between the inner and outer races of the release bearing. That is, when is the release bearing subject to wear?

(b) Under what conditions is there relative motion between the inner and outer races of the pilot bearing?

Q15.3　Briefly describe the differences between drum and disk brakes.

Q15.4　The constant power curve in Figure 15.6b theoretically touches the curve for each gear at only one point.

(a) At what condition is the engine operating when the constant power curve touches the curve for any one of the gears?

(b) Is it desirable for the engine to operate at or near the condition described in part a? Why?

Q15.5　Must there be an even or odd number of gear meshes for forward travel if the output shaft is to turn clockwise as viewed from the rear of (a) a transmission with in-line shafts and (b) a transmission with parallel shafts? Briefly explain the reasoning for your answers. Assume the engine rotates in the standard direction.

Q15.6　(a) What is the limitation of a manual shift transmission that a synchromesh transmission is designed to overcome?

(b) How does the synchronizer accomplish its task?

Q15.7　(a) What are the two basic types of power shift transmissions?

(b) What is the primary advantage of a power shift transmission over a synchromesh transmission?

(c) Is a manually operated clutch needed when a tractor has a power shift transmission?

Q15.8 Most hydrostatic transmissions in farm tractors include a variable displacement pump and a variable displacement motor.

(a) What capability would be reduced or lost if the pump was replaced with a fixed displacement pump?

(b) What would be reduced or lost if the motor was replaced with a fixed displacement motor?

(c) Why is a hydrostatic transmission usually placed in series with a manual shift transmission?

Q15.9 Hydrostatic and hydrokinetic transmissions both provide an infinite number of speed ratios.

(a) Assuming the engine speed remains constant, what determines the actual travel speed of a tractor with a hydrostatic transmission?

(b) What determines the actual travel speed of a tractor with a hydrokinetic transmission?

(c) Why is a hydrokinetic transmission usually placed in series with a manual shift transmission?

Q15.10 (a) What is the primary purpose of the differential in the rear axle of a tractor?

(b) What two other functions does the differential accomplish?

Q15.11 (a) What are the disadvantages of a differential that a differential lock is intended to overcome?

(b) How does a locked differential divide the power between the two axles?

Q15.12 Most automobiles and trucks do not have final drives. That is, the drive wheels run at the same speed as the side gears in the differential. Why do tractors have final drives, and what do the final drives accomplish?

Q15.13 The final drive on many tractors with four-wheel drive is an outboard planetary. Compare an outboard planetary to an inboard planetary.

(a) What advantages are provided by an outboard planetary?

(b) What capability is sacrificed?

Q15.14 (a) What is the standard direction of rotation of the rear pto shaft on a tractor?
(b) What are the standard rotational speeds?
(c) What factor determines which pto speed will be provided on a given tractor?

Q15.15 What are the three standard types of pto drives defined in ASAE standards, and how do they differ?

# PROBLEMS

P15.1 A certain tractor has a dry, single-disk clutch with a mean radius of 420 mm (16.5 in.). If the coefficient of friction is 0.3, what is the minimum clamping force required to transmit the peak engine torque of 1165 N·m (860 lb-ft)? (*Note*: A single-disk clutch has two friction-transmitting surfaces. Also, note that more than the minimum clamping force normally would be applied to provide some reserve torque capacity).

P15.2 In a certain planetary gear drive (Figure 15.5), the ring gear has 70 teeth and is held stationary. Power comes into the drive on the sun gear, which has 33 teeth and rotates clockwise at 100 rev/min. Power comes out of the gear set on the planet carrier.
(a) How fast does the planet carrier rotate?
(b) Does it rotate clockwise or counterclockwise?

P15.3 Assume the transmission of Figure 15.7 is operating in first gear.
(a) Trace the power flow through the transmission. That is, identify the gears that actually transmit the power.
(b) Calculate the transmission speed ratio, that is, the number of turns the input shaft must rotate for each revolution of the output shaft.
(c) Assuming the input shaft turns counterclockwise as viewed from the rear, which direction does the output shaft turn?
(d) Repeat steps a through c but with the transmission operating in 5th gear.

P15.4 Rework P15.3, but use 2nd and 6th gears.

P15.5      Rework P15.3, but use 4th and 8th gears.

P15.6      Rework P15.3, but use gears R1 and R2.

P15.7      Assume the transmission of Figure 15.7 is coupled to a differential with a ratio $R_D$ = 3.2:1. Each side gear of the differential is connected to a final drive with a ratio $R_{FD}$ = 4.1:1. The output shafts of the final drives are the rear axles of the tractor. Assume the transmission is in third gear and the efficiency of the power train is 0.87. If the engine delivers 575 N·m (424 lb-ft) of torque to the transmission at 2100 rev/min, calculate (a) the speed of the rear axles, (b) the total rear axle torque, and (c) the torque in each rear axle.

P15.8      Assume the transmission of Figure 15.13 is operating in 1st gear.
         (a) Trace the power flow through the transmission. That is, identify the gears that actually transmit the power.
         (b) Calculate the transmission speed ratio – that is, the number of turns the input shaft must rotate for each revolution of the output shaft.
         (c) Assuming the input shaft turns counterclockwise as viewed from the rear, which direction does the output shaft turn?
         (d) Repeat steps a through c but with the transmission operating in third gear.

P15.9      Rework P15.8, but use 2nd gear. For part d, calculate the speed ratio that would be obtained if $C_1$, $B_2$ and $B_4$ were engaged. Note that this available combination is not used as one of the 15 gears in Table 15.1.

P15.10      Rework P15.8, but use 4th and 8th gears.

P15.11      Rework P15.8, but use 5th and 9th gears.

P15.12      Rework P15.8, but use 6th and 10th gears.

P15.13      Rework P15.8, but use 12th and 14th gears.

P15.14      Rework P15.8, but use 7th and 13th gears.

P15.15      Rework P15.8, but use reverse gears 1R and 2R.

Power Trains 471

P15.16  Rework P15.8, but use reverse gears 3R and 4R.

P15.17  The inputs to a certain hydrostatic drive include torque of 250 N·m (184 lb-ft) and speed of 2500 rev/min. The drive includes a variable displacement pump, the displacement of which can vary from 42 cm$^3$/rev (2.56 in.$^3$/rev) to zero to 42 cm$^3$/rev (2.56 in.$^3$/rev) in the opposite direction. Assume the volumetric efficiency of the pump and motor are each 0.97, while the torque efficiencies are each 0.93. The maximum permissible pressure drop across the motor is 35 MPa (5100 psi).

If the motor has fixed displacement of 42 cm$^3$/rev (2.56 in.$^3$/rev), calculate the maximum (a) motor speed, (b) motor torque, (c) output power, and (d) transmission efficiency – that is, output power divided by input power.

Recalculate the (e) motor speed, (f) motor torque, and (g) output power when the pump displacement is reduced to 4.2 cm$^3$/rev (0.256 in.$^3$/rev).

[Note: If the efficiency in part d were to be recalculated, the pump input torque should be reduced first (because of the reduced displacement) to a value that could be calculated from Equation 14.11].

P15.18  Reconsider the situation in P15.17, but assume the hydrostatic transmission has a motor whose displacement can vary from 10 to 160 cm$^3$/rev (0.61 to 9.76 in.$^3$/rev). Calculate the (a) motor speed, (b) motor torque, (c) output power, and (d) transmission efficiency when the pump and motor displacements are each 42 cm$^3$/rev (2.56 in.$^3$/rev). Recalculate the (e) motor speed, (f) motor torque, and (g) output power when the motor displacement is increased to 160 cm$^3$/rev (9.76 in.$^3$/rev) and the pump displacement is reduced to 16 cm$^3$/rev (0.976 in.$^3$/rev).

P15.19  The differential in the rear axle of a farm tractor has a ring gear (Figure 15.23) with 39 teeth driven by a bevel pinion with 8 teeth. Each side gear is connected to a rear axle through a planetary gear set (Figure 15.25) that provides a 4.94:1 speed reduction. If the input torque to the bevel pinion is 1500 N·m (1100 lb-ft) and the input speed is 525 rev/min, calculate (a) the speed, (b) the torque, and (c) the power in each rear axle when the differential efficiency is 0.98 and the tractor is moving straight ahead on uniform, level ground. Now, assume that the left wheel encounters poorer traction so that the left axle torque drops 10% and the left wheel begins turning 50% faster than the right wheel. If the pinion speed and differential efficiency remain unchanged, calculate (d) the speed, (e) the torque, and (f) the power in each rear axle.

(*Note*: Both wheels are attached to the tractor and must move forward at the same speed. Thus, if the faster-turning wheel transmits more power, the excess compared to the slower-turning wheel is wasted in slippage. A differential lock would eliminate the loss by equalizing the axle speeds.)

# 16
# Weight Transfer, Traction, and Safety

## 16.1 INTRODUCTION

The word *tractor*, derived from the "traction engine", indicates the importance early tractor designers place on developing traction. That importance has not diminished. Engine power can be converted to drawbar power only if the drive wheels develop traction. Factors such as tire selection, hitching, ballasting, and implement selection determine whether engine power is transferred efficiently or inefficiently to the drawbar. By learning the traction terminology and principles presented in this chapter, you will gain useful insight about how to attain high pull and tractive efficiency from a tractor. A technique for estimating a tractor's potential pulling ability using data given in a Nebraska or OECD Tractor Test will be examined.

Statistics show that farming is one of the most dangerous occupations in the United States and that tractors are involved in a high percentage of farm accidents. Thus, there is continuing need to improve tractor safety. Accident prevention measures can be grouped into three categories: engineering, education, and enforcement. Examples of these three categories and their applicability to tractor safety are also considered in this chapter.

## 16.2 MOMENTS AND CENTER OF GRAVITY

Torque was described in Section 5.2 as a force acting perpendicular to a distance, as, for example, when a force is applied to the end of a wrench to tighten a nut on a bolt. When a force acts perpendicular to a distance on a tractor body, the result is called a *moment* rather than a torque. In calculating moments, it always is necessary to specify the center of moments – that is, the point from which the perpendicular distances to the forces are measured.

A tractor is shown resting on a smooth, horizontal surface in Figure 16.1. Three forces are applied to the tractor body. The tractor weight (W) is shown acting at the *center of gravity* of the tractor. The center of gravity can be considered a balance point. That is, if the tractor was lifted by a cable attached exactly at the center of gravity, the tractor would not tip in any direction. The weight of the tractor is supported by the ground through forces $R_r$ and $R_f$ applied at the rear and front wheels, respectively.

Suppose that point A in Figure 16.1 is chosen as a center of moments. The perpendicular distance from point A to the weight force W is shown as $X_{cg}$, the distance from the rear axle centerline to the center of gravity. The weight W produces a clockwise (CW) moment, $(W)(X_{cg})$, about point A. The force $R_r$ passes through point A and thus produces no moment. The force $R_f$ produces a counterclockwise (CCW) moment, $(R_f)(WB)$, about point A. The distance WB is the wheelbase of the tractor. For the tractor to be in equilibrium, the CW moment about point A must equal the CCW moments; therefore (using the quantities in Figure 16.1):

$$W * X_{cg} = R_f * WB \qquad (16.1)$$

where
    $W$  = weight of tractor in kN (lb)
    $X_{cg}$ = distance from rear axle centerline to center of gravity in mm (in.)
    $R_f$ = ground support force on front wheels in kN (lb)
    WB = wheelbase of tractor in mm (in.)

Dividing Equation 16.1 by the weight W provides a useful equation for calculating $X_{cg}$:

$$X_{cg} = \frac{R_f}{W} * WB \qquad (16.2)$$

We could place the front wheels of the tractor on a scale to measure $R_f$ and then place the entire tractor on the scale to measure W. The wheelbase could be measured with a ruler, and Equation 16.2 could then be used to calculate $X_{cg}$.

The center of gravity of a tractor can be changed by adding ballast weight to the tractor. Adding ballast to the tractor ahead of

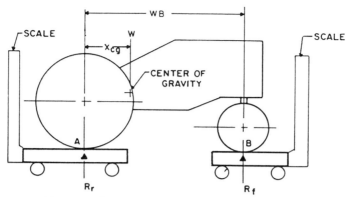
*Figure 16.1–Tractor weight force and ground support forces.*

the center of gravity increases $X_{cg}$; adding ballast behind the center of gravity decreases $X_{cg}$. Example Problem 16.1 illustrates the calculation of the location of the center of gravity.

## Example Problem 16.1

A tractor with a total weight of 28.5 kN (6400 lb) has a front wheel reaction of 9.0 kN (2023 lb) when the tractor is sitting on a horizontal surface. The wheelbase is 2083 mm (82 in.). Calculate the horizontal distance from the rear axle centerline to the center of gravity. Also, calculate the rear wheel reaction.

**Solution:** Equation 16.2 can be used to calculate the location of the center of gravity.

$$X_{cg} = [9.0/28.5]*[2083] = 658 \text{ mm}$$

or

$$X_{cg} = [2023/6400]*[82] = 25.9 \text{ in.}$$

The rear wheels must support that part of the weight not supported by the front wheels. Therefore, the rear wheel reaction is:

$$R_r = 28.5 - 9.0 = 19.5 \text{ kN}$$

or

$$R_r = 6400 - 2023 = 4377 \text{ lb}$$

Since this tractor has 68% of the weight carried by the rear wheels and 32% carried on the front, it is undoubtedly a rear-wheel-drive tractor. A four-wheel-drive tractor would have at least 50% of the weight carried by the front wheels.

## 16.3 WEIGHT TRANSFER

*Weight transfer* refers to the changes in the front and rear wheel reactions that occur when a tractor pulls a drawbar load. Figure 16.2 is used to illustrate weight transfer. This figure is similar to Figure 16.1, except that two new forces have been added. The force, $F_{db}$ represents the drawbar pull. The tractor can only produce drawbar pull if the ground provides a reaction force ($F_t$) against the periphery of the drive wheels. The drawbar pull is shown inclined so that the distance $Z_f$ from the drawbar pull to point B is longer than the distance $Z_r$ from the drawbar pull to point A. If point A is chosen as the center of moments, there are one CW moment and two CCW moments. Equating them gives the following equation (again, using the quantities shown in Figure 16.2):

$$R_f * WB + F_{db} * Z_r = W * X_{cg} \tag{16.3}$$

where
- $R_f$ = ground support force on front wheels in kN (lb)
- WB = wheelbase of tractor in mm (in.)
- $F_{db}$ = force on drawbar in kN (lb)
- $Z_r$ = distance from drawbar force to point a in mm
- W = weight of tractor in kN (lb)
- $X_{cg}$ = distance from rear axle centerline to center of gravity in mm (in.)

The equation can be solved for $R_f$ as follows:

$$R_f = \frac{W * X_{cg} - F_{db} * Z_r}{WB} \tag{16.4}$$

Notice that, if there was no drawbar pull ($F_{db} = 0$), the front wheel reaction would be:

$$R_{fo} = \frac{W * X_{cg}}{WB} \tag{16.5}$$

The force $R_f$ is called the *dynamic front wheel reaction*, while $R_{fo}$ is called the *static front wheel reaction*. The weight transfer ($\Delta R_f$) is the difference between the static and dynamic front wheel reactions:

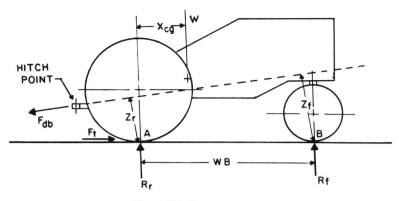

*Figure 16.2–Forces on a tractor.*

$$\Delta R_f = R_{fo} - R_f = \frac{F_{db} * Z_r}{WB} \tag{16.6}$$

By choosing point B as the center of moments and performing calculations similar to the preceding ones, it can be shown that:

$$R_r = \frac{W * [WB - X_{cg}] + F_{db} * Z_f}{WB} \tag{16.7}$$

and

$$R_{ro} = \frac{W * [WB - X_{cg}]}{WB} \tag{16.8}$$

and

$$\Delta R_r = R_r - R_{ro} = \frac{F_{db} * Z_f}{WB} \tag{16.9}$$

If the pull was parallel to the ground so that $Z_r = Z_f$, notice that the pull would reduce the front wheel reaction by the same amount the rear wheel reaction would be increased. Thus, the change in wheel reactions is termed *weight transfer*, even though no tractor mass is actually transferred. Often, the drawbar pull is inclined (see Figure 16.2), in which case the rear wheel reaction increases more than the front wheel reaction declines. Example Problem 16.2 illustrates the calculation of weight transfer.

### Example Problem 16.2
The tractor described in Example Problem 16.1 pulls a drawbar load of 12 kN (2700 lb). The pull is parallel to the ground, and the drawbar height is 580 mm (22.8 in.). Calculate the weight transfer.

**Solution:** The drawbar pull is parallel to the ground and is attached to the drawbar, therefore:

$$Z_r = Z_f = 580 \text{ mm (22.8 in.)}$$

Either Equation 16.6 or 16.9 can be used to calculate the weight transfer as follows:

$$\Delta R_r = \Delta R_f = 12*580/2083 = 3.34 \text{ kN}$$

or

$$\Delta R_r = \Delta R_f = 2700*22.8/82 = 751 \text{ lb}$$

Notice that the weight transfer of 3.34 kN (751 lb) would reduce the front wheel reaction from 9.0 kN (2023 lb) (see Example Problem 16.1) to 5.66 kN (1272 lb) and would increase the rear wheel reaction from 19.5 kN to 31.84 kN (4377 lb to 7128 lb). The weight transfer would improve traction.

## 16.4 TRACTOR TIRES

Tractor tire terminology was developed before tractors with four-wheel drive became popular. Therefore, lugged tires suitable for developing traction are called *rear tires*, while ribbed tires suitable for steering are called *front tires*. Perhaps the terminology, *lugged* and *nonlugged* would be more descriptive, but such terminology has not been adopted by the tire industry.

A cutaway view of a rear tractor tire is shown in Figure 16.3. The tire beads are rubber-enclosed bundles of wire that anchor the tire to the rim. The body plies are layers of rubber-cushioned fabric or cord that are tied to the beads and extend across the face of the tire. Tractor rear tires have from four to twelve plies separated from one another by resilient rubber compound. The outer edge of a rear tire has rubber lugs or treads that penetrate into the ground and provide improved traction. The tires should be mounted with the V-pattern pointing downward at the front of the tire, as shown in

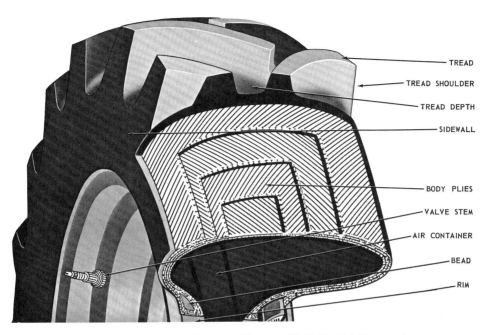

*Figure 16.3–A rear tire of a tractor. (Courtesy of B. F. Goodrich Company.)*

Figure 16.4. Sometimes, an arrow is molded into the side of the tire to show correct forward rotation.

Tractor front tires often have rubber ribs, as shown in Figure 16.5. the ribs penetrate into the ground and aid in turning the tractor.

Early tires all used *biased-ply construction*, in which the plies run from one bead to the other at an angle (Figure 16.6a). Belts can be included (Figure 16.6b). The cord belts are located between the plies and the tread and give increased rigidity to the tread. The resulting reduction in tread squirming during contact with the road gives increased tread life. *Radial ply tires* have gained popularity in recent years. Their construction is similar to that of the belted, biased ply tire, except that the plies are nearly perpendicular to the tire beads (Figure 16.6c). Radial tires can be operated at lower inflation pressures than can biased ply tires and thus have a greater area of contact with the ground. Both front and rear tractor tires are available with either radial or biased ply designs. Radial tires usually are more expensive, but they provide increased traction and a softer ride.

The codes listed in Table 16.1 have been developed by the tire industry for tires used on farm equipment. Code R designates a tractor rear tire, and an accompanying digit indicates the type of

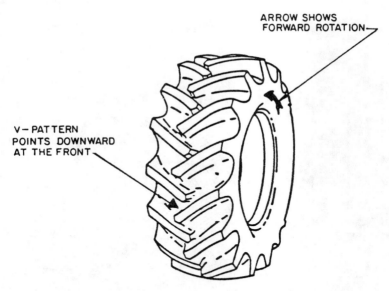

Figure 16.4–The tread pattern and direction of rotation of a tractor rear tire.

tread. Likewise, code F indicates a tractor front tire, and a digit indicates the type of tread.

Sizes of tractor tires are indicated by a code for the rim diameter

Figure 16.5–A tractor front tire.

# Weight Transfer, Traction, and Safety

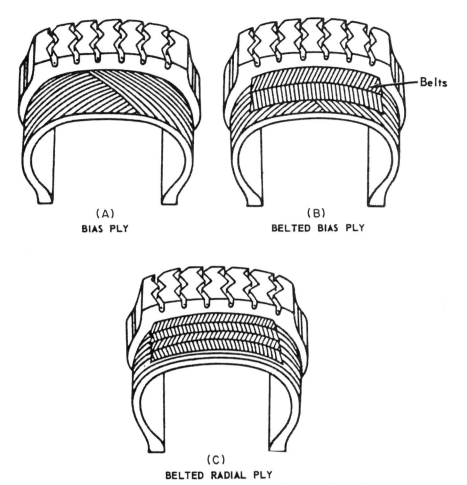

Figure 16.6–Biased ply and radial ply construction. (Courtesy of Deere & Company.)

and tire width when the tire is mounted on the recommended rim. For example, a tire marked 15.5-38 would have a width of 15.5 in. (394 mm) and a rim diameter of 38 in. (965 mm). Although at least one manufacturer has begun to make agricultural tires in metric sizes, the customary sizes still predominate and ASAE tire selection standard S220.4 still lists tires in customary units.

*Ballast* often is added to the drive wheels to improve traction. Two types of ballast are available. The ballast may be in the form of removable cast-iron weights that are bolted to the rim of the wheel. Ballast also can be provided by partially filling the tires with water. Calcium chloride is added to the water to prevent freezing. Not more than 75% of the tire volume should be filled with liquid because

TABLE 16.1. Standard industry codes for tire types

| Type of Tire | Code |
|---|---|
| **FRONT TRACTOR** | |
| Rice tread | F-1 |
| Single rib tread | F-2 |
| Dual rib tread | F-2D |
| Triple rib tread | F-2T |
| Industrial tread | F-3 |
| **DRIVE WHEEL TRACTOR (REAR)** | |
| Rear wheel, regular tread | R-1 |
| Cane and Rice, deep tread | R-2* |
| Shallow, non-directional tread | R-3 |
| Industrial, intermediate tread | R-4 |
| **IMPLEMENT** | |
| Rib tread | I-1 |
| Traction tread | I-3 |
| Plow tailwheel | I-4 |
| Smooth tread | I-6 |
| **OFF-THE-ROAD TIRES (INDUSTRIAL)** | |
| Rib | E-1 |
| Traction | E-2 |
| Rock | E-3 |
| Rock deep tread | E-4 |
| Rock intermediate | E-5 |
| Rock maximum | E-6 |
| Flotation | E-7 |

* Also includes similar treads for "G", "L", and "ML" series codes.

Source: Reprinted with permission. © 1970 Deere and Company, *Fundamentals of service—tires and tracks*, 4.

liquid is virtually incompressible. Retaining at least 25% air in the tire retains flexibility and allows the tire to absorb shocks. Use of excessive ballast can overload the tire or the tractor axles. Therefore, the amount of ballast should be selected in accordance with the tractor manufacturer's recommendations.

*Dual tires* (Figure 16.7) often are used to increase traction. They provide greater contact area with the soil and may permit the use of additional ballast. Use of dual tires improves floatation so the tractor is less likely to sink into soft soils. However, use of dual tires increases the stress on tractor axles, bearings, and the entire drive train. Only tires of equal diameter should be used as duals.

Weight Transfer, Traction, and Safety

*Figure 16.7–Dual tires on a tractor.*

## 16.5 BASIC CONCEPTS OF TRACTION

The ASAE has developed standard definitions for many terms relating to traction. Only a few of the most important of these terms will be discussed here.

### 16.5.1 Travel Reduction
Travel reduction refers to the reduction in forward speed that occurs due to increased slippage when a tractor pulls a drawbar load. The term slip often is used interchangeably with travel reduction, even though the true slip is slightly greater than the travel reduction. For example, although travel reduction is actually measured in Nebraska or OECD Tractor Tests, the results are reported as slip. Travel reduction can be calculated using the following equation:

$$TR = 100\left[1 - \frac{2\pi r}{2\pi r_o}\right] \quad (16.10)$$

where
- $TR$ = travel reduction in percent
- $r$ = effective rolling radius while pulling in mm (in.)
- $r_o$ = rolling radius on a specified surface in mm (in.) when tractor pulls no load

Measuring effective rolling radii is inconvenient. However, multiplying the rolling radius by the axle rotational speed gives the forward speed. If the engine is operating in the governor-controlled range (see Section 5.8.2) such that there is little change in axle speed due to the applied load, the approximate travel reduction can be calculated using the following equation:

$$TR = 100 * \left[1 - \frac{S_a}{S_o}\right] \quad (16.11)$$

where
- $S_a$ = actual speed in km/h (mph)
- $S_o$ = travel speed on a specified surface in km/h (mph) when tractor pulls no load

It is common practice to measure the no-load speed ($S_o$) when the tractor is running on a roadway or other rigid surface. The actual speed ($S_a$) must be measured in the field in which the tractor is working. Notice that the tractor cannot develop drawbar pull unless there is travel reduction. The tire lugs must move rearward and compress the soil to make it strong enough to support the tractive force $F_t$ (Figure 16.2); the rearward movement of the lugs and the consequent shearing of the soil causes travel reduction.

Note that Equation 16.11 applies to either wheeled tractors or crawler tractors. Because of the much larger "footprint" of a track compared to a tire, however, a crawler tractor will have much less travel reduction than a wheel tractor of the same weight that is pulling the same drawbar load.

### 16.5.2 Dynamic Traction Ratio

Dynamic traction ratio (DTR) refers to the ratio of drawbar pull over the dynamic weight on the driving wheels. A high DTR is needed to obtain high drawbar pull. Increasing dynamic weight also increases drawbar pull, but too much dynamic weight causes soil compaction and high stress in the tractor axles. Techniques to increase DTR include improved lug design and the use of radial ply construction. For a tractor with rear-wheel drive, the dynamic traction ratio is:

$$DTR_2 = \frac{F_{db}}{R_{ro} + \Delta R_r} \quad (6.12)$$

where
- $DTR_2$ = dynamic traction ratio in decimals
- $F_{db}$ = drawbar pull in kN (lb)

$R_{ro}$ = static weight on rear wheels in kN (lb)
$\Delta R_r$ = weight transfer to rear wheels in kN (lb)

For a tractor with four-wheel drive or a crawler tractor, the dynamic traction ratio is:

$$DTR_4 = \frac{F_{db}}{W} \tag{16.13}$$

where W = tractor weight in kN (lb).

### 16.5.3 Tractive Efficiency
*Tractive efficiency* refers to the fraction of axle power that is converted to drawbar power by the drive wheels. Thus, tractive efficiency is defined as:

$$TE = \frac{P_{db}}{P_A} \tag{6.14}$$

where
- TE = tractive efficiency in decimals
- $P_{db}$ = drawbar power in kW (hp)
- $P_A$ = axle power in kW (hp)

By making use of Equation 5.4 for drawbar power, the following equation for tractive efficiency can be developed:

$$TE = \frac{F_{db} * S_a}{K_{LP} * P_A} \tag{6.15}$$

where $K_{LP}$ = units constant = 3.6 (375).

The other variables in Equation 16.15 were previously defined. Equations 16.14 and 16.15 apply to tractors with 2WD, 4WD or crawler tractors. Any part of the axle power not converted to drawbar power is wasted. Therefore, high tractive efficiency is desirable. Maximum tractive efficiency can be achieved by ballasting for optimum travel reduction (see Sections 16.5 and 16.7).

### 16.5.4 Travel Reduction and Pull
Both dynamic traction ratio and tractive efficiency vary with travel reduction, as Figure 16.8 illustrates. The curves in Figure 16.8 are

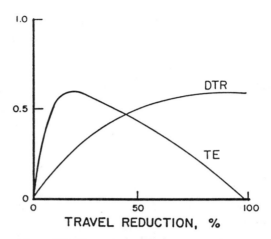

Figure 16.8–The variation of tractive efficiency and dynamic traction ratio with travel reduction on one specific soil.

valid for only one type of tractor and for only one condition of soil. The curves would be higher for firmer soils and lower for softer soils. The travel reduction at which peak tractive efficiency occurred would be least for crawler tractors and highest for 2WD tractors with 4WD tractors falling between.

Dynamic traction ratio cannot be greater than zero until the drive wheels have enough travel reduction to develop pull. The pull and dynamic traction ratio increase with travel reduction until a plateau is reached and essentially no further increases can occur. Figure 16.8 implies that DTR depends on travel reduction. It is useful to view the curve in the opposite light; that is, that travel reduction depends on and increases with drawbar pull. With the latter interpretation, it is clear the travel reduction of a given tractor can be increased by using a larger implement (with more draft) or decreased by using a smaller implement. Thus, as will be discussed further in Section 16.7, use of too large an implement will require the use of too much ballast on a wheeled tractor and/or will result in too much wheel slip. The slip of crawler tractors also increases with pull but, as mentioned in Section 16.5.1, the crawler tractor will have much less slip for a given drawbar pull.

### 16.5.5 Maximum Tractive Efficiency

Notice that the tractive efficiency cannot exceed zero until there is enough travel reduction to develop pull. Tractive efficiency must also be zero at 100% travel reduction because the drive wheels are spinning without moving the tractor forward. However, There is always one intermediate amount of travel reduction that provides maximum tractive efficiency. For the conditions illustrated in Figure 16.8, maximum tractive efficiency would occur at 12% travel reduction. It is important to remember that some travel reduction – that is, increased slippage – is necessary in order for traction to be efficient.

## 16.6 PREDICTING TRACTIVE PERFORMANCE

The chart in Figure 16.9 was developed for the ASAE by Frank Zoz of Deere & Company and frequently is referred to as the *Zoz chart*. The Zoz chart is used to predict the tractive performance of tractors with rear-wheel drive. It is based on Equations 16.11, 16.12, and 16.15 and on data from numerous drawbar tests in farm fields. Soil strength may vary considerably, depending on soil type, moisture content, and state of tillage. Zoz grouped all agricultural soils into three classes: firm soil, tilled soil and, soft or sandy soil. Because it lacks more precise definition of soil strength, the Zoz chart can provide only an approximate estimate of tractive performance. Other disadvantages of the Zoz chart are that it applies only to 2WD tractors with bias-ply tires. Zoz has developed a computer spread sheet which extends the traction predictions to include 4WD and FWA tractors with either bias or radial-ply tires. However, the Zoz chart will be used in this textbook for illustrating some important principles of traction.

Tractive performance is affected by weight transfer. It would be very difficult to measure the distances $Z_f$ and $Z_r$ (Figure 16.2) under field conditions and, therefore, Equations 16.6 and 16.9 are not of much use in the calculation of weight transfer. Zoz developed the following equation for calculating weight transfer:

$$\Delta R_r = DWC * F_{db} \qquad (6.16)$$

where
- $\Delta R_r$ = weight transfer to rear wheels in kN (lb)
- DWC = dynamic weight coefficient in decimals
- $F_{db}$ = drawbar pull in kN (lb)

Zoz estimated the following values for DWC:

> 0.65 for integral implements, such as plows fully mounted on the three-point hitch;
> 0.45 for semimounted implements, such as semimounted plows;

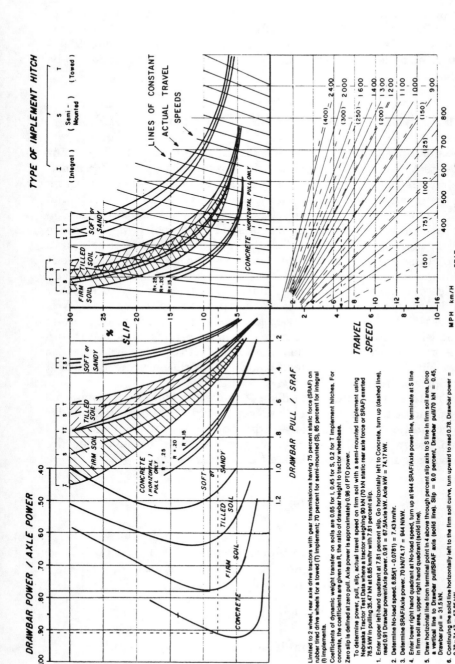

Figure 16.9–Traction prediction chart. (Reprinted from ASAE Data D230.4, *Agricultural machinery management*, revised December 1983.)

Weight Transfer, Traction, and Safety

0.20 for towed implements, such as plows hitched to the drawbar.

Because the weight transfer depends on the dynamic weight coefficient, use of the Zoz chart to predict tractive performance requires that the type of hitch be specified.

The Zoz chart can be used with data taken from Nebraska or OECD Tractor Tests. How the chart is used is illustrated in Example Problem 16.3.

## Example Problem 16.3

The tractor tested in Nebraska Test No 1441 (see Table 16.2) is to be used with full ballast to pull a semimounted plow on firm soil in ninth gear. Using the Zoz chart, determine the actual travel speed, travel reduction, drawbar pull, and drawbar power.

**Solution:** Before using the Zoz chart, it is necessary to consult the Nebraska test to find values for the static rear axle force (SRAF), travel speed without load ($S_o$), and axle power ($P_A$). The Nebraska Tractor Test shows 7035 kg mass (15,510 lb weight) at the rear axle. The SRAF (same as $R_{ro}$ in Equation 16.8) is equal to:

$$\text{SRAF} = [7035 \text{ kg}]*[9.80 \text{ m/s}^2] = 68\,943 \text{ N } (15{,}510 \text{ lb})$$

In the Nebraska test on a concrete track, the tractor produced 122.9 kW (164.8 hp) of drawbar power in ninth gear while traveling 8.48 km/h (5.27 mph) with 3.52% slip. The travel speed without load can be calculated from a modification of Equation 16.11:

$$S_o = S_a/[1 - \text{TR}/100] = 8.48/[1 - 0.0352] = 8.79 \text{ km/h}$$

or

$$S_o = S_a/[1 - \text{TR}/100] = 5.27/[1 - 0.0352] = 5.46 \text{ mph}$$

The Zoz chart includes curves relating tractive efficiency (drawbar power/axle power) to slip (the Zoz chart uses slip interchangeably with travel reduction). One of the curves can be used to estimate that, at 3.52% slip, the tractive efficiency on a concrete track would be approximately 0.905. Therefore, the axle power of the tractor is:

$$P_A = P_{db}/\text{TE} = 122.9/0.905 = 135.8 \text{ kW}$$

or

$$P_A = P_{db}/\text{TE} = 164.8/0.905 = 182.1 \text{ hp}$$

The ratio of SRAF over axle power is:

TABLE 16.2. Nebraska tractor test 1441 – International 5488 diesel, 18 speed (con't)

## POWER TAKE OFF PERFORMANCE

| Power Hp (kW) | Crank shaft speed rpm | Fuel Consumption | | | Temperature °F (°C) | | | Barometer inch Hg (kPa) |
|---|---|---|---|---|---|---|---|---|
| | | gal/hr (l/h) | lb/hp.hr (kg/kW.h) | Hp.hr/gal (kW.h/l) | Cooling medium | Air wet bulb | Air dry bulb | |

### MAXIMUM POWER AND FUEL CONSUMPTION
Rated Engine Speed—Two Hours (PTO Speed—1005 rpm)

| 187.22 (139.61) | 2400 | 11.555 (43.740) | 0.430 (0.262) | 16.20 (3.192) | 190 (87.7) | 61 (15.9) | 75 (23.9) | 28.873 (97.501) |

### VARYING POWER AND FUEL CONSUMPTION—Two Hours

| 165.46 (123.38) | 2496 | 10.665 (40.371) | 0.449 (0.273) | 15.51 (3.056) | 186 (85.6) | 61 (16.1) | 76 (24.4) | ...... |
| 0.00 (0.00) | 2614 | 3.446 (13.045) | ..... | ..... | 176 (80.0) | 60 (15.6) | 74 (23.3) | ...... |
| 84.88 (63.30) | 2556 | 6.935 (26.252) | 0.570 (0.347) | 12.24 (2.411) | 180 (82.2) | 60 (15.6) | 74 (23.3) | ...... |
| 186.88 (139.36) | 2400 | 11.517 (43.597) | 0.430 (0.261) | 16.23 (3.197) | 187 (87.2) | 60 (15.8) | 75 (23.9) | ...... |
| 42.84 (31.95) | 2590 | 5.184 (19.624) | 0.844 (0.513) | 8.26 (1.628) | 177 (80.6) | 60 (15.6) | 74 (23.6) | ...... |
| 125.58 (93.64) | 2524 | 8.841 (33.467) | 0.491 (0.299) | 14.20 (2.798) | 183 (83.9) | 61 (16.1) | 75 (23.9) | ...... |
| Av 100.94 (75.27) | 2530 | 7.765 (29.394) | 0.536 (0.326) | 13.00 (2.561) | 182 (83.2) | 60 (15.8) | 75 (23.8) | 28.897 (97.580) |

## DRAWBAR PERFORMANCE

| Power Hp (kW) | Drawbar pull lbs (kN) | Speed mph (km/h) | Crank-shaft speed rpm | Slip % | Fuel Consumption | | | Temp. °F (°C) | | | Barom. inch Hg (kPa) |
|---|---|---|---|---|---|---|---|---|---|---|---|
| | | | | | gal/hr (l/h) | lb/hp.hr (kg/kW.h) | Hp.hr/gal (kW.h/l) | Cooling med | Air wet bulb | Air dry bulb | |

### Maximum Available Power—Two Hours 9th (M3) Gear

| 163.44 (121.88) | 11642 (51.78) | 5.26 (8.47) | 2399 | 3.69 | 11.545 (43.701) | 0.493 (0.300) | 14.16 (2.789) | 187 (85.8) | 55 (12.5) | 67 (19.2) | 28.915 (97.642) |

### 75% of Pull at Maximum Power—Ten Hours 9th (M3) Gear

| 130.87 (97.59) | 8798 (39.14) | 5.58 (8.98) | 2512 | 2.57 | 9.949 (37.661) | 0.530 (0.322) | 13.15 (2.591) | 182 (83.4) | 56 (13.6) | 66 (18.8) | 28.951 (97.763) |

### 50% of Pull at Maximum Power—Two Hours 9th (M3) Gear

| 89.26 (66.56) | 5866 (26.09) | 5.71 (9.18) | 2549 | 1.76 | 7.959 (30.129) | 0.622 (0.378) | 11.21 (2.209) | 179 (81.7) | 57 (13.9) | 60 (15.6) | 28.945 (97.743) |

### 50% of Pull at Reduced Engine Speed—Two Hours 13th (H1) Gear

| 89.32 (66.60) | 5866 (26.09) | 5.71 (9.19) | 1530 | 1.58 | 6.023 (22.800) | 0.470 (0.286) | 14.83 (2.921) | 181 (82.8) | 59 (15.0) | 64 (17.8) | 28.895 (97.574) |

### MAXIMUM POWER IN SELECTED GEARS

| 154.52 (115.23) | 18646 (82.94) | 3.11 (5.00) | 2400 | 8.93 | 6th (L6) Gear | | | 181 (82.5) | 56 (13.3) | 58 (14.4) | 28.940 (97.726) |
| 162.73 (121.35) | 16001 (71.18) | 3.81 (6.14) | 2400 | 6.06 | 7th (M1) Gear | | | 185 (85.0) | 52 (11.1) | 63 (17.2) | 28.940 (97.726) |
| 164.58 (122.73) | 13536 (60.21) | 4.56 (7.34) | 2400 | 4.35 | 8th (M2) Gear | | | 186 (85.3) | 52 (11.1) | 62 (16.7) | 28.940 (97.726) |
| 164.82 (122.91) | 11731 (52.18) | 5.27 (8.48) | 2398 | 3.52 | 9th (M3) Gear | | | 186 (85.6) | 53 (11.7) | 60 (15.6) | 28.970 (97.827) |
| 164.43 (122.61) | 9879 (43.94) | 6.24 (10.04) | 2401 | 2.92 | 10th (M4) Gear | | | 186 (85.6) | 52 (11.1) | 63 (17.2) | 28.940 (97.726) |
| 162.54 (121.21) | 8373 (37.24) | 7.28 (11.72) | 2400 | 2.41 | 11th (M5) Gear | | | 188 (86.4) | 52 (11.1) | 64 (17.8) | 28.940 (97.726) |
| 160.12 (119.40) | 6987 (31.08) | 8.59 (13.83) | 2400 | 1.80 | 12th (M6) Gear | | | 187 (86.1) | 52 (11.1) | 64 (17.8) | 28.940 (97.726) |

### LUGGING ABILITY IN 9th (M3) GEAR

| Crankshaft Speed rpm | 2398 | 2162 | 1919 | 1682 | 1441 | 1204 |
|---|---|---|---|---|---|---|
| Pull—lbs (kN) | 11731 (52.18) | 13489 (60.00) | 14928 (66.40) | 15838 (70.45) | 15477 (68.85) | 13385 (59.54) |
| Increase in Pull % | 0 | 15 | 27 | 35 | 32 | 14 |
| Power—Hp (kW) | 164.82 (122.91) | 169.56 (126.44) | 165.14 (123.14) | 152.46 (113.69) | 127.90 (95.37) | 93.55 (69.76) |
| Speed—Mph (km/h) | 5.27 (8.48) | 4.71 (7.59) | 4.15 (6.68) | 3.61 (5.81) | 3.10 (4.99) | 2.62 (4.22) |
| Slip % | 3.52 | 4.35 | 5.18 | 5.66 | 5.50 | 4.52 |

**Department of Agricultural Engineering**

**Dates of Test:** May 26 to June 8, 1982

**Manufacturer:** INTERNATIONAL HARVESTER COMPANY, 401 North Michigan Avenue, Chicago, IL 60611

**FUEL, OIL AND TIME:** Fuel No. 2 Diesel Cetane No. 46.6 (rating taken from oil company's inspection data) Specific gravity converted to 60°/60° (15°/15°) 0.8375 Fuel weight 6.973 lbs/gal (0.836 kg/l) Oil SAE 30 API service classification CD/SE To motor 4.032 gal (15.262 l) Drained from motor 3.722 gal (14.088 l) Transmission and final drive lubricant I.H. Hy-tran fluid Total time engine was operated 38.5 hours.

**ENGINE:** Make International Diesel Type six cylinder vertical with turbocharger and intercooler Serial No. 467BT2U169510* Crankshaft lengthwise Rated rpm 2400 Bore and stroke 4.30" × 5.35" (109.2 mm × 135.9 mm) Compression ratio 16.3 to 1 Displacement 466 cu in (7636 ml) Starting system 12 volt Lubrication pressure Air cleaner two paper elements with aspirator Oil filter two full flow cartridges Oil cooler engine coolant heat exchanger for crankcase oil, radiator for hydraulic and transmission oil Fuel filter two paper cartridges Muffler underhood Exhaust vertical Cooling medium temperature control one thermostat.

**CHASSIS:** Type standard with duals Serial No. 2590002U001019* Tread width rear 64" (1625 mm) to 130" (3302 mm) front 62.5" (1588 mm) to 86.5" (2197 mm) Wheel base 111.6" (2835 mm) Center of gravity (without operator or ballast, with minimum tread, with fuel tank filled and tractor serviced for operation) Horizontal distance forward from center-line of rear wheels 26.9" (683 mm) Vertical distance above roadway 38.9" (988 mm) Horizontal distance from center of rear wheel tread 0" (0 mm) to the right/left Hydraulic control system direct engine drive Transmission selective gear fixed ratio with partial (2) range operator controlled powershift Advertised speeds mph (km/h) first 1.5 (2.4) second 1.8 (2.8) third 2.0 (3.2) fourth 2.4 (3.8) fifth 2.7 (4.4) sixth 3.2 (5.2) seventh 3.8 (6.1) eighth 4.5 (7.2) ninth 5.1 (8.3) tenth 6.0 (9.7) eleventh 7.0 (11.3) twelfth 8.2 (13.3) thirteenth 8.6 (13.8) fourteenth 10.1 (16.2) fifteenth 11.5 (18.5) sixteenth 13.6 (21.8) seventeenth 15.7 (25.3) eighteenth 18.5 (29.7) reverse 2.9 (4.6), 3.4 (5.4), 3.9 (6.2), 4.5 (7.3), 5.3 (8.5), 6.2 (9.9) Clutch wet multiple disc operated by foot pedal with hydraulic power assist Brakes wet multiple disc hydraulically power actuated and operated by two foot pedals which can be locked together Steering hydrostatic Turning radius (on concrete surface with brake applied) right 151.1" (3.84 m) left 151.1" (3.84 m) (on concrete surface without brake) right 199.5" (5.07 m) left 199.5" (5.07 m) Turning space diameter (on concrete surface with brake applied) right 316" (8.03 m) left 316" (8.03 m) (on concrete surface without brake) right 412" (10.47 m) left 412" (10.47 m) Power take-off 1005 rpm at 2400 engine rpm.

TABLE 16.2. Nebraska tractor test 1441 – International 5488 diesel, 18 speed (con't)

| TRACTOR SOUND LEVEL WITH CAB | dB(A) |
|---|---|
| Maximum Available Power—Two Hours | 78.0 |
| 75% of Pull at Maximum Power—Ten Hours | 78.5 |
| 50% of Pull at Maximum Power—Two Hours | 77.0 |
| 50% of Pull at Reduced Engine Speed—Two Hours | 73.0 |
| Bystander in 17th (H5) gear | 86.5 |

| TIRES, BALLAST AND WEIGHT | | With Ballast | Without Ballast |
|---|---|---|---|
| Rear Tires | —No., size, ply & psi (kPa) | Inner Two 20.8R38; 10; 12 (85) | Inner Two 20.8R38; 10; 12 (85) |
| | | Outer Two 20.8R38; 8; 12 (85) | Outer Two 20.8R38; 8; 12 (85) |
| Ballast | —Liquid (each inner) | 995 lb (452 kg) | None |
| | —Test Equip. (each) | 109 lb (49 kg) | None |
| Front Tires | —No., size, ply & psi (kPa) | Two 14L-16.1; 6; 28 (195) | Two 14L-16.1; 6; 28 (195) |
| Ballast | —Test Equip (each) | 130 lb (59 kg) | None |
| | —Cast Iron (each) | 40 lb (18 kg) | None |
| Height of Drawbar | | 21.5 in (545 mm) | 21.5 in (545 mm) |
| Static Weight with Operator | —Rear | 15510 lb (7035 kg) | 13085 lb (5935 kg) |
| | —Front | 4495 lb (2039 kg) | 4155 lb (1885 kg) |
| | —Total | 20005 lb (9074 kg) | 17240 lb (7820 kg) |

**REPAIRS and ADJUSTMENTS:** No repairs or adjustments.

**REMARKS:** All test results were determined from observed data obtained in accordance with SAE and ASAE test codes or official Nebraska test procedure. For the maximum power tests, the fuel temperature at the injection pump was maintained at 128°F (53.3°C). Seven gears were chosen between stability limit and 10 mph (16.1 km/h).

We, the undersigned, certify that this is a true and correct report of official Tractor Test **1441**.

LOUIS I. LEVITICUS
Engineer-in-Charge

K. VON BARGEN
W. E. SPLINTER
L. L. BASHFORD
Board of Tractor Test Engineers

*Source:* Reprinted from University of Nebraska Tractor Test Laboratory, Report 1441.

$$\text{SRAF}/P_A = 68\,943/135.8 = 508 \text{ N/kW}$$

or

$$\text{SRAF}/P_A = 15{,}510/182.1 = 85.2 \text{ lb/hp}$$

With these preliminary calculations completed, the Zoz chart can be used to predict the performance of the tractor while plowing in the field. Enter the chart at a travel speed of 8.79 km/h (5.46 mph) and move to the right to a force/power ratio of 508 N/kW (85.2 lb/hp) (interpolate between 500 and 600 N/kW or 75 and 100 lb/hp). At 508 N/kW (85.2 lb/hp), move vertically upward to the S curve (semimounted hitching) for firm soil. Then, move left to the slip axis (approximately 18%) and further left to the tractive efficiency curve for firm soil. The tractive efficiency is approximately 0.71. The data from the Zoz chart can now be used to calculate the tractor performance while pulling the plow. The actual speed can be calculated from another modification of Equation 16.11:

$$S_a = S_o * [1 - TR/100] = 8.79 * [1 - 0.18] = 7.21 \text{ km/h}$$

or

$$S_a = S_o * [1 - TR/100] = 5.46 * [1 - 0.18] = 4.48 \text{ mph}$$

The drawbar power can be calculated as follows:

$$P_{db} = TE * PA = 0.71 * 135.8 = 96.4 \text{ kW}$$

or

$$P_{db} = TE * PA = 0.71 * 182.1 = 129 \text{ hp}$$

Finally, the drawbar pull can be calculated from the following modification of Equation 5.4:

$$F_{db} = 3.6*Pdb/Sa = 3.6*96.4/7.21 = 48.1 \text{ kN}$$

or

$$F_{db} = 375*Pdb/Sa = 375*129/4.48 = 10,800 \text{ lbs}$$

The four quantities that were requested in the problem statement are summarized as follows:

actual travel speed = 7.21 km/h (4.48 mph)
travel reduction   = 18%
drawbar pull       = 48.1 kN (10,800 lb)
drawbar power      = 96.4 kW (129 hp)

Note that the preceding quantities represent the maximum potential performance of the tractor for the conditions stated and would be achieved only if the plow required exactly 48.1 kN (10,800 lb) of pull at 7.21 km/h (4.48 mph). Implement draft depends on the type, size, and speed of the implement and on the type and condition of the soil. The matching of implements to tractors is beyond the scope of this book, but the procedure is straightforward. Implement draft data are tabulated in the same section of the ASAE Standards book as the Zoz chart. To match a plow to the tractor in Example Problem 16.3, for example, you would use the ASAE data to calculate the width of plow that would require 48.1 kN (10,800 lb) of pull at 7.21 km/h (4.48 mph) on a firm soil. Then, because plows are available only with integer numbers of bottoms, you would select a plow whose pull did not exceed 48.1 kN (10,800 lb) but was as close to that figure as possible.

## 16.7 BALLASTING FOR TRACTION

The Zoz chart can be used to select the amount of ballast needed to give a desired amount of travel reduction. The first step is to select the desired travel reduction. We could select travel reduction that would maximize tractive efficiency (for example, see Figure 16.8). By selecting a somewhat larger travel reduction, however, an appreciable gain in dynamic traction ratio can be achieved with only a small loss in tractive efficiency. In practical terms, operating with a travel reduction somewhat greater than that for peak tractive efficiency can provide a substantial boost in drawbar pull with only a small loss in drawbar power. Use of the Zoz chart for ballast selection is illustrated in Example Problem 16.4.

## Example Problem 16.4

The tractor in Example Problem 16.3 is to be used to pull a towed disk on soft soil in ninth gear. How much ballast must be added to the unballasted tractor if the slip is to be 20%?

**Solution:** Some data from the previous problem can be used. The tractor operating in 9th gear has the same no-load travel speed as before – that is, 8.79 km/h (5.46 mph). The axle power is also the same – 135.8 kW (182.1 hp). However, the static rear axle force for the unballasted tractor is (from Table 16.2):

$$SRAF = [5935 \text{ kg}]*[9.80 \text{ mm/s}^2] = 58\,163 \text{ N } (13,085 \text{ lb})$$

With these preliminary data, the Zoz chart can be used to select ballast. First, enter the chart at 20% slip and go rightward to the T curve (towed hitch) for soft soil. From this intersection, draw a line (line A) straight down to the bottom of the Zoz chart. Next, enter the Zoz chart with a travel speed of 8.79 km/h (5.46 mph) and draw another line (line B) to the right. The intersection of lines A and B pinpoints a force/power ratio that, in this case, is equal to approximately 910 N/kW (153 lb/hp). The total SRAF is:

$$\text{total SRAF} = [910 \text{ N/kW}]*[135.8 \text{ kW}] = 123\,578 \text{ N}$$

or

$$\text{total SRAF} = [153 \text{ lb/hp}]*[182.1 \text{ hp}] = 27\,861 \text{ lb}$$

Since the tractor itself supplies 58 163 N (13,085 lb), the amount of additional ballast that must be added is:

$$\text{added ballast} = 123\,578 - 58\,163 = 65\,415 \text{ N}$$

or

$$\text{added ballast} = 27{,}861 - 13{,}085 = 14{,}776 \text{ lb}$$

The ballast could be added in the form of removable, cast-iron weight, as liquid in the rear tires, or as some combination. Adding ballast at the rear wheels moves the center of gravity of the tractor rearward. Many modern tractors have a rack on the front of the tractor for adding front-end ballast. Adding approximately 40% of the weight of the additional rear ballast on the front rack would restore the center of gravity to near its original position.

The reader may notice that the solution produced by the Zoz chart for the required ballast, although theoretically correct, is impractical. The required ballast is more than 85% of the mass of the entire unballasted tractor! The required ballast could be reduced by targeting for higher slip and/or by use of faster travel speeds. In

Example Problem 16.4, it was unrealistic to target for 20% slip on a soft soil and 30% slip would have been a better choice. The reader is encouraged to rework the example problem with higher slip and with several different travel speeds. Use of slower speeds requires larger amounts of added ballast to maintain the same travel reduction. Use of too much ballast causes excessive stress in the tractor axles and drive trains and also can cause excessive soil compaction. Travel speeds of at least 7.5 km/h (4.7 mph) should be selected for satisfactory use of the drawbar power of modern tractors, and a small enough implement should be selected to allow the tractor to attain or exceed this speed.

If traction were the only consideration, a tractor would be ballasted to put nearly all of the weight on the drive wheels. In the case of a 2WD tractor, as was used in Example Problems 16.3 and 16.4, enough of the static weight must be carried on the front wheels to achieve reliable steering. Generally, ballasting to put 25 to 30% of the static weight on the front wheels will assure enough dynamic weight on the front wheels with normal weight transfer. With 4WD tractors, approximately 55 to 60% of the static weight should be on the front wheels so that, with weight transfer, approximately half of the dynamic weight will be carried on each axle. Proper ballasting of tractors with FWA depends upon their use. When the FWA is disengaged, the tractor should be ballasted the same as a 2WD tractor. Conversely, when the FWA is engaged, ballasting should be the same as a 4WD tractor.

## 16.8 LIMITS TO PERFORMANCE

Typically, the pulling performance of a tractor is limited by one of three factors. First, the engine may not be able to deliver enough rear axle torque for the tractor to pull the load. This torque limit can nearly always be overcome by shifting the transmission to a lower gear. Second, traction may be insufficient to pull the load, and the drive wheels will spin. If traction is not limiting, stability may become the limiting factor. Stability is lost when the weight transfer becomes so large that the front wheels lift off the ground. Equation 16.4 can be used to calculate the critical drawbar pull at which stability is lost, that is, when $R_f = 0$. The critical pull is:

$$F_{db} = \frac{W * X_{cg}}{Z_r} \qquad (16.17)$$

For the tractor in Example Problem 16.2, the critical pull would be:

$$F_{db} = [28.5 \text{ kN}] * [658 \text{ mm}] / [580 \text{ mm}] = 32.3 \text{ kN}$$

or

$$F_{db} = [6400 \text{ lb}] * [25.9 \text{ in.}] / [22.8 \text{ in.}] = 7{,}270 \text{ lb}$$

If the tractor in Example Problem 16.2 has sufficient rear axle torque and sufficient traction to develop more than 32.3 kN (7270 lb) of drawbar pull, the front wheels would lift from the ground. Once the front wheels lift, the tractor could continue to tip over backwards or stop tipping, depending upon the location of the hitch point.

The *hitch point* is shown behind the rear axle on the tractor in Figure 16.2. Notice that, as the front end of this tractor rises, the hitch point moves closer to the ground. Therefore, the distance $Z_r$ decreases and, according to Equation 16.6, the weight transfer declines. Thus, the tractor can continue to pull without tipping over backwards. Such operation would not be safe, however, because the tractor could not be safely steered with the front wheels off the ground.

If the hitch point were at or ahead of the rear axle in Figure 16.2, notice that there would be no decrease in $Z_r$ as the front end of the tractor lifted. In such a situation, the tractor would quickly tip over backwards once the front end started to lift. Therefore, it is essential to safe operation that the hitch point be located well behind the rear axle. Generally, tractor drawbars and three-point hitches are designed to place the hitch point behind the rear axle. It is dangerous to hitch to points other than those recommended by the tractor manufacturer.

The pulling performance of a well-designed and properly ballasted tractor should be limited by torque in higher gears and by traction in lower gears. However, the hitch point should be located well behind the rear axle to prepare for the possibility that traction might momentarily improve and stability might become the limiting factor.

## 16.9  SIDEWAYS OVERTURNS

Tractors may overturn during high speed turns because of their high center of gravity. Figure 16.10 shows a tractor of weight W making a turn at high speed (S). The critical speed can be calculated by using the following equation:

$$S_c = K_S \sqrt{\frac{g * r * y}{h}} \qquad (16.18)$$

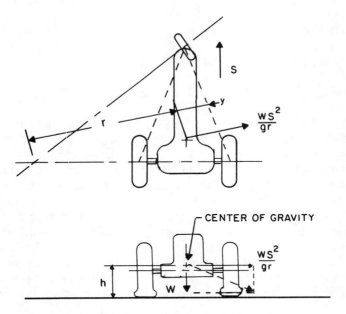

*Figure 16.10–Forces on a tractor in a high-speed turn.*

where
- $S_c$ = critical speed in km/h (mph)
- $g$ = acceleration of gravity = 9.8 m/s² (32.2 ft/s²)
- $r$ = radius of turn in m (ft)
- $y$ = distance from tractor center of gravity to tipping axis in m (ft)
- $h$ = height of tractor center of gravity in m (ft)
- $K_S$ = units constant = 3.6 (0.682)

The distance y can be estimated from Nebraska or OECD Tractor Test data using the following equation:

$$y = \frac{RTW * [WB - X_{cg}]}{2 * WB} \quad (16.19)$$

where RTW = rear tread width and WB and $X_{cg}$ are as defined in Section 16.2.

The tractor will tip over sideways if it makes a turn with a speed greater than the critical speed. Notice that the lower the center of gravity and the wider the turn, the higher the critical turning speed. Also notice that the tipping axis in Figure 16.10 passes through the center of the tire footprints. Faster safe turns can, therefore, be made if y is increased by increasing the spacing between the rear wheels or by using a tractor with a wide front end (see Figure 1.8). The wide front end is of no initial benefit because it is hinged to the front of the tractor. Initial tipping is like that for a tricycle tractor. However, when the axle hinge reaches the limit of its rotation, the tipping axis shifts out to the center of the front tire, and the increase in y may prevent further tipping.

## Example Problem 16.5

The tractor tested in Nebraska Test No. 1441 (Table 16.2) can turn with a radius of 5.07 m (16.6 ft) on concrete without use of wheel brakes. The height of the center of gravity is 988 mm (3.24 ft). Using Equation 16.19, the distance y can be calculated to be approximately 617 mm (2.02 ft) with minimum rear wheel spacing and 1253 mm (4.11 ft) with maximum rear wheel spacing. Calculate the critical turning speed at which side tipping would begin with minimum wheel spacing.

**Solution:** Equation 16.17 can be used to calculate the critical turning speeds. With the minimum rear wheel spacing, the critical speed is:

$$S_c = 3.6 \sqrt{\frac{9.8 * 5.07 * 0.617}{0.988}} = 20.1 \text{ km/h}$$

or

$$S_c = 0.682 \sqrt{\frac{32.2 * 16.6 * 2.02}{3.24}} = 12.5 \text{ mph}$$

Note that the tractor can attain 29.7 km/h (18.5 mph) in 18th gear. Thus, it is apparent that tractors can easily attain enough speed to tip over sideways during a turn. Tractor operators must use care to reduce speed and/or avoid sharp turns to avoid tipping.

Their high center of gravity makes tractors vulnerable to side overturns when they are operated on side slopes. For the tractor in Example Problem 16.5, the critical side slope would be approximately 60%. The rear wheel on the downhill side could encounter a hole, or the wheel on the uphill side could encounter a bump. Either occurrence would momentarily increase the effective slope. Therefore, the tractor should be operated on side slopes considerably less than the critical slope. The critical slope can be increased by widening the spacing of the rear wheels.

## 16.10 TRACTOR SAFETY

Statistics on the number of fatal accidents per 100,000 workers usually indicate that farming is more dangerous than most factory jobs. Typically, it ranks as one of the top three most dangerous occupations. Accident prevention measures can be grouped into three categories: engineering, education, and enforcement. Safety can be increased by designing or engineering equipment that is safer to operate. When workers are educated as to the proper use of equipment, they are less likely to have accidents. Finally, safety can be increased through the enforcement of safe work rules. The latter approach has limited applicability to tractor safety because farm tractors are often operated by independent, self-employed farmers who have no supervisors to enforce safety rules. Therefore, improvements in tractor safety must come through primarily engineering and education.

Early tractors had far fewer safety features than do tractors of today. For example, in the 1920s, when research led to a clearer understanding of the requirements for safe hitching, the frequency of rearward overturns experienced with some early tractors was diminished. Also, when it was learned that hand cranking a tractor could cause serious or fatal accidents if the tractor was left in gear and happened to start quickly, electric starters were introduced. Starters improved safety by allowing the operator to start the engine from the driver's seat. As a further improvement, interlocks were designed to prevent the engine from being cranked when the tractor was in gear.

The power shaft attached to the tractor pto is inherently dangerous. If a person's clothing comes in contact with an unshielded, rotating pto shaft, it can quickly wrap on the shaft, pull the person into the shaft and cause severe injury or death. Through engineering, power shafts were developed in which a permanent shield surrounds the shaft and is attached to the shaft with bearings. As long as the shaft is maintained in proper working condition so that the bearings are free to rotate, the shield will protect persons who come into inadvertent contact with the rotating shaft.

Many designs for increased safety were introduced during and following the 1950s. *Rollover protective structures* (ROPS) are among these and have been very effective in reducing fatalities from tractor overturns. The ROPS shown in Figure 16.11 can protect operators

Weight Transfer, Traction, and Safety

Figure 16.11–A ROPS (rollover protection structure) on a tractor. (Courtesy of Deere & Company.)

only if they remain in their seat; thus, seat belts should be worn. Some ROPS include an overhead canopy that serves as a sun shade. Some cabs (Figure 16.12) are designed to provide the strength of a ROPS. The ASAE has published standards for the design and testing of ROPS. During an impact, the ROPS must deform enough to absorb energy but not enough to allow the operator to be crushed.

Sometimes, tractor operators are forced to make quick decisions when using tractor controls. Therefore, the ASAE has developed a standard (S335.2) that "is based on the principle that a given direction of movement of any control produces a consistent and expected result". The location of many controls also is specified in the standard. For example, a foot clutch (if provided) should be actuated by the operator's left foot, with the direction of motion forward and/or downward for disengagement. Such a clutch could be operated more quickly in an emergency than could one that required an unfamiliar motion for disengagement. Locations and actions of other standard controls are similarly specified in the standard. A companion document describes standard symbols for operator controls.

A fatigued operator is more likely to make mistakes than one who is well-rested. Therefore, features that improve the convenience and comfort of the tractor operator also are safety features. Hydraulic controls and power steering have increased convenience by

Figure 16.12–A tractor cab with strength of a ROPS. (Courtesy of Ford-New Holland.)

greatly reducing the effort required from the operator for controlling the tractor and attached implements. Operator comfort has been improved through improved seats and by use of cabs to protect the operator from noise, dust, precipitation, and temperature extremes.

It is virtually impossible to design a tractor so safe that operators cannot cause injury to themselves or others. For example, if safety shields have been removed, they cannot protect operators. Pressures in hydraulic systems are high enough to cause skin penetration and severe injury if one attempts to disconnect a hydraulic coupler under full system pressure. Attempting to refill a fuel tank over a hot engine can start a fire if a spill occurs. There are numerous other possibilities for injury. Therefore, there is continuing need to educate tractor operators as to procedures for safe operation. Education takes many forms, including use of operator's manuals, safety decals, magazine and newspaper articles, and so forth. Some procedures for safe operation relate to specific tractors, while others apply to any tractor. One general rule is that only qualified persons should operate tractors. Sometimes, farm children are permitted to operate tractors as soon as they have enough physical strength to do so. However, they may lack the maturity to make sound decisions when unexpected events occur and, therefore, may cause an otherwise avoidable accident. Inexperienced operators should always be given some instruction before being permitted to operate a tractor.

It is likely that there will always be some element of risk in operating a farm tractor. For example, tractors have high centers of gravity because of the need to provide crop clearance under the axles. Therefore, the tractors are subject to tipping on side slopes. Continuing efforts will be needed to engineer more safety features for farm tractors and to educate operators as to their safe use.

## 16.11 SUMMARY

The primary purposes of a tractor are to provide drawbar pull and drawbar power. The fraction of the dynamic weight on the drive wheels that is converted to drawbar pull is called the dynamic traction ratio (DTR). Tractive efficiency is the fraction of axle power that is converted to drawbar power. Thus, both high DTR and high tractive efficiency are needed for achieving maximum drawbar pull and power. Drawbar pull also can be increased by increasing the dynamic weight on the drive wheels, for example, by ballasting or by weight transfer. Too much dynamic weight causes excessive soil compaction and axle stress.

Tractor tire terminology was developed before four-wheel-drive tractors became popular. Thus, lugged tires suitable for traction are known as rear tires, and nonlugged tires suitable for steering are called front tires. An arrow is provided on rear tires to show the proper direction of rotation for best use of the lugs in providing traction. Tire sizes are indicated by a code giving rim diameter and tire width in inches; currently, few metric sizes are available for tractor tires. Both front and rear tires are available with either biased ply or radial ply construction. Radial tires are more expensive, but they provide increased traction and a smoother ride. Dual tires can improve traction by providing increased contact area with the soil and improved floatation on soft soils.

Because soil is deformable, wheel slippage is necessary to compress and strengthen the soil enough to support drawbar pull. The reduction in forward speed accompanying pull and increased slippage is referred to as travel reduction. Travel reduction and drawbar pull increase together; therefore, a tractor cannot produce drawbar pull without travel reduction. For a given tractor on a given soil, there is only one optimum travel reduction that gives maximum tractive efficiency and drawbar power. With less travel reduction, drawbar power and efficiency decline because of reduced pull; with more travel reduction, efficiency declines because of reduced travel speed.

The many factors involved in traction have been incorporated into the Zoz chart for predicting tractive potential of tractors with rear-wheel drive. Nebraska or OECD Tractor Test data can be used to predict the potential drawbar pull and power for specific situations in the field. The potential pull and power can be achieved only with the perfect matching of an implement to the tractor, but data from the Zoz chart can provide a good starting point for implement selection.

The Zoz chart also can be used to select the amount of ballast needed for a desired amount of travel reduction, and the selection procedure gives insight into the importance of tractor speed. Too much ballast is needed to limit travel reduction when the tractor is used to pull very large implements at slow speeds. For satisfactory use of drawbar power, a small enough implement should be selected to permit travel speeds of at least 7.5 km/h (4.7 mph).

The pulling performance of a tractor usually is limited by axle torque in high gears and by traction — that is, excessive wheel slippage — in low gears. Stability can become the limiting factor in some situations; the tractor can develop enough weight transfer to lift the front wheels off the ground. Then, the hitch point becomes critical. Selection of an improper hitch point can cause the tractor to flip over backwards. Tractors also can turn over sideways due to operation on steep side slopes and/or turns at high speeds. Thus, accidents can occur easily if tractors are used incorrectly.

Accident surveys show that farming is one of the three most dangerous occupations in the United States and that tractors are involved in many of the farm accidents. Accident prevention measures can be grouped into the three categories of engineering, education, and enforcement. Enforcement has limited applicability in preventing farm accidents because independent, self-employed farm tractor operators have no supervisors to enforce safety rules.

Through careful engineering, many safety features have been incorporated into modern tractors. Examples include electric starters, rollover protective structures, and standardized controls. New safety features will continue to be introduced. Because there is inherent risk in unsafe operating procedures, there always will be a need for educating tractor users in accident prevention measures. Certainly, only qualified persons should be permitted to operated tractors.

## QUESTIONS

Q16.1   Would the location of the center of gravity of a tractor be affected if wheel weights were placed on the rear wheels? Briefly explain your answer.

Q16.2   What is the meaning of the word *weight transfer*?

Q16.3   If a tire on a tractor has the designation R13.9-36, what information does the designation convey?

Q16.4   Reconsider Q16.3, but assume the tire is an F2, 7.50-16 tire.

Q16.5   (a) What is travel reduction?
(b) Is the ideal travel reduction equal to zero? Briefly explain your answer.

Q16.6   (a) What is dynamic traction ratio?
(b) What relationship, if any, does it bear to travel reduction?

Q16.7   (a) What is tractive efficiency?
(b) What relationship, if any, does it bear to travel reduction?

Q16.8   Travel reduction can be controlled to some extent by ballasting a tractor. What amount of travel reduction would be a desirable goal in selecting ballast?

Q16.9   When modern farm tractors are used for pulling tillage implements, is 7.5 km/h (4.7 mph) a good upper limit or a good lower limit for travel speed? Why?

Q16.10  (a) Typically, the pulling performance of a tractor can be limited by one of what three factors?
(b) Normally, which factor should be limiting on a well-designed and ballasted tractor?

Q16.11  How is the critical tipping speed of a tractor in a high-speed turn affected by (a) increasing the tread width of the rear wheels and (b) switching from a tricycle front end to a hinged, wide front axle?

Q16.12  (a) Into what three categories are accident prevention measures grouped?
(b) Are all three categories as effective in preventing farm accidents as in preventing industrial accidents? Briefly explain your answer.

Q16.13  (a) What is an ROPS?
(b) Under what conditions is it effective?

Q16.14  If ASAE standards are followed, what principle should guide the design of tractor controls?

# PROBLEMS

P16.1  A certain tractor has a total weight of 133.3 kN (29,970 lb) and a wheelbase of 3251 mm (10.66 ft). The static weight on the front axle is 77.4 kN (17,400 lb).
(a) Calculate the horizontal distance from the rear axle centerline to the center of gravity.
(b) Does this tractor have rear-wheel drive or four-wheel drive?

P16.2  A certain rear-wheel-drive tractor has a total weight of 56.2 kN (12,634 lb). The wheelbase is 2692 mm (8.83 ft), and the horizontal distance from the centerline of the rear axle to the center of gravity is 777 mm (2.55 ft). Calculate the static weight on (a) the front axle and (b) the rear axle.

P16.3  The tractor described in P16.2 is pulling a level drawbar pull of 24.7 kN (5553 lb), and the drawbar height is 520 mm (1.71 ft). Calculate the weight transfer and the dynamic weight on (a) the front axle and (b) the rear axle.

P16.4  The tractor described in P16.1 is pulling a level drawbar load of 57.7 kN (12,970 lb), and the drawbar height is 430 mm (1.41 ft). Calculate the weight transfer and the dynamic weight on (a) the front axle and (b) the rear axle.

P16.5  A four-wheel-drive tractor with a total weight of 135.6 kN (30,480 lb) is pulling a level drawbar load of 55.4 kN (12,454 lb) on a concrete track. The actual travel speed is 11.09 km/h (6.89 mph), and the no-load travel speed is 11.40 km/h (7.08 mph). The axle power is 185.5 kW (248.7 hp). Calculate the (a) travel reduction, (b) dynamic traction ratio, and (c) tractive efficiency.

P16.6  A rear-wheel-drive tractor with a total weight of 52.3 kN (11,757 lb) has a wheelbase of 2662 mm (8.73 ft), and the center of gravity is 711 mm (2.33 ft) ahead of the rear axle centerline. The tractor is pulling a level drawbar pull of 25.8 kN (5800 lb) on concrete, and the drawbar height is 485 mm (1.59 ft). The actual travel speed is 8.31 km/h (5.16 mph) and the no-load travel speed is 8.69 km/h

Weight Transfer, Traction, and Safety

(5.40 mph). The axle power is 66.0 kW (88.5 hp). Calculate the (a) travel reduction, (b) dynamic load on the rear axle, (c) dynamic traction ratio, and (d) tractive efficiency.

P16.7   A certain rear-wheel-drive tractor has a static rear axle load of 60.3 kN (13,556 lb), axle power of 65.3 kW (87.5 hp), and no-load travel speed (in eighth gear) of 8.69 km/h (5.40 mph). The tractor is to be used to pull a towed disk on soft soil. Using the Zoz chart, find the (a) travel reduction, (b) actual travel speed, (c) drawbar power, and (d) drawbar pull.

P16.8   Rework Example Problem 16.3, but use a Nebraska or OECD Tractor test for a rear-wheel-drive tractor specified by your instructor.

P16.9   The unballasted tractor described in P16.6 has a static rear axle load of 52.3 kN (11,758 lb) and is to be used to pull a towed disk in soft soil in eighth gear. How much ballast must be added to the unballasted tractor if the slip is to be 17.5%?

P16.10  If the pull is level at a drawbar height of 520 mm (1.71 ft), calculate the critical pull at which the front wheels of the tractor described in P16.2 would just lift off the ground.

P16.11  If the pull is level at a drawbar height of 420 mm (1.38 ft), calculate the critical pull at which the front wheels of the tractor described in P16.1 would just lift off the ground.

P16.12  Rework Example Problem 16.4, but assume the tractor is working in eighth gear.

P16.13  Rework Example Problem 16.4, but assume the tractor is working in seventh gear.

P16.14  Rework Example Problem 16.4, but assume the tractor is working in sixth gear.

P16.15  Rework Example Problem 16.4, but assume the tractor is working in tenth gear.

P16.16  Reconsider Example Problem 16.5, but calculate the critical turning speed at which side tipping would begin with maximum wheel spacing.

# Appendix A

## SELECTED BIBLIOGRAPHY

Anonymous. 1988. Synthetic automotive gear lubricants. *Automotive Engineering* 96(11):49-53.

*ASAE Standards*, 39th Ed. 1992. St. Joseph, MI: ASAE.

ASTM. 1972. Single-cylinder engine tests for evaluating the performance of crankcase lubricants (abridged procedure). ASTM special publication 509. Philadelphia, PA: ASTM.

ASTM. 1981. Petroleum products and lubricants (I). Philadelphia, PA: ASTM.

ASTM. 1982. Petroleum products and lubricants (II). Philadelphia, PA: ASTM.

ASTM. 1991. Test methods for rating motor, diesel and aviation fuels. Philadelphia, PA: ASTM.

Benfaremo, N. and C. S. Liu. 1990. Crankcase engine oil additives. *Lubrication* 76(1):1-12.

Boldt, K. and B. R. Hall, 1977. *Significance of Tests for Petroleum Products*. Philadelphia, PA: ASTM.

Bosch. 1986. Automotive handbook. SAE Publication ISBN 0-89283-518-6. Warrendale, PA: SAE.

Bosch. 1988. Automotive electrical/electronic systems. SAE Publication ISBN 0-89883-509-7. Warrendale, PA: SAE.

Brady, R. N. 1981. *Diesel Fuel Systems*. Reston, VA: Reston Publishing Co.

Burchfield, G. 1991. New role for Nebraska lab. *Implement and Tractor* 106(10):1, 23.

Cummings, W. M. 1977. Fuel and lubricant additives. *Lubrication* 63(1).

Deere & Company. 1984. *Fundamentals of Service: Power Trains*. Moline, IL: John Deere Service Publications.

Deere & Company. 1984. *Fundamentals of Service: Electrical Systems*. Moline, IL: John Deere Service Publications.

Deere & Company. 1986. *Fundamentals of Service: Engines*. Moline, IL: John Deere Service Publications.

Deere & Company. 1986. *Fundamentals of Service: Tires and Tracks*. Moline, IL: John Deere Service Publications.

Deere & Company. 1992. *Fundamentals of Service: Hydraulics*. Moline, IL: John Deere Service Publications.

Deere & Company. 1992. *Fundamentals of Service: Fuels, Lubricants and Coolants*. Moline, IL: John Deere Service Publications.

Ellis, E. G. 1970. *Fundamentals of Lubrication*. Broseley, Shropshire, England: Scientific Publications.

Fein, R. S. 1971. Boundary lubrication. *Lubrication* 57:1-12.

Flynn, P. F. 1979. Turbocharging four-cycle diesel engines. In *Turbochargers and Turbocharged Engines*. SAE Publication SP-442. Warrendale, PA: SAE.

Gray, R. B. 1975. *The Agricultural Tractor, 1855-1950*. St. Joseph, MI: ASAE.

Herbstman, S. 1990. Diesel fuel additives to improve fuel quality. *Lubrication* 76(2):1-12.

Jones, F. K. and W. H. Aldred. 1980. *Farm Power and Tractors*, 5th Ed. New York: McGraw-Hill Book Company.

Kulhavy, J. T. 1964. Tractor engine cooling. ASAE Paper No. 64-637. St. Joseph, MI: ASAE.

Larsen, L. F. 1981. *The Farm Tractor, 1950-1975*. St. Joseph, MI: ASAE.

Lichty, L. C. 1967. *Combustion Engine Processes*. New York: McGraw-Hill Book Company.

Liljedahl, J. B., P. K. Turnquist, D. W. Smith and M. Hoki, 1989. *Tractors and Their Power Units*, 4th Ed. New York: Van Nostrand Reinhold.

McCormick, W. J. 1976. *Human Factors in Engineering and Design*, 4th Ed. New York: McGraw-Hill Book Company.

McKibben, E. G. 1927. The kinematics and dynamics of the wheel type farm tractor. *Agricultural Engineering* 8:15-16, 39-40, 43, 58-60, 90-93, 119-122, 155-160, 187-189.

Merritt, H. 1967. *Hydraulic Control Systems*. New York: John Wiley & Sons.

Muller, R. and S. Papageorge. 1988. Engine oil performance tests in the United States. *Lubrication* 74(1):1-28.

Obert, E. F., 1973. *Internal Combustion Engines and Air Pollution*. New York: Harper and Row.

Oliver, C. R. and H. B. Anderson. 1990. The operation and maintenance of high speed diesel engines. *Lubrication* 76(4):1-12.

Oliver, C. R., R. M. Reuter and J. C. Sendra. 1981. Fuel-efficient gasoline engine oils. *Lubrication* 67(1):1-12.

Promersberger, W. J., F. E. Bishop and D. W. Priebe. 1971. *Modern Farm Power*. Englewood Cliffs, NJ: Prentice-Hall.

Reuping, C. F. 1979. Antifreeze and coolants. *Lubrication* 65(3):25-40.

SAE. 1992. SAE Handbook. Warrendale, PA.

SAE. 1981. Synthetic automotive engine oils. SAE Publication PT-22. Warrendale, PA.

Sears, F. W. 1953. *Thermodynamics, The Kinetic Theory of Gases and Statistical Mechanics*. Reading, MA: Addison-Wesley.

Sequeira, A. 1989. Lubricant base oil processing. *Lubrication* 75(1):1-12.

Siemens, J. C. and J. A. Weber. 1958. Dry-type air cleaners on farm tractors. SAE Preprint No. 77A. Warrendale, PA: SAE.

Sporn, P. 1957. Energy requirements and the role of energy in an expanding economy. *Agricultural Engineering* 38(9):657, 677-79.

USDA. 1960. Power to produce. In *The Yearbook of Agriculture*. Washington, D.C.

Witte, A. C. 1991. Technology of modern greases. *Lubrication* 77(1):1-16.

Yahya, R. K. and C. E. Goering. 1977. Some trends in fifty-five years of Nebraska tractor test data. ASAE Paper No. MC77-1053. St. Joseph, MI: ASAE.

Zoz, F. M. 1972. Predicting tractor field performance. *Transactions of the ASAE* 15(2):249-255.

# Appendix B

## STANDARD HYDRAULIC CIRCUIT SYMBOLS

These symbols were established by a Joint Industry Conference (JIC) and first published in September 1948. They continue to be updated by the International Standards Organization. A more comprehensive set of symbols can be found in:

>ISO Standard 1219-1
>Fluid power systems and components -
>Graphic symbols and circuit diagrams -
>Part 1: Graphic symbols

>A copy of the standard may be obtained from:
>>The American National Standards Institute
>>11 West 42nd Street
>>New York, NY 10036

| LINES AND LINE FUNCTIONS | |
|---|---|
| LINE, WORKING | |
| LINE, PILOT (L>20W) | |
| LINE, DRAIN (L<5W) | |
| CONNECTOR (DOT TO BE 5X WIDTH OF LINES) | |
| LINE, FLEXIBLE | |
| LINE, JOINING | |
| LINE, PASSING | |
| DIRECTON OF FLOW | |
| LINE TO RESERVOIR ABOVE FLUID LEVEL BELOW FLUID LEVEL | |
| LINE TO VENTED MANIFOLD | |
| PLUG OR PLUGGED CONNECTION | |
| TESTING STATION (GAGE CONNECTION) | |
| POWER TAKEOFF (HYD.) | |
| RESTRICTION, FIXED | |
| RESTRICTION, VARIABLE | |

| MOTORS AND CYLINDERS | |
|---|---|
| MOTOR, ROTARY, FIXED DISPLACEMENT | MF |
| MOTOR, ROTARY, VARIABLE DISPLACEMENT | MV |
| MOTOR, OSCILLATING | MO |
| CYLINDER, SINGLE ACTING | |
| CYINDER, DOUBLE ACTING SINGLE END ROD DOUBLE END ROD | |

| MISCELLANEOUS UNITS | |
|---|---|
| ROTATING SHAFT (ARROW IN FRONT OF SHAFT) | |
| COMPONENT ENCLOSURE | |
| RESERVOIR | |
| PRESSURE GAGE | |
| OTHER * Insert appropriate letter combinations and add appropriate symbols to indicate shafts or connecting flow lines.  ACC ACCUMULATOR  ELEC MOT ELECTRIC MOTOR  ENG ENGINE  FLT FILTER  FM FLOW METER  HE HEAT EXCHANGER  INT INTENSIFIER  PS PRESSURE SWITCH  STR STRAINER  TACH TACHOMETER | |

| PUMPS | |
|---|---|
| PUMP, SINGLE, FIXED DISPLACEMENT | PF |
| PUMP, SINGLE, VARIABLE, DISPLACEMENT | PV |

# Appendix B

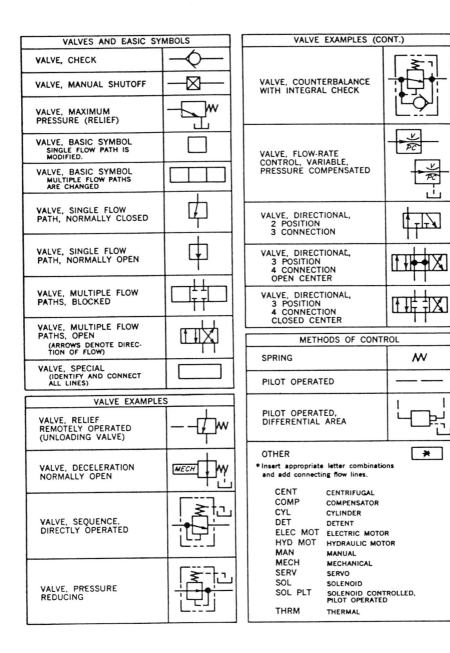

ASAE Standards, Engineering Practices and Data are informational and advisory only. Their use by anyone engaged in industry or trade is entirely voluntary. The ASAE assumes no responsibility for results attributable to the application of ASAE Standards, Engineering Practices and Data. Conformity does not ensure compliance with applicable ordinances, laws, and regulations. Prospective users are responsible for protecting themselves against liability for infringement of patents.

# Appendix C

## ASAE STANDARDS RELATING TO FARM TRACTORS AND TO POWERED LAWN AND GARDEN EQUIPMENT

### C.1 Standards Relating to Farm Tractors

**S201.4 (ANSI S201.4/SAE J716)**
Application of hydraulic remote cylinders to agricultural tractors and trailing-type agricultural implements.

**S203.11 (SAE J1170)**
Rear power take-off for agricultural tractors.

**S205.2 (SAE J722)**
Power take-off definitions and terminology for agricultural tractors.

**S207.11 (SAE J721)**
Operating requirements for tractors and power take-off driven implements.

**S209.5 (SAE J708)**
Agricultural tractor test code.

**S217.10 (ANSI/SAE J715)**
Three-point, free-link attachment for hitching implements to agricultural wheel tractors.

**S219.2 (SAE J712)**
Agricultural tractor and equipment disc wheels.

**S220.4 (SAE J711)**
Tire selection tables for agricultural machines of future design.

**S276.3 (ANSI 277.3/SAE J943)**
Slow-moving vehicle identification emblem.

**S278.6 (SAE J909)**
Attachment of implements to agricultural wheel tractors equipped with quick-attaching coupler.

**S296.3**
Uniform terminology for traction of agricultural tractors, self-propelled implements, and other traction and transport devices.

**S304.5 (ANSI 304.5/SAE J389b)**
Symbols for operator controls on agricultural equipment.

**S310.3 (SAE J167)**
Overhead protection for agricultural tractors – test procedures and performance requirements.

**S316.1**
Application of remote hydraulic motors to agricultural tractors and trailing-type agricultural implements.

**S318.10 (ANSI 318.10)**
Safety for agricultural equipment.

**S331.4 (ANSI 331.4)**
Implement power take-off driveline specifications.

**S332.2 (SAE J717)**
Agicultural tractor auxiliary power take-off drives.

**S335.4**
Operator controls on agricultural equipment.

**S338.2 (ANSI 338.2)**
Safety chain for towed equipment.

**S346.1 (SAE J884)**
Liquid ballast table for drive tires of agricultural machines.

**S349.1 (SAE J283)**
Test procedure for measuring hydraulic lift force capacity on agricultural tractors equipped with three-point hitch.

**S350 (ANSI 350)**
Safety-alert symbol for agricultural equipment.

**EP363.1**
Technical publications for agricultural equipment.

**S365.2 (SAE J1041)**
Braking system test procedures and braking performance criteria for agricultural field equipment.

**S366.1 (SAE J1036)**
Dimensions for cylindrical hydraulic couplers for agricultural tractors.

Appendix C

**S383.1 (SAE J1194)**
Roll-over protective structures (ROPS) for wheeled agricultural tractors.

**S390.1 (SAE J1150)**
Classifications and definitions of agricultural equipment.

**S430**
Agricultural equipment tire loading and inflation pressures.

**S434**
Aperture for entry of electrical wiring into agricultural tractor cabs.

**S441 (SAE J115)**
Safety signs.

**EP443**
Color coding hand controls.

**EP456**
Test and reliability guidelines.

**S489**
Hydraulic pressure available on agricultural tractors for remote use with implements.

**S493 (ANSI 493)**
Guarding for agricultural equipment.

**S495**
Uniform terminology for agricultural machinery managment.

**EP496**
Agricultural machinery management.

**D497**
Agricultural machinery management data.

**S513 (ISO 8759)**
Agricultural wheeled tractors – front-mounted linkage.

**S519 (ANSI 519/SAE J2194)**
Roll-over protective structures (ROPS) for wheeled agricultural tractors.

## C.2 Standards Relating to Powered Lawn and Garden Equipment

**S298.1 (ANSI 298.1)**
Drawbar for lawn and garden ride-on tractors.

**S320.1 (ANSI 320.1)**
Category "0" three-point, free-link attachment for hitching implements to lawn and garden ride-on tractors.

**S323.2 (ANSI 323.2)**
Definitions of powered lawn and garden equipment.

**S348.1 (ANSI 348.1)**
One-point tubular sleeve attachment for hitching implements to lawn and ride-on garden tractors.

**S370.2 (ANSI 370.2)**
2000-rpm power take-off for lawn and garden ride-on tractors.

**S377 (ANSI 377)**
Application of remote linear control devices to lawn and garden ride-on tractor attachments and implements.

**S418 (ANSI 418)**
Dimensions for cylindrical hydraulic couplers for lawn and garden tractors.

**S431**
2000 rpm front and mid pto for lawn and garden ride-on tractors.

**S440.1**
Safety for powered lawn and garden equipment.

---

These standards are published annually in the ASAE book of standards.

Note that some standards are jointly sponsored by other societies:

    ANSI  Co-sponsored by American National Standards Institute
    SAE   Co-sponsored by the Society of Automotive Engineers
    ISO   Co-sponsored by the International Standards Organization

# SUBJECT INDEX

Acceleration  22, 34, 58, 64, 145, 239, 246-247, 251, 311, 496
    definition  22
    of gravity  22, 496
Accelerator (see Carburetor)
Accessory circuit  161, 199
Accident prevention  473, 498, 502-503
Accumulator, hydraulic (see Hydraulic systems)
Additive  144, 151-152, 156-157, 325-326, 328, 331, 336-337, 342-346, 351, 356-361, 395
    antifreeze  316, 325-326, 328-329
        corrosion inhibitor  337, 343
        rust inhibitor  151, 325, 328, 337, 395
    fuel  144, 151, 150-151, 155-157, 346, 359
    hydraulic oil  336, 342-343, 346, 351, 357-361
    motor oil (see Lubricating oils)
Adiabatic process  26, 327
Aftercooler  304-308, 312
    intercooler  7, 304-305, 311, 313
Air cleaner  5, 233-234, 245, 293-297, 300, 310-311
    development of  293
    dry type  294-296, 311
    dust cup  295
    oil bath  294-295, 311
    precleaner  293-294, 311
Air cooling  304-305, 316, 321, 325
Air-fuel ratio  27, 29, 72-73, 81-82, 85, 105, 133-134, 149-150, 153, 158, 207, 210, 224, 232-233, 235-237, 241, 244-246, 250-253, 256, 262, 264, 283-284, 286-288, 296-297, 306-307, 312-313
Alcohol fuel  133-134, 155, 158
    ethanol  16, 153-155
    methanol  153
Alternator  7, 95, 98, 101, 179, 184, 188-191, 193-196, 201-202, 204
    delta-connected  191, 193-194
    diode-bridge  193-194, 221, 226
    principle of  189
    regulators (see Regulators)
    y-connected  192-194
Altitude compensator  310-312
American Petroleum Institute (API)  135-138, 147, 159, 346, 351, 356, 360, 362
American Society of Agricultural Engineers (ASAE)  3-6, 317, 402-403, 411, 461-462, 464, 466, 469, 481, 483, 487-488, 492, 499, 504

American Society for Testing Materials (ASTM)  135, 139, 144, 146, 235, 237, 341, 346, 351
Ampere  164, 177, 183
Antifreeze  316, 325-326, 328-329
    ethylene glycol  325-326, 328
API Service Classification (see Lubricating oils)
Automatic choke  237-238
Axle power (see Power)
Axle, wide front  9, 18, 503


Ballast  119, 209, 211, 214, 226, 474-475, 481-482, 486, 489, 492-494, 502-503, 505
    resistor  209, 211, 214, 226
    wheel weights  481
Battery  163-166, 169-170, 179-184, 186-189, 194-196, 198, 201-209, 214, 216, 219-220, 224-225, 248, 284
    charging  179-180, 183-184, 187, 189, 201, 203
    construction  179
    discharging  180, 184, 188, 194
    dry-charged  183, 201
    electrolyte  179-184, 201, 205
    lead-acid  179-180, 204
    maintenance-free  182, 201
    ratings  183, 201, 204-205
    specific gravity  180-181, 183, 205-206
    sulfation  182, 201, 204
Bearings  60-64, 66, 105-107, 110, 186, 258, 302, 310, 318, 333, 335-336, 352-353, 360-361, 371, 421, 425, 431, 465, 467, 482, 498
    cam  60, 63, 352
    main  60-64, 66, 258, 352, 431
    material  60, 66, 353
    rod  60-62, 64, 66, 352, 360
Bevel pinion  456-458, 471
Biased-ply tire  479, 501
Bleeding injection systems  283, 290
Block (see Cylinder)
Blowby  55, 64-65, 333
Boost  120, 151, 155, 299-301, 303, 306-314, 492
Boundary lubrication (see Lubrication)
Brakes  92, 96-98, 100-103, 110-111, 114, 120-125, 247, 252, 258, 291, 312-313, 315, 330, 365, 408, 419-425, 439-446, 456, 464-465, 467, 497
    vehicle  247, 419-424, 465
        caliper  422, 424
    in transmissions  121, 365, 419-420, 438-439, 445-446, 455-456, 464-465
Brake mean effective pressure (bmep) (see Pressure)

Brake power (see Power)
Brake thermal efficiency (see Efficiency)
Breaker points 207-210, 213-214, 216, 219-220, 225


Cab, tractor 500
Caliper (see Brakes, vehicle)
Camshaft 44-46, 51, 60, 63-65, 70-71, 77-78, 83, 85-86, 230, 275, 278, 286-287, 335
Capacitance 167
Capacitor 166-167, 203, 207, 209-210, 212, 217, 219-221, 224-227
Capacitor discharge ignition 227
Carburetor 5, 106, 127, 144, 152, 154, 211, 229, 231, 233-244, 248-253
    accelerator 151, 234, 237, 239
    accelerator pump 239
    bowl (float chamber) 233-234, 238-239, 250
    choke 235-238, 242, 250-253
    draft 234, 241, 250-251
    economizer 233, 235, 250
    idle adjustment 239, 251
    load screw 239, 241
    nozzle 234, 239, 241, 244, 250
    throttle 211, 233-234, 238-239, 241-242, 244, 249-251
    updraft 234-236, 238, 250
    Venturi 234, 238, 242, 249-252
Category, hitch (see Hitch)
Center of gravity 107, 473-476, 493, 495-497, 502, 504
Centrifugal advance 211-212, 216, 224-226
Cetane rating (Cetane number) 147, 149-151, 153, 156-157, 259, 286
Circuit, electrical 165, 177, 199-201, 205, 370
Clearance 8, 27-28, 30, 32, 35, 37, 47, 50, 55-56, 63-66, 260, 262, 268-269, 292, 357, 461, 501
    of rings 56, 64-65
    of valves 28, 47, 49-50, 63-64, 268-269
    volume 27, 30, 32, 35, 37, 66, 260, 262, 292
Closed-center (see Hydraulic systems)
Clutch 3, 120, 198, 319, 329, 408, 419-425, 430, 435, 437-446, 455, 459, 462-469, 499
    dry 420-421, 424, 465, 469
    free-travel 425, 465
    function of 446
    overcentering 420-421, 465
    pilot bearing 421
    pressure plate 421, 423-424
    release bearing 421, 425, 465, 467
        throw-out bearing 421

Clutch (continued)
    single-disk 421, 469
    spring-loaded 420-422, 465, 467
    wet 420, 424-425, 465
Coil 176-177, 184-188, 190-192, 194-198, 204, 207-209, 213-221, 223-226, 238
Compression ratio 27-28, 30-32, 34-35, 37-38, 66-67, 95, 98, 100, 120, 145-148, 150, 256, 258, 291-292
Conductor, electrical 161-164, 175-178, 177, 200-202, 204
Connecting rod 52-53, 57-58, 60-65, 78-79, 97, 259-260, 352, 360
CVT (see Transmission, CVT)
Coolants 40, 110, 200, 241, 246, 305-307, 313, 315, 320-321, 324-326, 328-331, 355, 361
Corrosion inhibitor (see Additives, antifreeze)
Cracking pressure 128, 379
Crankshaft 41, 46, 50-53, 57-66, 69-71, 73-79, 82-83, 85-87, 95, 97, 103, 110, 209, 211, 228, 245, 259, 263, 266, 278, 283, 291, 318-319, 334-335, 352
    balance 57, 64
    counterweights 57, 64-65
    types of 65, 85, 110
Crawler tractor 7-8, 484-486
    belted type 7-8, 479
    steel track 7
Critical speed (see Speed)
Crude oil (see Fuel)
Current, electrical 162, 164, 167, 171, 180, 185, 187, 202, 207, 210, 220
Current regulator 184, 186-188, 204
Cutout relay 186, 188, 194, 204
Cycles 4, 18, 28-38, 69, 71-73, 75, 77, 79-81, 83, 85, 87, 94-95, 97, 103, 121, 190, 193, 207, 210-211, 214, 218-219, 221, 256, 258, 267, 269-271, 277, 281-283, 286, 317, 391
    diesel 31-38, 69, 77, 83-85, 97, 256, 258, 269, 276, 283
    dual 32-35
    four-stroke 4, 18
    Otto 28-37, 97
    two-stroke 4, 69, 80-85
Cylinder 4, 27-30, 32, 37, 39-44, 51-53, 55, 57-58, 62-64, 66, 74-75, 77-79, 83-86, 95, 97, 111, 131, 139-140, 143, 145, 147, 207, 212, 214, 216, 223, 227, 240, 244-246, 248, 250, 252, 256, 260, 264-266, 269, 275, 283, 286, 291-293, 295, 297-298, 315-317, 321, 328-329, 352, 360, 363, 371-372, 382-388, 391, 397, 401, 404, 408-410, 412-417, 422-423, 437
    block 39, 384
    deglazer 41

Subject Index 523

Cylinder (continued)
    head  27, 42-43, 63-64, 223, 316
    hydraulic (see Hydraulic systems – cylinders)
    liners (see Liners, cylinder)
    numbering  79


Delivery valve  266-269, 271, 283, 287, 289
Density  25, 34, 36-37, 93-94, 103-104, 124-125, 135, 152, 155, 240, 247, 294, 300, 303, 306, 310-311, 317, 339, 363
Depth (position) control  365, 382, 404, 406-407
Detergent-dispersant (see Lubricating oils – additives)
Diesel cycle (see Cycles)
Diesel engine  4, 7, 15-17, 21, 26-27, 31-38, 74, 78, 80, 82-87, 94, 97, 99, 105-106, 133, 141, 148, 150, 153-157, 183, 204, 229, 255-259, 261, 263-265, 267, 269, 271, 273, 275-281, 283-291, 297-299, 303, 306, 308-313, 315, 327, 343, 346, 353, 361, 363
Diesel fuel  1, 16-17, 27, 31-32, 74, 86, 94, 124, 127, 129, 133, 135, 137, 141-144, 147, 149-151, 153-159, 255, 264-265, 268, 277, 281, 285, 290-292, 298, 330
Differential lock  408, 459-460, 466, 468, 472
Diodes (see Semiconductors)
Dipstick  354-355
Directional control valve (see Valves, hydraulic)
Displacement  22, 27-28, 30, 32, 35, 37, 66, 95-97, 103, 120, 248, 250-251, 262, 291-292, 306, 366, 368-375, 378-379, 381-382, 388-389, 396, 401, 410-412, 414-415, 447-450, 452, 466, 468, 471
    engine  22, 28, 30, 32, 37, 95-96, 103, 120, 248, 250, 291-292
    of hydraulic motors  388-389, 415, 447-450, 452, 468, 471
    of hydraulic pumps  369-375, 378, 381-382, 396, 401, 410-412, 414, 447-450, 452, 466, 468, 471
Distillation of fuels  138-139, 235
    temperature of vaporization  127-129
Distributor, ignition  207, 212, 214, 225
Draft (load) control  89, 107, 114, 119-120, 200, 404, 406-407
Draft of carburetors (see Carburetor)
Drawbar power (see Power – linear)
Drawbar pull (see Pull)
Dry-charged battery  183
Dual cycle (see Cycles)
Dual tires  482, 501
Dwell  210, 227
Dynamic traction ratio (see Traction – ratio, dynamic)
Dynamic weight coefficient  487, 489
Dynamometer  107, 109-113, 121, 123-125

Dynamometer (continued)
    eddy current 110-111
    electric 110-111, 121
    elements of 109, 121, 123
    portable 109-111, 113, 121, 123
    prony brake 110

Efficiency 7, 16-17, 21, 28-38, 89, 91, 93-95, 97, 99-105, 107, 109, 111, 113-115, 117, 119-125, 136, 138, 153, 240, 258, 262, 288, 291, 295, 297-304, 306-308, 310-311, 313-315, 319, 328, 375-379, 388-389, 397, 412, 414, 416, 427-429, 438, 446, 448, 452, 454-455, 457-458, 470-473, 485-487, 489, 491-492, 501, 503-505
    brake thermal 100-101, 103, 120-121, 123-124, 258, 291
    diesel cycle 32-36, 258
    dual cycle 32-35
    engine volumetric 103-105, 121-123, 125, 240, 295, 297-298, 300, 303-304, 306-308, 311, 313, 388
    hydraulic power 376-377, 389
    hydraulic volumetric (see Volumetric efficiency – of hydraulic motors)
    indicated thermal 99-101, 120, 122-124
    mechanical 100-102, 114, 121-124
    Otto cycle 30, 32, 34-35
    torque 376-378, 389, 412, 414, 448, 452, 454-455
    transmission 429, 438, 446, 454-455, 471
Electrical definitions and units 164
Electrolyte (see Battery)
Electromagnetism 161, 175, 201
Electronic ignition (see Ignition)
Electronic fuel injection (see Fuel injection)
Emissions 128, 131, 133, 143, 151, 153-155, 248, 250, 261, 283, 287
Energy 1, 14-15, 19, 23-24, 27, 29-32, 34-36, 57, 59, 69, 73-74, 82, 85, 89-90, 93-94, 99-101, 121, 127, 135, 145, 148-149, 152, 155, 162, 179, 196, 201-202, 207, 210, 219-220, 224-225, 233-234, 250, 262, 293, 299-300, 308-309, 315, 330, 369, 385, 389, 401, 411-412, 422, 446, 499
Engine balancers 65
Ethanol (see Alcohol fuel)
Ether 151, 285, 288, 323
Ethylene glycol (see Antifreeze)
Exhaust gas dilution 72, 232
Exhaust manifold (see Manifold)
Exhaust valve (see Valves, engine – exhaust)

Fan, cooling 316, 318-319, 325
Feeler gage 212, 224

Subject Index

Filters 144, 155, 229, 231, 245, 249-250, 264, 278, 283, 286, 295-296, 311, 352-355, 358, 360, 362, 390-391, 409-410, 413
  air 283, 295
  fuel 144, 155, 229, 231, 249, 264
  hydraulic oil 390-391, 409
  oil 353, 355, 358, 390-391
Final drive 120, 428-429, 459-462, 464-466, 468, 470
Firing interval 74-76, 78-80, 84-87
Firing order 57, 76-78, 80, 84-88
Fixed displacement 370-372, 396, 401, 410-412, 414, 447, 449-450, 468, 471
Fixed oils (see Lubricating oils)
Flash point of fuels 138, 141, 154, 156
Flux, magnetic (see Magnetic)
Flywheel 57, 59, 64, 74-75, 80, 92, 96, 100, 198, 202, 212, 216, 218-222, 225, 316, 420-421, 424
Flywheel power (see Power)
Force 22-23, 34, 49, 53, 67, 90-91, 105-108, 122-124, 164, 173-178, 184-185, 189-190, 197, 201-202, 204, 231, 235, 239, 270, 277, 298-299, 333-338, 360, 363, 366-367, 371, 386, 389, 404, 414, 422-424, 467, 469, 473-476, 484, 489, 491, 493
Forward bias 169-172, 193-194, 203, 479, 501
Four-stroke cycle 4, 18
Four-port valves (see Valves, hydraulic)
Free-travel (see Clutch)
Friction (see Lubrication – and friction)
Friction Power (see Power)
Four wheel drive 7, 9, 460, 468, 478, 485, 504
Fuel 1, 4, 7, 12-17, 23, 26-27, 29, 31-32, 34, 36-38, 69, 73-74, 78, 81-82, 84-86, 89, 92-95, 98-103, 105-107, 114, 118-122, 124, 127, 129, 131-145, 147-160, 207, 210, 224, 229-253, 255-256, 258-292, 296-298, 306-313, 315, 322, 327, 330, 335, 359, 500
  additives (see Additives)
  combustion of 13, 17, 27, 73-74, 85, 100-101, 127, 131-137, 139, 141-143, 145, 147-150, 153, 155, 157-159, 224, 232, 235, 242, 245-246, 256, 262, 268-269, 273, 277, 280, 282, 284-288, 327
  crude oil 127, 129, 143, 153, 156, 335
  cutoff ratio 32, 34, 38
  equivalent power (see Power – fuel equivalent)
  impurities 143
  molecular structure of petroleum 129, 335
  petroleum 14-15, 17, 143, 151-154, 248-249, 255
  properties 134, 154-155
  pump (see Pumps)
  refining 127, 143, 156-157, 335
  tank 23, 229-231, 242-243, 249, 251, 264, 277-278, 282, 286-287, 500

Fuel injection  32, 34, 84, 86, 144, 147, 229, 231, 244-245, 248, 250-251, 258, 263, 265-266, 268-269, 278-280, 283, 286-287, 289-290, 292, 308
    electronic  229, 231, 244-245, 248, 250, 278-280, 283, 287, 290
    for diesel engines  32, 34, 74, 84, 86, 141, 148, 255, 258-259, 263-265, 267, 271, 276, 278-280, 283, 286-287, 290-291
    for spark-ignition engines  244, 290
    nozzles  144, 245, 265
    pumps  231, 269, 289

Gas constant  25
Gasoline  5, 15, 21, 31-32, 35, 82, 97, 105-106, 127, 129, 131-134, 138, 140-141, 143-144, 146, 151-157, 159, 216, 229, 232, 236-237, 252-253, 256, 258-259, 264, 286, 288-289, 291, 296-298, 312, 335, 343, 346
Gear oil (see Lubricating oils – for gears)
Gears  3, 46, 51, 63, 102, 113, 115-120, 198, 202, 214, 225, 266, 275-276, 283-284, 287-288, 352, 356-357, 359-360, 370-371, 378-379, 395, 414, 420, 425-431, 433-446, 455-459, 465, 467-471, 489, 493-495, 497-498, 502, 505
    planetary  427-428, 439-440, 442-443, 459, 469, 471
        Sun  427-428, 439-445, 459, 469
    shifting  117, 356, 425, 434-437, 446, 455, 494
    speed ratio of  426, 430, 439-440, 442-443, 445, 469-470
    synchronized  435-436, 465
Generator  110, 164, 178-179, 184-189, 194-195, 201-202, 204, 206, 420
    armature  186, 204
    brushes  201
    commutator  185-186, 201, 204
    field  186-189, 204, 206
    principle of  184
    regulators (see Regulators – for generators)
    shunt  186, 189
Glow plugs  285, 288
Governors  5, 16, 89, 105-108, 113-116, 119-121, 123, 125, 232, 234, 252, 266, 270, 275-278, 308-309, 428, 430, 447, 453, 465
    development of  278
    droop  107
    function of  105, 430
    high idle setting  89, 121, 308
    maximum  89, 107-108, 113-115, 119-121, 123, 125, 232, 278, 308-309, 430, 447, 465
    regulation  89, 107-108, 121, 125
Grease  336-337, 360-361
    definition  336
    fitting  336-337

Subject Index 527

Grease (continued)
    gun 336-337, 360
    multipurpose 337


Head (see Cylinder)
Heating value of fuel 92-93, 103, 120, 124, 135-137, 156, 330
History of farm tractor 2, 17
Hitch 6-7, 17, 120, 200, 402-404, 406-411, 413, 487, 489, 493, 495, 502
    category of 402, 404, 411
    point 7, 404, 495, 502
    three-point 6-7, 17, 120, 200, 402-406, 408-411, 413, 487, 495
Hydraulic systems 7, 365-367, 369-371, 373, 375, 377, 379, 381, 383, 385, 387, 389, 391-393, 395-399, 401, 403, 405, 407, 409-411, 413, 415, 417, 500
    accumulators 389-390, 401-402, 410, 412-413, 416, 446
    classification 447
    closed-center 383, 399, 410
    cylinders 111, 372, 383-387, 391, 401, 408, 410, 413-414, 416-417, 422, 437
    fluids 392-393, 395
    lines 383, 391-392, 422
    maintenance and trouble shooting 357, 408-409
    motors 357, 365, 395, 399, 401, 410, 412, 415-416
    open-center 383-384, 396-399, 410, 413, 416
    pressure-compensated 372, 398-399, 410, 413
    pressure-flow-compensated 399-400, 410, 413
    principles 365-366, 369, 392, 411
    pumps 370, 376-377, 379, 390-391, 395, 410, 447
    symbols (see JIC symbols)
    valves (see Valves, hydraulic – systems)
Hydraulic valve lifters 50-51
Hydrodynamic lubrication (see Lubrication)
Hydrokinetic transmission (see Transmission)
Hydrostatic transmission (see Transmission)


Ideal gas law 24-26, 34, 389
Idle adjustment (see Carburetor)
Ignition 4-5, 73-74, 84-86, 145-146, 148-151, 156, 161, 166-167, 183, 207-227, 247, 256, 259, 262-263, 286, 288
    delay 74, 86, 145-146, 148-150, 259, 263
    electronic 85, 207, 213-217, 225-226
    pulse amplifier 214-215, 225
    spark 73, 85-86, 207, 209, 211-212, 216-217, 219-225, 227
    switch 209, 247

Ignition (continued)
    systems  5, 84–85, 166-167, 207-210, 212-227
    timing (see Timing)
Indicated mean effective pressure (see Pressure)
Indicated thermal efficiency (see Efficiency)
Indirect injection  259, 286
Injection, fuel (see Fuel injection)
Insulator, electrical  163, 202
Intake manifold (see Manifold)
Intake valves (see Valves, engine)
Intercooler (see Aftercooler)
Isothermal process  25


Jerk pump  265, 275
JIC symbols  369-370, 383-384, 389, 391, 411
Journal, crankshaft  60, 335


Kettering ignition system  207, 209-210, 212-213, 224, 226-227
Kinematic viscosity (see Viscosity)
Knock  30, 32, 127, 144-151, 157, 315


Lanchester balancer  59, 65
Lead-acid battery (see Battery)
Lifters, valve (see Valves, engine)
Liners, cylinder  42-44, 53, 57, 63-64, 66, 140, 143, 321, 328-329, 363
    dry  40, 63-64
    enbloc  39-40
    sleeves  40-41
    wet  63-64
Liquid cooling  142, 249
LP gas  15, 152, 154, 248-249, 251-252
Lubricating oils  41, 43, 47, 63, 82, 140, 321, 333, 335-336, 341-349, 351, 353, 355, 357, 361, 363
    additives  41, 43, 47, 63, 82, 140, 321, 333, 335-336, 339, 341-349, 351, 353, 355, 357-359, 361, 363
        detergent-dispersant  343, 360
        motor oil  343, 351
            oxidation inhibitor  343, 358
    fixed  335-336
    for gears  63, 357, 395
    low friction  337, 358, 362
    mineral  335-336, 343, 359-361

Lubricating oils (continued)
    service classification 346-351, 360-362
        API 346, 351, 360, 362
        synthetic 358-360, 362
            motor oil 358-359
    viscosity of (see Viscosity)
Lubrication 5, 47, 63-64, 82, 87, 141, 264, 273, 287, 326, 333, 335-338, 340, 342, 346, 352-356, 359-363, 371, 395, 408
    and friction 64, 333, 337, 359-360, 363
    boundary 335-337, 359-361, 395
    hydrodynamic 335-338, 359-361, 363
    mixed-film 335
    system 342, 352-355, 362


Magnetic 172-178, 184-186, 189-190, 194, 196-198, 200-204, 208-210, 214-216, 218-221, 224-225
    field 173-178, 184, 186, 189-190, 196-198, 201-204, 208-210, 214-216, 218-220, 224-225
    flux 177, 185, 190, 194, 201, 218, 221
    lines of force 173-178, 184-185, 189-190, 204
    poles 173-177, 186, 190, 194, 197-198, 214, 218
    reluctance 177, 190, 201, 214
Magnetism 172-174
Magneto 208, 216, 218-220, 225-227
Main Bearing (see Bearings)
Maintenance-free battery (see Battery)
Major thrust face (see Piston)
Manifold 42, 72, 211, 225, 233-236, 238, 240-241, 244-246, 249-250, 252-253, 276-277, 285, 287-288, 296-298, 300-305, 309-313
    exhaust 42, 72, 238, 240-241, 297-298, 300, 309, 311-312
    hot spot 241
    intake 42, 72, 211, 225, 233-236, 238, 240-241, 244-246, 249-250, 252-253, 285, 288, 296-298, 300-305, 310-313
    tuned 297, 312
Manual-shift transmission (see Transmission)
Mechanical efficiency (see Efficiency)
Methanol (see Alcohol fuel)
Mineral oils (see Lubricating oils)
Minor thrust face (see Piston)
Motor 19, 79, 83, 146, 167, 176, 179, 186, 196, 198, 201-202, 211, 213-215, 217, 231, 235, 276-277, 337, 340, 342-351, 355-360, 362-363, 365, 385, 388-389, 395, 399, 402, 410, 412, 415-416, 432-433, 447-450, 452, 466, 468, 471
    electric starter 196, 198

Motor (continued)
    hydraulic (see Hydraulic systems)
    starter  196, 198
Mufflers  298-299, 311-312
Mutual induction  208, 224


Naturally aspirated engine  48, 103, 105, 300, 305, 308, 310, 312-313
Nebraska tractor tests  6, 17, 115-119, 122-123, 473, 483, 489-491, 496-497,
    501, 505
Needle lift  245, 273, 275, 283
Nondetergent oil  343
Nozzles, diesel injection  74, 144, 264-265, 280, 288, 290-291
    pintle  287


Octane rating of fuel  144, 146, 149, 151-152, 155, 157
Ohm's law  164, 177, 195, 198, 201, 208
Oil (see Lubricating oils)
Oiliness  336, 360-361
Open-center hydraulic systems (see Hydraulic systems)
Organization of Economic and Community Development (OECD)  6, 113-118,
    122-123, 137-138, 159, 473, 483, 489, 496, 501, 505
Otto cycle (see Cycles)
Overcentering clutch (see Clutch)
Overlap, valve (see Valves, engine)
Oxidation inhibitor (see Additives, motor oil)
Oxygen sensor  224


Petroleum (see Fuel)
Pickup coil  214-215, 220, 225
Pilot bearing (see Clutch)
Pilot-operated valve (see Valves, hydraulic)
Pintle nozzle (see Nozzles, diesel injection)
Piston  27-29, 32, 39-40, 42, 52-53, 55-60, 62-65, 69, 71, 73-77, 80-82, 84-86,
        94-95, 103, 121, 131, 146, 150, 222-223, 233, 238, 242-243, 245, 256,
        262, 268, 272, 277, 289, 300, 333-335, 337, 352-353, 357, 360, 363,
        366-374, 379, 385-387, 398-400, 410-411, 414-415
    cam ground  55
    groove insert  55, 65
    major thrust face  53, 63, 65
    minor thrust face  53, 63
    pin  52-53, 55, 60, 63, 65, 272, 352, 360
    rings  52-53, 55, 57, 63-65, 333-335, 337, 352, 357, 360

Piston (continued)
    skirt taper 53, 65
    slap 63
    thrust faces of 53, 63, 65
Planetary gears (see Gears)
Polytropic process 25-26
Pop tester for injection nozzles 274, 290
Positive displacement 366, 369-370, 372, 411
Pour point 142-143, 151, 155, 157, 335, 346, 395
    of diesel fuel 143, 151
    of motor oils 346
Power 1-4, 6-8, 10, 12, 14-20, 22-24, 26, 28, 30, 32, 34, 36, 38, 40, 42, 44, 46, 48, 50-54, 56-60, 62, 64, 66, 68, 70-76, 78-126, 128, 130-134, 136, 138, 140, 142, 144, 146, 148, 150, 152, 154, 156, 158, 160, 162, 164, 166-168, 170, 172, 174, 176, 178, 180, 182, 184, 186, 188, 190, 192, 194, 196, 198, 200, 202, 204-206, 208, 210, 212, 214, 216, 218-220, 222, 224, 226, 228, 230, 232, 234, 236, 238, 240, 242, 244, 246-248, 250, 252-254, 256, 258, 260, 262, 264, 266, 268, 270, 272, 274, 276, 278, 280, 282-284, 286-288, 290-294, 296, 298-300, 302, 304-308, 310-316, 318-320, 322, 324, 326, 328, 330, 332-334, 336, 338, 340, 342, 344, 346, 348, 350, 352, 354, 356, 358, 360, 362-366, 368, 370-374, 376-380, 382, 384, 386, 388-392, 394-396, 398-404, 406, 408, 410, 412, 414-416, 418-474, 476, 478, 480, 482, 484-486, 488-494, 496, 498-502, 504-506
    axle 454, 457-459, 462, 468, 471-472, 485, 489, 493, 501, 504-505
    brake 92, 95-96, 98, 100, 102, 110, 114, 120-122, 124-125, 252, 258, 291, 312-313, 315, 330, 365, 419, 421, 423, 464, 467
    definition of 95-96
        Watts 167
    electrical 167, 198, 205, 247
    flywheel 64, 92, 100
    friction 95-96, 98, 101-102, 120-121, 124, 330, 363, 423
    fuel equivalent 92-94, 99-100, 102, 120, 122, 124
    hydraulic 96, 370, 376-378, 395-396, 401, 410, 437, 499
    indicated 94-97, 99-100, 102, 120, 122, 124, 330
    linear (drawbar) 16-17, 91, 96, 102-103, 115, 118, 120, 124, 403, 449-450, 473, 485, 489, 491-492, 494, 501-502, 505
    pto 6-7, 92, 96, 100, 102-103, 111, 114-115, 120, 122, 125, 408, 461-467, 469, 498
Power takeoff 6-7, 92, 96, 100, 102-103, 111, 114-115, 120, 122, 125, 408, 461-467, 469, 498
Power train 114, 360, 395, 419, 421, 423, 425, 427, 429, 431, 433, 435, 437-439, 441, 443, 445, 447, 449, 451, 453, 455, 457, 459, 461, 463-465, 467, 469-471
Power-shift transmission (see Transmission)

Precombustion chamber  260, 262, 285
Pressure
    absolute  24-25, 34, 37, 301, 390
    barometric  24-25, 36, 104, 114, 125, 303, 306, 313
    brake mean effective (bmep)  97-99, 121-122, 124, 312
    definition of  23
    friction mean effective  98, 121
    gage  24, 37, 111, 138, 274, 355, 376
    indicated mean effective  94-95, 97, 121, 298-299
Pressure-compensated (see Hydraulic systems)
Pressure plate (see Clutch)
Primary circuit  208
Primary current  208, 211, 213-214, 216, 218-220, 225
Prony brake (see Dynamometer)
PT injection system  276, 287, 290-291
Pull, drawbar  124, 476-478, 484, 486-487, 489, 491-492, 494-495, 501, 504-505
Pulse transformer  220
Pumps  78, 81-82, 95-96, 98, 101, 105-106, 111, 138, 141, 146, 229-231, 233, 239, 242-243, 245, 247-248, 250-251, 255, 264-278, 281, 283-284, 286-289, 299, 302, 304-305, 308-310, 316-320, 324, 328-329, 336, 343, 352-353, 355, 360, 369-384, 386, 388-392, 395-402, 409-416, 420, 446-450, 452, 466, 468, 471
    accelerator (see Carburetor)
    diesel injection  288
    fuel  105, 138, 141, 229-231, 233, 242-243, 247-248, 250-251, 264, 266-267, 269-270, 273-274, 277-278, 281, 286-287
    fuel transfer  230, 242, 251, 286
    hydraulic (see Hydraulic systems – pumps)
    oil  95-96, 98, 101, 302, 310, 343, 352-353, 355, 360, 384, 398, 410, 412, 415
    water  111, 304-305, 316-320, 324, 328-329, 355
Push rod (see Valves, engine)


Rack  266, 275-276, 287, 493
Radial piston pump  372, 374
Radial-ply tires  479, 481, 501
Radiator  241, 305, 316-330, 355, 361, 392
Rectifier  193-194, 217, 220
Refinery (see Fuel – refining)
Regulation (see Governors)
Regulators  184, 186-188, 194-196, 202, 204, 206, 245, 249, 251, 270, 276, 360
    for alternators  184, 194-196, 202, 204
    for generators  184, 186-188, 194-195, 202, 204, 206
    voltage  184, 186-188, 195, 206

Subject Index

Relief valve (see Valves, hydraulic)
Reluctance (see Magnetic)
Reservoir 243, 266, 269, 274, 286, 316, 336, 357, 360, 373, 379-384, 386, 388, 390-392, 395-397, 401, 409-410, 413, 415
Resistance, electrical 162, 177, 201
Resistors 110, 164-166, 170, 187-188, 193-195, 202-203, 209, 211, 214, 216, 226
Reverse bias 169-172, 193-194, 201, 203
Reverse idler 435, 438
Right-hand rule 177-178, 184-185, 189
Ring, piston 55, 333-334, 337, 352
    clearance 27-28, 32, 56, 65
    compression 27-29, 32, 55, 69, 77, 81, 86, 262, 277
    oil control 55, 352
Ring gear 198, 202, 427-428, 438-443, 445, 456, 458-459, 469, 471
    in planetary 427, 442
    starter 202
Rocker arms (see Valves, engine)
Rod bearings (see Bearings)
RollOver Protective Structure (ROPS) 7, 113, 498-500, 503
Rotators, valve (see Valves, engine)
Row-crop tractor 6-11, 14, 18
Rubber tires 478-479
Rust inhibitor (see Additives, antifreeze)


SAE number (see Viscosity)
Safety 141, 183, 201, 247, 387, 446, 473, 475, 477, 479, 481, 483, 485, 487, 489, 491, 493, 495, 497-503, 505
Saybolt universal seconds 339
    (SUS) (see Viscosity, units of)
Secondary circuit 208, 220
Secondary voltage (see Voltage)
Sediment bulb 231
Self-ignition temperature (SIT) (see Temperature)
Semiconductors 163, 167-168, 200-201, 203, 207, 216, 224
    definition of 163
    diodes 168
    holes 168, 203
    N-type 168, 201, 203
    P-type 168, 201, 203
    transistors 171-172, 195-196, 201, 203, 212-216, 225, 231
Series circuit 165
Shields, pto 464
Single-acting cylinder 385, 404, 412
Single-disk clutch (see Clutch)

Skirt taper (see Piston)
Slap (see Piston)
Sleeve metering  266, 269, 286
Sleeves (see Liners, cylinder)
Slippage of wheels (see Travel reduction)
Smoke, diesel  141, 284-285, 288
Society of Automotive Engineers (SAE)  54, 56, 135, 142-144, 148, 150, 155, 183, 207, 237, 285, 302, 337, 340-343, 346, 351, 356-363, 394
Solenoid, starter  198, 202
Spark advance (see Timing)
Spark arrester  298
Spark ignition (see Ignition)
Spark plug  29, 73, 78, 82, 84-85, 145, 147, 207-210, 212, 216, 218-227
    function  219, 226
    gap  210, 216, 222, 224-225, 227
    heat range  223, 225, 227
    reach  223-224
    sizes  223, 227
Specific fuel consumption  102-103, 121, 252, 287
Specific gravity  120, 135-137, 159, 180-184, 205-206, 325, 331
    of battery electrolyte  180-181, 183-184, 205-206
    of fuels  120, 135-137, 159
Speed  6, 15-17, 22, 34, 57, 59, 70-71, 73-74, 83-86, 91-92, 95, 98, 102-103, 105, 107-110, 114-116, 118-121, 123, 125, 145-146, 178, 190-191, 194-195, 200, 206, 209, 211-212, 224-227, 232, 238-239, 241, 245-247, 251-253, 256, 258, 262-263, 265, 270, 272, 278-279, 283, 286, 288, 291, 301, 306, 308-310, 312, 315, 330, 335, 338, 340, 357, 367-369, 375, 377-378, 386-388, 397, 399, 411-412, 414-415, 424-431, 433-450, 452-459, 461, 465-466, 468-472, 483-484, 489-497, 501-505
    critical  495-497, 503, 505
        overturning  495, 497
    definition of 22
    engine  17, 71, 73-74, 92, 95, 98, 102-103, 105, 107-108, 110, 114-116, 119, 121, 125, 200, 211, 224-225, 232, 239, 245-247, 253, 256, 262-263, 265, 272, 283, 286, 308, 312, 357, 429-430, 440-441, 443, 468, 484
    flame  73-74, 145
    of axles  200, 429, 457-459, 470, 484, 489, 504
    of gears  102, 116, 119, 425-430, 434-438, 440-443, 445-446, 456, 458, 465, 468-470, 489, 493, 505
    of hydraulic cylinders  256, 265, 386-388, 412
    of hydraulic motors  388, 399
    of hydraulic pumps  368-369, 377, 388, 411-412, 414, 448
    of power takeoffs  92, 114, 461, 466, 469
    of tractors  6, 15-17, 105, 116, 118-119, 121, 252, 262, 431, 461, 466, 468-469, 472, 483-484, 489-491, 493-495, 497, 502-504

Subject Index

Speed (continued)
    of turbochargers 308-310, 312
    ratio of differentials 429, 458
    ratio of transmissions 16, 429-430, 438, 445-447, 469-470
Spill port, in injector pumps 275
Stability of tractors 494, 502
Starter motor (see Motor)
Steam tractor 5, 18
Steering, articulated 11, 13
Stoichiometric mixture 247, 256
Sun gear (see Gears, planetary)
Supercharging 299, 311
Swirl ratio 262-264, 286
Synchronizer (see Transmission, synchromesh)
Synthetic motor oil (see Lubricating oils)


Tandem-center valve (see Valves, hydraulic)
Tappets (see Valves, engine)
Temperature
    absolute 22, 24-25, 27, 34, 302, 304, 307
    cloud point 143
    control in engines 316, 321, 323
    flash point 141
    in intake manifolds 236, 253, 302-304, 313
    of vaporization (see Distillation of fuels)
    pour point 143, 346, 395
    self-ignition (SIT) 27, 82, 145, 284
    units 21-22, 25, 135
Thermodynamics 21, 23, 25, 27, 29-31, 33, 35, 37
Thermosiphon cooling 316, 318
Thermostat 316, 323-324, 327-328
Three-point hitch (see Hitch)
Throttle (see Carburetor)
Throw-out bearing (see Clutch, release bearing)
Timing 44, 46, 50-51, 63, 65, 69-75, 77, 79, 81-87, 105, 121, 211-212, 216, 219-220, 224-226, 264, 266-267, 272, 278-284, 287-288, 290
    gears 46, 51, 63, 266, 283-284, 288
    ignition 72-73, 86, 211-212, 216, 219, 224-226
    injection 74, 264, 267, 272, 278, 282-283, 287
    spark advance 73-74, 86, 225
    valve 44, 50-51, 70-72, 83, 85, 87, 105, 121
Timing light 212, 225
Tires 6, 18, 24, 36-37, 473, 478-484, 487, 493, 497, 501, 503

Torque 43, 52, 60-61, 63, 74, 89-90, 92, 96, 98-99, 105, 107-111, 114-115, 120-125, 198, 233, 238, 273, 286, 340, 375-378, 388-389, 412, 414, 416, 420-425, 429-430, 448-450, 452-455, 457-459, 465-466, 469-474, 494-495, 502
   and bmep 98-99, 121-122
   and work 90, 92, 107, 122, 124
   capacity of clutch 423-425, 465
   definition 89, 120
   efficiency (see Efficiency)
   from hydraulic motors 412, 448
   input to pumps 471
   reserve 89, 108, 114, 120, 125, 273, 469
Traction 3, 5, 7, 11, 16-17, 120, 419-420, 430, 435, 437, 446, 458-459, 463, 465-466, 471, 473, 475, 477-479, 481-487, 489, 491-495, 497, 499, 501-505
   and ballast 481-482, 492-493
   basic concepts 478-484
   predictor chart 487, 501
   ratio, dynamic 484-486, 492, 501, 503-505
Tractive efficiency 473, 485-487, 489, 491-492, 501, 503-505
Tractor 1-2, 4-24, 26, 28, 30, 32, 34, 36-42, 44-46, 48, 50-52, 54-56, 58, 60-62, 64-66, 68, 70, 72, 74, 76, 78, 80, 82, 84, 86, 88-92, 94, 96, 98, 100, 102, 104-108, 110-126, 128, 130, 132-134, 136, 138, 140, 142, 144, 146, 148, 150, 152-156, 158, 160, 162, 164, 166, 168, 170, 172, 174, 176, 178, 180, 182-184, 186, 188-190, 192, 194, 196, 198-200, 202, 204-206, 208-212, 214, 216, 218, 220, 222, 224, 226, 228-230, 232, 234, 236-240, 242, 244, 246, 248-252, 254-256, 258, 260, 262, 264, 266, 268, 270, 272-274, 276, 278, 280, 282, 284, 286, 288, 290, 292-294, 296, 298, 300, 302, 304, 306, 308-312, 314, 316-318, 320, 322, 324, 326, 328, 330-334, 336, 338, 340, 342, 344, 346, 348, 350, 352, 354, 356-358, 360, 362, 364-366, 368-370, 372, 374, 376, 378-380, 382, 384, 386, 388, 390, 392-396, 398-404, 406-414, 416-420, 422, 424, 426, 428-434, 436-438, 440, 442, 444, 446-450, 452, 454-456, 458-466, 468-480, 482-506
   definition 7
   types 7, 39, 55, 64, 69, 111, 127, 133, 135, 171, 195, 203, 229, 231, 241, 250-252, 259, 266, 273, 286-287, 289, 298, 304, 312, 325, 335, 358, 360-361, 370, 381, 385, 392, 394-396, 419-421, 428, 430, 436-437, 447, 449-450, 462, 465-467, 469, 479-482, 486
Transistors (see Semiconductors)
Transmission 5, 7, 16, 120-121, 333, 356-357, 361, 365, 395, 408, 419-420, 425, 428-456, 462-471, 494
   CVT 447, 465
   hydrokinetic 430, 452-455, 466, 468
   hydrostatic 7, 16, 430, 447-452, 465-466, 468, 471
   manual shift 356-357, 430-433, 435, 437, 446, 450-452, 454, 465-468

Transmission (continued)
    power-shift 419, 430, 437-440, 445-446, 450, 465, 467-468
    synchromesh 419, 430, 435, 437, 465, 467-468
        synchronizer 436-437, 465, 467
    theory of 428, 447
Travel reduction 483-487, 489, 492, 494, 501-505
    and efficiency 485-487, 489, 492, 501, 503-505
    and pull 484-486, 489, 492, 501-502, 505
    definition of 483
    desired amount of 492, 502
    slippage of wheels 483, 487, 501
Tuned manifold (see Manifold)
Turbocharger 103, 293, 299-303, 306-313
    boost 299-300, 303, 306, 309-313
    compressor 300-302, 306-307, 313
    definition 300, 303
    efficiency 299-300, 302-303, 313
    turbine 300-301, 308-310
Two-stroke cycle (see Cycles)


Unit injector 275-277, 281-282, 287, 290
Unloading valve (see Valves, hydraulic)
Updraft carburetor (see Carburetor)


Vacuum advance 211-212, 216, 226
Valves, engine 45, 48-51, 64, 67, 83, 85, 246, 270, 272
    adjustment 49-50
    clearance 64
    cooling 47, 321, 328
    exhaust 49, 82-83, 85
    guides 46-47, 274, 357
    intake 49, 82, 85
    lifters 51
    overlap 85
    push rod 70
    rocker arms 45, 63, 67, 70, 230, 278-282, 352
    rotators 48-49, 64
    seats 67
    springs 46, 63, 67, 70, 230-231, 268, 280-282, 287, 400
    tappets 44-45, 50, 63, 70, 343
    terminology 46, 383, 396
    timing 51, 83, 85
    train 45, 85

Valves, hydraulic  50, 200, 379, 384, 391, 400, 413
    classification  379, 383
    closed-center  383, 410-411
    directional control  384
    flow-control  379, 382-383
    four-port  383-384, 412
    open-center  383-384, 396-398, 410, 413, 416
    pilot-operated  379, 381
    pressure-compensated  381-382, 398-399, 410
    relief  236, 320-321, 328, 352, 379-381, 397-398, 412, 416
    systems  5, 7, 52, 141, 151, 154, 161, 163-167, 169, 171, 173, 175, 177, 179, 181, 183, 185, 187, 189, 191, 193, 195-197, 199-203, 205, 207-209, 212-213, 216, 219-220, 224-226, 229, 231, 233-235, 237, 239, 241, 243-245, 247-253, 255, 264-268, 274, 278, 283, 287, 291, 293, 295, 297, 299, 301, 303, 305, 307-309, 311, 313, 315-317, 319-321, 323-325, 327-329, 331, 333, 335, 337, 339, 341, 343, 345, 347, 349, 351-357, 359-361, 363, 365-367, 369-371, 373, 375, 377, 379, 381, 383, 385, 387, 389, 391-393, 395-401, 403, 405-407, 409-411, 413, 415, 417, 423, 500
    tandem-center  384-385, 396, 410
    unloading  380-381, 401, 410, 412
Vane pump  270, 273, 370-371, 379, 395
Vapor lock  138, 141
Vapor pressure of fuels  138-139, 249, 251
Variable displacement  372-373, 375, 379, 381-382, 447, 449-450, 452, 465, 468, 471
    hydraulic motors  447, 449-450, 452, 465, 468
    pumps  371-373, 375, 379, 381-382, 447, 449-450, 452, 465, 468, 471
Venturi (see Carburetor)
Vibration dampener  59-60, 65
Viscometer  338-341
Viscosity  135, 141-142, 148, 153, 157, 259, 273, 286, 289, 335-343, 356-363, 392, 395, 412
   basic concepts of  337
   classification of oil  360
   dynamic  338-339, 361, 363
   index  335, 342-343, 356, 358-361, 395
   kinematic  339, 392
   of fuel  135, 141-142, 153, 157, 259, 273, 289, 359
   of hydraulic oil  395, 412
   of lubricating oils  335-336, 343, 361, 363
   SAE number  340, 342, 360-362
   units of  338-339
       Saybolt universal seconds (SUS)  339

Voltage  162, 164, 166-167, 170-171, 177-180, 183-184, 186-196, 198, 201-203, 205-211, 213-216, 218-225, 227, 248
    and power  164, 166-167, 170, 178, 186, 188, 190, 192, 194, 198, 202, 206, 208, 210, 219, 248
    definition of  164
    ignition secondary  216, 219, 221-222
    induced  177-178, 184, 189, 208, 210, 219, 221
    regulators (see Regulators)
    secondary  207-210, 213, 216, 218, 220-225
Volumetric efficiency  103-105, 121, 123, 125, 240, 295, 297-298, 300, 303-471
    of engines  103-105, 121-123, 125, 240, 295, 297-298, 300, 303-304, 306-308, 311, 313, 388
    of hydraulic motors  448
    of pumps  375, 377, 379, 397, 411-412, 448, 471


Water cooling  39, 43, 57, 63, 111, 315-317
Water pump (see Pumps)
Watts (see Power, definition of)
Wear  40, 46, 48, 52-53, 55, 60, 63-64, 71, 143-144, 216, 293, 322-323, 328, 333, 337, 343, 356-357, 359-361, 395, 425, 467
    and cooling  323
    and lubrication  64, 333, 337, 359-360, 395
Weight transfer  473, 475-479, 481, 483, 485, 487, 489, 491, 493-495, 497, 499, 501-505
Wet clutch (see Clutch)
Wheel base  120
Wheel weights (see Ballast)
Work, definition of  96


Y-connected alternator  193


Zener diode  170-171, 195-196, 201, 203
Zero absolute temperature  22, 24